$10

Light on Tantra in Kashmir Shaivism

Abhinavagupta's Tantrāloka Chapter One

Revealed by
Swami Lakshmanjoo

WITH ORIGINAL AUDIO

John Hughes, Editor

Lakshmanjoo Academy

Published by:

Lakshmanjoo Academy

First printing 2017

Printed in the United States of America

For information, address:
Lakshmanjoo Academy
http://www.lakshmanjooacademy.org

ISBN
ISBN 978-1-947241-01-5 (paperback)
ISBN 978-1-947241-00-8 (hardcover)
ISBN 978-1-947241-02-2 (ebook)

This sacred text is dedicated to Swami Lakshmanjoo,
our beloved teacher and spiritual father
who has given us everything.
Glory be to Thee!

Table of Contents

Tantrāloka chapter One

Invocations

General Introduction

Teachings of Tantrāloka

Appendix

Guide to Pronunciation

The following English words exemplify the pronunciation of selected Saṅskṛit vowels and consonants. The Romanized Saṅskṛit vowel or consonant is first listed and then an English word is given to aid you in its proper pronunciation.

a	as	a in ***A***merica.
ā	as	a in f***a***ther.
i	as	i in f***i***ll, l***i***ly.
ī	as	i in pol***i***ce.
u	as	u in f***u***ll.
ū	as	u in r***u***de.
ṛi	as	ri in mer***ri***ly.
ṛī	as	ri in ma***ri***ne.
e	as	e in pr***e***y.
ai	as	ai in ***ai***sle.
o	as	o in st***o***ne.
au	as	ou in h***ou***se
ś	as	s in ***s***ure.
ṣ	as	sh in ***sh***un, bu***sh***
s	as	s in ***s***aint, ***s***un

Preface

In the winter of 1971, I traveled with my wife and daughter to Kashmir, India, with the sole purpose of asking Swami Lakshmanjoo to teach me the philosophy of Kashmir Shaivism. At that time, I was in the process of writing my PhD thesis on this ancient philosophy. I wanted to study with Swami Lakshmanjoo as he was recognized worldwide as the foremost authority in Kashmir Shaivism. I met him personally for the first time at his ashram in November of that year. I must say that at that first meeting I was awestruck by his presence. I couldn't put my finger on it but I knew I was meeting a man who was special in ways that I couldn't quite comprehend. At that first meeting, I asked him if he would teach me Kashmir Shaivism and he said yes and that I should come the following Tuesday. Swami Lakshmanjoo began to reveal to my wife, Denise, and I this wondrous philosophy of reality that is Kashmir Shaivism. Swamiji told us that his lectures would be on the introductory topics of Kashmir Shaivism and that they would illumine the essential teachings of his philosophical and spiritual tradition.

It was my good fortune that, prior to traveling to Kashmir to begin my studies, I decided that it was important to record my meetings with Swami Lakshmanjoo. I wanted to make sure that these recordings be of high quality and long lasting. So, I scraped my money together and on the way to Kashmir I stopped in Germany to purchase a high quality portable tape recorder. Why this was so important to me at the time, I wasn't sure. Later, however, it made sense and a big difference.

Throughout the winter, spring, and summer of that first year, Swamiji gave us weekly lectures on the important topics of Kashmir Shaivism.[1] These lectures were eventually transcribed, edited, and published in 1985 as *Kashmir Shaivism–The Secret Supreme*, which was Swamiji's first English publication.[2] In the preface of that first book Swamiji says:

> This book consists of lectures that I delivered in 1971-1972. It began in 1969, when Mahesh Yogi came to our Valley. He had heard of me and wanted us to meet so he called on me. When he visited he asked if I would speak to his disciples and I agreed. He sent his transport and I was taken to where he was staying with his Western disciples. John and Denise Hughes were also present at that gathering, but at the time I had not yet met them. They must have been impressed with what they heard for, in 1971, they returned to Kashmir and came to see me at my Ashram. I asked them who they were. They said there were Maharishi's disciples. They explained that they had heard my discourse when they first came to Kashmir with Maharishi in 1969. John then told me that he had one problem: he wanted to learn Kashmir Shaivism and would I have time to teach him? I replied, "Yes, I have enough time." I instructed him that he should come to the Ashram on the next Tuesday and I would begin teaching him. So on Tuesday he arrived, along with his tape recorder, and I began giving him lectures in the Ashram hall. Denise, his wife, also attended these lectures.
>
> In the beginning, I taught John only the introductory topics of Kashmir Shaivism. As time passed, however, I came to know that John had good power of understanding and I became fond of him. I wanted to tell him more and

1 These initial lectures covered nineteen independent subjects, which included 15 hours of recorded material. At every lecture Swamiji spoke without the aid of textbooks or written material, which emphasized to me that here was a master who lived his tradition.

2 After its publication, it became apparent that *Kashmir Shaivism, The Secret Supreme*, was Swami Lakshmanjoo's succinct rendering of the important topics contained in Abhinavagupta's Tantrāloka. See Appendix 26.

more about Kashmir Shaivism. I wanted to teach him Shaivism's secrets, so I continued giving lectures which John recorded. This was the main starting point of his studies. It is these secrets, these major points which I taught him at that time, which comprise this book.

As I appreciated that John was assimilating the lectures very well, after they were completed, I started teaching him the theory, which is found in the Shaiva scriptures. In this manner, Kashmir Shaivism was taught to John.

I think, when these lectures are printed, it will be a great boon for mankind and will elevate the whole world. Also, I will consider myself blessed by Lord Shiva. I hope that John will continue writing on what I have delivered to him in theory and practice–*The Secret Supreme.* If he continues to expose it to the world, it will be a great help for everyone.

Swami Lakshmanjoo
1984

As time passed and our lectures continued, Swamiji indicated that he would like to continue revealing and commenting upon the most important sacred scriptures of this tradition. Naturally, I was thrilled by this new development. I knew from my previous studies that, due to events of the last eight hundred plus years, the teachings of Kashmir Shaivism had remained hidden. In addition, I also knew the keys necessary for unlocking this treasury of knowledge had, since ancient times, been passed down verbally from master to disciple. This oral transmission was the very life of this tradition and it was Swami Lakshmanjoo who was recognized as the last living exponent and guardian of the secret wealth of this knowledge. From the lessons he had already given, it was clear to me that here was a scholar and saint who possessed the understanding bestowed on him by the oral tradition, which was necessary for unlocking this treasure of knowledge that Kashmir Shaivism embodies.

After these initial lectures, he began translating and explaining the important texts that he had selected. As I was well prepared, I was able to audio record everything. I expressed to Swamiji that it was my intention to preserve his lectures and translations so that they would be available in the future for other students desiring to learn Kashmir Shaivism. He seemed quite pleased with this idea and possibility. He expressed his concern that the reality of this tradition should not be lost after his departure from this world.

As my studies continued, I realized that nothing was more important than being able to remain in Kashmir working with Swamiji. I discussed this with Denise and she agreed, so we took the steps necessary to move our family to Kashmir. Once this was accomplished, I was able to begin work in earnest. Swamiji had gathered a series of texts that he wanted to translate and comment upon. Over the next nineteen years, I recorded Swamiji's revelations of the following texts of Kashmir Shaivism:[3]

- *Bhagavad Gitartha Samgraha* of Abhinavagupta, Audio (1978 to 80).
- *Bhagavad Gitartha Samgraha* of Abhinavagupta, Video (1990).
- *Bodhapancadashika* of Abhinavagupta (1980).
- *Dehastadevatacakra* of Abhinavagupta (1980).
- *Janma Marana Vicara* (1975).
- *Kashmir Shaivism–The Secret Supreme* (1972).
- *Kashmiri Lectures on Practice and Discipline* (1980).
- *Kundalini Vijnana Rahasya* in Kashmiri (1980).
- *Paramarthasara*, Abhinavagupta's commentary, Audio (1972).
- *Paramarthasara*, Abhinavagupta's commentary, Video (1990).
- *Parapraveshika* of Kshemaraja (1980).

3 See Bibliography for details on these texts.

- *Questions on the Pratyabhijna Hridayam of Kshemaraja* (1972).
- *Questions on various text of Kashmir Shaivism* (1978).
- *Paratrishika Laghuvritti* of Abhinavagupta (1974).
- *Paratrishika Vivarana* of Abhinavagupta (1982 to 1985).
- *Shivastotravali* of Utpaladeva (1976 to 1978).
- *Shiva Sutra Vimarshini* of Vasugupta (1975).
- *Spanda Karika* of Vasugupta (1981).
- *Spanda Samdoha* of Kshemaraja (1981).
- *Special Verses on Practice* (1988).
- *Stavacintamani* of Bhatta Narayana (1980 to 1981).
- *Tantraloka* of Abhinavagupta, Chapters 1-19 (1976 to 1981).
- *Vatulanath Sutras* of Kshemaraja (1975).
- *Vijnana Bhairava* (1975).
- *Vijnana Bhairava Questions* (1985).

I also recorded the following lectures given by Swamiji in the Kashmiri Language:

- *Ishvarapratyabhijna Vimarshini* (selected verses).
- *Kundalini Vijnana Rahasya* (entire text).
- *Maharthamanjari* (selected verses).
- *Paratrishika Vivarana* (selected verses).
- *Shivastotravali* of Utpaladeva (20 chapters).
- *Shiva Sutra Vimarshini* (selected verses).
- *Stutikusmanjali* (selected verses).
- *Tantraloka* (selected chapters).
- *Patanjali*'s *Yamas and Niyamas*.

This resulted in over 800 hours of recordings among which over 200 hours were devoted to translating and commenting on what Swamiji considered to be the central text of Kashmir Shaivism: Abhinavagupta's *Tantrāloka*. This is a text filled with the secret wisdom from the *Mālinīvijaya Tantra*, a *tantra* that Abhinavagupta tells us is the basis for his *Tantrāloka*. It is an encyclopedia of the knowledge of Kashmir Shaivism, both practical and intellectual. Composed of thirty-seven chapters (*āhnikas*), it is so complete that it is said to be a book for masters. Each chapter has it's own distinct topic. In all of his teachings, Swamiji always sought to emphasize the practical aspects of Kashmir Shaivism along with it's intellectual content. In translating and revealing the *Tantrāloka*, Swamiji only completed those chapters that he felt were directly concerned with practice (chapters 1 through 19). For his teachings he used the *Kashmir Series of Texts and Studies*, *Tantrāloka* volumes 1-10, published by the Research Department of Jammu and Kashmir from 1918 to 1933. He also made numerous corrections to the original Sanskrit.

Swamiji's revelation of the *Tantrāloka* is truly masterful. He brings clarity to a text that Abhinavagupta purposely made obscure. He is so in sync with Abhinavagupta that it as if he is Abhinavagupta reborn. It took Swamiji seven years to complete his revelation of the first nineteen chapters of *Tantrāloka*, and even then he was not satisfied until we had gone through the original recordings to make sure that there were no missing parts. We re-recorded whatever sections were missing or damaged from the original recordings, which resulted in the complete record that we have today.

In conclusion, I feel humbled to have been involved in the publication of this first chapter of the Tantrāloka series.[4] I feel equally blessed to have been associated with Swami Lakshmanjoo, Abhinavagupta, the masters of this sacred tradition, and Lord Shiva, who in the reality of Kashmir Shaivism, are all one Being. May the grace of Lord Shiva unfold in the hearts and minds of all sincere students of this glorious teaching.

John Hughes
9th May, 2017

---

4 The Lakshmanjoo Academy will continue to publish the remaining 18 chapters of *Tantrāloka*, as commentated upon by Swami Lakshmanjoo.

Abhinavagupta[5]

The *Tantrāloka* is the voluminous masterwork of the 10th century philosopher-saint, Abhinavagupta. Years ago Swami Lakshmanjoo wrote the following about Abhinavagupta:

Abhinavagupta was one of the most outstanding *acharya*s (teachers) of the Shaiva philosophy. We learn from references about him in his *Tantrāloka* and *Parātrīśikā Vivaraṇa* that he lived in Kashmir at about the end of the tenth and the beginning of the eleventh century CE. The earliest ancestor of Abhinavagupta was a famous Brahmin, Atrigupta, who lived in Antarvedi, the ancient name of the tract of land lying between the Ganga and the Yamuna Rivers. Atrigupta, who was recognized as a great Shaiva teacher, was invited to come to live in Kashmir by King Lalitaditya, who ruled over Kashmir from 700-736 CE. He was given the old palace of Pravarasena on the banks of the Jhelum (Vitasta) River and a large parcel of land was granted to him for his maintenance. Many generations later, one of his descendants, Varahagupta, also became known as a learned scholar of Shaiva philosophy. His son, Narasiṁhagupta (alias Chukhala), also renowned as a great Shaiva teacher, was the father of Abhinavagupta.

Abhinavagupta became renowned as a formidable scholar and Shaiva teacher who possessed knowledge in all matters relating to Kashmir Shaivism. The versatility of his genius was recognized in his own time. He was considered to be one of the most knowledgeable authorities on Shaiva philosophy as well as on various other branches of Sanskrit literature. As a young man filled with a thirst for knowledge, he sat at the feet of many of the teachers of traditional and authoritative knowledge. His humility and devotion were such that these teachers imparted to him, without hesitation, all of the learning they

5 A paper on Abhinavagupta written by Swami Lakshmanjoo.

possessed. The celebrated author of Kavya Prakash, Rajanaka Mammatta, called Abhinavagupta "the Shankaracharya of Kashmir".

The *Mālinīvijayotara Tantra* list six important signs of spiritual advancement. These great spiritual signs were also observed in Abhinavagupta by knowledgeable individuals who looked upon him as Shiva incarnate.

1. Unswerving devotional attachment to Shiva.
2. Full attainment of Mantra Siddhi.[6]
3. Attainment of controlling power over all of the five elements.
4. Capacity to accomplish the desired end.
5. Mastery over the whole science of rhetoric and poetics.
6. The sudden dawning of knowledge of all the *shastra*s (scriptures).[7]

Lord Shree-Kantha-Nath Shiva Himself appeared in Kashmir in the form of Abhinavagupta to enlighten the people. Madhurāja also asserts that Abhinavagupta was, in fact, the incarnation of Bhairava-Nath Shiva. In conclusion I would say that Abhinavagupta was the pride of Kashmir. He is even now the pride of Kashmir, as his works and teachings continue to deeply influence discerning people.

END

---

6 "Whatever *mantra* he recites, or makes his disciple recite, that *mantra* will become fruitful in a very short period. It will never fail, his *mantra* never fails. If he gives you a *mantra*, it won't fail, it will carry you to God consciousness." Swami Lakshmanjoo, trans., *Tantrāloka* 13.215 (LJA archives).

7 The *Mālinīvijaya Tantra* recognizes only five spiritual signs which result from the elevated state of *rudra-śakti-samāveśa*, the fifth being mastery over poetics, or, knowledge of all *śāstras*. In the above paper, Swamiji has included the sixth sign, since Abhinavagupta clearly exhibited both of these qualities.

Tantrāloka

The word *Tantrāloka* means Light on the Tantra. It is concerned with the philosophy and practices of the monistic tradition which Abhinavagupta calls the Trika System,[8] now known as Kashmir Shaivism. On account of the size and scope of the *Tantrāloka*, it is a veritable encyclopedia of non-dual Shaivism. It is a treasure-text containing the synthesis of the monistic *Mālinīvijaya Tantra* and all of the four systems of Kashmir Shaivism: the Krama System, the Spanda System, the Kula System, and the Pratyabijñā System.[9]

8 *Trika* means, threefold. It is the threefold science of man and his world. This *Trika* contains the science of the individual (Nara), the energy (Śakti), and the universal being (Śiva). The purpose of *Trika* is to show how an individual rises to the state of the universal being through energy.

9 Abhinavagupta tells us that the *Krama* System is concerned with space and time. He explains that there is actually no space. When one deals with forms, then space appears. When one is established in the formless state of being, then for him there is no space. In the same way, when there is something to be done, only then does time exist, and when you have nothing to do, then time has no existence.

In explaining the *Spanda* System, Abhinavagupta says that it is that movement which actually is no movement. *Spanda* makes us realize that whatever is in movement actually is established in the unmoved point. So, although everything seems to be moving, it is not actually moving at all. When talking about the *Kula* System, he says that *kula* means "the science of totality". In each and every part of the universe, totality shines throughout. Take a small part of any object, and in that part you will see the universal energy existing.

Concerning the essence of the *Pratyabhijñā* System, The School of Recognition, Abhinavagupta explains that, at the time of God-realization, nothing new is realized. On the contrary, the *yogi* feels that the state of God-consciousness he is experiencing was already known to him.

Abhinavagupta tells us that *Pratyabhijñā* teaches us that the state

Why was the *Tantrāloka* written? In answer to this question, Abhinavagupta tells us in this first chapter that, although in the schools of Trika (Kashmir Shaivism) there are many wonderful and important ways for attaining the supreme Trika state (the supreme reality), yet in his time not even one was still existing – all of those ways were lost. It is for this reason that he was requested by his colleagues and disciples to create a text that would illuminate and clarify all of these ways of Trika. So, to accomplish this, Abhinavagupta composed the *Tantrāloka*, a text, which he tells us, is filled with the complete explanation of the ways associated with Trika.

That is to say that the philosophical understanding on the level of the intellect might have been existing, but the actual practical means or methods to be used to attain the supreme reality to which they all pointed, that was lost. Abhinavagupta was intent, therefore, to revive the true understanding of these very important teachings, to make the practices that they embodied live again. For what is the use of a map if you have no *way* to reach the destination? Thus, Abhinavagupta gave us the *Tantrāloka* to remedy this situation. When you examine the *Tantrāloka* as a whole, you'll find that it is primarily concerned with the means (*upāya*) to attain supreme oneness, oneness with the universe, oneness with the Universal Being.

The *Tantrāloka* is composed of thirty-seven chapters (*āhnika*s). Each chapter has it's own distinct topic. In this present volume, Abhinavagupta lays the groundwork for the rest of his *Tantrāloka*. In this first chapter he tells us that he has two objectives: to examine the differentiated perception of all of the practices/means (*upāya*s) and to name all of the topics that are to be explained in the body of the *Tantrāloka*.

of God-consciousness is always there. So, the conclusion is that, in this universe, you only have to see and realize the kingdom of God consciousness everywhere and nothing else.

Contents of Tantrāloka One

Invocations

a) To the supreme Consciousness embodied in Abhinavagupta's mother and father,

b) to the Goddesses of the three fold energies supreme (*parā*), medium (*parāparā*), and inferior (*aparā*) of which the Trika (threefold) System is comprised,

c) to the Masters of the various schools of Trika Shaivism.

The declaration that the *Tantrāloka* is based on the *Mālinīvijayottara Tantra*, the essence of which he learned from his foremost teacher, Śrī Śambhunātha.

Abhinavagupta offers a special invocation to his master Śambhunātha.

General Introduction

Having offered obeisance to everything that played a part in the creation of his *Tantrāloka*, Abhinavagupta begins his introduction to the *Tantrāloka* in which he explains a) the nature of knowledge and ignorance, b) the nature of liberation-*mokṣa* (the release from the repeating cycle of births and deaths), c) the two kinds of knowledge (*jñāna*) and ignorance (*ajñāna*).[10]

The explanation concerning the essence of what is to be recognized, the real object to be known. That real object is, in fact, Lord Śiva, and That real object is not away from the objective world. It is in this objective world that you find the essence of Lord Śiva because nothing can exist without the light (*prakāśa*) of Lord Śiva.

10 Self-knowledge (*pauruṣa jñāna*), ignorance of the Self (*pauruṣa ajñāna*), intellectual knowledge (*bauddha jñāna*) and intellectual ignorance (*bauddha ajñāna*).

The explanation concerning the question: are Siva and Sakti one? First, there is the question of Lord Śiva's innumerable energies. Although He has innumerable energies, all of those energies are one with His supreme energy, *svātantrya śakti*, the energy of absolute independence. But still then, there are two: Lord Śiva and His supreme energy–*svātantrya śakti*. If this is the case, the doctrine of monism (absolute oneness) is destroyed. Abhinavagupta resolves this mystery by telling us that this energy is, in fact, the reality of That being. It's separation is only a cognitive distinction to be accepted for the time being, for explanatory purposes. Otherwise, the energy and the energy-holder are one.

For instance, there is a fire. The burning energy is never separated from the fire, the lightening energy is not separated from the fire, the heating energy is not separated from the fire, the cooking energy is not separated from the fire. All of these energies are one with that fire.

The fourteen-fold states of *rāma*: moving (*gatiḥ*), *sthānam* (staying), going in dreams, staying in wakefulness, the twinkling of the eyes (*unmeṣa* and *nimeṣa*), running, jumping, not-knowing (*āyāsaḥ*, not knowing, ignorance), and knowing ones's own energies.

This is not Rāma the son of Daśaratha. This is the explanation of what is really "*rāma*".

The explanation of the various names attributed to Lord Śiva: a) "Bhairava", b) "Deva", c) "Pati", d) "Śiva", e) further explanations of the names – "Bhairava", "Deva", "Pati", and "Śiva".

The Teachings

Introduction to the teachings and theory of the *Tantrāloka*'s sacred texts (*śāstra*s)

The general introduction to the means and methods (*upāya*) for attaining the state of full and pure knowledge where you perceive your nature as one with the universe. This is the true liberation of Kashmir Shaivism.

The successive explanation of the three means (*upāya*): *śāmbhava upāya*, the means associated with will (*icchā*); *śākta upāya*, the means associated with knowledge (*jñāna*); and *āṇava ūpāya,*, the means associated with action (*kriyā*).

The explanation of the three variations of absorption or trance (*samāveśa*) as they apply to the means (*ūpāya*) of *śāmbhava*, *śākta*, and *āṇava* as mentioned in the *Mālinīvijaya Tantra* (chapter 1, verses 21-23).

A discussion of the means pertaining to *śāmbhava*.

A discussion of the means pertaining to *śākta*.

A discussion of the means pertaining to *āṇava*.

The understanding that the master and the disciple are one.

An examination of the theory of the three impurities (*mala*s).

A discussion of the fourfold means (*upāya*) for attaining liberation: *āṇavopāya*, *śāktopāya*, *śāmbhavopāya*, and the fourth supreme means, *anupāya*, where there are no means.

The examination of the application of logic in the *Tantrāloka* with respect to nomination (*uddeśa*), definition (*lakṣana*), and investigation (*parikṣa*).

Understanding the logical functions of nomination (*uddeśa*), definition (*lakṣana*), and investigation (*parikṣa*) as they apply to the three levels of speech: *paśyantī* (subtle, which relates to letters), *madhyamā* (medium, which relates to words), and *vaikarī* (gross, which relates to sentences).

Examination of the fivefold contacts of masters and disciples in Trika Shaivism.

Contents of Tantrāloka in brief

- Chapter one is where you get the differentiated knowledge of all of the means–*vijñānabhit*.
- Chapter two introduces the means where there is no means–*gatopāya* (viz., *anupāya*).
- Chapter three is a discussion of the supreme means–*śāmbhavopāya*.
- Chapter four is a discussion of *śāktopāya*.
- Chapter five onward is a discussion of some aspect of *āṇavopāya*, the means of the individual.
- Chapter six is a discussion of the means and method to cross time.
- Chapter seven is a discussion of the practice known as *cakrodaya*–the rise of the wheels (*cakra*s) of energy in your body.
- Chapter eight is the explanation of all one hundred and eighteen worlds that comprise our external reality.
- Chapter nine is the explanation of the thirty-six elements–*tattva*s.
- Chapter ten describes the various ways of rising through the thirty-six elements from earth (*pṛthvī*) to Śiva by the absorption of one in another. This is called *tattva bheda*, the differentiated process of the elements.
- Chapter eleven is the explanation of the five circles (*nivṛtti kalā*, *pratiṣṭhā kalā*, *vidyā kalā*, *śāntā kalā*, and *śāntātītā kalā*).
- In chapter twelve the main object to be held when one is treading on the path of the elementary world is described.
- In chapter thirteen the grace (*śaktipāta*) of Lord Śiva is explained.
- In chapter fourteen the concealing power (*tirodhāna śakti*) of Lord Śiva is explained.
- In chapter fifteen an introduction to initiation and the

initiation of discipline is described.

- Chapter sixteen explains how to become a *putraka* (son) of your master wherein you have authority to receive his spiritual property.
- Chapter seventeen describes how the master ties the disciple in order to free him later.
- Chapter eighteen describes subtle initiation.
- Chapter nineteen explains how to get rid of the physical body if it is not healthy or if you are experiencing unbearable and incurable pain. This is not suicide. It is done through initiation by your master.
- Chapter twenty explains how to perform the initiation of scale.
- Chapter twenty-one describes how a master can bring a disciple, who has unexpectedly died, back to life in order to initiate him properly so that he attains liberation.
- Chapter twenty-two explains how a master changes the spiritual sign (*liṅgoddhāra*) of a potential disciple so he can enter on the path of Shaivism.
- Chapter twenty-three first explains how a disciple is initiated to become disciplined (*samayī dīkṣa*), then how he is initiated to tread on the path of spirituality (*sādhaka dīkṣa*), then how he is initiated for achieving the inheritance of his master (*putraka dīkṣa*) and finally how he is initiated to become a master (*ācārya dīkṣa*) and he can initiate others.
- In chapter twenty-four we are told how a funeral for the master or disciple is to be prepared and carried out.
- In chapter twenty-five we are told how to celebrate a Shaivite death anniversary (*śrāddha*).
- Chapter twenty-six explains how a master who is elevated and absolutely one with Lord Shiva, must act in the remaining portion of his life.
- In chapter twenty-seven we are told how to worship a Shiva *linga*.
- In chapter twenty-eight we are told what special days are to be observed.
- In chapter twenty-nine we are taught secret worship.

- In chapter thirty the differentiation of all *mantras* is explained.
- In chapter thirty-one, we are told how to create spiritual symbols (*maṇḍalas*) for worship.
- Chapter thirty-two tells us what physical postures (*mudrās*) are needed in Shaivism.
- In chapter thirty-three we are told that the point is oneness, union, with all philosophies.
- In chapter thirty-four we are told how to enter in our real nature.
- In chapter thirty-five, we are told that all scriptures are actually united.
- In chapter thirty-six we are told about the tradition of masters and disciples of Abhinavagupta.
- In chapter thirty-seven, it is explained why we must get help from the scriptures.

Specific explanation of the contents of the *Tantrāloka.*

Concluding verses as a definition (*lakṣana*) of the *Tantrāloka.*

Concluding verses as a complete investigation (*parikṣa*) of the *Tantrāloka.*

Abhinavagupta's concluding verse for the first chapter (*āhnika*).

Jayaratha's concluding verse.

In 1966, Swamiji composed a brief commentary on the first 45 verses of *Tantrāloka*.[11] This work was started on the anniversary of the day Abhinavagupta composed his famous hymn, Bhairava Stotra.[12] In his preface Swamiji wrote:

> "Today is the anniversary of the auspicious day when our illustrious teacher, Abhinavagupta, a manifestation of Lord Shiva,[13] entered into the divine abode of universal consciousness and achieved the supreme state of Bhairava. In the Vedic calendar it was the tenth day of the waning moon in the month of December.[14] On this day, in a state of oneness with Bhairava, our beloved Abhinavagupta composed his famous hymn – the *Bhairava Stotra*.[15] Having been inspired by Shri Abhinavagupta Ji, I too have started my commentary on this auspicious day.
>
> "*Tantrāloka* is a grand epic, in which our revered teacher has expounded in detail and shed light on all the systems related to the *Trika Śāstras*, i.e., *non-dual*, *dual-nondual* and *dual*, branches of Shaivism. Abhinavagupta further narrates:

---

11 This was a hand written commentary in Hindi.

12 A hymn to Bhairava, traditionally sung by Kashmiri Pandits.

13 Literally, we consider Abhinavagupta our chosen deity (Iśtadevata), who is another form of Lord Śiva (Śivasvarūpa).

14 The month of Paush in the Hindi calendar.

15 In the second verse of the Bhairava Stotra, Abhinavagupta declares his experience.

tvanmayam etad, aśeṣam idānīṁ
bhāti mama tvad, anugraha śaktyā /
tvam ca maheśa, sadaiva mamātmā
svātma mayaṁ mama, tena samastam //2//

"By the energy of your grace (*anugraha śakti*) it has been revealed to me that this vibrating universe is your own existence. Thus, O Lord Śiva, this realization has come to me that you are my own soul and as such this universe is my own expression and existence."

adhyuṣṭasaṁtatisrotaḥ sārabhūtarasāhṛtim ।
vidhāya tantrāloko'yaṁ syandate sakalānrasān ।।[16]

"This *Tantrāloka* is a manifestation of a stream of divine nectar encompassing the essence of all spiritual wisdom. With its broad sweep, it embodies in its exposition the quintessence of all of the three and one half streams of wisdom."[17]

"Therefore, keeping in view the well known saying "*A sincere effort definitely bears fruit when done with utmost intention*," I am undertaking to write the explanatory commentary and exposition on this great epic of Tantric Literature – "*Tantrāloka*". It is my heart's desire that this auspicious undertaking be completed with the grace of the great Abhinavagupta (who is none other than Svacchandanātha – Lord Shiva). I will consider myself fulfilled of all desires if this work is materialized."

Paush Krishna Dashamī[18]
Samvat Vikrami: 2023
English Calendar: 1966
Sapatrishi Samvat: 5042

Resident of Ishwar Ashram
Servant of the devotees of Śiva
Rajanak Lakshmana[19]

16 *Tantrāloka* 36.15.
17 The three and a half streams of wisdom are the schools of Durvāsa Ṛṣi's mind-born sons, Tryambhakanātha, Śrīnātha, Āmardakanātha and his mind-born daughter Ārdhatryambhakā. See *Kashmir Shaivism, The Secret Supreme*, chpt 13, Birth of the *Tantras*, p90-91.
18 The 10th day of the waning Moon in the Vedic month of Paush - approximately late December.
19 Swami Lakshmanjoo

Acknowledgements

First of all I would like to thank our team of associate editors: Viresh Hughes, George Barselaar, Denise Hughes, and Stephen Benson. They took the raw unedited audio transcript and transformed it into a polished document ready for publication. Being closely attuned to Swamiji's vision they were able to lightly edit the manuscript without tarnishing the flow of the narrative. Recognizing that these revelations were meant to aid the student in gaining an understanding of the philosophy and practices of Kashmir Shaivism, comprehensive footnotes and an exhaustive appendix have been added to facilitate this quest. Lastly, I would like to thank Michael Van Winkle, our audio engineer who enhanced the original audio, Claudia Dose, our creative director who was responsible for the formatting and creation of the overall design of this book, and Shanna Hughes who coordinated this project.

Swami Lakshmanjoo

Swami Lakshmanjoo

Swami Lakshmanjoo was born in Srinagar, Kashmir, on May 9, 1907. He was the most recent and the greatest of the long line of saints and masters of the Kashmir Shaiva tradition. From a young age, Swami Lakshmanjoo spent his life studying and practicing the teachings of this unique and sacred tradition. Having a complete intellectual and spiritual understanding of the philosophy and practice of Kashmir Shaivism, he was a true master in every respect.

Being born with a photographic memory, learning was always easy for him. In addition to possessing a complete knowledge of Kashmir Shaivism, he had a vast knowledge of the traditional religious and philosophical schools and texts of India. Swamiji would freely draw upon other texts to clarify, expand, and substantiate his lectures. He could recall an entire text by simply remembering the first few words of a verse.

In time, his reputation as a learned philosopher and spiritual adept spread. Spiritual leaders and scholars journeyed from all over the world to receive his blessings and to ask questions about various aspects of Kashmir Shaiva philosophy. He gained renown as a humble devotee of Lord Shiva and as an accomplished master (*siddha*) of the non-dual tradition of Kashmir Shaivism.

Throughout his life, Swamiji taught his disciples and devotees the ways of devotion and awareness. He shunned fame and all forms of recognition. He knew Kashmir Shaivism was the most precious jewel and that, by God's grace, those who desired supreme knowledge would be attracted to its teachings. He taught freely, never asking anything in return, except that his students, young and old, should do their utmost to assimilate the teachings of his cherished tradition. His earnest wish was for Kashmir Shaivism to be preserved and made available to all humankind.

On the 27th of September, 1991, Swami Lakshmanjoo left his physical body and attained *mahāsamādhi*, the great liberation.

Swami Lakshmanjoo

Śrī Tantrāloka of Abhinavagupta

Chapter (*Āhnika*) One

Invocation to the Supreme Consciousness Embodied in Abhinavagupta's Mother and Father (1)

Audio 1 - 00:00

विमलकलाश्रयाभिनवसृष्टिमहा जननी
भरिततनुश्च पञ्चमुखगुप्तरुचिर्जनकः
तदुभययामलस्फुरितभावविसर्गमयं
हृदयमनुत्तरामृतकुलं मम संस्फुरतात्॥ १ ॥

vimalakalāśrayābhinavasṛṣṭimahā jananī
bharitatanuśca pañcamukhaguptarucirjanakaḥ /
tadubhayayāmalasphuritabhāvavisargamayaṁ
hṛdayamanuttarāmṛtakulaṁ mama saṁsphuratāt //1//

[Abhinavagupta]: My essence of being, which is filled with the supreme nectar of God consciousness, which has come forth by the union of my mother and father, let that essence of my being vibrate in this whole universe. My mother was named as Vimala because she was residing in the purity of God consciousness, and her only festival was my birth in her life. My father, who was full-bodied because he had no desires at all for sensual pleasures was named Pañcamukhagupta.

(Pañcamukhagupta means, Narasiṁhagupta).[1] His [given] name was Narasiṁhagupta and he was my father. [The union of] these two souls has [produced] the existence of Abhinava. And let the heart and the essence of my being vibrate in this whole universe.

INVOCATION TO THE GODDESSES OF THE TRIKA PARĀ - PARĀPARĀ - APARĀ (2-4)

Audio 1 - 02:12

नौमि चित्प्रतिभां देवीं परां भैरवयोगिनीम्।
मातृमानप्रमेयांशशूलाम्बुजकृतास्पदाम॥ २॥

naumi citpratibhāṁ devīṁ parāṁ bhairavayoginīm /
mātṛmānaprameyāṁśaśūlāmbujakṛtāspadām //2//

I bow to that supreme *parā* energy, which is the light of consciousness and which is one with the supreme Bhairava; that energy which is established in the lotus *āsana* in the three lotuses, which has three sharp spikes.

You know "spikes"?

SCHOLAR: Lotuses on the three points.

SWAMIJI: Points. One of subjective consciousness, the other of cognitive consciousness, and the other of objective conscious-

1 "Pañcamukhagupta means, he has five energies: *cit śakti* (the energy of consciousness), *ānanda śakti* (the energy of bliss), *icchā śakti* (the energy of will), *jñāna śakti* (the energy of knowledge), and *kriyā śakti* (the energy of action). These are the five faces of Lord Śiva. A great father is recognized by these five energies." *Parātriśikā Vivaraṇa*, with the commentary of Abhinavagupta, translation and additional commentary by Swami Lakshmanjoo (LJA archive, 1982-85).

ness.[2] On these three sharp spikes is seated that Bhairava *yoginī*, the supreme energy of God consciousness, *cit-pratibhā*.[3] I bow to That.[4]

---

2 *Pramātṛ bhāva*, *pramāṇa bhāva*, and *prameya bhāva*, respectively. See Appendix 3, p374.

3 *Pratibhā*: intuitive knowledge, intuition, divination. "*Pratibhā* means, the shining of knowledge within your own nature, within your own Self. The rise of this knowledge comes from your own Self without dependence on the *śāstra*s (scripture) and *ācarya*s (masters)." *Tantrāloka* of Abhinavagupta, translation and commentary by Swami Lakshmanjoo (original audio recording, LJA archives, Los Angeles, 1972-1981) 13.132.
"And that not-depending on any other agency is called supreme *Pratibhā devī*, that is the independent energy of His will (*svātantrya*), which is *anuttarām*, absolutely supreme." Ibid., 3.66. "*Pratibhā* is *nirvikalpa*." *Parātriśikā Vivaraṇa* (LJA archive). *Nirvikalpa* (thoughtless-ness) will be discussed throughout *Tantrāloka*. (See Appendix 4, p374.)

4 The following paraphrase from the *Parātriśikā Laghu Vṛtti* explains the relationship between Parabhairava (Supreme Bhairava) and the goddess (Bhairava *yoginī*) who governs the three energies of consciousness (*pramātṛ*, *pramāṇa*, and *prameya*; subjective, cognitive, and objective consciousness, respectively). "O Devī, *parabhairavīyaṁ śakti trayam*, these three energies are concerned with supreme Bhairava [because] this heart of Bhairava is always functioning in a threefold (triple) movement. Where there is will, there is knowledge; where there is knowledge, there is action; where there is action, there is everything. So, this is *trikoṇa maṇḍala*, and *trikoṇa maṇḍala* is always in movement, it is never *niṣpanda* (without movement). This is the heart of Bhairava and this Bhairavanātha is the essence of Bhairavī. The whole universe is the essence of Bhairava and Bhairava is the essence of the universe. There is not at all the slightest difference between Bhairava and the world. This is the philosophy of the Trika system. So, the attainment of the universal heart of Bhairava, which is no other than being in the trance of Bhairava and Bhairavī, bestows one liberation from repeated births and deaths, not in the end of life, but *jīvata eva*, in life also; not in this very life, [but] now!" *Parātriśikā Laghuvṛtti,* with the commentary of Abhinavagupta, translation and commentary by Swami Lakshmanjoo (original audio recording, LJA archives, Los

Now, the third [*śloka*]:

Audio 1 - 03:31

नौमि देवीं शरीरस्थां नृत्यतो भैरवाकृते।
प्रावृण्मेघघनव्योमविद्युल्लेखाविलासिनीम्॥ ३ ॥

naumi devīṁ śarīrasthāṁ nṛtyato bhairavākṛte /
prāvṛṇmeghaghanavyomavidyullekhāvilāsinīm //3//

I bow to that *devī* (goddess), *aparā*, the inferior energy of Lord Bhairava, who is situated in gross bodies, the gross body of Bhairava–Bhairava, the real dancer–and who is shining just like the lightening from the dense clouds of the rainy season. It is that light which has come out from the objective world; it shines from the objective world in the form of God consciousness. I bow to that *devī*.

Now, the fourth [*śloka*]:

Audio 1 - 04:46

दीप्तज्योतिश्छटाप्लुष्टभेदबन्धत्रयं स्फुरत्।
स्ताज्ज्ञानशलं सत्पक्षविपक्षोत्कर्तनक्षमम्॥ ४ ॥

dīptajyotiśchaṭāpluṣṭabhedabandhatrayaṁ sphurat /
stājjñānaśūlaṁ satpakṣavipakṣotkartanakṣamam //4//

Let the *triśūla* (trident), the three sharp-pointed *śūla* (weapon) of Lord Śiva–although it is filled with will, knowledge, and action,[5] it has predominance in knowledge only (that is *jñāna śūlaṁ*)[6] –let that *jñāna śūla* remain in such a

---

Angeles, 1982).

See Appendix 1 (p369) for a detailed explanation of Bhairava. See verse 95 for an understanding of why Lord Śiva is nominated as Bhairava. See Appendix 2 (p372) for an explanation of the 36 elements (*tattvas*) of Kashmir Shaivism.

5 *Icchā śakti*, *jñāna śakti*, and *kriyā śakti*, respectively.

6 The weapon of knowledge (*jñāna śakti*). In verses 2, 3, and 4, Abhinavagupta has given the order of the three energies of

way that it destroys the opposites [just as in] that supreme state of *jagat-ānanda*.[7] And let that *jñāna śūla* destroy all the three bondages[8] by its flame of absolute divine God consciousness (*dīpta jyoti*).

The fifth [*śloka*]:

INVOCATION TO THE SUPREME ENERGY SVĀTANTRYA ŚAKTI (5)

Audio 1 - 06:20

स्वातन्त्र्यशक्तिः क्रमसंसिसृक्षा
क्रमात्मता चेति विभोर्विभूतिः।
तदेव देवीत्रयमन्तरास्ता-
मनुत्तरं मे प्रथयत्स्वरूपम्॥५॥

svātantryaśaktiḥ kramasaṁsisṛkṣā
kramātmatā ceti vibhorvibhūtiḥ /
tadeva devītrayamantarāstām-
anuttaraṁ me prathayatsvarūpam //5//
[not recited]

Parabhairava as supreme (*parā*), inferior (*aparā*), and medium (*parāparā*), respectively, which differs from the order given in the *Mālinīvijaya tantra*. In his commentary on verses 192-193, Swamiji explains that this order is given by Abhinavagupta because *parāparā* cannot be explained without first explaining *aparā*.

7 Also spelled *jagadānanda*. Lit., "rejoicing the world." Kashmir Shaivism recognises seven states of *ānanda* (bliss), which are listed as *nijānanda*, *nirānanda*, *parānanda*, *brahmānanda*, *mahānanda*, *cidānanda*, and *jagadānanda*. See Appendix 5 (p378) for explanation of these seven states of *ānanda*.

8 *Āṇavamala*, *māyīyamala*, and *kārmamala*. (See Appendix 6 (p385) for explanation of *malas*.) See also *Kashmir Shaivism–The Secret Supreme*, Swami Lakshmanjoo, ed. John Hughes (Universal Shaiva Fellowship, Los Angeles, 1985-2015), "The Threefold Impurities – *Malas*," 7.47-49.

The energy filled with *svātantrya*, absolute independence, is first; *krama saṁsisṛkṣā*, just the will of desiring the world of succession, [is second]; and *kramātmatā*, the world of succession, [is third]. *Svātantrya śakti* is first (it is *abheda*), *krama saṁsisṛkṣā*, just [the will] to give rise to the successive world (it is *bhedābheda*), and *kramātmatā*, the successive world (it is *bheda*).[9] These three energies are the glory of my Lord, the glory of Lord Śiva. Let these three energies remain in my heart in such a way so that they reveal to me that supreme nature of God consciousness (*anuttaraṁ svarūpam prathaya*).

SCHOLAR: "*Svātantrya śakti*" is not *bahuvrīhi*.[10]

SWAMIJI: From my point of view, it is not *bahuvrīhi* as it is commentated by Jayaratha. "*Svātantrya śakti*" [Jayaratha] has put as Bhagavān, Lord Śiva, but it is not [in this instance]. [Abhinavagupta] says, "*Tadeva devī trayam*, these are the three energies of Lord Śiva." [Here], *svātantrya śakti* is an energy [among three], so it is not *bahuvrīhi*.[11] [Jayaratha] has not understood the way of Abhinavagupta.[12] [Jayaratha says], "*Svātantrya rūpā śaktiḥ'yasyāsau ananta śaktir bhagavān śivaḥ*." That is not it.

9 *Abheda* (monistic), *bhedābheda* (monistic-cum-dualistic), *bheda* (dualistic).

10 *Bahuvrīhi* is compound word that refers to a subject by nominating a particular attribute or quality of the subject. It is composed of an adjective followed by a noun, e.g., someone whose hair is red is called a redhead.

11 Although *svātantrya śakti* is generally understood to be the principal and defining energy/nature of Lord Śiva, in this instance Abhinavagupta lists *svātantrya śakti* as one amongst three energies of Lord Śiva. It cannot, therefore, be a *bahuvrīhi* compound.

12 Jayaratha wrote this commentary on the *Tantrāloka* about 200 years after its composition. To this day, his commentary is held as the authoritative work on the *Tantrāloka*. Although holding Jayaratha in high regard, Swamiji observed that since he was not connected with the oral tradition of Kashmir Shaivism, he had in numerous places misinterpreted Abhinavagupta's teaching.

DEVOTEE: *Svātantrya śakti* is *parā*.[13]
SWAMIJI: *Svātantrya śakti* is the supreme energy.[14]
Now, the sixth *śloka*:

13 *Svātantrya śakti* (absolute freedom) is *parā* (viz., *abheda*), *krama saṁsisṛkṣā* (the will to give rise to succession) is *parāparā* (viz., *bhedābheda*), and *kramātmatā* (the world of succession) is *aparā* (viz., *bheda*). "*Parā* is the monistic class of energies, the mono-dualistic class of energies is *parāparā*, and the dualistic class of energies is the *aparā* class." *Parātriśikā Vivaraṇa* (LJA archives).

14 "That is the *svātantrya* (absolute independence), that is *kartṛtvaṁ* (pure action), and that is *īśvaratā* (lordship), that is everything. When you see the outside situated inside and the inside situated outside, that is the reality of Lord Śiva. The real state of *jagadānanda* is that." *Tantrāloka* 6.238 (LJA archive). "*Svātantrya śakti* is His free will. Whatever He wishes, that is *svātantrya śakti*. *Svātantrya śakti* is the germ of all His five energies. He has got five energies: *cit śakti* (energy of consciousness), *ānanda śakti* (energy of bliss), energy of will (*icchā śakti*), energy of knowledge (*jñāna śakti*), and the energy of action (*kriyā śakti*). All these five energies of God consciousness are produced by His *svātantrya śakti* of freedom, of [His] free power. And *cit śakti* is actually based on His nature [viz., Śiva *tattva*], *ānanda śakti* is based on His Śakti (Pārvatī), *icchā śakti* is based on Sadāśiva, and *jñāna śakti* (the energy of knowledge) is based on Īśvara, and the energy of *kriyā* is based on Śuddhavidyā. All these five pure states of Lord Śiva are one with Lord Śiva. *Cit śakti* indicates Lord Śiva's actual position, *ānanda śakti* indicates Lord Śiva's position of Śakti, and *icchā śakti* indicates Lord Śiva's position of Sadāśiva, and *jñāna śakti* indicates His position in Īśvara, and Śuddhavidyā is [His] fifth position [viz., *kriyā śakti*]. All these five positions are filled with God consciousness. Below that is the scale of *māya*, illusion. That will go from *māya* to earth." Swami Lakshmanjoo, trans., *Special Verses on Practice, Selected Verses from Various Text on Kashmir Shaivism,* LJA archive, 1988, verse 13. See Appendix 7 (p387) for a further explanation of *svātantrya*.

Invocation to Cakreśvara – Ganeśa (6)

Audio 1 - 08:29

तद्देवताविभवभाविमहामरीचि-
चक्रेश्वरायितनिजस्थितिरेक एव।
देवीसुतो गणपतिः स्फुरदिन्दुकान्तिः
सम्यक्समुच्छलयतान्मम संविदब्धिम् ॥ ६ ॥

taddevatāvibhavabhāvimahāmarīci-
cakreśvarāyitanijasthitireka eva /
devīsuto gaṇapatiḥ sphuradindukāntiḥ
samyaksamucchalayatānmama saṁvidabdhim //6//

Let the offshoot of the supreme energy of *parā*, Gaṇapati,[15] . . .*

Gaṇapati means, the lord of the masses, the lord of classes (all classes), and that lord of classes is called Gaṇapati. He is an offshoot of *devī*, *parā devī*.

*. . . and that lord Gaṇapati, [who] is shining just like the full moon (*sphurat indu kāntiḥ*), and that Gaṇapati [who] is *sthitir*, is situated in his own nature, governing as the governor of the *śakti cakra*[16] of these three energies (*parā*,

15 Another name for Gaṇeśa, Lord Śiva and Pārvatī's son. "The creator of obstacles and the remover of the obstacles is Gaṇapati." *Tantrāloka* 6.69 (LJA archive). "Gaṇeśa is also [Lord Śiva and Pārvatī's] doorkeeper, and that is the breath. In the cycle of breathing in and out, this is the kingdom of Hanumān. At that junction point is the kingdom of Gaṇeśa." *Special Verses on Practice* (LJA archive).

16 Wheel (*cakra*) of energy (*śakti*).

parāparā, and *aparā*)–these three energies[17] have created glory and that glory is *parā*, *parāparā*, and *aparā*–and that glory, triple glory, has created innumerable *śakti cakra*s, and on that *śakti cakra* governs that Gaṇapati, who is *cakreśvara*,[18] . . .*

JOHN: What exactly is a "*cakra*" in this sense?

SWAMIJI: *Cakra* means, wheel. [*Śakti cakra* means], the wheel of energies. And he is Gaṇapati, [who is] *nijasthitir*, situated in his own nature, and is shining just like the moon.

*. . . let that Gaṇapati vibrate and penetrate my ocean of consciousness in such a way that it pervades the whole universe. That *saṁvit abdhiḥ* is, in other words, called the *Tantrāloka*. My *saṁvit abdhiḥ* (my ocean of consciousness) is filled in the *Tantrāloka*. Let that *Tantrāloka* shine everywhere and vibrate in the whole universe (*samucchalayatāt*).

The seventh [*śloka*]:

INVOCATION TO THE ANCIENT MASTERS OF TRIKA SHAIVISM (7-16)

Audio 1 - 11:42

रागारुणं ग्रन्थिबिलावकीर्णं
यो जालमातानवितानवृत्ति।
कलोम्भितं बाह्यपथे चकार
स्तान्मे स मच्छन्दविभुः प्रसन्नः ॥७॥

rāgāruṇaṁ granthibilāvakīrṇaṁ
yo jālamātānavitānavṛtti /
kalombhitaṁ bāhyapathe cakāra
stānme sa macchandavibhuḥ prasannaḥ //7//
[not recited in full]

17 *Svātantrya*, *krama saṁsisṛkṣā*, and *kramātmatā*, respectively.
18 The lord of the *cakras*.

Now he bows before all the masters of this school, directly and indirectly. First, he bows [before] the master, Macchandanātha.[19]

Let Macchandanātha remain happy with me–*prasanna*.

SCHOLAR: Favoring. Yes, show me his favor, let him . . .

SWAMIJI: . . . be favorable to me. Let Macchandanātha, the great master of Shaivism, be favorable to me always; Macchandanātha, who discarded this *jāla* of the universe, this net of the universe, in which net everybody is entangled and bound.

And that "net" he defines, what kind of net is that net of this universe.

It is *rāgāruṇaṁ*, it is red by that *geru* substance[20] (*rāga* means, *gairika ādi dravyeṇa,*[21] by that red color).[22] It is red because of that color [of *geru*]–red color. It is red because of that red color of this *jāla*, this net, the net of the universe in which net everybody is entangled, everybody is caught. And that net is called the *māyā* net, the net of *māyā*.[23] It is red

19 "The Kula System was introduced in Kashmir in the beginning of the fifth century A.D. by Śrī Macchandanātha. Later, in the ninth century, because its teachings had become distorted, it was reintroduced by Sumatinātha. In the line of masters that followed from Sumatinātha, Somanātha was his disciple. Śambhunātha was the disciple of Somanātha, and the great Abhinavagupta was the disciple of Śambhunātha." *Kashmir Shaivism–The Secret Supreme*, "The Schools of Kashmir Śaivism," 19.129.

20 A substance used in India to paint earthen pots and the bases of trees. *Geru* is a partially decomposed hematite (iron peroxide).

21 The substance (*dravya*) of red chalk (*gairika*), etc. (*ādi*).

22 Among the many definitions of *rāga* are: the act of coloring or dyeing; color, hue, tint, dye, esp. red color, redness; love, affection or sympathy for, vehement desire of, interest or joy or delight in.

23 "*Svātantrya śakti* and *māyā* are one, yet they are different in the sense that *svātantrya śakti* is that state of energy which can produce the power of going down and coming up again, both at will, whereas *māyā* will only give you the strength of going down and not the ability of rising up again. Once you have come down, you cannot move up again. This is the reality of the state of *māyā*. It binds you.

because of that color [of *geru*] and it is red also [because of] creating attachment also (that is *rāga*). It creates attachment. It creates curiosity to have it. Everybody wants to have that *jāla* because of the element of *rāga* (attachment), by *rāga tattva*, the element of *rāga*.[24] There, you should not explain [i.e., place significance upon] the color. It is the element of *rāga* (*rāga tattva*). By the element of *rāga tattva*, it creates attachment to this *jāla*. *Granthibilāvakīrṇam*, and it is filled with those holes of *granthi*, with knots. The outward *jāla* is filled with those holes. The *māyā jāla* is filled with the holes of that sex, where everybody is focused and wants to be attached with those *granthi*, *māyā granthi*.[25] And this *jāla* (this net) is *ātāna vitāna vṛtti*, wide in width and length. It is not only wide in width and length, it is also wide in width and length because of its innumerable variety of existence. And it is *kalombhitam*; this *jāla*, this net, is *kalombhitam*, artistically made.[26] Or, another meaning is, it is made from *kalā* [*tattva*][27]

Māyā śakti is that universal energy which is owned by the individual being, the individual soul, and when that same universal energy is owned by the universal Being, it is called *svātantrya śakti*. *Svātantrya śakti* is pure universal energy. Impure universal energy is *māyā*. It is only the formation that changes through a difference of vision. When you experience *svātantrya śakti* in a crooked way, it becomes *māyā śakti* for you, and when you realize that same *māyā śakti* in Reality, then that *māyā śakti* becomes *svātantrya śakti* for you." *Kashmir Shaivism–The Secret Supreme*, "The Three Impurities (*Malas*)," 7.47.

24 One of the five *kañcukas* (coverings), which are the productions of *māyā*, that comprise the limited individual. See Appendix 8 (p390) for a detailed explanation of the *kañcukas*.

25 "In Kashmir Shaivism, *māyā* has three aspects: *māyā śakti* (the energy of *māyā*), *māyā tattva* (the state or element of *māyā*), and *māyā granthi* (the illusive power of *māyā*). Abhinavagupta explains these three aspects of *māyā* at length in the 8th and 9th āhnika of Tantrāloka.

26 Bhaṭṭanārāyaṇa: "Lord Śiva is the greatest artist I have ever seen, I have ever come to know. Because He is such an artist that *nirupādāna saṁbhāram* and *abhittau eva tanvate*, He draws this

to earth (*pṛthvī*). From *māyā*, the element begins from *kalā*. So, from *kalā* to earth it is built.[28] And this *jāla* was discarded by Macchandanātha, outside. He didn't have it. He didn't possess it. Let Macchandanātha remain favorable to me always.

SCHOLAR: So, he bows first to the great master of the Kula system . . .

SWAMIJI: Kula system–Macchandanātha.

SCHOLAR: . . . to show precedence of the Kula system over Tantra system.

SWAMIJI: Yes.

Audio 1 - 16:40

त्रैयम्बकाभिहितसन्ततिताम्रपर्णी-
सन्मौक्तिकप्रकरकान्तिविशेषभाजः ।
पूर्वे जयन्ति गुरवो गुरुशास्त्रसिन्धु-
कल्लोलकेलिकलनामलकर्णधाराः ॥ ८ ॥

traiyambakābhihitasantatitāmraparṇī-
sanmauktikaprakarakāntiviśeṣabhājaḥ /

---

sketch of one hundred and eighteen worlds without any basis, without any paper, without any pen, without any ink, without any colors, without any pencils." *Stava Cintāmaṇi of Bhaṭṭanārāyaṇa*, translation and commentary by Swami Lakshmanjoo (original audio recording, LJA archives, Los Angeles, 1980-81), verse 9.

27 The *kañcuka* (covering) of limited action.

28 "All these elements from *māyā* to *pṛthvī* are just the expansion of His energy, His *svātantrya śakti*." *Tantrāloka* 9.156 (LJA archive). (See Appendix 2 (p372) for a list of the 36 elements (*tattvas*).) "Directly, universal consciousness can never travel to individual consciousness unless universal consciousness is absolutely disconnected. *Māyā* is the disconnecting element from God consciousness. *Kalā* (limited action) is the connecting element to that dead being in some limited thing. So, he does something by *kalā*. When he does something, then individuality shines. Otherwise, direct from God consciousness, individual consciousness would never come in existence." *Tantrāloka* 9.175-6 (LJA archive).

pūrve jayanti guruvo guruśāstrasindhu-
kallolakelikalanāmalakarṇadhārāḥ //8//

Let those ancient masters be glorified because they were selfless *karṇadhārāḥ*, selfless . . .

SCHOLAR: Helmsmen.

SWAMIJI: . . . helmsmen (*karṇadhārāḥ*, those who take you from the other [shore] on the boats). Selfless, *amala karṇadhārāḥ*, they were selfless, they didn't charge anything from their disciples, and they were capable of taking them from the deep ocean of the *śāstra*s (scriptures), the deep ocean of all theories, systems, schools, thoughts. Because those thoughts are so deep [that they] cannot be understood easily, but they made them easy to be grasped. So, they put those disciples on the other side of that ocean of *śāstra*.

SCHOLAR: *Kalana*, *kallolakelikalana*.

SWAMIJI: *Kelikalana*. *Kalana* means, the *racana*, the various ways of explanation, the various ways of describing and putting forth all clear things, and removing all doubts of the *śāstra*s. They were capable of that. Let those masters be glorified always, who had obtained the glory of those jewels, those rubies, . . .

SCHOLAR: *Mauktikā*?

SWAMIJI: *Mauktikā*.

SCHOLAR: Pearl? Is it pearl? A white one?

SWAMIJI: Pearl, yes.

. . . rubies out of the great Tāmraparṇī *nadī*,[29] out of that great stream which was flowing through the line, the succession, of Tryambakanātha.[30] So, Tryambakanātha created that Tāmraparṇī *nadī*. In that Tāmraparṇī river, those jewels,

29 A river that runs through the southern Indian state of Tamil Nadu.

30 Durvāsa Ṛṣi's son, Tryambakanātha, was the founder of the monistic school of Śaivism. See *Kashmir Shaivism–The Secret Supreme*, "The Birth of the *Tantra*s," 90.

those rubies and pearls, were possessed by those ancient masters who were *amala karṇadhārā* (*amala* means "selfless" *karṇadhārā*, helmsmen).

Now, the ninth [*śloka*]:

Audio 1 - 20:21

जयति गुरुरेक एव श्रीश्रीकण्ठो भुवि प्रथितः।
तदपरमूर्तिर्भगवान् महेश्वरो भूतिराजश्च॥९॥

jayati gurureka eva śrīśrīkaṇṭho bhuvi prathitaḥ /
tadaparamūrtirbhagavān maheśvaro bhūtirājaśca //9//

Let that unique master, Śrīkaṇṭhanātha, who appeared in this universe, let him be glorified always.[31] And another formation of His being who was Maheśvara and Bhūtirāja, let those two masters also be glorified.[32]

Now, he bows before–in the tenth and eleventh [*śloka*s]–before those masters who were ancient masters of logic on Shaivism.[33]

Audio 1 - 21:08

श्रीसोमानन्दबोधश्रीमदुत्पलविनिःसृताः।
जयन्ति संविदामोदसन्दर्भा दिक्प्रसर्पिणः॥१०॥

31 Śrīkaṇṭhanātha was an incarnation of Lord Śiva who appeared at the beginning of Kaliyuga. He initiated Durvāsa Ṛṣi in the *Bhairava tantra* and instructed him to disseminate its teachings throughout the world. Ibid.

32 Maheśvara was Abhinavagupta's teacher of Śrīsantāna, the school of mono-dualistic thought in Shaivism. This mono-dualistic school of Shaivism was founded by Śrīnātha, one of the three mind-born sons of Durvāsa Ṛṣi. Bhūtirāja revealed the meaning of the *Bhagavad Gītā* to Abhinavagupta and also taught him *Brahmavidyā*, the technique of leaving one's body at the time of death (*utkrāntiḥ*). See *Tantrāloka* 14.32-41. Though Bhūtirāja was a revered master of the Krama System, it is said that he was not Abhinavagupta's teacher in that particular system.

33 That is, the Pratyabhijñā system. See *The Secret Supreme*, "The Schools of Kashmir Shaivism," 130.

तदास्वादभरावेशबृंहितां मतिषट्पदीम्।
गुरोर्लक्ष्मणगुप्तस्य नादसंमोहिनीं नुमः ॥ ११ ॥

śrīsomānandabodhaśrīmadutpalaviniḥsṛtāḥ /
jayanti saṁvidāmodasandarbhā dikprasarpiṇaḥ //10//
tadāsvādabharāveśabṛṁhitāṁ matiṣaṭpadīm /
gurorlakṣmaṇaguptasya nāda saṁmohinīṁ numaḥ //11//
[not recited]

I bow to *mati ṣaṭ padī* (*ṣaṭ padī* means, that black bee), the black bee of the intellect, the black bee of the intellect of Lakṣmaṇagupta. I bow to the black bee of the intellect of Lakṣmaṇagupta. Lakṣmaṇagupta's intellect was just like a black bee, which was captivating everybody's heart by its sound (by its sound, *parāmarśa*). By its sound (*parāmarśa*), that black bee, the sound of the black bee of the intellect of Lakṣmaṇagupta, which was *nāda saṁmohinīm* (*nāda saṁmohinīm* means, captivating the heart of all disciples by that sound, buzzing sound), . . .*

SCHOLAR: And in a second sense, *parāmarśa*.

SWAMIJI: *Parāmarśa*, the sound that is *parāmarśa*.[34]

*. . . and which was filled with the nectar, with the entry of nectar, spread all over the world and expanded from the knowledge of Somānanda and Utpaladeva.[35] Somānanda and Utpaladeva created that fragrance, which spread all around

34 Swamiji generally defines *parāmarśa* as "supreme awareness." In Kashmir Shaivism, *parāmarśa* is synonymous with *nāda* (sound) and *vimarśa* (awareness). See Appendix 9 (p392) for an explanation of *parāmarśa*.

35 Somānanda was the master of Uptaladeva. "Somānanda was the reproducer of the Pratyabhijñā system, the Theory of Recognition. It was lying secretly in the *tantras*." Swami Lakshmanjoo, trans., *Spanda Samdoha* (LJA archive). Although Somānanda was considered to be the founder of the Pratyabhijñā system, it was his disciple Utpaladeva who introduced the title Pratyabhijñā, the Theory of Recognition, and it was Utpaladeva who wrote extensively on that system.

the world, and that fragrance was captivating the black bee of the intellect of Lakṣmaṇagupta[36] (the black bee is always fond of that fragrance), and that fragrance was the fragrance of God consciousness. And I bow to that Lakṣmaṇagupta who was the black bee of the intellect, an intellectual black bee.

Now he bows before his father:

Audio 1 - 23:54

यः पूर्णानन्दविश्रान्तसर्वशास्त्रार्थपारगः।
स श्रीचुखुलको दिश्यादिष्टं मे गुरुरुत्तमः॥ १२॥

yaḥ pūrṇānandaviśrāntasarvaśāstrārthapāragaḥ /
sa śrīcukhulako diśyādiṣṭaṁ me gururuttamaḥ //12//

My father also was my master of spirituality because he was resting in complete and universal *ānanda* (*pūrṇa ānanda*)[37] and he had mastered, and he had the information of, all the *śāstra*s–my father. And his name was Cukhulakanātha. Although his name was Narasiṁhagupta, his other name was Cukhulakanātha. Let that Cukhulakanātha, who was my great master, bestow to me whatever I desire in the spiritual world.

SCHOLAR: *Diśyādiṣṭaṁ.*

SWAMIJI: *Diśyāt*, bestow to me.

SCHOLAR: Aha, *diśyād iṣṭaṁ.*

SWAMIJI: *Iṣṭam*, whatever is desired by me (*iṣṭam*, desired, my desired thing). My desired object, let him bestow to me my desired object. That desired object is Lord Śiva.

Now the thirteenth *śloka*:

36 Lakṣmaṇagupta was Utpaladeva's chief disciple and Abhinavagupta's teacher in the Pratyabhijñā system.
37 The fullness (*pūrṇa*) of bliss (*ānanda*).

Audio 1 - 25:22

जयताज्जगदुद्धृतिक्षमोऽसौ
भगवत्या सह शंभुनाथ एकः ।
यदुदीरितशासनांशुभिर्मे
प्रकटोऽयं गहनोऽपि शास्त्रमार्गः ॥ १३ ॥

jayatājjagaduddhṛtikṣamo'sau
bhagavatyā saha śaṁbhunātha ekaḥ /
yadudīritaśāsanāṁśubhirme
prakaṭo'yaṁ gahano'pi śāstramārgaḥ //13//
[not recited]

Now his immediate [master], he bows before his immediate master of the Kula system. [His] immediate master of the Kula system was Śambhunātha–[the master] of Abhinavagupta. And [Śambhunātha] had a *dūti*[38] with him. And he was *jagat uddhṛtikṣama*, he was capable of uplifting the whole universe, not only one or two disciples. He could uplift the whole universe in one minute. *Jayatāt*, let him be glorified. Let him be glorified because he was the only unique master of mine. Let him be glorified along with his *dūti*–let his *dūti* also be glorified–by whose pointing out the important points of *śāstra*s, all *śāstra*s have become clear to me, although this *śāstra* is very deep (*gahano api śāstra mārga ayam prakaṭaḥ na abhavat*).

Now, he decides to explain the way of *śāstra* now.

JOHN: In the fourteenth.

SWAMIJI: In the fourteenth.

---

38 Lit., a female attendant. In Kashmir Shaivism, particularly in the Kaula system, it was required for the master to have a *dūti*. With reference to Kula system, Swami Lakshmanjoo tells us that, "If a lady (*dūti*) is not there along with the master, then the master has no authority to initiate." (*Tantrāloka 5*, LJA archive, concluding remarks.)

Audio 1 - 26:58

सन्ति पद्धतयश्चित्राः स्रोतोभेदेषु भूयसा।
अनुत्तरषडर्धार्थक्रमे त्वेकापि नेक्ष्यते॥ १४॥

santi paddhatayaścitrāḥ srotobhedeṣu bhūyasā /
anuttaraṣaḍardhārdhakrame tvekāpi nekṣyate //14//

Although in these triple flows of the schools of Trika[39] there

---

39 "The Trika system (Kashmir Shaivism) is comprised of four sub-systems: the Pratyabhijñā system, the Kula system, the Krama system, and the Spanda system. These four systems, which form the one thought of the Trika system, all accept, and are based on, the same scriptures. Kashmir Śaivism is known as the Pure Trika System. The word Trika means, the threefold science of man and his world. In the idea of Trika, there are three energies: *parā* (supreme), *aparā* (lowest), and *parāparā* (the combination of the lowest and the highest). These three primary energies represent the threefold activities of the world. In the thought of Trika, therefore, it is admitted that this whole universe and every action in it, whether spiritual, physical, or worldly, is existing in these three energies. The Trika philosophy is meant for any human being without restriction of caste, creed, or color. Its purpose is to enable you to rise from individuality to universality." *Kashmir Shaivism–The Secret Supreme*, 19.129.

naraśaktiśivātmakaṁ trikaṁ hṛdaye yā vinidhāya bhāsayet /
praṇamāmi parāmanuttarāṁ nijabhāsāṁ pratibhācamatkṛtim //

"*Nara śakti śivātmakaṁ trikaṁ*. In fact, this whole universe is threefold. Either it is in the state of Nara (individual soul), or it is in its energy (Śakti), or it is Śiva, i.e., Śiva, Śakti, and Nara (supreme, medium, and inferior). The inferior state of God consciousness is found in the individual soul, and the medium state of God consciousness is found in Śakti, and the supreme state of God consciousness is established in the state of Śiva. And this is the philosophy of Trika. Trika does not mean that it is the state of Śiva only. Trika absorbs, digests, Nara and Śakti, these both elements in one–that is Trika. When these threefold elements are digested in one nature, that is Trika." *Parātriśikā Vivaraṇa*, introduction, verse 3, (LJA archive).

are many ways, many important ways, and many wonderful and important ways,[40] for attaining the supreme Trika system, for attaining the supreme Trika state, but not even one is existing now. All those ways are lost. Not even one way is existing.

Audio 1 - 27:55

इत्यहं बहुशः सद्भिः शिष्यसब्रह्मचारिभिः ।
अर्थितो रचये स्पष्टां पूर्णार्थां प्रक्रियामिमाम् ॥ १५ ॥

ityahaṁ bahuśaḥ sadbhiḥ śiṣyasabrahmacāribhiḥ /
arthito racaye spaṣṭāṁ pūrṇārthāṁ prakriyāmimām //15
[not recited]

Ityahaṁ, so, it was necessary for me to explain those ways because those ways are all lost. All those ways are existing in the various schools of the Trika system, [but] not even one way is found now existing in this time. For this reason, all my disciples and all my colleagues (*sabrahmacāri* means, colleagues who have only one master), . . .

Those are called "colleagues"?

. . . by those colleagues also and by many disciples, I have been requested to make such a *śāstra* that would explain before the public all the ways, clarify all the ways (*arthita*). So, I *racaye*, I compose, *spaṣṭām* (clearly), this way of Trika in the formation of the *Tantrāloka*, which is filled with the complete explanation.

Audio 1 - 29:30

श्रीभट्टनाथचरणाब्जयुगात्तथा श्री-
भट्टारिकांघ्रियुगलाद्गुरुसन्ततिर्या
बोधान्यपाशविषनुत्तदुपासनोत्थ-
बोधोज्ज्वलोऽभिनवगुप्त इदं करोति ॥ १६ ॥

40 *Paddhataya*.

śrībhaṭṭanāthacaraṇābjayugāttathā śrī-
bhaṭṭārikāṁghriyugalādgurusantatiryā /
bodhānyapāśaviṣanuttadupāsanottha-
bodhojjvalo'bhinavagupta idaṁ karoti //16//
[not recited]

But this work I do only by the grace of my masters, not with my power. This was not in my power to do it. This power I got from the two feet, the two lotus feet, of Bhaṭṭanātha[41] (Śaṁbhunātha)[42] and the two lotus feet of his *dūti*[43] (his *dūti* was also so much, extremely, divine, and he himself was also divine).[44] From their two lotus feet, by the grace of [their] two lotus feet, and *guru santatiḥ*, all the line of masters, which have come out from those two lotus feet of both,[45] that *santati* is really destroying the poison of *pāśa*,[46] the poison of becoming entangled in this universe, which is absolutely away from supreme consciousness, supreme God consciousness.[47] And by that *upāsanā*, by worshipping that *bodha*, by worshipping that God consciousness, which has come out from the line of those masters [who] were gracefully graced by these two feet of my Śambhunātha and his *dūti*, Abhinavagupta has become

41 A title of respect. Bhaṭṭa means "my lord" and *nātha* means "refuge."

42 "[Śambhunātha] was a complete master for all the schools of Śaivism." *Tantrāloka* 13.346 (LJA archive). "[Abhinavagupta] says that Śambhunātha was the sun of the *maṭhikā,* [where disciples reside with master], of Trayambaka, the Trayambaka school. Tryambaka is a monistic school." *Tantrāloka* 6.88 (LJA archive). *Kashmir Shaivism–Secret Supreme*, "The Schools of Kashmir Shaivism," 19.129.

43 *Bhaṭṭārikā*, a noble lady.

44 See footnote 40.

45 Śambhunātha and his *dūti*.

46 A snare, trap, noose, tie, bond, cord, chain, or fetter.

47 "Because their mind is distracted towards worldly pleasures. The more you are entangled in worldly pleasures, the more you remain away from God consciousness." Swami Lakshmanjoo, trans., *Bhagavad Gita–In the Light of Kashmir Shaivism* (with original video), ed. John Hughes (LJA, 2013), verse 2.45.

enlightened by that supreme *bodha*, and being enlightened in such a way [that] *idaṁ karoti*, this *śāstra* is being composed by him.

Abhinavagupta has not said that his [only] master was Śambhunātha and [that] his *dūti* was his [only] master. [Śambhunātha's] disciples were also his masters–[Śambhunātha's] other disciples. Śambhunātha had not only one disciple, Abhinavagupta. So, [Abhinavagupta] collected knowledge from all of [Śambhunātha's] disciples. Abhinavagupta was unique in that way. It is why he says, "*bodhānya pāśa viṣanut tad upāsanottha*," all those Kula *santatiḥ* masters, he got information from them also, those colleagues also.

SCHOLAR: So, when he says, "*bhaṭṭārikāṁ-ghri-yugalād guru-santati*," it's *guru santatir* . . .

SWAMIJI: *Gurupāram pariyam.*[48]

SCHOLAR: And it arises from the lotus feet.

SWAMIJI: Yes. So, it is cent-per-cent correct that this *Tantrāloka* is divine [because] it has come from the mouth of all masters!

Now the seventeenth [*śloka*]:

THE MĀLINĪVIJAYOTTARA TANTRA (17-20)

Audio 1 - 33:20

न तदस्तीह यन्न श्री-मालिनीविजयोत्तरे।
देवदेवेन निर्दिष्टं स्वशब्देनाथ लिङ्गतः ॥ १७ ॥

na tadastīha yanna śrīmālinīvijayottare /
devadevena nirdiṣṭaṁ svaśabdenātha liṅgataḥ //17//
[not recited]

In this *Tantrāloka*, that object does not exist that does not

48 Knowledge flowing through the line of masters.

exist in the *Mālinīvijaya* [*tantra*].[49] Whatever is in the *Mālinīvijaya*, that you will find in the *Tantrāloka*, nothing else, because the *Mālinīvijaya* is explained by the Lord of lords to Devī by His direct words and by His signs.

SCHOLAR: So, there is nothing here which has not been taught by the God of gods, either directly or implicitly . . .

SWAMIJI: Yes.

SCHOLAR: . . . in the *Mālinīvijayottara tantra*.

SWAMIJI:

Audio 1 - 34:05

दशाष्टादशवस्वष्टभिन्नं यच्छासनं विभोः।
तत्सारं त्रिकशास्त्रं हि तत्सारं मालिनीमतम्॥ १८॥

daśāṣṭādaśavasvaṣṭabhinnaṁ yacchāsanaṁ vibhoḥ /
tatsāraṁ trikaśāstraṁ hi tatsāraṁ mālinīmatam //18//
[not recited]

This *śāstra* of Lord Śiva is classified in ninety-two *tantra*s: ten-fold, eighteen-fold, and sixty-four-fold. And all of these ninety-two *tantra*s are explained by Lord Śiva Himself. In ninety-two *tantra*s, ten *tantra*s are said to be explained in a dualistic way, and eighteen *tantra*s are said to be explained in a mono-dualistic way, and sixty-four *tantra*s are explained in the monistic way of Trika.[50] And the essence of these ninety-two *tantra*s is the Trika *śāstra*, the Trika *śāsana*. And the essence of that Trika *śāstra* is the *Mālinīvijaya*. So, there is nothing beyond the *Mālinīvijaya tantra*.

JOHN: That was the end of the eighteen [*śloka*].

SWAMIJI: Yes, the end of the eighteen [*śloka*].

---

49 "The *Mālinīvijaya tantra* is the chief *tantra* for Kashmir Śaivism." *Tantrāloka* 13.198 (LJA archive).

50 Viz., Śiva *tantra*s, Rudra *tantra*s, and Bhairava *tantra*s, respectively.

Audio 1 - 35:32

अतोऽत्रान्तर्गतं सर्वं संप्रदायोज्झितैर्बुधैः।
अदृष्टं प्रकटीकुर्मो गुरुनाथाज्ञया वयम्॥ १९॥

ato'trāntargataṁ sarvaṁ saṁpradāyojjhitairbudhaiḥ /
adṛṣṭaṁ prakaṭīkurmo gurunāthājñayā vayam //19//

So, we will explain clearly what was not understood by those *jñānis,*[51] by those *paṇḍits*, who were away from the *saṁpradāya,*[52] the *guru-śiṣya krama,*[53] of their masters–who were away from that *saṁpradāya*, tradition. So, *atrāntargatam*, so, in the ninety-two *tantra*s, whatever is in the body of the ninety-two *tantra*s, whatever is existing, whatever tradition of thought and school and explanation is existing, that object is not found by those masters who were away from the grace of their masters. And that *saṁpradāya* I will clarify in this *Tantrāloka* by *ājñā*, by the command, of my master. My master has commanded me to do this. Because, without . . .

SCHOLAR: Śambhunātha.

SWAMIJI: Śambhunātha.

JOHN: That's the end [of the] nineteenth [*śloka*].

SWAMIJI: End nineteenth, yes. Now the twentieth [*śloka*]:

Audio 1 - 37:20

अभिनवगुप्तस्य कृतिः
सेयं यस्योदिता गुरुभिराख्या।
त्रिनयनचरणसरोरुह-
चिन्तनलब्धप्रसिद्धिरिति॥ २०॥

---

51 Although *jñānis* are considered to be more elevated than *yogis* in Shaivism, in this case Swamiji is referring to those who are just scholars (*paṇḍits*), who are not necessarily given to practise.

52 An established doctrine or tradition transmitted from one teacher to another.

53 The succession (*krama*) of masters (*guru*) and disciples (*śiṣya*).

abhinavaguptasya kṛtiḥ
seyaṁ yasyoditā gurubhirākhyā /
trinayanacaraṇasaroruha-
cintanalabdhaprasiddhiriti //20//

Whatever Abhinavagupta has created, whatever Abhinavagupta has explained or composed (any *śāstra,* any *śloka*), for that composition, Abhinavagupta has got, achieved, the title from his masters. His masters have bestowed [upon] him this title that, "Abhinavagupta has got this kind of power to create and explain in a clear way because he is given to the contemplation of the feet of Lord Śiva. He is always contemplating on the feet of Lord Śiva, so he has achieved that power to explain things." This title was bestowed to me, Abhinavagupta, by my masters. So, I think this *Tantrāloka* will be really explained in its real way.

Invocation to Śambhunātha (21)

Audio 1 - 38:45

श्रीशम्भुनाथभास्कर-
चरणनिपातप्रभापगतसङ्कोचम्
अभिनवगुप्तहृदम्बुज-
मेतद्विचिनुत महेशपूजनहेतोः ॥ २१ ॥

śrīśambhunāthabhāskara-
caraṇanipātaprabhāpagatasaṁkocam /
abhinavaguptahṛdambujam-
etadvicinuta maheśapūjanahetoḥ //21//
[not recited]

So, let this–the twenty-first [*śloka*]–let this lotus, one hundred petal lotus, of the heart of Abhinavagupta–this heart of Abhinavagupta, this *Tantrāloka* is the heart of Abhinavagupta–let this heart of Abhinavagupta be *vicinuta* (plucked one-by-one), plucked one-by-one by the readers. Let the readers of the *Tantrāloka* pluck one-by-one the lotus of this heart of Abhinavagupta, that is, the *Tantrāloka*. The *Tantrāloka* is the heart of Abhinavagupta.

SCHOLAR: Why one-by-one? Why do you say "one-by-one"?

SWAMIJI: *Vicinuta. Vicinuta* is not to pluck it [as a whole].

SCHOLAR: It means?

SWAMIJI: Just to open it, one-by-one. Because, on some plate, you have to put those [petals] for the worshipping of Lord Śiva.

SCHOLAR: You put the petals . . .

SWAMIJI: Those leaves, petals, one-by-one. "One-by-one" means, you must go in the depth of this thought of the *Tantrāloka*, in the depth of all those schools [that are discussed in the] *Tantrāloka*. This heart of Abhinavagupta, which is a lotus, let this lotus be *vicinuta*, plucked, plucked one-by-one.

SCHOLAR: To paraphrase it.

SWAMIJI: Analyze it. Analyze it separately just to worship Lord Śiva. Because this lotus of Abhinavagupta, which is the *Tantrāloka*, is *apagata saṁkocam*, is opened, has opened, is opened, has bloomed out, in the *Tantrāloka* by the touch of the sun of Śambhunātha.

SCHOLAR: *Caraṇa*, rays.

SWAMIJI: Rays, the rays of Śambhunātha (Śambhunātha was his master). *Ādi vākyam*, this is *ādi vākya*: "*śambhunātha bhāskara caraṇanipāta prabhāpagata saṁkocam.*" This is the most important *vākya*[54] of Abhinavagupta.

JOHN: This *śloka*?

SWAMIJI: This *śloka*, because this [*śloka*] will create enthusiasm, curiosity, in people to read it. Because, by reading it, this will become worship of Lord Śiva–by reading it clearly.

SCHOLAR: So, "*ādi vākyam*" refers not only to this verse

54 *Vākya*: Speech, saying, assertion, statement, command, words.

but to all the preceding verses?

SWAMIJI: No, this [verse] is *ādi vākya*.

SCHOLAR: Just the one?

SWAMIJI: Just the one.

SCHOLAR: *Mahāvākyatena*.[55]

SWAMIJI: *Mahāvākyatena*, yes.

SCHOLAR: *Ekamevādi vākyam*.

SWAMIJI: *Ekamevādi vākyam*, this is only one *ādi vākya*.

SCHOLAR: Yes, alright. I've seen it.[56]

JOHN: Twenty-two?

SWAMIJI: Twenty-two. From [verse] twenty-two begins the *Tantrāloka*, the *śāstra* of the *Tantrāloka*.

General Introduction
A) The nature of Ignorance (22-30)

Audio 1 - 42:04

इह तावत्समस्तेषु शास्त्रेषु परिगीयते।
अज्ञानं संसृतेर्हेतुर्ज्ञानं मोक्षैककारणम्॥ २२॥

iha tāvatsamasteṣu śāstreṣu parigīyate /
ajñānaṁ saṁsṛterheturjñānaṁ mokṣaikakāraṇam //22//

In this world of spirituality, everywhere, in each and every *śāstra*, it is sung that ignorance is the cause of repeated births and deaths and knowledge is the cause of liberation from it.

55 Here [in this text], it is the principal statement. Note: Abhinavagupta has also used this same verse in praise of his master, Śambhunātha, as one of the introductory *śloka*s of his *Tantrasāra*, his brief version of the *Tantrāloka*.

56 In his commentary, Jayaratha has concluded that all the previous verses were *ādi vākya*.

This I have not explained from my mind. It is explained by Śiva in *tantra*.

For this he explains this twenty-third *śloka*:

Audio 1 - 43:01

मलमज्ञानमिच्छन्ति संसाराङ्कुरकारणम्।
इति प्रोक्तं तथा च श्रीमालिनीविजयोत्तरे॥ २३॥

malamajñānamicchanti saṁsārāṅkurakāraṇam /
iti proktaṁ tathā ca śrīmālinīvijayottare //23//
[not recited in full]

Mala is ignorance. *Mala* is not some dirt.[57] *Mala* is [literally] "dirt," but that dirt is ignorance, and that ignorance becomes the cause of *māyīyamala* and *kārmamala*. *Malam* is called *āṇavamala*. *Āṇavamala* is called *ajñāna* (ignorance) and that *ajñāna* is the cause of *māyīyamala* and *kārmamala*.[58] This is explained by Lord Śiva in the *Mālinīvijayottara* [*tantra*].[59]

Audio 1 - 43:50

विशेषणेन बुद्धिस्थे संसारोत्तरकालिके।
संभावनां निरस्यैतदभावे मोक्षमब्रवीत्॥ २४॥

viśeṣaṇena buddhisthe saṁsārottarakālike /
saṁbhāvanāṁ nirasyaitadabhāve mokṣamabravīt //24//

Lord Śiva has explained, told, that *mokṣa* (liberation) will only come into being, into existence, by the depriving of the *ajñāna* (ignorance) of *puruṣa*.[60] [Now], this *ajñāna* has got two

57 "The *malas* are just the absence of knowledge and not something substantial." *Tantrāloka* 9.75 (LJA archive).
58 See Appendix 6 (p385) for detailed explanation of the *malas*. See also *Kashmir Shaivism–The Secret Supreme*, 7.47-49.
59 The first line of verse 23 is a direct quote from the *Mālinīvijaya tantra* 1.23cd.
60 The individual soul.

qualifications, this ignorance has got two qualifications: one ignorance is attached to the intellect[61] and another ignorance is attached to *puruṣa* (being).[62] But if we would say that that *ajñāna*, [which is explained] there in *Mālinīvijaya*, [if it] is explained as that ignorance which is attached to the intellect, [then] that cannot be [said to be the cause of *puruṣa's* bondage] because the intellect has come out into existence after the world was created. When the world was created, after the creation of the world, the intellect took place, the intellect was created. How, by removing the intellectual ignorance, can you get liberation? There is still *saṁsāra* yet.

SCHOLAR: When you say that it is created after *saṁsāra* . . .

SWAMIJI: It is created after *saṁsāra*.

SCHOLAR: . . . you don't mean in the sense of time but in the sense of that *āṇavamala*, *nirvikalpa* [thoughtless-ness], precedes ideation always.

SWAMIJI: Yes, after *āṇavamala* it was created; the intellect was created after *saṁsāra*. So, how can that intellectual knowledge be the cause of the removal of ignorance? Because [the intellect] is *saṁsāra uttara kālike*, it has come into existence after *saṁsāra* was created.[63]

SCHOLAR: It presupposes *saṁsāra*.

SWAMIJI: Yes. So, *saṁbhāvanāṁ nirasya*, this *saṁ-*

---

61 *Bauddha ajñāna*.

62 *Pauruṣa ajñāna*.

63 Swamiji tells us that, "The creative course is beginning from Śiva to *pṛthvī*" (*Parātriśikā Vivaraṇa*, LJA archive) and also that these 36 elements "flash forth simultaneously in a successive way." *Tantrāloka* 9.215, (LJA archive). As Swamiji explains in his translation of verse 9.94 of the *Tantrāloka* (LJA archive), *āṇavamala* first arises in the state of Sadāśiva. The intellect (*buddhi tattva*) is created after the creation of *āṇavamala* (viz., Sadāśiva) and after the creation of the limited individual/*saṁsāra* (viz., *māyā* and the *kañcukas*) and therefore cannot be the cause of the individual's bondage. See Appendix 2 (p372) for a list of the 36 elements.

bhāvanā[64] you should put away, you should cast this *saṁbhāvanā* aside. *Etat abhāve* [means], *pauruṣa ajñāna abhāve*, when *pauruṣa ajñāna*[65] is destroyed, *mokṣam abravīt*, *mokṣa*[66] is likely to happen.

JOHN: It is not certain that *mokṣa* will happen, it's only likely.

SWAMIJI: No, no, it is certain. *Abravīt*, He has told that *mokṣa* will take place, not likely [take place].

Audio 1 - 46:38

अज्ञानमिति न ज्ञानाभावश्चातिप्रसङ्गतः।
स हि लोष्टादिकेऽप्यस्ति न च तस्यास्ति संसृतिः॥२५॥

ajñānamiti na jñānābhāvaścātiprasaṅgataḥ /
sa hi loṣṭādike'pyasti na ca tasyāsti saṁsṛtiḥ //25//
[not recited in full]

But ignorance is not the complete absence of knowledge. The complete absence of knowledge is not [what is meant by] "ignorance" here.

SCHOLAR: It is not a merely negative thing.

SWAMIJI: It is not the complete absence of knowledge [because] there is some knowledge. In ignorance, there is some knowledge, but not complete ignorance. *Ajñānamiti na jñānābhāva*, the complete negation of knowledge is not ignorance here because *ati prasaṅgataḥ*, if we accept that ignorance is the complete negation of knowledge, there will be *ati prasaṅga*[67] . . .

SCHOLAR: Lack of specificity.

SWAMIJI: . . . because *sa hi loṣṭādike api asti*, that kind of

64 Opinion or assumption.
65 Spiritual ignorance.
66 Liberation.
67 The logical fault of over-extension; an unwarrantable stretch of a principle.

ignorance you would find in rocks also. *Na ca tasyāsti saṁsṛtiḥ*, but rocks have no *saṁsāra*, they are not moving in the wheel of repeated births and deaths. The mover who moves in repeated births and deaths is only *puruṣa*, not these rocks and earth. Earth has no *saṁsāra*, rocks have no *saṁsāra*, only being, that individual being, has *saṁsāra*. And so the individual being has that knowledge which is incomplete knowledge. So, *ajñāna* (ignorance) is that incomplete knowledge, *ajñāna* is not the negation of knowledge.

Number twenty-six [*śloka*]:

Audio 1 - 48:28

अतो ज्ञेयस्य तत्त्वस्य सामस्त्येनाप्रथात्मकम्।
ज्ञानमेव तदज्ञानं शिवसूत्रेषु भाषितम्॥ २६ ॥

ato jñeyasya tattvasya sāmastyenāprathātmakam /
jñānameva tadajñānaṁ śivasūtreṣu bhāṣitam //26//
[not recited]

So, in the *Śiva Sūtra*s also, it is explained that that ignorance is knowledge but [knowledge] in differentiated form. *Jñeyasya tattvasya*, when the reality of the worth-knowing object . . .

The worth-knowing object is Lord Śiva; *jñeyasya tattvasya*, worth-knowing, what is to be known, that is Lord Śiva.

SCHOLAR: Not "*nīlasukhādi jñeyasya*"?[68]

SWAMIJI: Yes, that is also [applicable]. Whatever you find in this universe (*nīla sukhādi*, all this objective world), that objective world is really the nature of Lord Śiva.

. . . so when this objective world, [when] you don't feel the nature of Lord Śiva in this objective world (*sāmastyena āprathātmakam*, when you don't feel Lord Śiva's formation in

68 A reference to Jayaratha's commentary: by the knowledge of (*jñeyasya*) the color blue (*nīla*) and pleasure (*sukha*), etc.

this objective world), that kind of knowledge is called ignorance. And it is said in the *Śiva Sūtra*s.

Audio 1 - 49:44

चैतन्यमात्मा ज्ञानं च बन्ध इत्यत्र सूत्रयोः ।
संश्लेषेतरयोगाभ्यामयमर्थः प्रदर्शितः ॥ २७ ॥

caitanyamātmā jñānaṁ ca bandha ityatra sūtrayoḥ /
saṁśleṣetarayogābhyāmayamarthaḥ pradarśitaḥ //27//

This very point is explained in the first two *sūtra*s of the *Śiva Sūtra*s: "*caitanyamātmā*" (verse 1.1) and "*jñānam bandha*" (verse 1.2). *Caitanyam ātmā*, consciousness is the Self. *Jñānam bandha*, perception is bondage. In these two *sūtra*s, by *saṁśleṣa* and *itara*, by combining them together or keeping them separately, these *sūtra*s, they point out the same explanation: consciousness is the Self and perception is bondage. What kind of perception is bondage? That he will explain. And non-perception is bondage, too. If you keep these two *sūtra*s combined, then [it means], "consciousness is the Self and non-perception is bondage." If you keep these two *sūtra*s separately, then [it means], "consciousness is the Self and perception is bondage" (when it will [read] "*jñānam bandha*"). If [they are] combined, then it will be "*ajñānaṁ bandha*."[69]

---

69 "In the first reading, when you unite these two *sūtra*s with the letter *a*, it reads "*caitanyam ātmā, ajñānaṁ bandha*." When you do not unite them [with the letter *a*], then the reading will be "*caitanyam ātmā, jñānaṁ bandha*." So, the author defines the meaning of *jñāna* in two ways: *jñānaṁ bandha* (knowing is bondage) and *ajñānaṁ bandha* (not knowing is bondage). Thus, the meaning of the verse is, knowing differentiatedly is bondage and not knowing undifferentiatedly is bondage. So, knowing (*jñānaṁ*) is bondage and not knowing (*ajñānam*) is bondage. These two meanings arise from combining and not combining the words in the first two verses–"*caitanyam ātmā*" from the first verse and "*jñānaṁ bandha*" from the second verse. Knowledge is bondage. What knowledge is

Now he explains the same in the twenty-eighth, twenty-ninth, and thirtieth *śloka*s:

Audio 1 - 51:30

चैतन्यमिति भावान्तः शब्दः स्वातन्त्र्यमात्रकम्।
अनाक्षिप्तविशेषं सदाह सूत्रे पुरातने॥ २८॥
द्वितीयेन तु सूत्रेण क्रियां वा करणं च वा।
ब्रुवता तस्य चिन्मात्ररूपस्य द्वैतमुच्यते॥ २९॥

caitanyamiti bhāvāntaḥ śabdaḥ svātantryamātrakam /
anākṣiptaviśeṣaṁ sadāha sūtre purātane //28//
dvitīyena tu sūtreṇa kriyāṁ vā karaṇaṁ ca vā /
bruvatā tasya cinmātrarūpasya dvaitamucyate //29//
[not recited]

Caitanyam,[70] this [word] *caitanyam* is *bhāvāntaḥ śabda.*[71] "*Cetanā*" is not *bhāvān śabda.*[72] *Cetanasya bhāvaḥ caitanyam.*

SCHOLAR: So it's an abstract noun.

SWAMIJI: Yes. Because, the existing reality of consciousness is *caitanya*–the existing reality–that is, *bhāvāntaḥ śabda.* This *bhāvāntaḥ śabda* explains to you only *svātantrya mātrakam*, only *svātantrya*, only absolute independence, without touching all the other aspects of the Lord, for

---

bondage? Differentiated knowledge. What not-knowing is bondage? Not knowing your own undifferentiated Self. So, knowing individual consciousness as one's own nature and not knowing universal consciousness as one's own nature are both bondage."
Swami Lakshmanjoo, trans., *Shiva Sutras–The Supreme Awakening*, ed. John Hughes (LJA, 2002-2015), 1.2.18-19.

70 *Caitanyam* means, the independent state of consciousness. Ibid., 1.1.12.

71 An abstract noun, which refers to something that cannot be grasped by the senses.

72 A concrete noun, which refers to something that can be grasped by the senses.

instance, all-pervading-ness, all-knowledge, etc.[73] *Anākṣipta viśeṣaṁ*, and this is explained in that ancient *sūtra*.[74] And the next *sūtra* also there, "*jñānaṁ bandha*," explains that *cinmātra rūpaḥ*[75] has two aspects of action: one is *kriyā* and the other is *karaṇa*. *Kriyā* means, perception (perception is *jñāna*) and [that] by which you perceive [i.e., *karaṇa*], that is [also] *jñāna*. By which you perceive, that is the objective world. When your perception is adjusted to the objective world, that perception is also bondage. That perception is also bondage and [that] by which you perceive is bondage. So, differentiated knowledge is explained in this way [with respect] to that conscious Being.

Now the thirtieth [*śloka*]:

Audio 1 - 53:32

द्वैतप्रथा तदज्ञानं तुच्छत्वाद्बन्ध उच्यते।
तत एव समुच्छेद्यमित्यावृत्त्या निरूपितम्॥ ३०॥

dvaitaprathā tadajñānaṁ tucchatvādbandha ucyate /
tata eva samucchedyamityāvṛttyā nirūpitam //30//
[not recited]

And that *dvaita prathā*, that differentiated perception, is *ajñāna* (ignorance), and it is *tucchatvāt* (*tucchatvāt* means, it is to be discarded).

SCHOLAR: It is worthless.

---

73 "The author would use the word *cetanā* if he were to declare that other aspects, in addition to the aspect of complete independence (*svātantrya*), also existed in the state of Lord Śiva. But only one aspect exists and that is *svātantrya*." *Shiva Sutras–The Supreme Awakening*, 1.1.12. "When *caitanya* becomes limited, it is transformed into the nature (*svarūpa*) of the intellect, and it becomes the intellect." Ibid., 1.3.24, fn10.

74 "*Caitanyamātmā*." Ibid., verse 2.

75 The formation or embodiment (*rūpa*) of consciousness (*cinmātra*), i.e., Lord Śiva.

SWAMIJI: Worthless. So, [differentiated knowledge] is to be discarded, and this is explained by the repetition of these [two] *sūtras* again, twice repetition.[76]

B) The nature of Liberation – Mokṣa (31-35)

Now the thirty-first [*śloka*]:

Audio 2 - 0:02

स्वतन्त्रात्मातिरिक्तस्तु तुच्छोऽतुच्छोऽपि कश्चन।
न मोक्षो नाम तन्नास्य पृथङ्नामापि गृह्यते॥ ३१ ॥

svatantrātmātiriktastu tuccho'tuccho'pi kaścana /
na mokṣo nāma tannāsya pṛthaṅnāmāpi gṛhyate //31//

Now, he explains in this *śloka*, the thirty-first *śloka*, what is really liberation (*mokṣa*). *Mokṣa*, he explains, *mokṣa* is only *svatantrātma*, when your being becomes absolutely independent from all sides. That is *mokṣa*, that is liberation, then you are liberated. Without that absolute independence, whatever is existing in this world, if it is *tuccha* or if it is *atuccha*, if it is empty (worthless) or if it is worthy, . . .

JOHN: Valuable.

SWAMIJI: . . . whatever it is, that is not *mokṣa*. So, there is nothing separately explained as *mokṣa* except *svatantrātma*.

The thirty-second [*śloka*]:

Audio 2 - 01:23

यत्तु ज्ञेयसतत्त्वस्य पूर्णपूर्णप्रथात्मकम्।
तदुत्तरोत्तरं ज्ञानं तत्तत्संसारशान्तिदम्॥ ३२ ॥

yattu jñeyasatattvasya pūrṇapūrṇaprathātmakam /
taduttarottaraṁ jñānaṁ tattatsaṁsāraśāntidam //32//

76 That is, as combined and as separated.

The essence that we have to perceive [of that which is] worth perceiving, that essence [of that] which is to be perceived (that is, Lord Śiva), and that perception, as long as it becomes full by-and-by, in succession, as much as it is full, you are near *mokṣa*. If it is not full, if it is incomplete, you are away from *mokṣa*. So, that [incomplete] fullness is differentiated fullness. For some masters of some other schools, they consider that full, but in other systems it is not, it is incomplete. So that complete fullness lies only in Shaivism, although they[77] are liberated from that *saṁsāra* of their own (*tattat saṁsāra śāntidam*[78]).

Now he explains the same in the thirty-third *śloka*:

Audio 2 - 03:01

रागाद्यकलुषोऽस्म्यन्तःशून्योऽहं कर्तृतोज्झितः।
इत्थं समासव्यासाभ्यां ज्ञानं मुञ्चति तावतः॥ ३३॥

rāgādyakaluṣo'smyantaḥśūnyo'haṁ kartṛtojjhitaḥ /
itthaṁ samāsavyāsābhyāṁ jñānaṁ muñcati tāvataḥ //33//
[not recited]

Some masters of [other] schools say that, "*rāgādi akuluṣo asmi*," the reality of the Self is [realized] when you are absolutely away from the bondage of *rāga* (attachment), *kāma* (desire), *krodha* (wrath), etcetera (*rāgādi akaluṣo asmi*).

77 The masters of other schools who have an incomplete knowledge and understanding of what liberation is.

78 *Saṁsāra* generally refers to the cycle of repeated births and deaths and every school agrees that *kārmamala* (the erroneous sense of doership) is the primary cause of reincarnation. Kashmir Shaivism, however, proclaims the existence of two subtler *mala*s (*āṇavamala* and *māyīyamala*), which continue to inhibit the soul from realizing absolute freedom even after being released from the cycle of repeated births and deaths.

SCHOLAR: Free of *kleśāvaraṇa*–the Yogācāras.[79]

SWAMIJI: Yes, it is for Yogācāras. Another school of thought explains that the reality of the Self is just to become deprived or away from all substance. When you are an absolute void, [when] you become an absolute void, you are free. Absolute voidness is freedom.

SCHOLAR: *Śūnya svabhāvako'ham.*

SWAMIJI: Yes, *śūnya svabhāvako'ham*.

JOHN: Which school is this?

SCHOLAR: Mādhyamikā.[80]

SWAMIJI: Mādhyamikā. And another school explains that the reality of the Self is when the Self becomes absolutely away from *kartṛ bhāva* (action).

JOHN: This would be Sāṁkhya?

SWAMIJI: It is Sāṁkhya.[81]

SCHOLAR: And Patañjali *yoga*.

SWAMIJI: Patañjali *yoga* also.[82] So this way (*ittham*),

---

79 Literally, "*yoga* practice," Yogācāra is one of the two principal schools of Mahāyana Buddhism that prescribes the overcoming of *kleśa*s (afflictions) as the means towards liberation.

80 Literally, "intermediate," Mādhyamikā is the second principal school of Mahāyana Buddhism, which was founded by Nāgārjuna.

81 The third among the six classical systems of Indian philosophy, Sāṁkhya literally means "pertaining to numbers." Founded by Ṛṣi Kapila, the doctrine of Sāṁkhya posits the existence of 25 *tattva*s (elements), all which are incorporated in the 36 *tattva*s of Kashmir Shaivism. According to this dualistic system, there exists a multiplicity of souls (*puruṣa*s), each of which exist independent of one another and of material nature (*prakṛti*). Sāṁkhya is the most widely incorporated systems in Indic philosophy. According to Sāṁkhya, knowledge alone is sufficient for the achievement of liberation (*mokṣa*).

82 The fourth of the six classical systems of Indian philosophy was formulated by Patañjali in his *Yoga Sūtra*s. This system, which is considered to be an atheistic doctrine, wholly incorporates the doctrine of Sāṁkhya and provides systematic and practical guide-

samāsavyāsābhyāṁ jñānaṁ, this knowledge, this perception, relieves them from that bondage of their own, collectively[83] or separately.[84] Some become aware and that *jñāna* (knowledge) removes the bondage of those people collectively, . . .

SCHOLAR: Up to that point.

SWAMIJI: Up to that point.[85]

. . . and to some, one-by-one (*vyāsābhyām*).

SCHOLAR: What does that mean?

SWAMIJI: That means, some people are freed from *māyīyamala*, some people are freed from *kārmamala*, and some are freed from all these *mala*s. Those who are freed from all these *mala*s, it is *samāsena*.[86]

SCHOLAR: But none of these three are freed completely.

SWAMIJI: They are not freed completely.

---

lines for the achievement of liberation (*mokṣa*).

83 *Samāsa*.

84 *Vyāsa*.

85 Up to the point of their particular understanding of liberation.

86 In general, the Buddhist conception of liberation is the experience of *pralayākala** (viz., *sūnya* or *suṣupti*), which, according to Kashmir Shaivism, is a condition still mired by *āṇavamala* and *māyīyamala*. It is agreed, however, that the cycle of repeated births and deaths ceases at this stage on account of being freed from *kārmamala*. The *pralayākalin*, however, will again enter the cycle of *saṁsāra* after *mahāpralaya* (the great destruction). For Sāṁkhyā-Yoga and Advaita Vedānta, the highest conception of liberation is the experience of *vijñānākala*, which is still mired by *āṇavamala*. As such, these conceptions of liberation are said to be incomplete. According to Kashmir Shaivism, complete liberation is not merely the cessation of repeated births and deaths (*saṁsāra*), but more significantly, the achievement of absolute freedom (*svātantrya śakti*), which is achieved only when *āṇavamala* has been completely destroyed, and this occurs only at the state of Śiva/Śakti. Swamiji tells us: "When *āṇavamala* is gone, everything is gone, and you have got entry in God consciousness." *Tantrāloka* 9.120 (LJA archive). *See Appendix 10 (p394) for a discussion of the seven perceivers and their associated *mala*s (impurities).

SCHOLAR: So, how can he say "*samāsa*" in that sense?

SWAMIJI: From their point of view, [it is] *samāsa* [totality].

JOHN: And, at the same time, is it possible to be liberated from, say, *māyīyamala* and not from *kārmamala*?

SWAMIJI: If there is *māyīyamala*, there is *kārmamala* also.

SCHOLAR: *Ārāṅkurakāraṇam.*[87]

SWAMIJI: Yes.

JOHN: So, it goes in . . . it's successive.

SWAMIJI: Successive, yes, these two *malas*. *Āṇavamala* is the most subtle *mala*.

SCHOLAR: So, *vyāsa*[88] would be just from *āṇavamala*.

SWAMIJI: *Āṇavamala*.

SCHOLAR: Just from that.

SWAMIJI: Yes.

SCHOLAR: Or from *māyīyadmalad aṁśāṁśikāya*.[89]

SWAMIJI: *Aṁśāṁśikāya*.

SCHOLAR: That would be *vyāsa*.

SWAMIJI: Yes. The thirty-fourth [*śloka*]:

Audio 2 - 06:21

तस्मान्मुक्तोऽप्यवच्छेदादवच्छेदान्तरस्थितेः ।
अमुक्त एव मुक्तस्तु सर्वावच्छेदवर्जितः ॥ ३४ ॥

tasmānmukto'pyavacchedādavacchedāntarasthiteḥ /
amukta eva muktastu sarvāvacchedavarjitaḥ //34//
[not recited]

Tasmāt mukto'pyavacchedāt. So, although he is liberated

87 The seed of *kārmamala* lies in *māyīyamala*.

88 Separately.

89 *Aṁśa* means a portion, and *aṁśāṁśikāya* means forming a part of that portion. Here the sense is that *māyīyamala* and *kārmamala* are parts of *āṇavamala*.

from these bondages, but another class of bondages appears to him on his way, on his path. So, from that point of view, he is not liberated at all. The really-liberated person is that person who is liberated from these *mala*s from all sides.

So, next, the thirty-fifth *śloka*:

Audio 2 - 07:07

यत्तु ज्ञेयसतत्त्वस्य ज्ञानं सर्वात्मनोज्झितम्।
अवच्छेदैर्न तत्कुत्राप्यज्ञानं सत्यमुक्तिदम्॥ ३५॥

yattu jñeyasatattvasya jñānaṁ sarvātmanojjhitam /
avacchedairna tatkutrāpyajñānaṁ satyamuktidam //35//
[not recited]

The perception of that worthy-[to-be]-known object, Śiva (*jñeyasatattvasya*), that perception, when it is *sarvātmanā ujjhitam avaccheda*, when it is absolutely away, absolutely away from all bondages, that kind of perception is nowhere [non]-perception [of the undifferentiated Self], nowhere ignorance, and it gives you the real liberation (*satya muktidam*), and that is the Shaivite liberation.

C) The two ways of Knowledge and Ignorance (36-45)

Now, he explains in the following *śloka*s what is knowledge and what is ignorance.

Audio 2 - 08:09

ज्ञानाज्ञानस्वरूपं यदुक्तं प्रत्येकमप्यदः।
द्विधा पौरुषबौद्धत्वभिदोक्तं शिवशासने॥ ३६॥

jñānājñānasvarūpaṁ yaduktaṁpratyekamapyadaḥ /
dvidhā pauruṣabauddhatvabhidoktaṁ śivaśāsane //36//

In the *Śiva śāstra*s, the reality of knowledge and ignorance is said to be, is explained to be, in two ways: *pauruṣa jñāna* and *pauruṣa ajñāna*, *bauddha jñāna* and *bauddha ajñāna*–in the *Śiva śāstras*. *Pauruṣa ajñāna* [and *pauruṣa jñāna* are] concerned with that of *puruṣa* (the Self): the ignorance of the Self (*pauruṣa ajñāna*) and the knowledge of the Self (*pauruṣa jñāna*), these two. *Bauddha ajñāna* and *bauddha jñāna* are the ignorance of intellectual apprehension and the knowledge of intellectual apprehension, these two.[90]

Now he explains them fully in the following *śloka*s, thirty-seventh and a half:

Audio 2 - 09:28

तत्र पुंसो यदज्ञानं मलाख्यं तज्जमप्यथ।
स्वपूर्णचित्क्रियारूपशिवतावरणात्मकम्॥ ३७॥
संकोचिदृक्क्रियारूपं तत्पशोरविकल्पितम्।

tatra puṁso yadajñānaṁ malākhyaṁ tajjamapyatha /
svapūrṇacitkriyārūpaśivatāvaraṇātmakam //37//
saṁkocidṛkkriyārūpaṁ tatpaśoravikalpitam /

In those two perceptions and two ignorances, the perception concerning *puruṣa*, that non-perception (*ajñāna*), is *āṇavamala*, is *malākhyam*. *Tajjamapi atha*, although that *āṇavamala* has come out from *puruṣa* itself–*āṇavamala* has come out, come forth, from *puruṣa*–but that *āṇavamala* covers the real state of Śiva, which is filled with consciousness and filled with action (filled with knowledge and action). Complete knowledge and complete action is the formation of *śivatā* (Śiva), and that *śivatā* is covered by this *āṇavamala*. And in place of this complete knowledge and complete action, He puts

90 For more on these two types of knowledge and ignorance, see Appendix 11 (p397).

incomplete knowledge and incomplete action at its place, and that is owned by *paśu*[91] (the limited being). That incomplete knowledge and incomplete action is owned by the limited being.

SCHOLAR: It is *avikalpitam,*[92] it is *a-priori* for him.[93] It is *avikalpitam*.

SWAMIJI: *Avikalpitam*, [it seems] real. He[94] considers that, "It is my own real knowledge. That differentiated knowledge and differentiated perception of being is my own." That is *avikalpitam*. It is *vāstavam*[95] from his point of view.

SCHOLAR: But also in the sense of, for him, at the limited level, it is *nirvikalpam.*[96]

SWAMIJI: Yes.

SCHOLAR: It is like *prathamālocanātmakam.*[97]

SWAMIJI: No, no, not *prathamālocanātmakam*.

SCHOLAR: Well, the commentator takes it like that I think.

SWAMIJI: Where?

SCHOLAR: *Kriyāsvābhāsālocanātmakaṁ jñānam*.

SWAMIJI: *Ālocanātmakaṁ*, [not] *prathama ābhāsa*. It is *ālocanātmakaṁ*, just "perceiving."

---

91 Lit., a beast.

92 Lit., undoubted.

93 *A-priori*: reasoning or knowledge which proceeds from theoretical deduction, inference, or postulation, rather than from observation or experience.

94 Lord Śiva who has assumed the condition of an individual (*paśu*).

95 Substantial, real, true, genuine.

96 According to Kashmir Shaivism, the foundation of ignorance (*āṇavamala*) itself is a thought-less (*nirvikalpa*) condition because *nirvikalpa* always precedes, and is the very life of, ideation (*vikalpa*).

97 The scholar is referring to the first flow of perception (*prathama ābhāsa*, *prathama prasara*, *prathama ālocana*, *prathama anusaṁdhāna*), which is the initial "appearance of God consciousness in universal objectivity." Swami Lakshmanjoo, trans., *Śhivastotrāvalī–Hymns to Shiva* by Utpaladeva, ed., John Hughes (Universal Shaiva Fellowship, Los Angeles, 2014), 9.5.

SCHOLAR: Well, that is the first perception, direction perception, of objects?

SWAMIJI: Not the direct perception.

SCHOLAR: Because *āṇavamala* limits you into that *saṅkoca dṛkkriyā*[98] . . .

SWAMIJI: Yes, yes.

SCHOLAR: . . . spontaneously without . . .

SWAMIJI: Yes, yes. Yes, from that point of view it is. The thirty-eighth [*śloka*]:

Audio 2 - 12:30

तदज्ञानं न बुद्ध्यंशोऽध्यवसायाद्यभावतः ॥ ३८ ॥

tadajñānaṁ na buddhyaṁśo'dhyavasāyādyabhāvataḥ //38//
[not recited]

And that perception [i.e., ignorance] is not concerned with the intellect (*na buddhyaṁśa*) because *adhyavasāyābhāvataḥ*, the *adhyavasāya* is not existing there [in *pauruṣa ajñāna*].

SCHOLAR: So in that sense, too, it is *avikalpitam*.

SWAMIJI: Yes, in that sense.

JOHN: What is that word?

SWAMIJI: *Adhyavasāya*. *Adhyavasāya* means, judgment, differentiated judgment. Differentiated judgment has not come into existence at that time of *pauruṣa ajñāna*.

JOHN: In *āṇavamala*.

SWAMIJI: In *āṇavamala*. After *āṇavamala*, *buddhi* has come into existence.

Audio 2 - 13:11

अहमित्थमिदं वेद्मीत्येवमध्यवसायिनी।
षट्कञ्चुकाबिलाणूत्थप्रतिबिम्बनतो यदा ॥ ३९ ॥

98 Contracted perception.

धीर्जायते तदा तादृग्ज्ञानमज्ञानशब्दितम्।
बौद्धं तस्य च तत्पौंस्नं पोषणीयं च पोष्टृच॥ ४० ॥

ahamitthamidaṁ vedmītyevamadhyavasāyinī /
ṣaṭkañcukābilāṇūtthapratibimbanato yadā //39//
dhīrjāyate tadā tādṛgjñānamajñānaśabditam /
bauddhaṁ tasya ca tatpauṁsnaṁ poṣaṇīyaṁ ca poṣṭṛca //40//

Now, he explains in the thirty-ninth and fortieth *śloka*s, what is actually the knowledge of *bauddha* and the ignorance of *bauddha* (intellectual knowledge and intellectual ignorance).

SCHOLAR: As opposed to inherent ignorance and inherent knowledge.[99]

SWAMIJI: Yes. That intellect which perceives that, "I am perceiving this object, such and such object, this way (*aham ittham, idaṁ vedmi*)," this kind of intellectual perception, when it comes into existence by the reflection that has come out from *puruṣa* who is entangled by the six coverings, . . .*

JOHN: Ah, *kañcuka*s.

SWAMIJI: *Ṣaṭ kañcuka. Ābila* means, he who is covered by these six coverings.[100] From that *puruṣa*, it is reflected. That reflection is penetrated in that intellect and that intellect then perceives that, "I perceive this in this way."

*. . . and this kind of perception of the intellect, when it comes forth, that kind of knowledge is called *ajñāna*, and that *ajñāna* is *bauddha ajñāna*. And that *bauddha ajñāna* is already strengthened and gets more and more life by *pauruṣa*

---

99 The scholar is referring to *pauruṣa ajñāna* and *pauruṣa jñāna*, respectively.

100 See Appendix 8 (p390) for an explanation of the six (*ṣaṭ*) coverings (*kañcuka*s). *Ābila* refers to the *puruṣa* who becomes confounded, confused, and who suffers pain and misfortune because of the *kañcuka*s.

ajñāna in the coming future. *Pauruṣa ajñāna* strengthens, nourishes, feeds, that *bauddha ajñāna*. And it is *poṣaṇīyaṁ ca poṣṭṛ ca*, *pauruṣa ajñāna* strengthens the intellectual ignorance and intellectual ignorance strengthens the *pauruṣa ajñāna*.

SCHOLAR: As in the state of great grief, eventually the object of grief appears before you. Is that what he means here?

SWAMIJI: Yes.

SCHOLAR: It's the example [given by Jayaratha].

SWAMIJI: This is *bauddha ajñāna*. Now, what is *bauddha jñāna*?

JOHN: Forty-one.

SWAMIJI: Forty-one and forty-two:

Audio 2 - 16:08

क्षीणे तु पशुसंस्कारे पुंसः प्राप्तपरस्थितेः।
विकस्वरं तद्विज्ञानं पौरुषं निर्विकल्पकम्॥४१॥
विकस्वराविकल्पात्मज्ञानौचित्येन यावसा।
तद्बौद्धं यस्य तत्पौंस्नं प्राग्वत्पोष्यं च पोष्टृ च॥४२॥

kṣīṇe tu paśusaṁskāre puṁsaḥ prāptaparasthiteḥ /
vikasvaraṁ tadvijñānaṁ pauruṣaṁ nirvikalpakam //41
vikasvarāvikalpātmajñānaucityena yāvasā /
tadbauddhaṁ yasya tatpauṁsnaṁ
prāgvatpoṣyaṁ ca poṣṭṛ ca //42// [not recited]

When the impressions of a limited being are destroyed (*kṣīṇe tu paśu saṁskāre*; *saṁskāre* means, these impressions, traces of limitedness), when the traces of limitedness are destroyed and *puruṣa* is situated in his own real nature, *prāpta parasthite*, that knowledge which *puruṣa* holds, that is *vikasvaraṁ* (*vikasvaraṁ* means, all-round shining), and that knowledge is called *pauruṣa* knowledge, and that is *nirvikalpakam*, not *avikalpitam*. There is a difference between *nirvikalpakam* and *avikalpitam*. *Avikalpitam* means, from his [limited] point of view it is *avikalpitam*.

SCHOLAR: For the limited subject.

SWAMIJI: From the limited subject['s point of view]. *Nirvikalpakam* is for the unlimited subject.[101] *Vikasvara avikalpātma jñānaucityena yāvasā*, and, to that *puruṣa*, who is filled with that real knowledge, that intellect which is existing in that *puruṣa* according to the existence of his own knowledge of *pauruṣa*, which is *vikasvara* and *avikalpa* (all-round shining and thoughtless; without any impressions, without any differentiated impressions), that intellect is called *bauddha jñāna*. And that intellectual knowledge is nourished by that *pauruṣa jñāna* and *pauruṣa jñāna* is nourished by that intellectual knowledge, side-by-side.

JOHN: So, this *avikalpa*, that is not "thought-less" in the same way as *nirvikalpa* is "thought-less."

SWAMIJI: *Avikalpakam* is "thought-less," yes, *nirvikalpa*. *Avikalpitam*, [as described] previously in that [*pauruṣa*] *ajñāna*, that is not "thought-less." This [*avikalpakam*] is "thought-less."

SCHOLAR: The difference being that, in the first case, there is no awareness . . .

SWAMIJI: There is no awareness.

JOHN: It's like *śūnya* (voidness)!

SCHOLAR: . . . and no judgment, but here there is awareness but no judgment.

JOHN: So that other one is *śūnya*.

SWAMIJI: That other one[102] is exactly like *śūnya*; not *śūnya*, but like *śūnya*.

---

101 *Nirvikalpa*: thought-less or undifferentiated. Lit., not admitting an alternative, free from change or differences, admitting no doubt, not wavering, without hesitation or reflection. See Appendix 4 (p375).

102 The *avikalpitam* of *āṇavamala* (*pauruṣa ajñāna*) as explained in verse 38a.

Audio 2 - 18:53

तत्र दीक्षादिना पौंस्नमज्ञानं ध्वंसि यद्यपि।
तथापि तच्छरीरान्ते तज्ज्ञानं व्यज्यते स्फुटम्॥ ४३ ॥

tatra dīkṣādinā pauṁsnamajñānaṁ dhvaṁsi yadyapi /
tathāpi taccharīrānte tajjñānaṁ vyajyate sphuṭam //43//

[Among] these two perceptions,[103] this ignorance of *puruṣa* is destroyed by being initiated by masters. When you get initiation from your master, then that ignorance concerned with the *puruṣa* is destroyed. Although it is destroyed there, the fruit of that destruction is perceived only at the end of the body, not in his lifetime. Although it is there, that knowledge is there, *pauruṣa jñāna* is there, but the fruit of *pauruṣa jñāna* [i.e., liberation] is found, is perceived, only at the end of leaving that physical body.

SCHOLAR: Swamiji, when he says "*dīkṣādinā*," is he only meaning *kriyā dīkṣā*[104] and these *dīkṣās*, or also higher *dīkṣās*?

SWAMIJI: Higher *dīkṣās* (initiations) also.

SCHOLAR: *Vedha dīkṣā* as well?

SWAMIJI: Yes, *vedha dīkṣā.*[105]

SCHOLAR: So, how can *vedha dīkṣā* occur and *bauddha jñāna* not appear?

SWAMIJI: *Vedha dīkṣā. Bauddha jñāna* will appear only by knowledge, by book knowledge.

JOHN: Does he explain later why it is the case that you don't attain *mokṣa* [while embodied] if you don't have *bauddha*

---

103 *Pauruṣa ajñāna* (spiritual ignorance) and *bauddha ajñāna* (intellectual ignorance).

104 Physical initiation.

105 Abhinavagupta explains the subject of *vedha dīkṣā* (the initiation of piercing) in the 29th *āhnika* of the *Tantrāloka*. See Appendix 12 (p398) and also *Kashmir Shaivism–The Secret Supreme*, chapter 18, "Variations in the Rise of Prāṇa Kuṇḍalinī."

jñāna? What it is . . .

SWAMIJI: Yes, he will explain it. Now, the forty-fourth *śloka*:

Audio 2 - 20:35

बौद्धज्ञानेन तु यदा बौद्धमज्ञानजृम्भितम्।
विलीयते तदा जीवन्मुक्तिः करतले स्थिता॥ ४४॥

bauddhajñānena tu yadā bauddhamajñānajṛmbhitam /
vilīyate tadā jīvanmuktiḥ karatale sthitā //44//

Now, if *pauruṣa jñāna* is there existing, *pauruṣa jñāna* is there, and *bauddha jñāna* is also [there]–*bauddha jñāna* has completely destroyed the *bauddha ajñāna* (intellectual ignorance)–when that intellectual ignorance is also destroyed in his lifetime (if *pauruṣa jñāna* is there and intellectual ignorance is also destroyed by intellectual knowledge), then *jīvan mukti*[106] is there, *karatale*, in his hand. Then he is *jīvan mukta*; he has not to wait for leaving his body. So, *bauddha jñāna* has got this kind of power to make him *jīvan mukta*, but only in the case [that] there is *pauruṣa jñāna* existing in his nature.

JOHN: So at the time of *dīkṣā*, that *pauruṣa jñāna* isn't fully manifested.

SWAMIJI: *Pauruṣa jñāna* is manifested, but it cannot manifest . . .

JOHN: Completely.

SWAMIJI: . . . [as long as] there is the limitation of the body.

SCHOLAR: It is still *avikalpitam*.

SWAMIJI: It is still *avikalpitam*.[107]

106 Embodied liberation.

107 His *pauruṣa ajñāna* (spiritual ignorance) is still *avikalpitam*. "He considers that, 'It is my own real knowledge; that differentiated knowledge and differentiated perception of being is my own.' That is *avikalpitam*. It is *vāstavam* (real) from his point of view." Extract from Swamiji's commentary on verse 37 above.

SCHOLAR: For him at that level, too. It[108] doesn't affect the awareness of the mind.[109]

SWAMIJI: Now, the forty-fifth *śloka*:

Audio 2 - 22:08

दीक्षापि बौद्धविज्ञानपूर्वा सत्यं विमोचिका।
तेन तत्रापि बौद्धस्य ज्ञानस्यास्ति प्रधानता॥४५॥

dīkṣāpi bauddhavijñānapūrvā satyaṁ vimocikā /
tena tatrāpi bauddhasya jñānasyāsti pradhānatā //45//

Now he explains in this forty-fifth *śloka* the [greater] importance of *bauddha jñāna* from the Śaiva point of view. *Bauddha jñāna* is a must here! If *bauddha jñāna* is not there, then nothing is there. If *bauddha jñāna* is there, everything is there. So, intellectual knowledge is to be achieved from all sides. Because, *dīkṣāpi*, this initiation also becomes successful if there is intellectual power in the disciple to receive it. At the time of receiving initiation from his master for attaining *pauruṣa jñāna*, you need the intellectual power. The disciple needs intellectual power to receive it, to grasp it–how to meditate, how to concentrate on the Self. If he has not that intellectual power, that *dīkṣā* won't be successful. So, in that way also, *bauddha jñāna* is predominant.

SCHOLAR: So this *bauddha vijñāna* is not as Jayaratha takes it: the *bauddha jñāna* which is necessary in the master in order to be able to initiate the disciple.

SWAMIJI: No, no, that is not it.[110]

---

108 *Pauruṣa jñāna* alone.

109 Abhinavagupta will explain in verse 49 how the acquisition of spiritual knowledge alone, although short-lived without the support of intellectual knowledge, is indeed capable of liberating an individual at the point of death.

110 Although that is not what is meant in this instance, Swamiji tells us: "The master must be established in God consciousness which has come in his experience by getting entry in *svātantrya*; *svātantrya*,

SCHOLAR: But surely if intellectual knowledge (*bauddha jñāna*) is required for . . .

SWAMIJI: For the disciple.

SCHOLAR: . . . for *dīkṣā*–right?–then how could it be the case that he would remain un-liberated until death if he already had *bauddha jñāna* to some extent? If he already had *bauddha jñāna*, which is the prerequisite of . . .

SWAMIJI: Only *bauddha jñāna*.

SCHOLAR: . . . adept *yogis*. You said, if [*dīkṣā*] is preceded by *bauddha vijñāna*, *dīkṣāpi bauddha vijñāna pūrvā* . . .

SWAMIJI: *Dīkṣā*. *Dīkṣā* means, *pauruṣa jñāna sambandhini*. *Dīkṣā* means, initiation that will create *pauruṣa jñāna* in you.

SCHOLAR: Yes.

SWAMIJI: That initiation will take place, it will be successful, only when there is intellectual knowledge, some intellectual knowledge, some traces of intellectual knowledge, in the disciple. Otherwise, it won't be understood.

SCHOLAR: Not complete *śāktopāya* awareness, not complete intellectual knowledge . . .

SWAMIJI: Not complete but . . .

SCHOLAR: . . . like in *śāktopāya*.[111]

SWAMIJI: No (affirmative). You must have some intellectual

---

which makes him one with Lord Śiva. *Sa eva hi guruḥ kārya*, that guru you must find out for getting initiation in these rituals. *Tato asau dīkṣaṇe kṣamaḥ*, he is the perfect master to handle these rituals, no other master. That master who is only authorized in rituals without [personally] getting entry in God consciousness is not fit to become a master. He knows rituals but he has not *āveśa*, he has not experienced the entry of God consciousness, so he is not a fit master for this." *Tantrāloka* 15.38 (LJA archive).

111 The three *upāyas* (practical means) that are prescribed in Trika are *śāmbhavopāya*, *śāktopāya*, and *āṇavopāya*. Abhinavagupta introduces the subject of the *upāyas* in verse 70, and discusses the three *upāyas* in great detail from verse 139 onwards. See Appendix 25 (p418) for a detailed explanation of the *upāyas*.

power to receive it. When there is no intellectual power, that *pauruṣa jñāna* won't be understood. That *dīkṣā* (initiation) won't be understood.

JOHN: So Shaivism excludes duffers.

SWAMIJI: Duffers, yes, absolutely (laughs).

SCHOLAR: Bhairava *śāstra*.[112]

SWAMIJI: *Tena tatrāpi bauddhasya jñānasya asti pradhānatā*. So, the predominance lies only in *bauddha jñāna* there, not in *pauruṣa jñāna*.[113]

[In the following verse, Abhinavagupta says], "This two-fold knowledge and two-fold ignorance is not my own invention":

D) Confirmation of Knowledge and Ignorance From various Śāstras (46-51)

Audio 2 - 25:20

ज्ञानाज्ञानगतं चैतद्द्वित्वं स्वायम्भुवे रुरौ।
मतङ्गादौ कृतं श्रीमत्खेटपालादिदैशिकैः ॥४६॥

jñānājñānagataṁ caitaddvitvaṁ svāyambhuve rurau /
mataṅgādau kṛtaṁ śrīmatkheṭapālādidaiśikaiḥ //46//
[not recited]

This is explained in the *Svāyambhu śāstra*, in the *Ruru śāstra*, in the *Mataṅga śāstra*, by Kheṭapāla, etcetera, masters.

SCHOLAR: That's commentators.

SWAMIJI: Yes, commentators. [Abhinavagupta says], "So this is not new. So this is not my invention regarding this knowledge and ignorance."

112 Monistic scripture/doctrine.

113 That is, in order for an initiation to produce the desired result: embodied liberation.

Audio 2 - 25:50

तथाविधावसायात्मबौद्धविज्ञानसम्पदे।
शास्त्रमेव प्रधानं यज्ज्ञेयतत्त्वप्रदर्शकम्॥ ४७॥

tathāvidhāvasāyātmabauddhavijñānasampade /
śāstrameva pradhānaṁ yajjñeyatattvapradarśakam //47//

That *śāstra* which carries you to the essence, to the reality, of that which is to be known,[114] that *śāstra* is concerned [with] maintaining, for experiencing, or attaining, the glory of *bauddha vijñāna*. This *śāstra* is needed for that, i.e., that *śāstra* which will carry you to that point of That [which] is to be known. So, *advaita śāstra*[115] is concerned . . . *advaita śāstra* is a must for attaining the glory of *bauddha jñāna*.

SCHOLAR: But *dīkṣā* is a necessary prerequisite for that.

SWAMIJI: Yes, previously you must have *dīkṣā* (initiation). Only *bauddha jñāna* won't liberate you.

JOHN: Can you gain the fullness of *bauddha jñāna* without *pauruṣa jñāna*? Can a person have *pūrṇa* (complete) *bauddha jñāna* without . . .

SWAMIJI: Without *pauruṣa jñāna*? No.

JOHN: So, there is a very close correlation . . .

SWAMIJI: Yes. *Pauruṣa jñāna* is first. *Pauruṣa jñāna* must be there first, existing, and then *bauddha jñāna* is glorious. *Bauddha jñāna* will glorify itself and *pauruṣa jñāna* also. If there is only *bauddha jñāna*, not *pauruṣa jñāna*, *bauddha jñāna* is of no use and the holder of that *bauddha jñāna* is useless.

SCHOLAR: But isn't it more than no use? Isn't it just impossible to have *bauddha jñāna* unless you have already destroyed *āṇavamala*? You can think those thoughts, but can

---

114 Lord Śiva (*jñeyatattva*).

115 *Advaita śāstra* (non-dual scripture) refers to the Bhairava *śāstras*, the monistic scriptures of Kashmir Shaivism, which are the substance of the *Tantrāloka*.

you have *bauddha jñāna*? It's impossible to have *bauddha jñāna*, surely. How can you think, "I am all this . . ."?

SWAMIJI: Complete *bauddha jñāna* won't exist until there is *pauruṣa jñāna*. That is true.

SCHOLAR: So, it is really *bauddhājñāna* (intellectual ignorance).

SWAMIJI: Yes.

JOHN: So, they grow together then?

SWAMIJI: They grow together. It is already explained previously.

JOHN: So then, the whole function of Śaiva *sādhanā* (practice) is, on the one hand, practice and devotion to the master, and on the other hand, this . . .

SWAMIJI: Intellectual power, yes.

Audio 2 - 28:24

दीक्षया गलितेऽप्यन्तरज्ञाने पौरुषात्मनि।
धीगतस्यानिवृत्तत्वाद्विकल्पोऽपि हि सम्भवेत॥४८॥

dīkṣayā galite'pyantarajñāne pauruṣātmani /
dhīgatāsyānivṛttatvādvikalpo'pi hi sambhavet //48//

Although, by the initiation of masters, this ignorance concerned with *puruṣa* has disappeared, but as long as *dhīgata ajñāna*, *dhīgatasya anivṛttatvāt*, when *bauddha ajñāna* is not destroyed, has not disappeared, *vikalpo api hi sambhavet*,[116] there is the possibility of *pauruṣa ajñāna* also to rise. Again, after attaining the *pauruṣa jñāna*, there is an apprehension that *pauruṣa jñāna* would be destroyed after some period if *bauddha ajñāna* is existing there throughout. If *bauddha ajñāna* is existing there, there is the possibility of *pauruṣa jñāna* also to be destroyed–*pauruṣa jñāna* will also vanish.

116 On account of the production (*sambhava*) of differentiated thoughts (*vikalpa*).

SCHOLAR: That is possible, is it?

SWAMIJI: This is possible.

JOHN: It is possible because of what? The person becomes . . .

SWAMIJI: So, *bauddha jñāna* you must hold.

JOHN: So, the disappearance of Self-knowledge[117] would be because the individual would become side-tracked or had the wrong ideas or . . .

SWAMIJI: Yes, wrong ideas, and it will carry him downwards, downwards, downwards by-and-by, and there will be *ajñāna*; instead of *jñāna* (knowledge), there is *ajñāna*.[118]

SCHOLAR: Back to Śaiva Siddhānta, Vaiṣṇavas, the Vedas, . . .

SWAMIJI: Yes.

SCHOLAR: . . . *bhūta pūjā*.[119]

SWAMIJI:

Audio 2 - 30:07

देहसद्भावपर्यन्तमात्मभावो यतो धियि।
देहान्तेऽपि न मोक्षः स्यात्पौरुषाज्ञानहानितः ॥४९॥

dehasadbhāvaparyantamātmabhāvo yato dhiyi /
dehānto'pi na mokṣaḥ syātpauruṣājñānahānitaḥ //49//
[not recited]

Deha sadbhāva paryantam. And there is another point also to be discussed. Because, as long as his physical frame is

117 *Pauruṣa jñāna.*

118 "Ignorance is knowledge but [knowledge] in differentiated form," viz., differentiated thoughts (*vikalpas*). From Swamiji's translation of verse 26 above. This will be discussed further in verse 51.

119 Traditionally the word *bhūta* means, ghosts or spirits, but Swamiji tells us, "By *bhūta* you must know that *śarīra* (the body) is *bhūta*, breath (*prāṇa*) is *bhūta*, and objects are *bhūta*. *Shiva Sutras–The Supreme Awakening*, 1.20.63

existing and he has achieved the *pauruṣa jñāna*–and his physical frame, as long he holds this physical frame up to death–*ātmabhāvo yato dhiyi*, and this intellectual ignorance is shining there as long as his physical [body is existing], there is one possibility of *pauruṣa jñāna* [alone] to liberate you: if you achieve *pauruṣa jñāna* and die! If you achieve *pauruṣa jñāna* and [immediately] die, then there is no fear of returning again to *ajñāna*.

SCHOLAR: Like in *brahmavidyā*[120], . . .

SWAMIJI: Yes, *brahmavidyā*.

SCHOLAR: . . . the moment-of-death rituals, meditations.

SWAMIJI: Yes. Otherwise, if *pauruṣa ajñāna* is there in his lifetime, *pauruṣa ajñāna* is there, *ātmabhāvo yato dhiyi dehānte api na mokṣa syāt*, after leaving his physical frame also, he won't become liberated, because *pauruṣa ajñāna hānitaḥ*, *pauruṣa jñāna* will be destroyed by *bauddha ājñāna*.

SCHOLAR: So you've explained that Jayaratha is wrong in a big way . . .

SWAMIJI: Yes, absolutely.

SCHOLAR: . . . because he doesn't accept the possibility of *jñāna*, *pauruṣa jñāna*, could disappear.

SWAMIJI: No, no, he is not right there.

SCHOLAR: Your explanation is so much clearer.

SWAMIJI: *Bauddha ajñāna nivṛttau tu* . . . the fiftieth *śloka*:

Audio 2 - 31:47

बौद्धाज्ञाननिवृत्तौ तु विकल्पोन्मूलनाद्ध्रुवम्।
तदैव मोक्ष इत्युक्तं धात्रा श्रीमन्निशाटने॥५०॥

120 *Brahmavidyā* is the procedure to be adopted at the time of death. This technique known as *utkrānti* was taught to Abhinavagupta by the illustrious master, Bhūtirāja. Chapter 19 of the *Tantrāloka* gives details of *utkrānti*. See verse 280.

bauddhājñānanivṛttau tu vikalponmūlanāddhruvam /
tadaiva mokṣa ityuktaṁ dhātrā śrīmanniśāṭane //50//
[not recited in full]

When *bauddha ajñāna* has vanished, *bauddha ajñāna* has vanished, intellectual ignorance is gone, and *vikalpa unmūlanāt*, and *pauruṣa ajñāna* is also uprooted, then *tadaiva mokṣa*, then there and then you get liberation. This is explained by Lord Śiva in the *Niśāṭana tantra*.

Vikalpayuktacittastu piṇḍapātā . . . the fifty-first *śloka*:

Audio 2 - 32:28

विकल्पयुक्तचित्तस्तु पिण्डपाताच्छिवं व्रजेत्।
इतरस्तु तदैवेति शास्त्रस्यात्र प्रधानतः ॥५१॥

vikalpayuktacittastu piṇḍapātācchivaṁ vrajet /
itarastu tadaiveti śāstrasyātra pradhānataḥ //51//
[not recited in full]

The one [who has been initiated and] who has got *vikalpa*,[121] *vikalpa* in his intellectual sphere of knowledge, when he has got *vikalpa* (*vikalpa yukta cittastu*), it means [that although] he has got *pauruṣa jñāna*, [he also has] *bauddha ājñāna* (*pauruṣa* [*jñāna*] and at the same time *bauddha ājñāna*, that is *vikalpa yukta cittastu*).

SCHOLAR: Because he still thinks, *"Kṛśo'ham."*

SWAMIJI: Yes. *"Kṛśo'ham," "sthūlo'ham," "kṣāma," "sukhi aham," "duḥkhi aham," "kṛṣṭo'smi."*[122]

DEVOTEE: It is *bauddha vikalpa*?

SWAMIJI: Yes, *bauddha vikalpa*.[123] *Piṇḍapātāt śivam*, it is said that he will get liberation at the time of death only. *Itarastu*, but the one who has got intellectual knowledge also

121 Differentiated thoughts.

122 "I am thin," "I am stout," "I am emaciated," "I am happy," "I am sad," "I am weak," respectively. In other words, he has differentiated thoughts.

123 Intellect limited by differentiated thought.

at the same time, *tadaiva*, he becomes liberated there and then in his lifetime. *Iti śāstrasyātra pradhānataḥ*, so, the [knowledge of the] *śāstra*s are more valid than your experience of the Self. *Śāstrasyātra pradhānataḥ*, intellectual knowledge is more predominant there.

JOHN: In this regard.

SWAMIJI: In this regard.

JOHN: If you want to gain *mokṣa* in your life.

SWAMIJI: Yes, there and then.

SCHOLAR: Because there is no real Self-knowledge without intellectual knowledge.

SWAMIJI: *Bas*,[124] the explanation of *ājñāna* (ignorance) and *jñāna* (knowledge) is over.

The Essence of What is to be Realized (52-67)

Now he explains here the essence of what is to be recognized, the real object to be known:

Audio 2 - 34:33

ज्ञेयस्य हि परं तत्त्वं यः प्रकाशात्मकः शिवः।
नह्यप्रकाशरूपस्य प्राकाश्यं वस्तुतापि वा॥५२॥

jñeyasya hi paraṁ tattvaṁ yaḥ prakāśātmakaḥ śivaḥ /
nahyaprakāśarūpasya prākāśyaṁ vastutāpi vā //52//
[not recited]

The real object is, in fact, Lord Śiva. That real object is not away from the objective world. It is in this objective world that you find the essence of Lord Śiva there, because nothing can

124 A Hindi expression, which literally means "enough," is often used by Swamiji to signify the end of a topic or subject.

exist without the light of Lord Siva.[125]

Now, the fifty-third *śloka*:

Audio 2 - 35:13

अवस्तुतापि भावानां चमत्कारैकगोचरा।
यत्कुड्यसदृशी नेयं धीरवस्त्वेतदित्यपि॥ ५३ ॥

avastutāpi bhāvānāṁ camatkāraikagocarā /
yatkuḍyāsadṛśī neyaṁ dhīravastvetadityapi //53//
[not recited]

If anybody says and if anybody believes that this is not existing, [that] Lord Śiva is not existing or [that] this pot is not existing, this [recognition of non-existence] also will make it exist, will prove the existence of this. For instance, you say, "There is not a pot" or "There is not a book here," but this negation of [the pot or] the book is existing in consciousness, so there is the Lord in the negation of that also.

Audio 2 - 35:53

avastutāpi bhāvānāṁ camatkāraikagocarā /
yatkuḍyāsadṛśī neyaṁ dhīravastvetadityapi //53 (repeated)

When the intellect perceives that this[126] is not existing, this non-existence, this recognition of non-existence, also proves the existence of Lord Śiva.

SCHOLAR: Why does he say, "*yat kuḍyasadṛśī neyaṁ*"?

SWAMIJI: It is not *kuḍya sadṛśī,*[127] this [notion of the] intellect.[128]

125 See Appendix 13 (p399) for an explanation of "the light of God-consciousness," *prakāśa* and *vimarśa*.
126 Any given object.
127 It is not similar (*sadṛśa*) to an inert object such as a wall (*kuḍya*).
128 Every notion, be it an affirmation or a denial, occurs in the field of consciousness, which is full of life, and is therefore unlike an inert object.

SCHOLAR: It's not like something . . . ?

SWAMIJI: It is not just like a *kuḍya*, just like *jaḍa* (*kuḍya* means *jaḍa*[129]).

SCHOLAR: It is not like some inert object.

SWAMIJI: Yes (agreement). The fifty-fourth *śloka*:

Audio 2 - 36:43

प्रकाशो नाम यश्चायं सर्वत्रैव प्रकाशते।
अनपह्नवनीयत्वात् किं तस्मिन्मानकल्पनैः ॥५४॥

prakāśo nāma yaścāyaṁ sarvatraiva prakāśate /
anapahnavanīyatvāt kiṁ tasminmānakalpanaiḥ //54//
[not recited]

And this *prakāśa* of Lord Śiva, which is existing in each and every object of the world, because you cannot ignore That, *anapahnavanīyatvāt*, so, there is no need to put proofs on It to make It's existence proved. There is no need of proofs [because] It is already there.

Audio 2 - 37:20

प्रमाणान्यपि वस्तूनां जीवितं यानि तन्वते।
तेषामपि परो जीवः स एव परमेश्वरः ॥५५॥

pramāṇānyapi vastūnāṁ jīvitaṁ yāni tanvate /
teṣāmapi paro jīvaḥsa eva parameśvaraḥ //55// [not recited]

The proofs also–the fifty-fifth *śloka*–the proofs also exist, the proofs also get life from This. Whatever proof you put on Lord Śiva (on that object which is to be recognized), that proof itself has no value without the existence of Lord Śiva. So, all these proofs, the life of all these proofs, is *jīva* (the conscious being), and that conscious being is Parameśvara, Lord Śiva.

---

129 Inert, lifeless.

Audio 2 - 38:11

सर्वापह्नवहेवाकधर्माप्येवं हि वर्तते।
ज्ञानमात्मार्थमित्येतन्नेति मां प्रति भासते॥५६॥

sarvāpahnavahevākadharmāpyevaṁ hi vartate /
jñānamātmārthamityetanneti māṁ prati bhāsate //56//
[not recited]

Now, if you take [the theory] for the Buddhists [into consideration], they negate the objective world, the subjective world, and the cognitive world, but this negation of the objective, subjective, and cognitive worlds also proves the existence of knowledge because they *know* that this not existing, [that] this object is not existing, [that] cognition is not existing, [and that] the *grāhaka* (the subject) is not existing. [So this [notion of] "not-existing," this knowledge proves, it carries you to, that real Being [who is possessed] of all-knowledge and all-action,[130] because this negation also exists in that existence of Lord Śiva.

Audio 2 - 39:18

अपह्नुतौ साधने वा वस्तूनामाद्यमीदृशम्।
यत्तत्र के प्रमाणानामुपपत्त्युपयोगिते॥५७॥

apahnutau sādhane vā vastūnāmādyamīdṛśam /
yattatra ke pramāṇānāmupapattyupayogite //57//
[not recited]

Because–in the fifty-seventh [*śloka*]–when you negate this whole universe, this whole objective world, cognitive world,

130 "*Cetayati iti cetanaḥ*, the conscious Being is that who makes others conscious, and *sarva jñāna kriyā svatantraḥ*, who is independent in each and every knowledge and each and every action." *Śiva Sūtras* of Vasugupta, with the *Vimarśinī* (commentary) of Kṣemarāja, translation and commentary by Swami Lakshmanjoo (original audio recording, LJA archives, Los Angeles, 1975), 1.1.

and subjective world, or [when] you prove this cognitive world, subjective world, and objective world, in proving or in negating you feel that the topmost shining existence is there of Lord Śiva. So, neither there is the necessity of putting proofs on Him, nor is it worth to put proofs on Him.

SCHOLAR: It's neither logical nor useful.

SWAMIJI: Yes. The fifty-eighth [*śloka*]:

Audio 2 - 40:20

कामिके तत एवोक्तं हेतुवादविवर्जितम्।
तस्य देवातिदेवस्य परापेक्षा न विद्यते॥५८॥
परस्य तदपेक्षत्वात्स्वतन्त्रोऽयमतः स्थितः।

kāmike tata evoktaṁ hetuvādavivarjitam /
tasya devātidevasya parāpekṣā na vidyate //58//
parasya tadapekṣatvātsvatantr'yamataḥ sthitaḥ /59a/
[not recited]

In the *Kāmika tantra*, it is therefore explained that This is *hetuvādavivarjitam*, It is deprived of, It is away from, *hetuvāda* (*hetuvāda* means, why, why this is existing or how this is existing–this is *hetuvāda*[131]). It is beyond that. There is no "why" and there is no "how." It is there, It is already existing there. [For] that Lord of lords, there is no *apekṣā* (support) of any other agent, any other agency, to prove It. That agency [itself] is supported by this supreme Lord. [That] agency is existing, the agency gets life, from This. So, It is absolutely independent, all-round.

Audio 2 - 41:40

अनपेक्षस्य वशिनो देशकालाकृतिक्रमाः॥५९॥
नियता नेति स विभुर्नित्यो विश्वाकृतिः शिवः।

131 Lit., statements of reasons or arguments, assigning a cause, disputation.

anapekṣasya vaśino deśakālākṛtikramāḥ //59b//
niyatā neti sa vibhurnityo viśvākṛtiḥ śivaḥ /60a/

This Lord Śiva is *anapekṣa*, He does not need any support from any other agency. And It is *vaśina*, He is *vaśina* (*vaśina* means, *svātantrya*, absolutely independent). So for Him, the succession of space, the succession of time, and the succession of formation, *niyatā na*, do not exist at all. There is no succession of *deśa* (place) as we have the succession of *deśa*, e.g., we reside in Gupta Ganga. We have the succession of time, e.g., we are seventy years old, sixty years old, forty years old (this is the succession of time). The succession of *ākāra* means, formation, e.g., we are beautiful, we are ugly, we are long-shaped or we are short-shaped–it is all *ākṛtiḥ*.[132] These successions do not exist to Him. He is beyond the succession of space, beyond the succession of time, and beyond the succession of formation. It is why He is called "all-pervading" because of being above the succession of space, "eternal" because It is above the succession of time, and "universal" because It has no limited formation.

Now, the sixtieth *śloka*:

Audio 2 - 43:39

विभुत्वात्सर्वगो नित्यभावादाद्यन्तवर्जितः ॥ ६० ॥
विश्वाकृतित्वाच्चिदचित्तद्वैचित्र्यावभासकः ।

vibhutvātsarvago nityabhāvādādyantavarjitaḥ //60b//
viśvākṛtitvāccidacittadvaicitryāvabhāsakaḥ /61a/

As He is all-pervading, He is everywhere. As He is eternal, He is without beginning and end. As He is universal, He is the founder and lighter . . .

SCHOLAR: Revealer.

SWAMIJI: . . . revealer, revealer of everything that is *cit* and *acit* (*jaḍa*).

132 Constituent parts; form, figure, shape, appearance, or aspect.

SCHOLAR: Conscious and unconscious.

SWAMIJI: Yes, conscious and unconscious.[133] Sixty-one now:

Audio 2 - 44:35

ततोऽस्य बहुरूपत्वमुक्तं दीक्षोत्तरादिके ॥ ६१ ॥

tato'sya bahurūpatvamuktaṁ dīkṣottarādike //61b//
[not recited]

It is why in the *Dīkṣottara*, etcetera, *tantras*, He is nominated as "*bahurūpa*." *Bahurūpa* means, having all formations. He reads now [from the] *Kāmika tantra* for explaining this same thing:

Audio 2 - 45:01

भुवनं विग्रहो ज्योतिः खं शब्दो मन्त्र एव च।
बिन्दुनादादिसम्भिन्नः षड्विधः शिव उच्यते ॥ ६२ ॥

bhuvanaṁ vigraho jyotiḥ khaṁ śabdo mantra eva ca /
bindunādādisambhinnaḥ ṣaḍvidhaḥ śiva ucyate //62//

Bhuvanaṁ means, *bhogādhāra,*[134] not exactly "the world." The one who resides in that world is *bhuvanaṁ*, not the *bhuvana* itself. The "world" [is not meant] by "*bhuvana*" here. You should know that *bhuvana* is *bhuvanādhāra*, the one who lives in that *bhuvana*.

SCHOLAR: But *bhuvana ādhāra* means *bhuvanāśraya.*[135]

SWAMIJI: *Bhuvanāśraya–bhuvaneśvara*, that is *bhuvaneśvara.*[136]

133 *Cit* and *acit* (*jaḍa*), respectively.
134 The substratum of enjoyment.
135 *Āśraya*: that to which anything is annexed or with which anything is closely connected or on which anything depends or rests.
136 The lord (Īśvara) of the world (*bhuvana*).

SCHOLAR: But it's *adhiṣṭheyaṁ*,[137] not *adhiṣṭātṛ*[138]*–tattad-bhuvanādhiṣṭheyaṁ*.

SWAMIJI: *Tattat bhuvanādhiṣṭheyaṁ bhogādhāra rūpam*. That is, in those *bhuvana*s (worlds), [those] who are *adhiṣṭheya*, who reside [in the world]–that is *bhuvaneśvara*.

SCHOLAR: It's *bhogādhāra* in the form of the various occupied worlds.

SWAMIJI: Yes. He has not commented on it very clearly–Jayaratha. But here, Abhinavagupta means that *bhuvana* means, *bhuvaneśvara*, not *bhogādhāra*, not exactly *bhogādhāra*. [*Bhuvanaṁ* refers to] the one who rules, who governs, on that [*bhuvana*].

SCHOLAR: *Bhoktā*, in fact.

SWAMIJI: *Bhoktā*, *bhoktā*.[139] *Vigraha*: *Vigraha* means, the body. By "bodies" you must not say that the body is Lord Śiva, [but rather], the body-holder is Lord Śiva (*vigraha dhārī*; *vigrahiṇa pramātaraḥ*). [*Vigrahin*s are] not those *pramātā*s (subjects) who are not elevated, [but those who are] elevated *pramātā*s, elevated ones. [They are] *rūdra*s, not *kṣetrajña*s,[140] not *paśu pramātāra*s.[141]

SCHOLAR: *Rudrādīni kāraṇānyeva*,[142] just Rudra, Brahmā, and Viṣṇu.

SWAMIJI: Yes, *kāraṇā*–Rudra, Viṣṇu, Brahmā, Śiva, all these [causal agents].

137 The superintended or governed.

138 The superintendent or governor.

139 The enjoyer.

140 "*Kṣetrajña* means, this body is the field for sowing the seeds of *karma*. *Etadyo veda*, and the person who indulges in this body, he is *kṣetrajña*. *Kṣetrajña* means, he is *jīva*, a limited soul. This body is *kṣetra* (*kṣetra* means, the field in which you sow your *karma*s) and *kṣetrajña* is the limited soul who is entangled in actions and he gets its fruits." *Bhagavad Gita in the Light of Kashmir Shaivism*, Swami Lakshmanjoo, ed. John Hughes (Lakshmanjoo Academy Book Series, Los Angeles, 2015), 13.2.

141 Lit., beast-like, or limited subjects.

142 Jayaratha's commentary.

Now *jyoti*: *jyoti* means, *bindu*, that center of that light which is found in each and every junction of the universe.[143] That is *jyoti*. There you find the existence of the Lord. *Khaṁ*: *khaṁ* means, those states which are void, absolutely void. [Jayaratha] has commentated nicely [by relating *khaṁ* to] *śakti*, *vyāpinī*, and *samanā*. *Śakti*, *vyāpinī*, and *samanā* are absolutely void from all the differentiated world.[144] So, in "*khaṁ*," you should know that. *Śabda*: *śabda* is *parāmarśa* (*nāda*, the supreme *nāda*), that sound which carries you to the state of God consciousness. That is [the meaning of] "*śabda*."[145]

143 "This junction is actually the fourth state, *turya*." *Kashmir Shaivism–The Secret Supreme*, 107. See Appendix 14 (p401) for an explanation of *turya* and *turyātītā*.

144. "[*Śakti*] is potential energy and [*vyāpinī* is the energy of] potential expansion (*vyāpinī* is universal potential expansion)." *Tantrāloka* 6.164a (LJA archive). "*Samanā* is that energy which digests time, the sphere of time; time is no more existing." Ibid., 8.190a. "According to our Trika system, they reside in the thirty-fifth element–[the energies of] *śakti*, *vyāpinī*, and *samanā*." Ibid., 15.314. "*Śakti* is *aparā*, *vyāpinī* is *parāparā* energy, *samanā* is *parā* energy. Is this the correct [order of] *śakti*, *vyāpinī*, and *samanā*, [that] the lowest one is *śakti*, [then] *vyāpinī*, and [then] *samanā*? It cannot be understood because it is *svātantrya*, which is *akrama*, it is beyond succession." *Parātriśikā Vivaraṇa* (LJA archive). "There is no difference between *śakti*, *vyāpinī*, and *samanā*. They are not one above another. In no case are they one above another. They are in one level." *Tantrāloka* 15.313 (LJA archive).

145 "*Nāda* (sound) means, I-consciousness, God consciousness, supreme I-consciousness (*ahaṁ parāmarśa*). There are two positions of Śiva: one is *prakāśa* and another is *vimarśa*, one is *bindu* and another is *nāda* (*bindu* is *prakāśa*, *nāda* is *vimarśa*). When *bindu* is there, He is in full bliss. When He understands [i.e., is aware of] that full bliss, there is *nāda*, that is *nāda*. When He feels this blissful state as His own nature, that is *prakāśa*. When He feels, "That blissful state is My glory," that is *vimarśa*. When He feels that, "This blissful state is My being," that is Śiva. When He believes that, "This is My glory," that is Śakti. The cycle of glory is residing in Śakti and the cycle of *prakāśa* is residing in Śiva–both are in one. That is indicated by *visarga* in Śiva, [the vowel] '*aḥ*' (:). So, *vimarśa śakti* is

Mantra is any *mantra*. It may be *praṇava,*[146] it may be *vaidika praṇava*, it may be Śakti *praṇava,* or it may be Śiva *praṇava*. *Vaidika praṇava* is "*oṁ-kāra*," Śakti *praṇava* is "*hrīṁ-kāra*," and Śiva *praṇava* is "*ahaṁ*." These will all go in *mantra*, in the world of *mantras*.

SCHOLAR: So, *oṁ*, *hrīṁ*, and *ahaṁ*.

SWAMIJI: *Oṁ* is *vaidika*, *hrīṁ* is Śakti, and *ahaṁ* is Śiva *praṇava*.[147] These are all *praṇavas*. So these are six. So, in this way, *ṣaṭ vidhaḥ śiva ucyate*, the sixfold Śiva is explained in this *Dīkṣottara tantra*. Because this Śiva is already mixed with *bindu* and *nāda* everywhere (*prakāśa* and *vimarśa*), so *prakāśa* and *vimarśa* won't [be listed among] these numbers [of states]. The numbers are finished up to *mantra*. *Bhuvana*, *vigraha*, *jyoti*, *khaṁ*, *śabda*, and *mantra*, these sixfold states are concerned with Śiva. And, in these sixfold [states of] Śiva, Śiva is absolutely one with *bindu* and *nāda*; *prakāśa* and *vimarśa* are not away from Him.

SCHOLAR: So Jayaratha is incorrect here because he says this is only *mantra* that is *bindunādādisambhinnaḥ*.[148]

SWAMIJI: Yes.

---

the supreme *parā parameśvarī* attributed to *svātantrya śakti*. It is the intensity of the independence of the *svātantrya* of Bhairava–this *vimarśa śakti*." *Parātriśikā Vivaraṇa* (LJA archive). "*Vimarśa* and *parāmarśa* will go in one sense. *Parāmarśa* is the same and *vimarśa* is the same here. *Parāmarśa* means, complete I-consciousness." *Tantrāloka* 3.200 (LJA archive). See See Appendix 9 (p392) for an explanation of *parāmarśa*, and also Appendix 13 (p399) for an explanation of *prakāśa* and *vimarśa*.

146 Lit., a mystical or sacred syllable.

147 In Kashmir Shaivism, Śiva *praṇava* is also referred to as '*hūṁ*'. See Swami Lakshmanjoo, trans., *Vijñāna Bhairava–The Manual for Self Realization* (with original audio), ed. John Hughes (LJA, Los Angeles, 2007-2015), verse 39.

148 According to Jayaratha, only *mantra* is in contact (*sambhinna*) with *bindu* and *nāda*.

Audio 2 - 50:53

यो यदात्मकतानिष्ठस्तद्भावं स प्रपद्यते।
व्योमादिशब्दविज्ञानात्परो मोक्षो न संशयः ॥ ६३ ॥

yo yadātmakatāniṣṭhastadbhāvaṁ sa prapadyate /
vyomādiśabdavijñānātparo mokṣo na saṁśayaḥ //63//

Any *sādhaka* (aspirant) who is meditating on any of these formations of Lord Śiva–say, *bhuvana* (*bhuvaneśvara*), or *pati pramātā* (*vigraha*, *vigrahiṇī*), or *jyoti*, or void (*khaṁ*), or *śabda*, or *mantra*–separately, *tadbhāvam sa prapadyate*, he goes to that, he achieves that state. [For example], he becomes *bhuvaneśvara*; he who meditates on *bhuvaneśvara*, he becomes one with that *bhuvaneśvara*. The one who meditates on *rūdra*s (*pati pramātā*s), they become one with those beings. In the same way, in *jyoti*, in *khaṁ*, in *śabda*, and in *mantra*. But, universally, there are some other *sādhaka*s who pervade (*vyoma*) the recognition (*vijñānāt*) of Śiva in all the six. They don't find *bhuvaneśvara* there; they find Lord Śiva there. They don't find *rūdra*s there; they find Lord Śiva there. They don't find *jyoti* there; they find Lord Śiva. In the same way, in voidness (*śakti*, *vyāpinī*, and *samanā*), and in *śabda* (in *nāda*), in *mantra* also (in *vaidika mantra*, and Śakti *mantra*, and Śiva *mantra*), they find Lord Śiva in them. It is why he says, "*vyomādi śabda vijñānāt*." Why has he put "*vyoma*"[149] first here? Because, [in the previous verse], he had to put "*bhuvanādi śabda vijñānāt*." *Bhuvana* was the first, *vigraha* was second, *jyoti* is third, *khaṁ* is fourth, *śabda* is fifth, and *mantra* is sixth. *Khaṁ* is fourth, [but in this verse] he has said, "*vyomādi śabda vijñānāt*." [Here], he has begun with *vyoma* (with *khaṁ*) because, absolutely, *bhuvaneśvara* and all these *rūdra*s, etc., are nothing [other] than Lord Śiva. It is why he has put *vyoma* first: "*vyomādi śabda vijñānāt*," [*vyoma* is achieved by] *vijñānāt*, by recognition, by knowing that all

149 Swamiji is using *vyoma* in the sense of "expansion' or 'pervasion' of all the six states.

these six states of these *bhuvaneśvaras*, etc., are nothing but Lord Śiva.

SCHOLAR: So, he breaks the order given in the previous verse in order to show that they are equal.

SWAMIJI: Yes, they are equal. For him, *paro mokṣo na saṁśayaḥ*, supreme *mokṣa* (supreme liberation) is there [by this recognition]. There is no doubt about it.

Now, the six states of Lord Śiva he has explained here, but in fact these six states are not only six states [because] they lead you to the universal states of Lord Śiva. This is what he says in the following *śloka*:

Audio 2 - 54:30

विश्वाकृतित्वे देवस्य तदेतच्चोपलक्षणम्।
अनवच्छिन्नतारूढाववच्छेदलयेऽस्य च॥ ६४॥

viśvākṛtitve devasya tadetaccopalakṣaṇam /
anavacchinnatārūḍhāvavacchedalaye'sya ca //64//
[not recited in full]

This is *upalakṣaṇam*[150] for the Lord of lords. This is *upalakṣaṇa*–these sixfold states, this explanation of the sixfold states, is *upalakṣaṇa* for Him, as He is universal. And this *upalakṣaṇa* is meant for the state of Lord Śiva for *anavacchinnatā rūḍhāu*, because He is established in *anavacchinnatā* (*anavacchinnatā*, where there is no bondage, no limitation at all) and *avacchedalaye*, [where] all limitations melt in oneness. For that, these sixfold states of Lord Śiva are explained, not for [explaining] the six only, but for [explaining] the universal states of Lord Śiva.

Audio 2 - 55:25

उक्तं च कामिके देवः सर्वाकृतिर्निराकृतिः।
जलदर्पणवत्तेन सर्वं व्याप्तं चराचरम्॥ ६५॥

150 A figure of speech in which the nomination of a part refers to the whole.

uktaṁ ca kāmike devaḥ sarvākṛtirnirākṛtiḥ /
jaladarpaṇavattena sarvaṁ vyāptaṁ carācaram //65//
[not recited]

In the *Kāmika tantra*, this is said that the Lord is *sarvākṛti*, possesses all formations of the world and possesses no formation at all (*sarvākṛti* and *nirākṛti*). If, from one point of view, you experience Him, you will see that He is *sarvākṛti*, all formations are His. And, from another point of view, if you perceive Him, you will find that He has no formation at all.

SCHOLAR: Because all forms are His, He has no forms.

SWAMIJI: Yes. *Jaladarpaṇavattena sarvaṁ vyāptaṁ carācaram*, as the whole universe is reflected in water [or as] the whole universe is reflected in a mirror, in the same way, the whole *carācara* universe is reflected in His own nature.

SCHOLAR: *Carācara*, moving and unmoving.

SWAMIJI: Moving and unmoving.[151]

Audio 2 - 56:38

न चास्य विभुताद्योऽयं धर्मोऽन्योन्यं विभिद्यते।

na cāsya vibhutādyo'yaṁ dharmo'nyonyaṁ vibhidyate /66a

In fact, these aspects of Lord Śiva (three aspects: all-pervading, being eternal, and consisting of universal forms[152]), these three aspects also are not occupied by Lord Śiva because He is [also] not universal, He is [also] not all-pervading, He is [also] not eternal. If He were all-pervading and [not] not all-pervading, [then] not-all-pervading-ness would be excluded. So, there is not real pervasion [if that were the case].

SCHOLAR: There is nothing for Him to pervade.

SWAMIJI: No. "There is nothing for Him to pervade"–not that! If He is [only] all-pervading, then not-all-pervading is

151 Viz., animate and inanimate (conscious and inert).
152 Omniform.

excluded there (the negation of all-pervading-ness is excluded), [but] there is no negation at all for Him: He is all-pervading and He is not all-pervading. That is the reality of His Being. He is eternal and He is not eternal at the same time. He is universal and not universal also. [Otherwise], the classes of not-universality [would be] excluded there. So, you can't say that He is all-pervading only. You can't say that He is eternal only. You can't say that He is universal only. He is the negation of the universal also. He is the negation of all-pervading-ness also. He is the negation of universality.

SCHOLAR: He says in this verse that these attributes of Lord Śiva are not in reality distinct from each other (*anyonyaṁ vibhidyate*).

SWAMIJI: *Anyonyaṁ na vibhīyate*, yes. These are not separated aspects of Lord Śiva.

SCHOLAR: His being is not divided by the fact that He can be seen in these three ways.

SWAMIJI: Yes. Only one aspect He has occupied: that aspect which includes each and every aspect of God.

SCHOLAR: This is the next verse now.

SWAMIJI: Yes.

Audio 2 - 59:26

एक एवास्य धर्मोऽसौ सर्वाक्षेपेण वर्तते॥ ६६ ॥
तेन स्वातन्त्र्यशक्त्यैव युक्त इत्याञ्जसो विधिः।

eka evāsya dharmo'sau sarvākṣepeṇa vartate //66b//
tena svātantryaśaktyaiva yukta ityāñjaso vidhiḥ /67a
[not recited]

And that real aspect is *svātantrya*.[153] *Svātantrya* He has possessed. He is the possessor of *svātantrya śakti*. So, "He possesses *svātantrya śakti*," this is the real way of explaining

153 Absolute freedom, independence. See Appendix 7 (p387) for an explanation of *svātantrya*.

His energy.

SCHOLAR: And this implies all the others.

SWAMIJI: Yes.

SCHOLAR: *Sarvākṣepeṇa vartate.*

SWAMIJI: Yes. This implies [that] all other energies are there. The sixty-seventh [*śloka*]:

Audio 2 - 01:00:00

बहुशक्तित्वमप्यस्य तच्छक्त्यैवावियुक्तता ॥ ६७ ॥

bahuśaktitvamapyasya tacchaktyaivāviyuktatā //67b//
[not recited]

Although Lord Śiva has innumerable energies, but all those innumerable energies are one with that *svātantrya śakti* (*tat śaktyaiva āviyuktatā*).

SCHOLAR: Inseparability from that energy.

SWAMIJI: Inseparable, yes. But still then, there are two, there remain two.[154] The monistic [doctrine] is destroyed by this theory.

JOHN: By Śiva and having . . .

SWAMIJI: . . . having His *svātantrya* energy. There are two, so there is not oneness. For this, he explains in the next *śloka*, the sixty-eighth:

Śiva and Śakti are One (68-85)

Audio 3 - 00:00

शक्तिश्च नाम भावस्य स्वं रूपं मातृकल्पितम्।
तेनाद्वयः स एवापि शक्तिमत्परिकल्पने ॥ ६८ ॥

154 Śiva and His energy (*svātantrya śakti*).

śaktiśca nāma bhāvasya svaṁ rūpaṁ mātṛkalpitam /
tenādvayaḥ sa evāpi śaktimatparikalpane //68//
[not recited in full]

This energy is, in fact, the reality of that Being, and it is *mātṛkalpitam*, it is just for the time-being to be accepted. Otherwise, the energy and the energy-holder are one.

SCHOLAR: It's a cognitive distinction (*mātṛkalpitam*).

SWAMIJI: Yes. For instance, there is a fire. Burning energy is there. Burning energy is never separated from the fire, or lightening energy is not separated from fire, heating energy is not separated from fire, cooking energy is not separated from fire. All these energies are one with that fire. So, He is only one. Although *śaktimat parikalpane*, you call Him the energy-holder, although He holds the *svātantrya śakti*, He is one.

JOHN: Sixty-nine.

SWAMIJI: Sixty-nine:

Audio 3 - 01:19

मातृक्लृप्ते हि देवस्य तत्र तत्र वपुष्यलम्।
को भेदो वस्तुतो वह्नेर्दग्धृपक्तृत्वयोरिव॥ ६९॥

mātṛklṛpte hi devasya tatra tatra vapuṣyalam /
ko bhedo vastuto vahnerdagdhṛpaktṛtvayoriva //69//

This *mātā* (*mātā* means, anyone[155]), *devasya tatra tatra vapuṣi alam klṛpte*, the formation of the Lord is variously imagined [*klṛpte*] by *mātā*, by the one who needs it that way. For instance, if you need [the energy of] cooking from fire, you believe that this fire has the energy of cooking and you ignore the energy of lightening, you ignore all other energies of fire. That is *mātṛ klṛpte*. So, . . .

Do you understand?

155 *Mātā* is derived from *mātṛ*, which means "measurer" or "knower," viz., *pramātā*.

JOHN: So, people take one energy out of . . .

SWAMIJI: One energy according to your needs.

JOHN: Needs and tastes, yes.

SWAMIJI: [When] you have got the energy [of heating], [then] there is no [need for the] energy of lightening[156] here. The energy of heating is only [there] because you need that energy of heating. But, in fact, this fire has not only the energy of heating. *Ko bhedo vastuto vahner dagdhṛpaktṛtvayoriva*, in fact, the energy of *dagdhṛ* (*dagdhṛ* means, burning energy) or *paktṛ* (cooking energy), all these energies are not separated from fire. So, fire is one. All energies are included in that, included in it, they are not excluded. In the same way, Lord Śiva has innumerable energies and all those innumerable energies are one with Him.

SCHOLAR: So, when you speak of fire and say that fire has various capacities, various *śakti*s, you can always reduce them to one which is still namable.

SWAMIJI: Yes.

SCHOLAR: But you can't with Śiva because *svātantrya śakti* . . . all you can say is that It's *svātantrya*.

SWAMIJI: *Svātantrya śakti* creates all energies because there is *svātantrya*.

SCHOLAR: It is absolutely non-specific. There is no *viśeṣa*.

SWAMIJI: Yes, there is no *viśeṣa*.[157]

Audio 3 - 03:57

न चासौ परमार्थेन न किंचिद्भासनादृते।
नह्यस्ति किंचित्तच्छक्तितद्वद्भेदोऽपि वास्तवः ॥७०॥

na cāsau paramārthena na kiñcidbhāsanādṛte /
nahyasti kiñcittacchaktitadbhedo'pi vāstavaḥ //70//

156 That is, illumination.
157 Differentiated-ness.

In reality, *asau* (*asau* means, the classes of energies), *na kiñcid bhāsanādṛte*, these classes of energies of Lord Śiva are nothing [other] than the existence of Lord Śiva; *bhāsana*, . . .

SCHOLAR: His appearance.

SWAMIJI: . . . only the appearance of Lord Śiva. All energies are appearing in the formation of those energies, and Lord Śiva is, in fact, appearing in the form of all energies. This is the formation of the appearance of Lord Śiva through energies. *Nahyasti kiñcit tat śakti tadbhedo'pi vāstavaḥ*, so, this differentiation of *śakti* and *śaktimān* (energy and energy-holder) is not real.

Now he'll go to this fact that energy is the thing by which you can perceive Lord Śiva. You can recognize Lord Śiva through energy, through Its energy, not direct. You can't perceive Lord Śiva directly. These are energies that carry you to Its recognition. So, energies are the means, energies have become the *upāya*s. For instance, the energy of His will is supposed [to be], is explained as, *śāmbhavopāya*, the energy of knowledge is supposed to be *śāktopāya*, and the energy of action is *āṇavopāya*.[158] From the energy of action, you will be carried to the state of Lord Śiva. For instance, the energy of action is breathing, breathing exercise, reciting of *mantra*s, these are all in the world of actions. Reciting of *mantra*s, reciting of *śloka*s (hymns), and *pūjā* (worship), all these are in action, in the world of action. So, all these things are included in *āṇavopāya*, and they will carry you to the state of Lord Śiva. And knowledge, for instance, knowledge, this is *śāktopāya*, the energy of knowledge. Perceiving, "middle-ing" (centering), all these are in the world of *śāktopāya*. They will also carry you to the state of Lord Śiva. And will, the first start, the first start of each and every action,[159] that is *śāmbhavopāya* and that will

158 Consequently, these three *upāya*s are also known as *icchopāya*, *jñānopāya*, and *kriyopāya*, respectively. The *upāya*s will be explained in detail from verse 139 onwards.

159 "At the first start, there is only sensation, *nirvikalpa* (thoughtless). You can't understand what it is. It is just one with Śiva."

carry you to Siva's state.

SCHOLAR: So, then you'll have complete freedom of action, complete freedom of knowledge, because you are grounded in *icchā*.

SWAMIJI: Yes.

SCHOLAR: In this verse, Swamiji, did you say that this collection of energies is nothing at all? Doesn't the verse say, "In reality, it is not nothing . . ."

SWAMIJI: It is nothing.

SCHOLAR: ". . . because it appears–*na na kiñcit*"?

SWAMIJI: *Na cāsau paramārthena na kiñcit*, it is existing in the state of Lord Śiva.

SCHOLAR: Because it appears.

SWAMIJI: Yes, because *daunanyo prakṛtarthe dhardhyambhrutā*, two negatives make an affirmation.[160]

Nahyasti kiñcit tat śakti tadvad bhedo'pi vāstavaḥ. This *śakti* and *śaktiman*, this differentiation is not real.

JOHN: That was seventy.

SWAMIJI: Yes, seventy now.

DEVOTEE: *Asau paramārthena na na kiñcit.*

SWAMIJI: *Api tu kiñcit, api tu sarvaṁ–prakāśa rūpatvāt.*[161]

JOHN: Now, seventy-one.

Parātriśikā Vivaraṇa (LJA archive). "That is *prathamā ābhāsa, prathamā prasara*, the first flow, the first flow outside. At that first flow, you have to watch. You can't watch That, because It is not watched, It is the watcher." Ibid. (LJA archive). See verses 145-6.

160 Referring to the two instances of '*na*' (not) in "*na cāsau paramārthena na kiñcidbhāsanādṛte.*"

161 But also (*api tu*) something (*kiñcit*), but also (*api tu*) everything (*sarvaṁ*)–the formation (*rūpatvāt*) of the light of God-consciousness (*prakāśa*).

SWAMIJI:

Audio 3 - 08:06

स्वशक्त्युद्रेकजनकं तादात्म्याद्वस्तुनो हि यत्।
शक्तिस्तदपि देव्येवं भान्त्यप्यन्यस्वरूपिणी ॥ ७१ ॥

svaśaktyudrekajanakaṁ tādātmyādvastuno hi yat /
śaktistadapi devyevaṁ bhāntyapyanyasvarūpiṇī //71//

Svaśakti udreka janakam, vastunaḥ yat svaśakti udreka janakam. Vastunaḥ means, the substance of that Being. That which is *svaśakti udreka janakam*[162] will create that energy, one nominated energy, from that [one substance of Being].[163]

SCHOLAR: An emphasis (*udreka*) of those energies.

SWAMIJI: Only one energy, . . .

SCHOLAR: One prominent.

SWAMIJI: . . . one [energy] from That universal energy-holder, that any one energy will be created. That is the reality of *upāya* and *upeya bhāva*.[164] That [particular *upāya*/energy] becomes the means to be carried to That.

JOHN: Taking one energy . . .

SWAMIJI: Taking one energy out of It.

JOHN: Using that.

SWAMIJI: Only one energy is meant for you from your master, not all the energies.

JOHN: At one time.

SWAMIJI: You must not try each and every *upāya*.

---

162 That which is vividly or predominantly (*udreka*) produced (*janaka*) from self-power (*svaśakti*).

163 Just as one particular energy can be utilized (nominated) out of the many energies inherent to fire, in the same way, a particular energy can be nominated out of the infinite energies inherent to *svātantrya śakti*.

164 The means (*upāya*) and the state of the meant (*upeya*). In his commentary on verse 165, Swamiji explains that, "These means are many, but the meant is only one."

JOHN: You do one and then another, but not simultaneously. Is that . . . ?

SWAMIJI: No, you do one as you are asked by your masters–*bas*, only one energy.[165]

JOHN: But what about when you are practicing *āṇavopāya* in *śāmbhavopāya*?

SWAMIJI: You will be carried to *śāmbhavopāya* by itself, by that energy.

JOHN: By the energy of *icchā* (will), not the energy of *kriyā* (action).

SWAMIJI: By the energy of *kriyā*, you will reach to the energy of *icchā*.

JOHN: But you were saying that the man in *śāmbhavopāya* can practice *āṇavopāya* in *śāmbhavopāya*.

SWAMIJI: Afterwards, yes.

JOHN: Afterwards. So then, in that state, the energy of *icchā śakti* is . . .

SWAMIJI: *Icchā* is pervading in the energy of *jñāna śakti* and in the energy of *kriyā śakti* also, in that way. But the energy of action, the energy of *kriyā*, is not pervading in the energy of knowledge, is not pervading in the energy of *icchā*. *Icchā* is pervading in the energy of knowledge and in the energy of action. Don't you understand?

JOHN: Yes, I do.

SWAMIJI:

Audio 3 - 10:25

शिवश्चालुप्तविभवस्तथा सृष्टोऽवभासते।
स्वसंविन्मातृमकुरे स्वातन्त्र्याद्भावनादिषु॥ ७२ ॥

---

165 "Be attached to your own practice. It will cary you to *śāktopāya* and *śāmbhavopāya* by its own way. There are thousand ways, and the way that has been selected by your master is the best, is the divine way for you." *Vijñāna Bhairava–The Manual for Self Realization*, page 3, fn 9.

śivaścāluptavibhavastathā sṛṣṭo'vabhāsate /
svasaṁvinmātṛmakure svātantryadbhāvanādiṣu //72//

This is the outcome of His independence, the absolute independence of Lord Śiva, that Śiva also becomes an object in *samādhi*. In *samādhi*, you perceive Him in the objective field. You become the perceiver of Lord Śiva in *samādhi*. This is His *svātantrya śakti*. This is from His *svātantrya śakti* that He becomes the object–by His *svātantrya śakti*. *Ālupta vibhava*, although His *vibhava*, His glory of subjectivity, is never absent, still, by His freedom of *svātantrya śakti*, He becomes an object.

JOHN: And this is in the state of *samādhi*.

SWAMIJI: Yes.

SCHOLAR: "*Bhāvanādiṣu*," he says here.

SWAMIJI: *Bhāvanādiṣu* (in contemplation, in meditation, in *samādhi*).

SCHOLAR: So in *śāktopāya* . . .

SWAMIJI: In *śāktopāya*, you can perceive Him in an objective way; in *śāmbhavopāya* also, in *āṇavopāya* also. In *śāmbhavopāya* also!

JOHN: "See Him" means?

SWAMIJI: Perceive Him, that "I am Lord Śiva." In *śāmbhavopāya*, you will perceive Him as "I am Lord Śiva." In *śāktopāya*, you will perceive Him as "Lord Śiva."

JOHN: So, limitation then, what is . . .

SWAMIJI: And in *āṇavopāya*, you will perceive Him as "This is Lord Śiva." There is a difference only in perceiving this way. In *āṇavopāya*, you perceive Him as "This is Lord Śiva. This is the formation of Lord Śiva." It is *āṇavopāya*'s result. *Śāktopāya*'s result is, "Lord Śiva." *Śāmbhavopāya*'s result is, "I am Lord Śiva." This is the difference of perceiving.

SCHOLAR: But also in *śāktopāya*, doesn't the *yogi* have to develop that awareness of identification with the Absolute?

SWAMIJI: Yes, so he sees Lord Śiva only. He doesn't see who is the subject and who is the object.

JOHN: In *śāktopāya*.

SWAMIJI: In *śāktopāya*. In *śāmbhavopāya*, he sees, he perceives, that, "I am subjective; I am Lord Śiva." He does not perceive Lord Śiva as "This." He perceives Lord Śiva as "I."

JOHN: Full "I."

SWAMIJI: Yes. In *āṇavopāya*, he perceives Lord Śiva as "This."

JOHN: Who is the cognizer in *āṇavopāya*? The *āṇavopāya* cognizer doesn't realize himself as one with . . . ?

SWAMIJI: No, he perceives that, "This is Lord Śiva," separated from his being, in *āṇavopāya*.

SCHOLAR: So, how can that be a real . . . ?

SWAMIJI: That will carry him. If he persists to get establishment in that, it will carry him to the *śāktopāya* state, and then in the *śāmbhavopāya* state, by-and-by.

SCHOLAR: But how can he have that false conviction that, "This is Lord Śiva"?

SWAMIJI: In *āṇavopāya*, this results like that.

JOHN: Is that a form of Śiva? You see this is Lord Śiva in some *mūrti*, or is it, are you . . . ?

SWAMIJI: Because he perceives both beings that, "I am perceiving Lord Śiva. How beautiful and how glamorous."

JOHN: In other words, he experiences some duality.

SWAMIJI: Some duality, yes, in *āṇavopāya*, in *āṇavopāya samādhi*.

JOHN: But he doesn't experience Śiva in some *mūrti*. He's not thinking of a form.

SWAMIJI: No, not a formation. There is no question of formation at all in this Shaivism.

SCHOLAR: But, you said that the fullness of . . . when *āṇavopāya* is realized, . . .

SWAMIJI: Yes.

SCHOLAR: . . . then that *yogi* experiences *cidānanda* and even *jagadānanda.*[166]

SWAMIJI: *Jagadānanda* he won't experience . . .

SCHOLAR: Only slightly.

SWAMIJI: . . . until he enters in the *śāmbhava* state. *Jagadānanda* is experienced only in the *śāmbhava* state.

SCHOLAR: And *cidānanda*?

SWAMIJI: *Cidānanda* is experienced in the *śākta* state.

SCHOLAR: Not in . . . ?

SWAMIJI: No, only traces of that *cidānanda* are found in *āṇava samādhi*.

SCHOLAR: But I thought that you said that *cidānanda* was *nimīlanā samādhi*.

SWAMIJI: Yes, that is *nimīlanā samādhi.*[167]

SCHOLAR: Is that not achieved in *āṇavopāya*?

SWAMIJI: That is achieved in *āṇavopāya* [but] that is not the complete achievement. That is not, in fact, the complete achievement.

SCHOLAR: So when *kuṇḍalinī* rises and the *yogi* experiences that *cidānanda*, how can he be said to be having objective knowledge of Śiva if he is in pure subjectivity?

---

166 "The difference between *turya* and *turyātītā* is, in *turya*, you find in *samādhi* that this whole universe is existing there in a seed form, a germ. The strength, the energy, of universal existence is existing there, but here he has [yet] to come out [into activity]. In *turyātītā*, he comes out in action and feels universal consciousness. This is the difference between *turya* and *turyātītā*. So, *turyātītā* is just like *jagadānanda* and *turya* is *cidānanda*." *Tantrāloka* 10.288 (LJA archive). See Appendix 14 (p401) for more on *turya* and *turyātītā*.

167 "*Unmīlanā samādhi* is experienced in *turyātītā* and *nimīlanā samādhi* is experienced in *turya*. This is the difference between *turya* and *turyātītā*. *Nimīlanā samādhi* means, absorption of universal consciousness. When universal consciousness is absorbed in your nature, that is *turya*. When universal consciousness is expanded everywhere, that is *turyātītā*." Ibid., 10.288. See Appendix 15 (p403) for explanation of *unmīlanā* and *nimīlanā samādhi*.

SWAMIJI: Because he comes out from it.

SCHOLAR: But at the moment of his realization, he's not having . . .

SWAMIJI: He remembers as "This."

SCHOLAR: In the ongoing movement of his practice, he has that flavor.

JOHN: Oh, I see. Not in the moment of . . .

SCHOLAR: That is the flavor of his awareness when he is in *āṇavopāya*.

SWAMIJI: Yes.

Audio 3 - 15:30

तस्माद्येन मखेनैष भात्यनंशोऽपि तत्तथा।
शक्तिरित्येष वस्त्वेव शक्तितद्वत्क्रमः स्फुटः ॥७३॥

tasmādyena mukhenaiṣa bhatyanaṁśo'pi tattathā /
śaktirityeṣa vastveva śaktitadvatkramaḥ sphuṭaḥ //73//

So, *yena mukhena*, by which means, this *anaṁśa* of Lord Śiva, although He has no *aṁśa*s, . . .

SCHOLAR: Though "part-less," "undivided."

SWAMIJI: . . . He is undivided (undivided in *śāmbhavopāya*, undivided in *śāktopāya*, and undivided in *āṇavopāya*), but *tat tathā*, but He reveals Himself like that.[168] So, this is the reality of *śakti* and *śaktimat krama*.[169] So, *śaktimat* and *śakti krama* is the absolute truth.

Audio 3 - 16:35

श्रीमत्किरणशास्त्रे च तत्प्रश्नोत्तरपूर्वकम्।
अनुभावो विकल्पोऽपि मानसो न मनः शिवे॥७४॥
अविज्ञाय शिवं दीक्षा कथमित्यत्र चोत्तरम्।

168 That is, He reveals Himself with *aṁśa*s (with parts, divisions).
169 The energy-holder (*śaktimat*) and the course (*krama*) of His energies (*śakti*).

śrīmatkiraṇaśāstre ca tatrāśnottarapūrvakam /
anubhāvo vikalpo'pi mānaso na manaḥ śive //74//
avijñāya śivaṁ dīkṣā kathamityatra cottaram / 75a
[not recited]

In the *Kiraṇa śāstra* also, lord Garuḍa asked Nārāyaṇa [a question] and Nārāyaṇa gave him an *uttara* (answer) in this connection:[170]

"*Anubhāvo vikalpo'pi mānaso*, although this *anubhāva*, this experiencing of Lord Śiva, the state of Lord Śiva, is to experience Lord Śiva through the mind (it is *man*, by mind), but, O Nārāyaṇa, You have already explained to me that through the mind there is no possibility of reaching to the state of Lord Śiva. But as this *anubhāva* is done by the mind, how can this *anubhāva* be the truth, real, as long as it is functioned by the mind?" This is the question of Garuḍa for Nārāyaṇa. "*Avijñāya śivam*, so, in the end, when the master has not experienced the state of Lord Śiva because he has experienced It through the mind (by *vikalpa*)–by *vikalpa* that experience is untrue, it is false–so, how can he initiate others?" This is the question. "How can he initiate others if he is incomplete himself? If the master is incomplete himself, how can he initiate others and elevate them to God consciousness?"

To this, in answer, [Nārāyaṇa] has put the following thing:

Audio 3 - 18:42

क्षुधाद्यनुभवो नैव विकल्पो नहि मानसः ॥७५॥

kṣudhādyanubhavo naiva vikalpo nahi māsanaḥ //75b//

"Your question is not correct (*naiva*, your question is not correct). You have not come to the real point, O Garuḍa." This is the saying of Nārāyaṇa to Garuḍa. "*Kṣudhādi anubhavo mānasaḥ vikalpa na*, when you feel thirst, when you feel

170 "It is not a Vaiṣṇava *tantra*, it is a dualistic *tantra*–the *Kiraṇa tantra*. Nārāyaṇa is teaching His driver (Lord Garuḍa)." *Tantrāloka* 15.18 (LJA archive).

hunger, you can't feel it in the mind, you don't feel that hunger and thirst in the mind. It is *nirvikalpa*. You just say that, 'I am hungry'."

SCHOLAR: You recognize it in the mind.

SWAMIJI: You recognize it . . . not in the mind!

SCHOLAR: But the mind says, "I am hungry!"

SWAMIJI: The mind does not say [anything]. Some feeling comes [first].

SCHOLAR: Yes.

SWAMIJI: There are no thoughts.

SCHOLAR: But Garuḍa has been confused by the fact that he says, "I am hungry," therefore, he thinks it is a purely mental phenomenon, but really it's pre-discursive.

SWAMIJI: No, this is the answer. This is the answer of Nārāyaṇa.

JOHN: It's pre-discursive. First comes the feeling of being hungry and then comes the thought.

SWAMIJI: And then comes thought, afterwards. How can a mad [person] become hungry? His thoughts are *bilkul* (absolutely) away from his being. Hunger, thirst, etc., or craving for sex, that desire, that does not come in the mind first. That is only just a . . .

JOHN: Comes.

SWAMIJI: It comes. It is just like a fountain.

SCHOLAR: *Svayameva prasara.*[171]

SWAMIJI: Yes.

SCHOLAR: This is Śiva.

SWAMIJI: And that is the *nirvikalpa* state. That is the *nirvikalpa* state. That is not the *anubhava*[172] of the mind.

JOHN: This is the seventy-six now.

SWAMIJI:

171 That desire flows (*prasara*) within oneself (*svayameva*).
172 Perception, experience.

Audio 3 - 20:35

रसाद्यनध्यक्षत्वेऽपि रूपादेव यथा तरुम्।
विकल्पो वेत्ति तद्वत्तु नादबिन्द्वादिना शिवम्॥ ७६ ॥

rasādyanadhyakṣatve'pi rūpādeva yathā tarum /
vikalpo vetti tadvattu nādabindvādinā śivam //76//

Just as any tree (for instance, it is a tree of oranges), when you perceive some orange tree with oranges [although] you don't taste that orange, . . .

Rasādi anadhyakṣatve'pi, the *rasa* (the taste) of that orange is not in your mouth. Only you perceive that inside, that this is the fruit of oranges. *Rasādi anadhyakṣatve'pi*, if it is not *pratyakṣa,*[173] but *rūpād eva*, by only a glance you say that, "It is the tree of oranges."

. . . in the same way, *nāda bindvādinā*, by *nāda* and *bindu* (*prakāśa* and *vimarśa*)[174] you can perceive Lord Śiva although you don't taste It. Without tasting It, you can perceive It, and that perceiving is real. Because that perceiving of that orange tree is real although you don't [actually] taste that [orange]. By only a mere glance, you say that it is [an orange tree].

SCHOLAR: Because each implies the other (*sarvākṣepeṇa vartate*).[175]

SWAMIJI: Yes, *sarvākṣepeṇa vartate.*

SCHOLAR: When he says, "*nāda bindvādinā*," . . .

SWAMIJI: *Nāda bindvādinā.*

SCHOLAR: . . . he doesn't mean, just *prakāśa* and *vimarśa.* He says, "*ādinā.*"

SWAMIJI: Yes, *nāda bindvādinā* means, [the perception of] *nāda* and *bindu* is from the *śāmbhava* point of view, *jñāna* and

173 Directly perceptible.
174 *Nāda* is *vimarśa* and *bindu* is *prakāśa.*
175 See verse 66.

kriyā[176] is from the *śākta* point of view, *prāṇa* and *apāna*[177] is [from the] *āṇava* point of view. "*Nādabindvā*[*dinā*]" will [signify] all.

SCHOLAR: So, "*ādi*" refers to that?

SWAMIJI: Yes. *Nāda* and *bindu*–he has put the predominant thing first–*nāda* and *bindu* will go to *śāmbhavopāya*.

SCHOLAR: *Prakāśa* and *vimarśa*.

SWAMIJI: *Prakāśa* and *vimarśa*. And *jñāna* and *kriyā* will go to *śāktopāya*, and *prāṇa* and *apāna* will go to *āṇavopāya*.

SCHOLAR: And in *śāktopāya*, there can be an emphasis on *jñāna* or an emphasis on *kriyā*.

SWAMIJI: *Jñāna* and *kriyā*.

SCHOLAR: One is an emphasis outside, one is an emphasis inside.

SWAMIJI: Yes.

Audio 3 - 23:02

बहुशक्तित्वमस्योक्तं शिवस्य यदतो महान्।
कलातत्त्वपुराणाणुपदादिर्भेदविस्तरः ॥७७॥

bahuśaktitvamasyoktaṁ śivasya yadato mahān /
kalātattvapurāṇāṇupadādirbhedavistaraḥ //77//[178]

[not recited]

Lord Śiva is said to hold, or possess, numberless energies. It is why He is so great. Besides this, [He possesses] the expanding, or courses, of *kalā*, [which] means the five circles (*nivṛtti kalā*, *pratiṣṭhā kalā*, *vidyā kalā*, *śāntā*, and *śāntātītā*); *tattva* means, the courses of the thirty-six elements; *purā* means, one hundred and eight[teen] worlds; *arṇa* means, *varṇādhva*, the courses of all [letters]; *aṇu* means, *mantra-adhva*, the courses of all [*mantra*s/words]; . . .*

176 Knowledge and action, respectively.
177 Exhale and inhale, respectively.
178 See *Special Verses on Practice*, vs. 14 (LJA archives).

SCHOLAR: Is *varṇa* "letters" and *aṇu* "*mantra*"?

SWAMIJI: *Aṇu* is "*mantra*," yes.

SCHOLAR: And *varṇa* is "letter."

SWAMIJI: *Varṇa* is letters.

JOHN: So [*mantrādhva*] would be the course of all *mantra*s.

SWAMIJI: *Mantra*s.

*. . . and *padādir*, the course of all sentences.[179]

Audio 3 - 24:32

सृष्टिस्थितितिरोधानसंहारानुग्रहादि च।
तुर्यमित्यपि देवस्य बहुशक्तित्वजृम्भितम्॥ ७८॥

sṛṣtisthititirodhānasaṁhārānugrahādi ca /
turyamityapi devasya bahuśaktitvajṛmbhitam //78//[180]
[not recited]

In addition to this, the creative, the protective, the destructive, the energy of concealing, and the energy of revealing, and the basis of these five acts (*turya*), are the expansion of the innumerable energies of Lord Śiva.[181]

179 All are possessed by Lord Śiva. For a detailed explanation of the six-fold path (*ṣaḍadhvan*), which consists of five circles, thirty-six elements, and one hundred and eighteen worlds, along with letters, words, and sentences, see Appendix 16 (403). See also *Kashmir Shaivism–The Secret Supreme*, chapter 2, "The Sixfold Path of the Universe (*Saḍadhvan*)."

180 See *Special Verses on Practice*, (LJA archives), verse 12.

181 "These five acts of Lord Śiva, *turyamityapi*, actually these five acts are residing in *turya*, in His God consciousness. *Sṛṣṭi* (creation) is in God consciousness, protection (*sthiti*) is in God consciousness, and *saṁhāra* (destruction) is in God consciousness, concealing is in God consciousness, and revealing is in God consciousness. For this purpose, [Abhinavagupta] has put the sixth one. The sixth one is *turya*. *Turya* is the basis of all these five acts of Lord Śiva. These five acts are *devasya* (of the Lord), *bahu-śakti-tva-jṛmbhitam*, just the glamour of His energies." Ibid., 12. See *Kashmir Shaivism–The*

Audio 3 - 25:02

जाग्रत्स्वप्नसुषुप्तान्यतदतीतानि यान्यपि।
तान्यप्यमुष्य नाथस्य स्वातन्त्र्यलहरीभरः ॥ ७९ ॥

jāgratsvapnasuṣuptānyatadatītāni yānyapi /
tānyapyamuṣya nāthasya svātantryalaharībharaḥ //79//[182]
[not recited]

In addition to this, these five states: *jāgrat* (state of wakefulness), the state of dreaming (*svapna*), the state of sound sleep (*suṣupti*), and *turya* ("the fourth"),[183] *tadatītāni*, and beyond the fourth, the state which is beyond the fourth state,[184] these five states also represent the fullness of Lord Śiva's *svātantrya*, the fullness of the tides of Lord Śiva.

Secret Supreme, 110.65-66, "The Five Great Acts of Lord Śiva (*Pañcakṛtyavidhiḥ*)."

182 See *Special Verses on Practice*, (LJA Archives), verse 10.

183 "This state of *turya* is all-active because this state of *turya* operates *jāgrat*, operates *svapna*, operates *suṣupti*. These three states are operated by *turya*. And [*turya*] is *anāmayā*, without any sickness, there is no trouble. If there is trouble in *jāgrat* and *svapna*, then it is connected with *jāgrat* [and *svapna*], it is not connected with *turya*. *Turya* is without trouble, there is no trouble. If you are once situated, established, in the *turya* state, [then] in *jāgrat avastha* you will find always bliss, in *svapna* you will find bliss, and in *suṣupti* also you will be blissful." *Tantrāloka* 10.271-278 (LJA archive). "This state of *turya* is *rūpakatvāt udāsīnāt cyuteyaṁ*, it is beyond *rūpa*, beyond the individual surface of consciousness, and it has gone beyond the level of ignoring the universal energies [as in *suṣupti*]. . . . Universal energies are existing there but in another coating; the coating is divine in *turya*. *Pūrṇatūnmukhyī daśā*, it is towards the fullness of God consciousness. [*Turya*] is situated towards the fullness of God consciousness. It is not the fullness of God consciousness. It is situated *towards* the fullness of God consciousness." Ibid., 10.271-278. See Appendix 14 (p401).

184 *Turyātītā*. "*Turya* is the tide of God consciousness and *turyātītā* is the tide of God consciousness in its fullness." *Special Verses on Practice*, vs. 11. See Appendix 14 (p401).

SCHOLAR: *Laharī*, wave.

SWAMIJI: Yes, tides. *Laharī*, big waves.

Audio 3 - 26:00

महामन्त्रेशमन्त्रेशमन्त्राः शिवपुरोगमाः ।
अकलौ सकलश्चेति शिवस्यैव विभूतयः ॥ ८० ॥

mahāmantreśamantreśamantrāḥ śivapurogamāḥ /
akalau sakalaśceti śivasyaiva vibhūtayaḥ //80//[185]

Besides this, [the seven perceivers that begin] from Lord Śiva, then *mahā mantreśa* (*mantra maheśvaraḥ*, the state of *mantra maheśvara*[186]), the state of *mantreśvara*,[187] the state of the *mantras*,[188] and *akalau* means, *vijñānākala* and *pralayākala*, *sakalaśceti*, and the state which is called *sakala*, these seven states are nothing [other] than the glory of Lord Śiva (*śivasyaiva vibhūtayaḥ*).[189]

---

185 Ibid., vs. 11.

186 The state is Sadāśiva. The perceiver of this state is *mantra maheśvara*.

187 The state is Īśvara. The perceiver of this state is *mantreśvara*.

188 The state is Śuddhavidyā. The perceiver of this state is *mantra*.

189 "So, if you have to see the glory of Lord Śiva, see the glory of Lord Śiva in wakefulness, etc., see the glory of Lord Śiva in all seven *pramātṛ bhavas*. *Sakala*, we are in *sakala*. At the time of deep sleep, we are in *pralayākala*. At the time of entrance to God consciousness, we are in *vijñānākala*. At the time of experiencing God consciousness, we are in Śuddhavidyā. At the time of [experiencing the] fullness of God consciousness, we are in Īśvara. At the time of [experiencing the] complete fullness of God consciousness, we are in Sadāśiva. At the time of [experiencing the] glamour of Śiva, we are in Śiva *bhava*. And all these are no less than each other. They are just *vibhūti*, they are the glamour, seven ways of the glamour, of God consciousness. So, don't worry about experiencing Śiva. If you are experiencing *sakala*, that is also fine. No worry." *Special Verses on Practice*, vs. 11. See also *Kashmir Shaivism–The Secret Supreme*, 8, "The Seven States of the Seven Perceivers (*Pramātṛn*)." See Appendix 10 (p394) for explanation of the Seven Perceivers.

Audio 3 - 26:50

तत्त्वग्रामस्य सर्वस्य धर्मः स्यादनपायवान्।
आत्मैव हि स्वभावात्मेत्युक्तं श्रीत्रिशिरोमते॥ ८१ ॥

tattvagrāmasya sarvasya dharmaḥ syādanapāyavān /
ātmaiva hi svabhāvātmetyuktaṁ śrītriśiromate //81//

It is explained in the *Triśirobhairava āgama*[190] that all these classes of *tattvas* (elements, etc.), the real aspect of all these elements, etc., is only one, that is *Ātmā* (the Self), which is *svabhāvātmā*, which has become the nature of all these states (*tattvas*, *bhuvanas*, *kalās*, all that what he has explained in the previous *ślokas*).

SCHOLAR: It is an invariable attribute (*anapāvayān*).

SWAMIJI: *Anapāvayān*, yes, which cannot be removed, which cannot be excluded in any way.

JOHN: Eight-two.

SWAMIJI: Now he quotes the *Triśirobhairava āgama*:

Audio 3 - 28:00

हृदिस्थं सर्वदेहस्थं स्वभावस्थं सुसूक्ष्मकम्।
सामूह्यं चैव तत्त्वानां ग्रामशब्देन कीर्तितम्॥ ८२ ॥

hṛdisthaṁ sarvadehasthaṁ svabhāvasthaṁ
susūkṣmakam /
sāmūhyaṁ caiva tattvānāṁ grāmaśabdena kīrtitam //82//
[not recited]

Really, that reality of Lord Śiva, is nominated as "*grāma*", (*grama śabdena kīrtitam*) because *grāma* means, *sāmūhyam*

190 "[*Āgama* means] from the original source, that is Śiva." *The Mystery of Vibrationless-Vibration in Kashmir Shaivism,* Vasugupta's *Spanda Kārikā and* Kṣemarāja's *Spanda Sandoha*, Revealed by Swami Lakshmanjoo, Lakshmanjoo, ed. John Hughes, Lakshmanjoo Academy, Los Angeles, 2016. (additional questions, p. 268.)

caiva tattvānām, the collective state of all the elements etc., and which is situated in the heart, which is situated in each and everybody, which is situated in one's own nature (*svarūpa*), and which is most subtle (*susūkṣmakam*), and which is the collective state of all the *tattvas*. This is why He is nominated as "*grāma*."

JOHN: The literal [meaning] of "*grāma*" is?

SWAMIJI: Collection (*samūha*). "*Samūha*" is in Sanskrit, "collection" is in English.

Audio 3 - 29:15

आत्मैव धर्म इत्युक्तः शिवामृतपरिप्लुतः।

ātmaiva dharma ityuktaḥ śivāmṛtapariplutaḥ /83a
[not recited]

And the [real] aspect (*dharma*) of all these collective things, what we see in this universe, the real aspect of all these is *Ātmā*, that Self, which is bathed in the nectar of Śiva. It is not the individual self, it is the universal Self. So it is the universal Self which is the real aspect of this whole universe (*śiva āmṛta pariplutaḥ ātma*).

JOHN: Eight-three.

SWAMIJI: Now, eighty-three:

Audio 3 - 30:01

प्रकाशावस्थितं ज्ञानं भावाभावादिमध्यतः ॥८३॥
स्वस्थाने वर्तनं ज्ञेयं द्रष्टृत्वं विगतावृति।
विविक्तवस्तुकथितशुद्धविज्ञाननिर्मलः ॥८४॥
ग्रामधर्मवृत्तिरुक्तस्तस्य सर्वं प्रसिद्ध्यति।

prakāśāvasthitaṁ jñānaṁ bhāvābhāvādimadhyataḥ //83b//
svasthāne vartanaṁ jñeyaṁ draṣṭṛtvaṁ vigatāvṛti /
viviktavastukathitaśuddhavijñānanirmalaḥ //84//
grāmadharmavṛttiruktastasya sarvaṁ prasiddhyati /85a

The one who is established permanently in the aspect of this collective state of Lord Śiva the one who is established in this state is said to be established in *grāma dharma.*[191] That *yogi* who is established in this state is said to be established in the [real] aspect of *grāma*. It is held, It is to behold, as knowledge between two objects, as knowledge [that is] one with conscious light; *prakāśāvasthitam jñānam*, knowledge filled with the light of one's own consciousness, and that is to be held in the center of two objects or in the center of existing and non-existing [objects].

SCHOLAR: *Bhāvābhāva.*

SWAMIJI: *Bhāvābhāva. Bhāva abhāva* or *bhāvayoḥ*. And this is not to be held in-between these two objects or in[-between] existing and non-existing objects, It is to be held in one's own Self (*svasthāne vartamānaṁ jñeyam*, It is to be held in one's own nature) because It is *draṣṭṛtvam*, It is the subjective state. It is not an objective state that It could be observed in[-between] two objects.

JOHN: It is the seer.

SWAMIJI: It is the seer. It is not the seen. And It is *vigatāvṛti*, It has no covering, It is without covering. All coverings end up to *samanā*. *Unmanā* has no covering, so this is really the state of *unmanā*.[192] This is really the state of not inhale or exhale, but the center of these two.[193]

---

191 The real aspect (*dharma*) of the collection of every element (*grāma*).

192 In his commentary, Jayaratha quotes two verses from the fourth chapter of the *Svacchanda Tantra*, "*ākaraśca ukaraśca* . . .," depicting the divisions (*kalās*) of the *praṇava mantra* '*auṁ*' (*oṁ*). *Samanā* and *unmanā* make up the last two parts of this division. See Appendix 17 (p405) for a detailed explanation of the twelve divisions of the *praṇava mantra* '*auṁ*' (*oṁ*). Later, Abhinavagupta addresses the ten-fold division of '*auṁ*' in verses 186 and 187.

193 To explain how one is to enter into the center of two objects, Jayaratha quotes a verse from the *Vijñāna Bhairava tantra*: "While entering in the center of these two objects, you have to take the support, every now and then, of these two objects. For instance,

SCHOLAR: Beyond even *parāparā kāla*.

SWAMIJI: It is not the state of past, present, and future. It is the state which gives life to these three times (past, present, and future). That is *parāparā kālātīta*. All these others are *āvṛtiḥ* (coverings), they cover that real nature of Lord Śiva. It is without cover. And It is purified with pure knowledge of the Self (*śuddha vijñāna nirmalaḥ*). And It is *vivikta vastu kathita*, an absolutely discriminating state.

SCHOLAR: Discriminat*ed*?

SWAMIJI: Discriminated state (*vivikta*), discriminated from all individualities (*vivikta*).[194] The one who is established in this state is said to be established in *grāma dharma*. That *yogi* who is established in this state is said to be established in the [real] aspect of *grāma*.

SCHOLAR: He moves in That, he has *vṛtti* in That.

SWAMIJI: *Vṛtti* means, established, the establishing state.

SCHOLAR: Is it the same as *sthiti* or is it . . . ?

SWAMIJI: *Sthiti*. It is *sthiti*, yes, It does not move. *Vṛtti* means, he is situated in That. For him, nothing is unsolved; *tasya sarvam prasiddhyati*, everything is solved.

SCHOLAR: Perfected for him.

SWAMIJI: Perfected.

---

while you concentrate on that center, this center will disappear, and you have to take the support of these two objects again; and then again and again, see this and see this, see this and see this, and see what is in-between, and focus your mind in the center, and when that center is established well, then you have to discard the impression of both these objects and be established in the center, and then the Universal center will be revealed. Or, take the support of breathing in and breathing out for establishing your center. When the center of these two breaths is established well, then leave the breath aside and enter in that center, and that Universal center will be revealed." *Vijñāna Bhairava–The Manual for Self Realization, Dhāraṇā* 38, vs. 61.

194 Differentiation.

Audio 3 - 34:26

ऊर्ध्वं त्यक्त्वाधो विशेत्स रामस्थो मध्यदेशगः ॥ ८५ ॥

ūrdhvaṁ tyaktvādho viśetsa rāmastho madhyadeśagaḥ // 85b//[195] [not recited]

And that *yogi* who is established in the [real] aspect of *grāma*, when he leaves behind *ūrdhva* and *adhaḥ* (up and down)–when he leaves behind up and down, the states which are situated in the upper state and the lower state, when he leaves those away–and *ūrdhvaṁ adhaḥ tyaktvā*, when he leaves these two states, he must *viśet*, he gets entry, he gets entry. *Sa madhyadeśagaḥ rāmasthaḥ*, that person, that *yogi*, who has got entry in the universal center is [said] to be established in "*rāma*" also. It is not only establishment in the aspect of *grāma*, it is establishment in the state of *rāma*.[196]

JOHN: Which is? What is the state of *rāma*?

SWAMIJI: *Rāma*. *Rāma* is *paramātmā*, the supreme God consciousness. Now he explains fully the state of *rāma*, what is "*rāma*" really.

SCHOLAR: Swamiji, this up and down is . . .

SWAMIJI: *Prāṇa* and *apāna*.

SCHOLAR: . . . in *āṇavopāya*?

SWAMIJI: Up and down is not only in *āṇavopāya*. Up and down in *āṇavopāya* is breath, the two breaths. In *śāktopāya*, it is *pramāṇa* (cognition) and *prameya* (objectivity).[197]

SCHOLAR: That would be *cit kuṇḍalinī*.[198]

---

195 See *Special Verses on Practice*, (LJA archives) verse 57.

196 "And that is the establishment held in the central vein (*madhya nāḍī*)." Ibid.

197 "Or," as Swamiji will explain later, "*jñāna* and *kriyā*."

198 "*Cit kuṇḍalinī* is experienced by *yogins* by means of concentrating on the center between any two breaths, thoughts, or actions; between the destruction and creation of any two things." *Kashmir Shaivism–The Secret Supreme*, 17.118-122. See Appendix 19 (p410) for an

SWAMIJI: Yes. And in *śāmbhavopāya*, it is *prakāśa* and *vimarśa*.[199] Up and down . . .

SCHOLAR: But in each case the breath is stopped, so it means that always, throughout.

SWAMIJI: Breath is stopped. *Prakāśa* and *vimarśa* merge in that one Being [in the *śāmbhavopāya* state]. *Jñāna* and *kriyā* merges in that *jñātṛ bhāva*[200] [in the *śāktopāya* state].

SCHOLAR: But when it is *prakāśa* and *vimarśa*, there is no succession. It is instant . . .

SWAMIJI: Instantaneously.

SCHOLAR: . . . establishment in that center.

SWAMIJI: Yes. So he explains now what is really "*rāma*." *Rāma* is not the son of Daśaratha.[201]

THE FOURTEEN-FOLD STATES OF RĀMA (86-93)

Audio 3 - 36:52

गतिः स्थानं स्वप्नजाग्रदुन्मेषणनिमेषणे।
धावनं प्लवनं चैव आयासः शक्तिवेदनम्॥ ८६ ॥
बुद्धिभेदास्तथा भावाः संज्ञाः कर्माण्यनेकशः।
एष रामो व्यापकोऽत्र शिवः परमकारणम्॥ ८७ ॥

gatiḥ sthānaṁ svapnajāgradunmeṣaṇanimeṣaṇe /
dhāvanaṁ plavanaṁ caiva āyāsaḥ śaktivedanam //86//

---

explanation of *kuṇḍalinī* in Kashmir Shaivism.

199 For explanation of *prakāśa* and *vimarśa* see Appendix 13 (p399). *Śāmbhavopāya, śāktopāya* and *āṇavopāya* are discussed in detail from verse 139 onwards.

200 The state (*bhāva*) of the knower (*jñātṛ*).

201 Rāma (Viṣṇu incarnate), the principal hero of the *Rāmāyana* epic.

buddhibhedāstathā bhāvāḥ sañjñāḥ karmāṇyanekaśaḥ /
eṣa rāmo vyāpako'tra śivaḥ paramakāraṇam //87//[202]
[not recited]

[The fourteen-fold states of *rāma*]: Moving (*gatiḥ*), *sthānam* (staying),[203] going in dreams, staying in wakefulness, the twinkling of the eyes (*unmeṣa* and *nimeṣa*[204]), running, jumping, not-knowing (*āyāsaḥ*, not knowing, ignorance), and knowing one's own energies.[205] *Śakti vedanam* is actually when he is aware of all his senses. That is *śakti vedana* when he is aware of all his senses, when he does not follow the movement of the senses, but [rather], he makes the senses follow him, he makes his senses follow him. Do you understand? All these sensual organs, when they move on their objects, he does not move with them, but [rather], these [senses] follow him.[206]

JOHN: So he is the actor, not the acted.

SWAMIJI: He is the actor, not the acted. And in addition, *buddhi bhedā*, all differentiated states of knowledge,[207] all

---

202 See *Special Verses on Practice*, vs. 55 and 56.
203 "Just walk and you'll find the state of *rāma*; *sthānaṁ*, just sit and you'll find the state of *rāma*." Ibid., vs. 55.
204 Lit., opening and closing the eyes, respectively. In his commentary, Jayaratha explains *unmeṣa* and *nimeṣa* in connection with the cosmic operation of Sadāśiva and Īśvara as described in *Spanda Sandoha*, (LJA archive), vs 1. Here, these terms may, in fact, simply refer to the mundane movement of the eyelids, which is consistent with the mundane nature of the other states described.
205 *Śakti vedanam.*
206 Swamiji also explains *śakti vedanam* as, "deriving strength from within for some [forceful activity], that strength, with force you want to [commit an action], that is *rāma*." *Special Verses on Practice*, (LJA archives), verse 55.
207 "*Buddhi bhedā* means, the eight-fold sections of *buddhi* (intellect): *dharma*, *jñāna*, *vairāgya*, *aiśvarya* and *adharma*, *ajñāṇa*, *avairāgya*, *anaiśvarya*." Ibid., vs. 56. The general meaning of these states and their opposites are: *dharma* (duty), *adharma* (negation of duty), *jñāna* (knowledge), *ajñāna* (ignorance), *vairāgya* (detachment), *avairāgya* (attachment), *aiśvarya* (glorious), and *anaiśvarya* (absence

moods,[208] all names, all actions (all various actions), all this collectively is called "*rāma*," because *vyāpako'tra śiva*, He pervades all these movements. So, hence, *rāma* is Śiva, and He is the supreme *kāraṇa*, the real cause of this whole universe.[209]

JOHN: Is there some literal sense of "*rāma*" that they're driving this idea of permeating in all actions?

SWAMIJI: *Rāma* means "*rāmu krīḍāyāma*," who plays, . . .

JOHN: Who plays.

SWAMIJI: . . . who plays in this universe–the player. Now he explains in the next *śloka* how you can get entry in the state of *rāma*:

Audio 3 - 39:33

कल्मषक्षीणमनसा स्मृतिमात्रनिरोधनात्।
ध्यायते परमं ध्येयं गमागमपदे स्थितम्॥ ८८॥

kalmaṣakṣīṇamanasā smṛtimātranirodhanāt /
dhyāyate paramaṁ dhyeyaṁ gamāgamapade sthitam //88//
[not recited]

You have just to stop *smṛti* (*smṛti* means, *vikalpa*). Just stop various *vikalpa*s (thoughts). You have to stop them, not by the mind, [not] by the ordinary mind, but by that mind which is *kalmaṣa kṣīṇa manasā*, which is an absolutely pure mind, an "un-dotted" mind, that mind which is absolutely pure. By that mind, you have to see that all thoughts are put away.

---

of being glorious, i.e., pitiable, degraded, etc.).

208 Although "*bhāvāḥ*" can refer to "moods," Swamiji also says: "*Stathā bhāvāḥ*, whatever objective world you see before you, that is *rāma*, that is *bhāvāḥ*." Ibid., vs. 56.

209 This reference to the 'fourteen fold universe' (*etat caturdaśa vidhaṁ)* is from the *Triśirobhairava Tantra*, which Abhinavagupta has quoted almost verbatim in verses 86 to 89.

"*Etat caturdaśa vidhaṁ*, this fourteen-fold everything, *rāmaḥ tu parikīr*, is the position, the state, of *rāma*. So, in each and every activity, positive or negative, in all activities, you will find the state of *rāma*." Ibid.

JOHN: This mind is existing at what level? In *vijñānākala* or Śuddhavidyā?[210] What . . . ?

SWAMIJI: Yes.

JOHN: Not in *sakala*.

SWAMIJI: No, it is not in *sakala*. It must be in *vijñānākala*–just entry. *Vijñānākala* is the entry. The entry begins from *vijñānākala*, the entry in one's own nature. And *dhyāyate paramaṁ dhyeyaṁ*, there he contemplates on that supreme object which is established, that is established, in *gama* and *agama*:[211] *prāṇa* and *apāna* from the *āṇavopāya* point of view, *pramāṇa* and *prameya* (or *jñāna* and *kriyā*) from the *śāktopāya* point of view, and *prakāśa* and *vimarśa* from the *śāmbhavopāya* point of view.

SCHOLAR: So, you here differ from Jayaratha, who takes "*gamāgama*" as *upalakṣaṇa*[212] for the fourteen different aspects of *rāma*.

SWAMIJI: That is also *gamāgama* because all these . . . it is not only *prāṇa* and *apāna*, it is one step and another step, it is one talk and another talk. So, this whole will be found only in this fourteen-fold universe.

SCHOLAR: But still your interpretation differs from Jayaratha's.

SWAMIJI: Yes.

JOHN: This is *śāktopāya*.

SWAMIJI: It is *śāktopāya*, it is *āṇavopāya*, it is *śāmbhavopāya*.

JOHN: In these.

SWAMIJI: Yes.

JOHN: This *dhyāna* (meditation), this is Shaivite *dhyāna*,

---

210 See Appendix 10 (394) for explanation of the seven perceivers (*pramātṛs*).

211 Going and not going, respectively.

212 A figure of speech in which the nomination of a part refers to the whole.

this is not that *dhyāna* with *mūrti*.[213]

SWAMIJI: No (affirmative).

JOHN: So, how does the Shaivite exactly define this *dhyāna*, this contemplation? Is he contemplating *prakāśa-vimarśa*, contemplating *jñāna-kriyā*, contemplating *apāna-prāṇa*?

SWAMIJI: It is only awareness. Through awareness he contemplates.

JOHN: So it doesn't mean any kind of thinking about it in terms of *mūrti*.

Audio 3 - 42:18

SWAMIJI: Just be attentive. Don't lose your own subjective consciousness. *Bas*, that is all. You just have to observe and hold what you are really. Nothing is to be practiced. Everything is there.[214]

JOHN: So, Shaivism never means, by "*dhyāna*," this *mūrti*.

SWAMIJI: No.

JOHN: Thinking of Śiva with form or . . .

SWAMIJI: No [agreement].

SCHOLAR: Except in lower forms of meditation.

SWAMIJI: In *āṇavopāya* also, you have to be aware. Without awareness, *āṇavopāya* will be no use.

SCHOLAR: But you can have that *mūrti dhyāna*[215] with awareness.

SWAMIJI: *Mūrti dhyāna*, yes, with awareness. But *mūrti dhyāna* is discarded [here]. Only the subtle way of *dhyāna* of *āṇavopāya* is here mentioned–the subtle way.

SCHOLAR: In the *tantras*, say in the *Netra tantra*, [where] he describes meditation on Bhairavī and Bhairava with all

---

213 *Mūrti*: form; usually used to refer to the image of a deity, whether external or imagined or perceived internally.

214 "*Śivatvam*, He is Śiva. If you know Him, He is there. If you don't know Him, He is still there. Don't worry about it." *Special Verses on Practice*, vs. 57. See commentary of verse 137 for a full explanation of this quote from Somānanda's *Śivadṛṣṭi*.

215 Meditation on some image or form of a chosen deity (*Iṣṭa Devatā*).

their arms.

SWAMIJI: Yes, that is also . . .

SCHOLAR: Accepted.

SWAMIJI: . . . in *āṇavopāya*, yes. In the inferior state of *āṇavopāya*, not in the real state of *āṇavopāya*. In the real state of *āṇavopāya*, you have to be aware between two breaths. Move in and out, move in and out, with awareness of the subjective state. That is awareness.

JOHN: So this *dhyāna*, this lower *dhyāna* with *mūrti*, would just hold oneself in *vikalpa*.

SWAMIJI: But it purifies one's mind, and so he becomes capable of this entry.

SCHOLAR: You create that image and then you draw it into yourself. Is that right?

SWAMIJI: Yes, yes.

SCHOLAR: So it also purifies and elevates.

SWAMIJI: It purifies, absolutely.

Audio 3 - 44:14

परं शिवं तु व्रजति भैरवाख्यं जपादपि।

paraṁ śivaṁ tu vrajati bhairavākhyaṁ japādapi /89a

It is not only by *dhyāna*, by this contemplation full of awareness, that he enters in that supreme state of Lord Śiva (or in that supreme state of *rāma*), but by recitation also, by the state of reciting *mantra*s also, he enters in the state of Śiva, which is one with Bhairava. But what is that recitation? Recitation is:

Audio 3 - 44:51

तत्स्वरूपं जपः प्रोक्तो भावाभावपदच्युतः ॥८९॥

tatsvarūpaṁ japaḥ prokto bhāvābhāvapadacyutaḥ //89b//

Recitation is to feel one object, to observe one object, and then observe another object, then observe another object. These are the "beads" that are existing in this universe.

JOHN: So the *japa* is to have that point between those beads?

SWAMIJI: Between those beads.

SCHOLAR: The thread–*śakti sūtram*.

SWAMIJI: Yes, thread. The thread, *śakti sūtram*, the thread is the reality of all these beads.

JOHN: *Mālā*.

SWAMIJI: Yes. *Tatsvarūpam japaḥ prokto bhāvābhāva-padacyutaḥ*, because [the thread] is away from *bhāva* and *abhāva*,[216] It is away from one bead and another bead. "This is one bead, this is another bead, this another bead, this is another bead," go on observing this whole universe, not only by appearance, [but also] by *śabda* (sound), *sparśa* (touch), *rūpa* (form), *rasa* (taste), and *gandha* (smell).

SCHOLAR: Every sensation.

SWAMIJI: Every sensation. One sensation is one bead, another sensation is another bead–see in-between.

SCHOLAR: This is *śāktopāya*.

SWAMIJI: This is *śāktopāya*, and this is real *japa*.

JOHN: Some senses are harder to use. It seems like taste would be more difficult than sight, for example.

SWAMIJI: Taste is also one bead.

SCHOLAR: So, when they talk of *lakṣa japa* and all this tens of thousands of recitations of *mantra*s, what is meant in Shaivism?

SWAMIJI: *Lakṣa japa* is innumerable, innumerable. Just go on with full awareness through all the beads of the universe.

SCHOLAR: But when it says that this *yāga* is, say, *pañca lakṣa*, there are five points of awareness, the five centers, in the Kula system . . .

216 Existence and non-existence, respectively.

SWAMIJI: Yes, the five centers: *sṛṣṭi* (creation), *sthiti* (preservation), *saṁhāra* (destruction), *pidhāna* (concealing), and *anugraha* (revealing).[217] This also.

SCHOLAR: But *lakṣa* there really means, the center of intense awareness.

SWAMIJI: *Lakṣa* means, what is to held with awareness. That is *lakṣa* (*lakṣyate iti lakṣa*).

JOHN: So, in the terms of five . . .

SWAMIJI: Don't go to that [meaning]. ["*Lakṣa*"] is not there [with the suffix] "*ya*."[218]

SCHOLAR: *Lakṣa* in Shaivism doesn't mean that, just ten thousand recitations.

SWAMIJI: Ten thousand or one *lakh* (100,000). *Lakṣa* means, that point [to aim at].

SCHOLAR: Pandey thinks that it means that.

SWAMIJI: Yes. He's wrong.

SCHOLAR: It would even be too low for *āṇavopāya*.

SWAMIJI: Yes (laughs).

Audio 3 - 47:28

तदत्रापि तदीयेन स्वातन्त्र्येणोपकल्पितः ।
दूरासन्नादिको भेदश्चित्स्वातन्त्र्यव्यपेक्षया ॥ ९० ॥

tadatrāpi tadīyena svātantryeṇopakalpitaḥ /
dūrāsannādiko bhedaścitsvātantryavyapekṣayā //90//

But in this state also, this is the freedom of His *svātantrya śakti* that He has, Lord Śiva has, established the differentiated-ness of these means. Some means are away, far away, from His existence, and some ways are near His existence. Those which are far away from His existence, they are that

217 See Appendix 22 (p414).

218 Swamiji is saying, "Don't go to the literal meaning of *lakṣa* (100,000), because the word is not there with the suffix '*ya*', in which case *lakṣyate* means, what is to be held with awareness.

lakṣa japa, etc., *pūjā* (worship), recitation of *mantras*, and observing that sacrificial fire, etc. These also are means but they are away, far away (*dūra*). *Āsanna* means, those [means which] are very near to It. And this is also the glory of His *svātantrya* [that] He has kept all these means. Some means are very near to Him and some means are very far away from Him.

Evaṁ svātantryapūrṇatvād . . . next, the ninety-first [*śloka*]:

Audio 3 - 48:55

एवं स्वातन्त्र्यपूर्णत्वादतिदुर्घटकार्ययम्।
केन नाम न रूपेण भासते परमेश्वरः ॥९१॥

evaṁ svātantryapūrṇatvādatidurghaṭakāryayam /
kena nāma na rūpeṇa bhāsate parameśavaraḥ //91//

So, that Lord Śiva, who is *atidurghaṭa kāryayam*, whose actions are not understandable, whose acts you cannot imagine (beyond imagination, His actions are beyond imagination), . . .*

SCHOLAR: *Atidurghaṭa*, impossible.

SWAMIJI: Impossible. He makes the impossible possible.[219]

*. . . so, *kena nāma na rūpeṇa*, *kena rūpeṇa parameśvaraḥ na bhāsate*, He appears, He reveals His own nature, from

219 "The greatest *svātantrya* (independence) of Lord Śiva is *durghaṭa saṁpādana*: [that] which is possible, that becomes impossible; [that] which is impossible, that becomes possible (laughs). This is the *svātantrya* of Parabhairava. It was not possible for Parabhairava to become *jīva* (the limited individual). And [for] *jīva* to become Parabhairava, it is not possible. But *jīva* becomes Parabhairava and Parabhairava becomes *jīva*. Parabhairava just covers his own body and he is nowhere available in the market. You cannot find [Him] although you go on searching day and night, with no news." *Paramārthasāra–Essence of the Supreme Reality*, by Abhinavagupta, with the commentary of Yogarāja, translation by Swami Lakshmanjoo, ed. John Hughes (Lakshmanjoo Academy, Los Angeles, 2015), verse 15.

every side, from those sides also which are away from Him and those sides which are very near to Him. So He reveals His nature *sarvena rūpeṇa*, by each and every means.

JOHN: Ninety-two.

SWAMIJI: Ninety-two and ninety-three, collectively:

Audio 3 - 50:11

निरावरणमाभाति भात्यावृतनिजात्मकः।
आवृतानावृतो भाति बहुधा भेदसंगमात्॥ ९२ ॥
इति शक्तित्रयं नाथे स्वातन्त्र्यापरनामकम्।
इच्छादिभिरभिख्याभिर्गुरुभिः प्रकटीकृतम्॥ ९३ ॥

nirāvaraṇamābhāti bhātyāvṛtanijātmakaḥ /
āvṛtānāvṛto bhāti bahudhā bhedasaṁgamāt //92//
iti śaktitrayaṁ nāthe svātantryāparanāmakam /
icchādibhirākhyābhirgurubhiḥ prakaṭīkṛtam //93//

Nirāvaraṇamābhāti, He appears without any interruption; *nirāvaraṇam*, without any foreign agency.

SCHOLAR: Obscuration.

SWAMIJI: Without any foreign agency. There is no foreign agent in-between, in-between the *sādhaka* and the *sādhya*,[220] Parameśvara and the *yogi*.

SCHOLAR: In *śāmbhavopāya*.

SWAMIJI: In *śāmbhavopāya*. *Nirāvaraṇamābhāti*, He appears without *āvaraṇa*, without . . .

JOHN: Covering.

SWAMIJI: . . . without covering [in *śāmbhavopāya*]. *Bhāti āvṛta nijātmaka*, He appears also with covering in *āṇavopāya*. *Avṛta anāvṛto bhāti*, He appears somewhat covered and somewhat revealed in *śāktopāya*. *Bahudhā bheda saṁgamāt*, because His differentiated states of means are innumerable

220 The contemplator (*sādhaka*) and the contemplated (*sādhya*).

(*bahudhā*). So these threefold energies, which are *parā*, *parāparā*, and *aparā*, . . .*

[Abhinavagupta lists the energies in this order]: *parā*, *aparā*, and *parāparā* [because] *parāparā* cannot be explained without explaining *aparā* first.[221]

SCHOLAR: This is why at the beginning he . . .

SWAMIJI: In the beginning also, yes.[222] The supreme energy is explained first, then the inferior energy, and then the energy in-between.

*. . . and these threefold energies in that Lord, for that Lord, [are] for revealing His nature (*nāthe–naimittiki vyākhyātā*; "*nāthe*" is *naimittiki saptamī*,[223] "for," for achieving the state of *nātha*[224]).

SCHOLAR: *Nātha pada prāptyartham.*

SWAMIJI: *Nātha pada prāptyartham.*[225] *Svātantryāpara-nāmakam*, these threefold energies of Lord Śiva are nominated as *svātantrya*, collectively. *Icchādibhirākhyābhirgurubhiḥ prakaṭīkṛtam*, and our ancient masters have revealed and explained that these are the energies of *icchā* (will), *jñāna* (knowledge), and *kriyā* (action). The energy of *icchā* is supreme, the energy of *kriyā* is inferior, and the energy of *jñāna* is medium.

JOHN: Ninety-four.

SWAMIJI: The ninety-fourth [*śloka*]:

---

221 Abhinavagupta has given a different sequence for the three-fold energies than what is given in the *Mālinīvijaya Tantra*. Later, in verses 167-169, he also list the *upāyas* in a different sequence than what is given in the *Mālinīvijaya*.

222 Referring to the invocatory verses 2, 3 and 4.

223 Special causal locative case.

224 An appellation of Lord Śiva, which literally means, refuge, a protector, or lord.

225 In order to attain (*prāptyartham*) God consciousness (*nātha pada*).

Various Names Attributed To Lord Śiva (94-105)

Audio 3 - 53:11

देवो ह्यन्वर्थशास्त्रोक्तैः शब्दैः समुपदिश्यते।
महाभैरवदेवोऽयं पतिर्यः परमः शिवः ॥९४॥

devo hyanvarthaśāstroktaiḥ śabdaiḥ samupādiśyate /
mahābhairavadevo'yaṁ patiryaḥ paramaḥ śivaḥ //94//[226]

This Lord, who is *deva*, that *paramaśiva* (supreme Śiva), is explained as "*deva*" by *sārthaka* meanings,[227] which are found in the *śāstras* (scripture).

JOHN: *Sārthaka* means?

SWAMIJI: *Sārthaka* means, with meaning. For instance, my name is Lakṣmaṇa. It has no *sārthaka*, it has no meaning.

JOHN: Without meaning.

SWAMIJI: It is *rūḍhiḥ.*[228] My name is *brahmacārī*–it has meaning. This *brahmacārī* name is *sārthaka* and the Lakṣmaṇa name is *rūḍhiḥ.* And "*deva*" for Lord Śiva is a *sārthaka* name, it has got a meaning. Why He is "*deva*"? It is explained.

Mahābhairavadeva, He is nominated as Mahābhairava (supreme Bhairava *deva*), He is nominated as *patiḥ* (universal husband), and supreme Śiva (*paramaśiva*). These are His *śārthaka* names.

SCHOLAR: *Mahābhairavadeva* (inaudible) *paramaśiva.*

SWAMIJI: "*Mahābhairavadeva*" is another.

JOHN: What is the meaning of "*mahābhairavadeva*"?

226 See *Special Verses on Practice*, (LJA archives), verse 28.
227 ". . . and by the statement of grammar." Ibid., vs. 28.
228 A conventional name.

SWAMIJI: Supreme Bhairava *deva*. He has to explain it. He will explain it one-by-one. He will explain first [the meaning of] "Mahābhairava," then "Deva," then "Pati," and then "Śiva," and then what *"parama"* means.

SCHOLAR: And *"mahā."*

SWAMIJI: *"Parama"* and *"mahā."*[229]

JOHN: So, ninety-five.

SWAMIJI: Yes, ninety-five and onwards:

BHAIRAVA (95-99)

Audio 3 - 55:11

विश्वं बिभर्ति पूरणधारणयोगेन तेन च भ्रियते।

viśvaṁ bibharti pūraṇadhāraṇāyogena tena ca bhriyate / 95a[230]

Lord Śiva is called "Bhairava" because Bhairava means, He who protects this whole universe by holding it, filling it with His nature, and protecting it from all sides.

SCHOLAR: Preserving it.

SWAMIJI: Preserving it. And Bhairava means, the one who is filled and protected by the universe is Bhairava. The one who protects and fills the universe is Bhairava and the one who is protected and filled *by* the universe is Bhairava–both ways. This universe protects Him and He protects this universe–this Bhairava.[231]

---

229 "*Avacchedunade*, limitation is negated from that supreme Bhairava, so '*parama*' and '*mahāt*', these qualifications are added in that name of Bhairava." *Special Verses on Practice*, vs. 28.

230 See *Special Verses on Practice*, (LJA Archives), verse 29.

231 "How He protects this universe? *Pūraṇa dhāraṇa yogena*, He fills it, all gaps are filled in this universe by Bhairava. Where there is a

Audio 3 - 56:08

सविमर्शतया रव रूपतश्च संसारभीरुहितकृच्च ॥९५॥

savimarśatayā rava rūpataśca saṁsārabhīrūhitakṛcca // 95b// [not recited in full]

And when He creates *rava* in individuals, . . .*

Rava means, sound, that supreme sound filled with consciousness. *Savimarśatayā* means, filled with consciousness. When, in that sound, there is consciousness, that conscious sound is called "Bhairava." "*O-o-o-o-o-o-ṁ*," when you recite this "*oṁ*" with consciousness, it is Bhairava, it is one with Bhairava–this sound. This is *rava rūpataśca*. Another way of explaining what Bhairava is: *saṁsāra bhūruhitakṛcca* (this is the third meaning).

*. . . in the one who is afraid from the universe, who is afraid from *saṁsāra* (*saṁsāra bhīru*), who wants to abandon this universe, who is afraid from *saṁsāra*, for him, who is the protector? Who protects him? The one who is afraid from *saṁsāra*, he is protected by that being who is Bhairava. Bhairava is [that Being] who protects those people who are afraid from *saṁsāra*, who are afraid from repeated births and deaths. Those persons are protected by that Being, which being is Bhairava.[232]

---

lacking of something, it is filled with That element. So, this whole universe becomes full, it possesses the fullness, just like Bhairava, and that fullness is derived from Bhairava in this universe. *Tena ca bhriyate*, this universe also produces fullness for Bhairava, the universe also creates fullness for Bhairava. Bhairava creates fullness for the universe [and the] universe creates fullness for Bhairava. So, these two elements, Bhairava and the universe, are actually one in its right manner. Why they are one? This universe is the embodiment of His energy (*śakti*) and Bhairava is the embodiment of Śiva. Bhairava is Śiva and the universe is Śakti." Ibid., vs. 29.

232 "*Savimarśatayā rava rūpataśca*, Bhairava is also that Being who creates, just like a loud speaker, who creates that loud speaking element in your nature for asking the help of Lord Śiva at the time of

Audio 3 - 57:48

संसारभीतिजनिताद्रवात्परामर्शतोऽपि हृदि जातः।

saṁsārabhītijanitādravātparāmarśato'pi hṛdi jātaḥ /96a[233]

JOHN: Ninety-six.

SWAMIJI: Yes, ninety-six now.

When a sound comes automatically from the fear of the universe, by the fear of the universe a sound comes, e.g., "*Ohhhh*, we are gone now, there is no hope of our living," and there also, because *spanda* is existing there,[234] . . .

SCHOLAR: The vibration of awareness.

SWAMIJI: . . . the vibration of awareness is existing in that intensity of that *parāmarśa*,[235] when you are absolutely . . .*

---

being tortured or trodden down. When you are trodden down, you cry and ask His mercy in that [situation]. And the abode of mercy is Bhairava, from whom this mercy is produced for you." Ibid., vs. 29.

233 Ibid., vs. 31.

234 Lit., vibration. Swamiji is here referring to *sāmānya spanda*. "There are two kinds of movements (*spanda*s) existing in God consciousness. One is *sāmānya spanda* and another is *viśeṣa spanda*." *Parātriśikā Vivaraṇa* (LJA archive). "*Viśeṣa spanda* is distinctive movement. Distinctive movement is found in the daily activity of life–going here and there, talking, eating, sleeping, joking, laughing, going to movies, etc. All these activities are distinctive ("distinctive" means, they are separated from each other). And there is another *spanda*, that is *sāmānya spanda*, universal *spanda*. *Sāmānya spanda* is found everywhere, just unchangeable and just in one formation. *Sāmānya spanda* is one, *viśeṣa spanda*s are many, but that elevated soul takes hold of that *sāmānya spanda*, not *viśeṣa spanda*. In the activity of *viśeṣa spanda*, he takes hold of *sāmānya spanda*. So he is fine, he does not go down, he is not trodden down from the kingdom of God consciousness. His kingdom of God consciousness is still prevailing there in *viśeṣa spanda* also. That is what is called *karma yoga* (*yoga* in action)." *Spanda Kārikā & Spanda Sandoha*, (LJA), 1.19.

235 Swamiji generally defines *parāmarśa* as "supreme awareness."

You have already been explained in the *Spanda Nirṇaya*.[236]

SCHOLAR: An expansion of the . . .

SWAMIJI: The expansion of *kiṁ karomīti vā mṛśan*, . . .

SCHOLAR: *Atikruddhaḥ*, . . .

SWAMIJI: *Atikruddhaḥ, prahṛṣṭo vā, kiṁ karomīti*, there is the establishment of the Bhairava state.[237] It is the same point he touches here.

*. . . *saṁsārabhītijanitād ravāt*, when [you are] afraid from *saṁsāra*, and some sound comes (that sound of fear), and when you are established in that fear [and you seek to find out] what that fear is actually, *parāmarśato'pi hṛdi jātaḥ*, He appears in your own heart, there, at that point. He is Bhairava.[238]

Here, *parāmarśa* is being used more in the literal sense, i.e., the vibration (*spanda*) of intense awareness produced by the crying that comes as the result of an overwhelming fear. See Appendix 9 (p392) for an explanation of *parāmarśa*.

236 *Spanda Nirṇaya* is Kṣemarāja's commentary on Vasugupta's *Spanda Kārikā*. Kṣemarāja also composed the *Spanda Sandoha*, which is a commentary on the first verse of the *Spanda Kārikā*.

237 *Atikruddhaḥ* (extreme wrath), *prahṛṣṭo vā* (extreme joy), *kim karomiti* ("what shall I do?," when you are in a fix what to do). "This *sāmānya spanda* you will find easily existing in these, at these points. . . . [because] your breath does not work, your actions also just stop, they don't function, at that period." *Spanda Kārikā*, (LJA), 1.22, p35.

238 An alternate translation of this verse from Swamiji's *Special Verses on Practice* runs thus: "*Saṁsāra bhīti janitāt ravāt*, the *bhīti* means, when the greatest fear rises from this world, *saṁsāra bhīti janitāt*, and, at that time, you see some disasters, some floods, and in those floods everybody is drowned–these kind of disasters also take place in this world; you experience this [sometimes]–or a terrible earthquake kills millions of people in one second–these kind of disasters–*saṁsāra bhītijanitāt*, by the fearful act in *saṁsāra*, *ravāt*, and that [resultant] cry of people, *parāmarśato'pi hṛdijātaḥ*, when, by crying repeatedly, crying again and again, He gives consolation in

SCHOLAR: Because of awareness.

SWAMIJI: Because of awareness.

Audio 3 - 59:50

प्रकटीभूतं भवभयविमर्शनं शक्तिपाततो येन ॥ ९६ ॥

prakaṭībhūtaṁ bhavabhayavimarśanaṁ śaktipātato yena // 96b//[239]

[He is Bhairava] by whose grace the discrimination of the universe [takes place] and Lord Śiva appears, *bhavabhaya vimarśanaṁ*, [by wondering], "The fear of *saṁsāra*, is it really existing?"[240]

End of Audio 3 - 60:22

So, when you conclude that, ["It is the way of the universe; [I] should not mind about it,"[241] this understanding is] the grace of Lord Śiva, Bhairava. He is Bhairava.

Audio 4 - 00:08

नक्षत्रप्रेरककालतत्त्वसंशोषकारिणो ये च।
कालग्राससमाधानरसिकमनःसु तेषु च प्रकटः ॥ ९७ ॥

nakṣatraprerakakālatattvasaṁśoṣakāriṇo ye ca /
kālagrāsasamādhānarasikamanaḥsu teṣu ca prakaṭaḥ // 97//[242]

your heart, in the heart of those who are caught in this torture. That is Bhairava who gives consolation at that moment." *Special Verses on Practice*, vs. 31.

239 Ibid., vs. 32.

240 "By His *śaktipāta*, the *vimarśanaṁ* (the analyzing) of this [takes place]: 'What is this fear? Wherefrom this fear has risen?'" Ibid., vs. 32.

241 Extracted from Swami Lakshmanjoo's *Special Verses on Practice*, vs. 32.

242 Ibid., vs. 33.

Now, the ninety-seventh *śloka*.

Nakṣatraprerakakāla, the time which is observed and ruled out [i.e., measured], governed, by all these *nakṣatra*s, . . .*

SCHOLAR: Celestial bodies.

SWAMIJI: Celestial bodies, these *nakṣatra*s (*tāraka*s), these stars, . . .

JOHN: Stars, the moon, . . .

SCHOLAR: Planets.

SWAMIJI: All these. Because, this time is established by these, by the movement of all these–the sun, the moon, everything.[243]

*. . . and the one who dries that time to nothingness, *tattva saṁśoṣakāriṇo*, those who dry it off, those who destroy this factor of time, the span of time, are called *yogi*s.[244]

SCHOLAR: *Bheravā*s.

SWAMIJI: *Bheravā*s. And those *yogi*s are nominated as "*bheravā*s" because *bhāṇi–nakṣatrāṇi īrayati prerayati iti bheraḥ*,[245] . . .*

SCHOLAR: Time.

---

243 "The lord of death governs those planets to see that everything is going on all right and everybody dies on time (*kāla tattva* means, the lord of death). Time is death. Because, when there is time, the existence of time in this universe–[when] there was no time, there was no death–as long as time is alive, death is alive. Because time goes on, time slips, and there will be death in the end." Ibid., vs. 33.

244 "Those who are bent upon destroying this ruler of time (that is, the lord of death), *kāla grāsa samādhāna rasikamanaḥsu*, they are happy to digest in their own nature, in nothingness, the position of the lord of death, they just eat the lord of death, they just finish the lord of death, and they are bent upon finishing that lord of death–who are they?–those are *yogi*s. [For] those *yogi*s who are bent upon destroying the position of the lord of death, the one who is available to them at all times is Bhairava. So, Bhairava is side-by-side [with] them, existing." Ibid.

245 Jayaratha's commentary.

SWAMIJI: *. . . *bheraṁ śoṣyanti iti bheravāḥ, tāsām ayam prakaṭa iti bhairava*, for whom that revealing state of nature is held is called Bhairava. Bhairava is revealed by them, by those who destroy the factor of time, that time which is governed by those stars and all these planets. *Teṣu ca prakaṭaḥ*, to those, He is revealed, He is there, He is always present.

Audio 4 - 02:15

संकोचिपशुजनभिये यासां रवणं स्वकरणदेवीनाम्।
अन्तर्बहिश्चतुर्विधखेचर्यादिकगणस्यापि ॥९८॥
तस्य स्वामी संसारवृत्तिविघटनमहाभीमः।
भैरव इति गुरुभिरिमैरन्वर्थैः संस्तुतः शास्त्रे ॥९९॥

saṁkocipaśujanabhiye yāsāṁ
ravaṇaṁ svakaraṇadevīnām /
antarbahiścaturvidhakhecaryādikagaṇasyāpi //98//[246]
tasya svāmī saṁsāravṛttivighaṭanamahābhīmaḥ /
bhairava iti gurubhirimairanvarthaiḥ saṁstutaḥ śāstre //
99//[247] [not recited in full]

And these collective masses of organs, sensual organs,[248] which are shrunk at the time of fear, [from the] fear of the world–*saṁkoci paśu janabhiye yāsām ravaṇam*, [they are] shrunk and they cry, these masses of sensual organs cry, and those masses of organs [cry] first–and *antar bahiḥ caturvidha khecaryādi gaṇakasyāpi*, and the internal and external [energies], all these *khecarī*, etc., all these energies, which are

246 See *Special Verses on Practice*, (LJA archives), verse 34.
247 Ibid., vs. 35.
248 "Which organs? The cognitive organs and the organs of action, the *karmendriya* and *jñānendriya* of every individual. Every individual has got these ten organs, and they are shrunken; these organs are shrunken in their own way in each and every individual." Ibid., vs. 34.

governing behind these sensual organs,[249] *tasya svāmī*, the master of all these organs is Bhairava.

And the last meaning of Bhairava is, *saṁsāra vṛtti vighaṭana mahābhīmaḥ*, He who is furious, that Being who is furious because of destroying all the differentiated states of the universe (*saṁsāra vṛtti vighaṭa*; *vighaṭana* means, *saṁharaṇa*).[250] *Bhairava iti gurubhirimair anvarthaiḥ saṁstutaḥ śāstre*, in that *Śivatanu śāstra*, in that *śāstra* which is nominated as *Śivatanu*, in that *Śivatanu śāstra*, our masters have explained in this way the reality of Bhairava.

DEVA (100-102)

Now [Abhinavagupta] explains the word "*deva*," why He is called "Deva."

Audio 4 - 04:16

हेयोपादेयकथाविरहे स्वानन्दघनतयोच्छलनम्।
क्रीडा सर्वोत्कर्षेणवर्तनेच्छा तथा स्वतन्त्रत्वम्॥ १००॥
व्यवहरणमभिन्नेऽपि स्वात्मनि भेदेन संजल्पः।

249 "All these organs have, in their own way, their [respective] gods who are governing them. Those are *khecarī*, *gocarī*, *dikcarī*, and *bhūcarī*, these four *śaktis*. They are produced by God for governing all these organs so that the activity of these organs should be experienced properly. [For example], if you see something [pertaining to] sex, it gives a sensation in the sexual organ." Ibid., vs. 35. "*Khecarī* is the cycle of energies which reside in the cycle of voidness. *Gocarī* is the cycle of energies that reside in the organs of cognition. *Dikcarī* means, those energies which reside in the organs of action. *Bhūcarī* are the energies which reside in the outside world." *Parātriśikā Vivaraṇa* (LJA archive).

250 Drawing or bringing together, collecting, gathering; also, destroying.

निखिलावभासनाच्च द्योतनमस्य स्तुतिर्यतः सकलम्॥ १०१
तत्प्रवणमात्मलाभात्प्रभृति समस्तेऽपि कर्तव्ये।
बोधात्मकः समस्तक्रियामयो दृक्क्रियागुणश्च गतिः॥ १०२॥

heyopādeyakathāvirahe svānandaghanatayocchalanam /
krīḍā sarvotkarṣeṇavartanecchā tathā svatantratvam //100
vyavaharaṇamabhinne'pi svātmani bhedena sañjalpaḥ /
nikhilāvabhāsanācca dyotanamasya stutiryataḥ sakalam //101
tatpravaṇamātmalābhātprabhṛti samaste'pi kartavye /
bodhātmakaḥ samastakriyāmayo dṛkkriyāguṇaśca gatiḥ //102

He explains that the verbal root of the word "*deva*" is "*divu*." *Divu* is really the verbal root from which "*deva*" has been formed. And that verbal root, *divu*, is meant for "play." *Heyopādeya kathā virahe*, it is not play when you go for business, when you go and collect money, when you earn money–it is not play.

JOHN: That is for some reason.

SWAMIJI: [It is not play] because it is for the reason to have and to disown something–disown what you don't like, own what you like. This is *heya* (rejecting) and *upādeya* (accepting). When that *kalana* (behavior) is over, when you just play, just like a boy, or, just like Shanna,[251] . . .*

> Shanna has no purpose. If she has one piece of candy in her hand, or [rather], a piece of gold in her hand, and you replace it with candy, she will be more happy. She will be more happy because she has no discrimination of what is to be held and what is to be thrown away–*heya updeya kathā virahe*.

*. . . so, *svānandaghanatayā ucchalanam*, just to jump and

251 The daughter of John and Denise Hughes. Shanna was a young girl at the time.

play in the universe because of His own freedom, because of His own happiness, joy, . . .

SCHOLAR: Undivided ecstasy.

SWAMIJI: Yes.

. . . that is "play." [*Divu* also] is meant for being established in that state from which there is no higher state–the highest state, establishment in the highest state. The meaning of "establishment in the highest state" is the meaning of "*divu*." This is the second meaning.

JOHN: The first meaning is "play."

SWAMIJI: Play.

SCHOLAR: *Krīḍā.*

SWAMIJI: *Krīḍā. Vijīgīṣā* is the second meaning. *Vijīgīṣā* means, he who is bent upon subsiding each and every being–down.

SCHOLAR: Transcending every . . .

SWAMIJI: Transcending, the real transcendental state.

JOHN: *Anuttara.*

SWAMIJI: *Anuttara.* And [*vijīgīṣā* also means], *svatantratyam*, being absolutely independent, absolutely independent.

SCHOLAR: That is the explanation of "*vijīgīṣā*."

SWAMIJI: *Vijīgīṣā*, yes. And *vijīgīṣā* is absolute independence in subsiding all, everything, and rising in transcendental Being, state.

SCHOLAR: *Kathaṁ nu nāma sarvānevābhibhūya ahaṁ varte.*[252]

SWAMIJI: Yes. This is the second meaning. The second meaning is over now. The third meaning [of *deva* is], *vyavaharaṇa*, He who moves in the universe; *abhinne'pi svātmani bhedena sañjalpaḥ*, He who moves in this universe in such a way as if He is differentiated in differentiated states. He is not actually differentiated in differentiated states. If He moves in

252 From Jayaratha's commentary.

differentiated states, He is undifferentiated. This is *abhinne'pi svātmani, sañjalpa vyavahāraṇam*. That is *vyavahāraṇam*.

SCHOLAR: *Sañjalpa.*[253]

SWAMIJI: *Vyavahāraṇam, abhinne'pi svātmani bhedena sañjalpa. Vyavahāra* is, although this whole universe is differentiated, in that differentiated state, [He is] the one who is undifferentiated. The one who observes the undifferentiated state is *vyavahāra* (it is His daily routine of His actions). [The fourth meaning of *deva* is], *nikhilāvabhāsanāt ca dyotanam*, as He shines, He is shining, and He makes everything shine in glory, it is the meaning of *dyotana* (*dyotana* means, shining, splendor). And *stuti*, the one who is worshipped and sung by people is [the fifth meaning of] *deva*. The one who is worshipped and sung . . .

JOHN: In *pūjā*, etc.

SWAMIJI: . . . in *pūjā*, etc., by people, is *deva*. What is worshipping and what is singing? Singing is, *yataḥ sakalam tatpravaṇāmāmalābhātprabhṛti samaste'pi kartavye*, whatever is being [performed] in action, whatever you act (you go for business, you go and light the stove, you go and take food), this is His worship, this is the worship of Lord Śiva in the actual state, in the real state.

JOHN: In the real way.

SWAMIJI: In the real way, everything, each and every act that we do, is His worship (*dyotanam asya sakalam*). *Bodhātmakaḥ samastakriyāmayo dṛkkriyāguṇaśca gatiḥ*, and His being everywhere, this is the last meaning of *deva*, because *samasta kriyāmayo dṛk kriyā guṇaśca*, He has the qualification of knowing and doing [everything], so He is all-doer and all-knowledge. This is His *gatiḥ*, this is His act, this is His movement.

Audio 4 - 11:18

इति निर्वचनैः शिवतनुशास्त्रे गुरुभिः स्मृतो देवः।

253 See verse 117 for an explanation of *sañjalpa*.

iti nirvacanaiḥ śivatanu śāstre gurubhiḥ smṛtau devaḥ /
[commentary introduction to verse 103]

This way our masters have explained the meaning of this word "*deva*" in the *Śivatanu śāstra.*

SCHOLAR: Bṛhaspati *pāda* . . .

SWAMIJI: Bṛhaspati *pāda.*[254]

SCHOLAR: . . . is *bheda-śaiva.*

SWAMIJI: Yes, *bheda-śaiva,*[255] yes. But, as he has explained this [word] "*deva,*" It is to be owned, It is to be respected.

SCHOLAR: Likewise, Abhinavagupta explains "*devī*" in same way . . .

SWAMIJI: Yes.

SCHOLAR: . . . in the *Parātriśikā.*

SWAMIJI: Yes, in *Parātriṁśikā Vivaraṇa.*

Now he explains "*pati,*" what is the meaning of "*pati.*" He is the universal husband. Lord Śiva is the universal husband. All others are His wives.

Pati and Śiva (103)

Audio 4 - 12:12

शासनरोधनपालनपाचनयोगात्स सर्वमुपकुरुते।

śāsanarodhanapālana-
pācanayogātsa sarvamupakurute / *103a*[256]

[He is Pati] by *śāsana*, by governing, by directing, this whole

254 Bṛhaspati *pāda* was considered to be a great master in the Shaiva tradition. See verse 199 of this text.

255 A dualistic Śaiva text.

256 *Special Verses on Practice*, (LJA archives), verse 26.

universe. [He is Pati by] *rodhana*; *rodhana* means, by keeping them in a standstill state. They don't move upward and they don't go down by that action of Lord Śiva.

SCHOLAR: He blocks them.

SWAMIJI: Blocks them. That is *rodhana*. And *pālana* also; He protects them, protects this whole universe. *Pācana*, and He completes the fruit of all actions, He ripens the fruit of actions. So, actually, He benefits this whole universe by governing (*śāsana*), by *rodhana* (by keeping them in a standstill way),[257] . . .*

SCHOLAR: He favors this whole universe.

SWAMIJI: He favors. *Upakārati* is "favors." "Favors" is the exact word for this.

*. . . and *pācana*, by completing and ripening the fruit of actions.[258]

---

257 "And *pālana* also; He protects them, protects this whole universe." *Tantrāloka* 1, additional audio (LJA archive).

258 "He actually, *sarvam upakurute*, He elevates each and every individual who is created by Him in this field of the universe. In this field of the universe, whoever is created by Lord Śiva, He elevates him, He goes on elevating them. But there are so many ways to elevate. By *śāsana*, by putting him to task, He elevates him. When he is mislead in *saṁsāra*, [when] he is doing some mischievous actions, when he commits mischievous actions, [Lord Śiva puts] *śāsana* on [him to] discipline and [punish] him. Punishment for what? Just to elevate him. That is *śāsana*. *Rodhana* means, when [someone] is stuck in some misbehaviour, doing mischievous actions continuously, and he is stuck somewhere and he doesn't go up or down, he is stuck there, Lord Śiva [makes] him stay there in a [stuck] position just to give him some punishment, threatening that he will never come out of this, so that he will, in the next life or in near future of his life, he'll be cautious in [how he] behaves. That is *rodhana*. And *pālana*; *pālana* means, the one who recites His name wholeheartedly, with great devotion, with great love, [for him, Lord Śiva] keeps him in His lap and kisses him and gives him hugs. This is also one way of elevating him. This is the nearest way to elevate. And *pācana yoga*, some do actions but not so wholeheartedly. They

Audio 4 - 13:35

तेन पतिः श्रेयोमय एव शिवो नाशिवं किमपि तत्र ॥ १०३ ॥

tena patiḥ śreyomaya eva śivo nāśivaṁ kimapi tatra //103//
[not recited]

It is why He is called, "the husband of the universe." And He is called "Śiva" also because He is all-round glorious; *śreyomaya eva śivo*, the un-glorified state is absolutely absent there.

SCHOLAR: He is explaining "Śiva" here?

SWAMIJI: Yes, "Śiva."

SCHOLAR: *Nāśivam.*

SWAMIJI: *Nāśivam vidyate kimapi tatra.*[259]

BHAIRAVA-DEVA-PATI-ŚIVA (104-105)

[Abhinavagupta now] illuminates why Lord Śiva is "Bhairava," why only Lord Śiva is "Pati," and why only Lord Śiva is "Śiva":

---

do actions but the result does not come soon, so they are waiting for that result [and wonder] why that result has not come. [They ask], "Am I not doing wholeheartedly this action?" *Pācana*, he elevates him by *pācana*, by ripening his actions, his activities. Unless it is ripe, the fruit does not come, this fruit is not revealed to him. So, it comes in time. So, you should not get worried about it. Lord Śiva elevates everybody; He is bent upon doing this thing." *Special Verses on Practice,* vs 26.

259 "*Nāśivam kimapi tatra*, the negation of protection is not born there in the kingdom of Lord Śiva; protection is never ignored there." Ibid., vs 26.

Audio 4 - 14:18

ईदृग्रूपं कियदपि
रुद्रोपेन्द्रादिषु स्फुरेद्येन।
तेनावच्छेदनुदे
परममहत्पदविशेषणमुपात्तम्॥ १०४॥

īdṛgrūpaṁ kiyadapi
rudropendrādiṣu sphuredyena /
tenāvacchedanude
paramamahatpadaviśeṣaṇamupāttam //*104*//[260]
[not recited in full]

As we see, this state of being Bhairava, this state of being Deva, this state of being Pati, and this state of being Śiva, is observed in Indra, in Brahmā, in Viṣṇu, in all these deities. So, [in order] to discriminate this state, *tena avacchedanude*, to discriminate that state of Bhairava, to discriminate that state of Śiva, and Pati, and Deva, *parama mahat pada viśeṣaṇam upāttam*, so he has adjusted, he has added, the qualification of "*parama*" and "*mahā*."

SCHOLAR: The adjectives.

SWAMIJI: So, He is not Bhairava; He is Mahābhairava. He is not Śiva; He is Paramaśiva. He is not *deva*; He is Parama-deva.

SCHOLAR: Mahādeva.

SWAMIJI: Mahādeva.

Audio 4 - 15:36

इति यज्ज्ञेयसतत्त्वं दर्श्यते तच्छिवाज्ञाया।
मया स्वसंवित्सत्तर्कपतिशास्त्रत्रिकक्रमात्॥ १०५॥

iti yajjñeyasatattvaṁ darśyate tacchivājñāyā /
mayā svasaṁvitsattarkapatiśāstratrikakramāt //*105*//

260 Ibid., vs. 27.

So this way, what is placed as the essence of what is to be got, what is to be recognized (*iti yat jñeya satattvam*, the essence of what is to be obtained), that state will be explained now in the *Tantrāloka*. That state will be explained in the *Tantrāloka* by the order of Lord Śiva. [Abhinavagupta says:] "Lord Śiva has ordered me to explain it in the universe, to explain the essence of what is to be got, what is to be obtained, by taking the help of my own experience (*svasaṁvit*), by taking the help of the pointing notes (*sattarka*) of my master, and by taking the help of the *dvaita śāstra*s and the *dvaitādvaita śāstra*s,[261] and by taking the help of the Trika *śāstra*s (*advaita śāstra*s)." [262]

SCHOLAR: When he says, "*śivājñāyā*," does he mean "*svagurvajñayā*"?

SWAMIJI: *Śivo'tra guruḥ*,[263] that can be, yes. There is no difference between Śiva and the master.

SCHOLAR: *Ādi vākyam*.

SWAMIJI: This is also *ādi vākyam*.[264] Now the *śāstra* will be explained. It is very beautiful. The *Tantrāloka* is very beautiful.

SCHOLAR: Great! That thing on Bhairava is magnificent.

SWAMIJI: Yes. Now here he begins to lay down the explanation of *śāstra*, what *śāstra* is here in the *Tantrāloka*– the theory.

END OF INTRODUCTION

---

261 Dualistic and dualistic-cum-monistic scriptures, respectively. "*Patiśāstra* means, *dvaita śāstra*s and the *dvaitādvaita śāstra*." *Tantrāloka* 1, additional audio (LJA archive).

262 Monistic scriptures.

263 Jayaratha's commentary.

264 An important (*ādi*) assertion or statement (*vākya*).

THE TEACHINGS OF TANTRĀLOKA (106-138)

Audio 4 - 17:38

तस्य शक्तय एवैतास्तिस्त्रो भान्ति परादिकाः।
सृष्टौ स्थितौ लये तुर्ये तेनैता द्वादशोदिताः ॥ १०६ ॥

tasya śaktaya evaitāstisro bhānti parādikāḥ /
sṛṣṭau sthitau laye turye tenaitā dvādaśoditāḥ //106//[265]

Lord Śiva's three energies–*parā*, *parāparā*, and *aparā*, [which are] *abheda*, *bhedābheda*, and *bheda*[266] [respectively]–shine in their own nature in the states of creation, protection, destruction, and in the transcendental state of these three (*turya* means, that transcendental state).[267]

JOHN: Fourth.

SWAMIJI: In this way, these energies (*parā*, *parāparā*, and *aparā*) shine in a twelve-fold formation, they become twelve [*kālīs*].[268] These three shine in each act: in *sṛṣti* (creation), in *sthiti* (protection), in *laya* (destruction), and in the transcendental state (*turya*).[269]

265 See *Special Verses on Practice*, (LJA archives), verse 13.

266 *Abhedha* (monistic), *bhedābheda* (monistic-cum-dualistic), *bheda* (dualistic).

267 "These three *śaktis* are manifested by His *svātantrya* in *sṛṣṭau* (in the act of creation), *sthitau* (in the act of protection), *laye* (in the act of destruction), and in the act of God consciousness (*turye*)." *Special Verses on Practice*, vs. 13.

268 "*Tena*, this way, *itāḥ*, these energies become *dvādaśo*, twelve energies, and those are supposed to be the twelve *kālīs* of Lord Śiva which have been produced by his three energies (*parā*, *parāparā*, and *aparā*). By the the unification of creation, protection, destruction, and *turya* (God consciousness), so they become twelve." Ibid.

269 "The Krama System is primarily attributed to *śāktopāya* and to

Now in this next *śloka*, he clears the doubt of why there are only twelve states of energies, why not innumerable states of energies, because Lord Śiva is possessing innumerable energies, not only twelve. For this he explains in this *śloka*:

Audio 4 - 19:20

तावान्पूर्णस्वभावोऽसौ परमः शिव उच्यते।
तेनात्रोपासकाः साक्षात्तत्रैव परिनिष्ठिताः ॥ १०७॥

tāvānpūrṇasvabhāvo'sau paramaḥ śiva ucyate /
tenātropāsakāḥ sākṣāttatraiva pariniṣṭhitāḥ //107//

This supreme Lord Śiva is said to be full by explaining these twelvefold energies of His.[270] So, in these twelvefold energies, those who are given to contemplation, those who contemplate on these twelvefold energies, really are established in His nature.[271]

One hundred and eight now:

Audio 4 - 20:07

तासामपि च भेदांशन्युनाधिक्यादियोजनम्।
तत्स्वातन्त्र्यबलादेव शास्त्रेषु परिभाषितम्॥ १०८॥

---

the twelve *kālī*s. The twelve *kālī*s are said to be the twelve movements of any one cognition. For example, if you look at any object such as a pot, the sensation travels from your thought to the place of the pot and then returns again from the place of the pot to your thought, giving you the sensation whereby you realize this pot. You do not realize this pot at the place of the pot, you realize this pot in your mind. Your perception has moved from inside to the pot and then returned again from the pot to your thought. And these movements are distributed in twelve ways, as the twelve *kālī*s, in the Krama System." *Kashmir Shaivisim–The Secret Supreme*, p133. See Appendix 20 (p412) for an explanation of the twelve *kālī*s.

270 The twelve *kālī*s describe the fullness of Lord Śiva. The twelve *kālī*s will be further explained in *ānika*s 3, 4, and 15.

271 See Appendix 20 (p412) for an explanation of the twelve *kālī*s.

tāsāmapi ca bhedāṁśanyūnādhikyādiyojanam /
tatsvātantryabalādeva śāstreṣu paribhāṣitam //108//

In these twelvefold energies, there are many and various ways of contemplation. There are *nyūna* energies and *ādhikya* energies; less energies than twelve (*nyūna*) and more energies than twelve (that is *ādhikya*). And those energies also shine by His independent freedom (*svātantrya*). It is described in the *śāstra*s.

The next [*śloka*]:

Audio 4 - 20:56

एकवीरो यामलोऽथ त्रिशक्तिश्चतुरात्मकः।
पञ्चमूर्तिः षडात्मायं सप्तकोऽष्टकभूषितः॥ १०९॥
नवात्मा दशदिक्छक्तिरेकादशकलात्मकः।
द्वादशारमहाचक्रनायको भैरवस्त्विति॥ ११०॥

ekavīro yāmalo'tha triśaktiścaturātmakaḥ /
pañcamūrtiḥ ṣaḍātmāyaṁ saptako'ṣṭakabhūṣitaḥ //109
navātmā daśadikchaktirekādaśakalātmakaḥ /
dvādaśāramahācakranāyako bhairavastviti //110//

JOHN: 109 and 110.

SWAMIJI: 109 and 110, yes.

In some states, He shines just like *ekavīra (eka vīra*, only one), sometimes He shines as two (*yāmala*), sometimes He shines in the triple formation (*triśakti*), sometimes fourfold (*catur*), at some places *pañca mūrti* (fivefold), *ṣaḍātmā* (sixfold), *saptaka* (sevenfold), *aṣṭaka bhūṣita* (eightfold), *navātmā* (ninefold), *daśa dikśaktir* (tenfold), *ekādaśa kalātmaka*, and elevenfold.

SCHOLAR: Eleven *kalā*s.

SWAMIJI: Eleven *kalā*s (divisions or aspects), yes.

SCHOLAR: And ten directions (*daśa dik śaktir*).

SWAMIJI: And He Himself becomes, He Himself is established, there in the twelfth energy, *dvādaśa* energy, and

He governs all these eighteen.[272]

SCHOLAR: He is established as the Lord of the great *cakra*, . . .

SWAMIJI: *Dvādaśāra mahā cakra nāyakāḥ*.

SCHOLAR: . . . of the *cakra* of twelve.

SWAMIJI: Twelvefold energies. Energies!

SCHOLAR: As the thirteenth.

SWAMIJI: *Eka vīra* means, when there is only Śiva everywhere. *Yāmala*, when there is Śiva and Śakti. *Triśakti*, when there are three energies shining (*parā*, *parāparā*, and *aparā*). *Caturātmā*, when there are four states: wakefulness, dreaming, dreamless [sleep], and *turya*.

SCHOLAR: Not that *jayā*, *vijayā*, *aparājitā* etc.?[273]

SWAMIJI: No, that I don't accept. *Pañcamūrti*–so you'll come to understanding–*pañcamūrti*; *pañcamūrti* means, *sṛṣṭi*, *sthiti*, *saṁhāra*, *pidhāna*, and *anugraha* (creation, protection, destruction, concealing, and revealing). *Ṣaḍātma*–*ṣaḍātma* [are the] sixfold energies. The sixfold energies are these [goddesses], what Jayaratha has explained.

JOHN: What are they?

Audio 4 - 23:39

SWAMIJI: Viśvā, Viśveśā, Raudrī, Vīrakā, Tryambikā, Gaurvī. These are the six energies of Lord Śiva shining in the sixfold states.

SCHOLAR: And where do these shine? Where are these six realized?

SWAMIJI: They are realized in His own nature, in the nature of Lord Śiva.

SCHOLAR: But from the point of view of the *sādhaka*, from the *sādhaka*'s point of view?

---

272 These twelve-fold *cakras* along with the six-fold *cakras* mentioned in verse 113 make a total of eighteen.

273 Referring to Jayaratha's commentary regarding the fourfold formation: "*caturātmā jayādibhedena*."

JOHN: What are these energies?

SCHOLAR: What do they represent? This is *anvartha kalpanā*, isn't it?

SWAMIJI: Yes, yes. They are those [energies] who shine and protect the *sādhaka* from all sides. Viśvā energy is the universal energy. Viśveśā energy is that energy which is above the universe. Raudrī is that energy which is keeping the *sādhaka* in a standstill position. Vīraka means, that which inserts heroic power in the *sādhaka*. Tryambikā means, that energy which puts the threefold (*parā*, *parāparā*, and *aparā*) states in the *sādhaka*. Gurvī means, that who commands the *sādhaka*. These are the sixfold energies that the *sādhaka* experiences in his *sādhanā*. And sevenfold are these: Brāhmī, Māheśvarī, Kaumārī, Vaiṣṇavī, Vārāhī, Indrāṇi, and Cāmuṇḍā. These govern His states of organic action. *Aṣṭakena* (eightfold) means, when Aghorā is also there.[274] The tenfold energies are Umā, Durgā, Bhadrakālī, Svastī, Svāhā, Śubhāṅkarī, Śrīḥ, Gaurī, Lokadhātri, Vāgīśī.

SCHOLAR: *Dik śakti*.[275]

SWAMIJI: *Aṣṭaka madhyavartī navātmā*,[276] he who governs these eightfold energies is *navātmā*. Jayaratha, the comment-

---

274 Aghorā is there in addition to the sevenfold energies. "They rule out this section of the eight organs: the five organs of knowledge, mind, intellect, and ego." *Parātriśikā Vivaraṇa* (LJA archive). "By these eight energies also, for an elevated soul, what do they do? For instance, Brāhmī energy will make you Brahmā, Vaiṣṇavī energy will make you Viṣṇu, Raudrī energy will make you Rudra, etc. In this way, they will push you up and up." Ibid.
In the *Dehasthadevatācakrastotram*, Abhinavagupta has explained that "these eight goddesses are always present (*sadoditam*) and shining in one's own body, and by our understanding (*anubhava*), they can be perceived and achieved." *Dehasthadevatācakrastotram* of Abhinavagupta, translation and commentary by Swami Lakshmanjoo (original audio recording, LJA archives, Los Angeles, 1980), vs 15.

275 The *śakti*s of the ten directions.

276 Jayaratha's commentary.

ator, says *ekā daśa*[277] is [discussed] in the *Khaṇḍa-cakra śāstra*. This is up to *eka daśa* energies (eleven-fold energies), i.e., *nyūna* energies. It is *nyūna saṁkhyā*, it is less than twelve. Now, *dvādaśāraṇam mahā cakra nāyako bhairava*, Bhairava is *nāyaka*, the leader of the twelvefold energies. Here, he has explained [that] this is *adhikā saṁkhyā*.

SCHOLAR: Thirteen.

SWAMIJI: Thirteenth.

SCHOLAR: But *śāradeva*, It is not really the thirteenth, though.

SWAMIJI: No, It is the thirteenth and onwards, not only the thirteenth.

SCHOLAR: It is explained in great length in book four [of the *Tantrāloka*] that really there is no thirteenth.

SWAMIJI: Thirteen *kālī*s. There it is described in the explanation of the *kālī*s. The *kālī*s are only twelve, not thirteen–either one or twelve.

SCHOLAR: But this *sarvotīrṇa* (all-transcending) Bhairava is not more that those twelve.

SWAMIJI: It is more than twelve.

SCHOLAR: In a substantial sense?

SWAMIJI: He is beginning to enter in the innumerable states of His being from the thirteenth. It is not concerned with the twelve *kālī*s here.

SCHOLAR: Although the *dvādaśāra* is the twelve *kālī*s.

SWAMIJI: Up to *dvādaśāra*.[278]

SCHOLAR: *Dvādaśāraṇam mahā cakra nāyako*, He is the leader of that *cakra*.[279]

SWAMIJI: He is the leader of that *cakra* and then He leads onwards also. It is why he says:

277 Elevenfold.
278 Twelvefold. See Appendix 20 (p412) for and explanation of the twelve *kālī*s as nominated in Kashmir Shaivism.
279 He is leader of the twelvefold *cakra*. See Appendix 21 (p413).

Audio 4 - 27:35

एवं यावत्सहस्त्रारे निःसंख्यारेऽपि वा प्रभुः।
विश्वचक्रे महेशानो विश्वशक्तिर्विजृम्भते॥ १११॥

evaṁ yāvatsahasrāre niḥsaṁkhyāre'pi vā prabhuḥ /
viśvacakre maheśāno viśvaśaktirvijṛmbhate //111//

In this very way–the one hundred and eleventh [*śloka*]–in this very way, when He attains and governs the *sahasrāra cakra*, thousandfold energies–not only thousandfold, *niḥ-saṁkhyāre*, "numberless-fold," more than a thousand–and that becomes *viśva cakra*, the universal wheel, and in that universal wheel, this Maheśvara, the possessor of universal energies, shines completely (*vijṛmbhate*; *viśeṣaṇa vijṛmbhate*). So, It is *adhikā saṁkhyā* (*adhikā saṁkhyā* is "innumerable"). [Maheśvara is] after twelve–thirteen-fold and onwards.

SCHOLAR: Śiva is never really, Bhairava is never really, a number in that sense–*kalayiti*.

SWAMIJI: He is not really the thirteenth, He is not the fourteenth, He is *asaṁkhya* (numberless)!

The next [*śloka*]:

Audio 4 - 28:45

तेषामपि च चक्राणा स्ववर्गानुगमात्मना।
ऐक्येन चक्रगो भेदस्तत्र तत्र निरूपितः॥ ११२॥

teṣāmapi ca cakrāṇāsvavargānugamātmanā /
aikyena cakrago bhedastatra tatra nirūpitaḥ //112//

In many *śāstras*, in here and there, in so many *śāstras*, this differentiation established in these wheels is explained by taking hold of each class. For instance, if *catuḥ-ṣaḍ-dvir-dvigaṇanā* . . . the next [*śloka*]:

Audio 4 - 29:23

चतुष्षड्द्विर्द्विगणनायोगात्त्रैशिरसे मते।
षट्चक्रेश्वरता नाथस्योक्ता चित्रनिजाकृतेः ॥ ११३ ॥

catuṣṣaḍdvirdviganaṇāyogāttraiśirase mate /
ṣaṭcakreśvaratā nātha syoktā citranijākṛteḥ //113//

First take the sixfold energies:[280] fourfold (*catuṣ*), *ṣaḍ* (sixfold), *dvir-dviganaṇāt*; *dviganaṇā yogena*, (*dviganaṇā yogena* means, six into two),[281] i.e., twelvefold and twenty-four.[282]

So, *ṣaṇṇāṁ cakrāṇām īśvaratā*,[283] so He governs and rules and possesses the kingdom of these sixfold [wheels of] energies, sixfold *cakras*.[284]

SCHOLAR: So, that's four, six, eight, twelve, sixteen, and twenty-four.

SWAMIJI: Yes. These are six, these are *ṣaṭ cakras*.[285] It is defined in the *Triśirobhairava* [*tantra*].

The next [*śloka*]:

---

280 The sixfold wheels (*cakras*).

281 When each are doubled and then re-doubled.

282 viz., 6-12-24. In the same way, when four is doubled, it is eightfold, and when eight is doubled, it is sixteen-fold, thus totalling six wheels of energies. The six wheels are the combination of 4, 8, 16 and 6, 12, 24, which together make up the sixfold *cakra* of 4, 6, 8, 12, 16, and 24.

283 Jayaratha's commentary.

284 As the Lord of six *cakras*, "*citra nijākṛteḥ*, His nature has become various, innumerable." *Tantrāloka* 1, additional audio (LJA archive).

285 "Because It is shining in six forms of wheels–fourfold of wheels, sixfold of wheels, eightfold of wheels, twelvefold of wheels, sixteen-fold of wheels, and twenty-four-fold of wheels; and It starts from the four-fold wheels. This is *ṣaṭcakra*, this is the real *ṣaṭ cakra*. The *ṣaṭ cakras* found by *yogis* in from *mūlādhāra* to *brahmarandhra*, those are also *ṣaṭ cakras*, but those are inferior *ṣaṭ cakras*. These are the real *ṣaṭ cakras*–fourfold, sixfold, eightfold, twelvefold, and sixteen-fold, and twenty-fourfold." *Tantrāloka*, 5.89 (LJA archive).

Audio 4 - 30:30

नामानि चक्रदेवीनां तत्र कृत्यविभेदतः।
सौम्यरौद्राकृतिध्यानयोगीन्यन्वर्थकल्पनात्॥ ११४॥

nāmāni cakradevīnāṁ tatra kṛtyavibhedataḥ /
saumyaraudrākṛtidhyānayogīnyanvarthakalpanāt //114//

These *devīs* of these *cakras* (wheels) are nominated according to the need of the *sādhaka* in their meditation, in their particular meditation, or particular *dhyāna*, or particular *havan*, *homa*, etc., oblations.

Audio 4 - 31:08

एकस्य संविन्नाथस्य ह्यान्तरी प्रतिभा तनुः।
सौम्यं वान्यन्मितं संविदूर्मिचक्रमुपास्यते॥ ११५॥

ekasya saṁvinnāthasya hyāntarī pratibhā tanuḥ /
saumyaṁ vānyanmitaṁ saṁvidūrmicakramupāsyate //115//

This wheel of the tides of energies are said to be held by Lord Śiva in the way of [supporting or fulfilling] the action of *sādhakas* in the way of *saumya*[286] or *raudra*.[287] If [the *sādhaka*] wants that, "Let the energy of Lord Śiva destroy such and such person" or "Let the energy of Lord Śiva protect such and such person," in this way, [for] those who meditate and contemplate and do some oblations, that also takes place.

SCHOLAR: You didn't explain the first part of the verse–*ekasya saṁvit nāthasya hyāntarī pratibhā tanuḥ*.

SWAMIJI: This is internal *pratibhā*,[288] this is the internal embodiment of consciousness, the conscious creative energy that creates protection or destruction in beings according to

286 Lit., placid, gentle, or mild; *saumya* is being used here as auspicious or protective.
287 Lit., violent, impetuous, or fierce; *raudra* is being used here as inauspicious or that which brings destruction and misfortune.
288 See verse 2, footnote 3, for explanation of *pratibhā*.

the needs of *sādhakas*. For instance, he explains in the next *śloka* [the procedure] for protection:

Audio 4 - 32:36

अस्य स्यात्पुष्टिरित्येषा संविद्देवी तयोदितात्।
ध्यानात्संजल्पसंमिश्राद्व्यापाराच्चापि बाह्यतः ॥ ११६ ॥

asya syātpuṣṭirityeṣā saṁviddevī tayoditāt[289] /
dhyānātsañjalpasaṁmiśrād vyāpāràccāpi bāhyataḥ //116//
[not recited]

For instance, "*asya syāt puṣṭiḥ*," somebody may think that, "Let this man get fattened. Let this man get strength. He is so weak, let him get strength." *Ityeṣā saṁviddevī*, this feeling in his consciousness is the subjective hero for this, for doing that.

SCHOLAR: Subjective . . . ?

SWAMIJI: Subjective hero. I mean to say that this consciousness, internal consciousness, will do the needful, not the meditation.

SCHOLAR: *Saṁviddevī tayoditāt.*

SWAMIJI: The *saṁvit devī*[290] in his internal consciousness [will fulfil] that [desire of] "Let him be protected."

SCHOLAR: *Āntarīpratīka.*

SWAMIJI: *Āntarīpratīka.*[291] "*Asya syāt puṣṭiḥ*, let this man become fat or strong." *Ityeṣā saṁvid devī*, this [thought or desire] you have to maintain first. The *sādhaka* has to maintain first this consciousness in his mind: "Let this man be protected by putting more weight in him."

"*Tathoditāt*" is incorrect. [It should read] "*tayoditāt*"–*tayāt saṁvittyā*, *saṁvit devyā*.

289 Swamiji corrects "*tathoditāt*" to read "*tayoditāt*."

290 The goddess or energy (*devī*) of knowledge or consciousness (*saṁvit*). That is, the force of the *sādhaka*'s thought or desire will itself manifest the desired effect.

291 Lit., turned or directed towards (*pratīka*) the interior (*āntarī*).

By that *saṁvit devī*, what[ever desire] is put forth, *dhyāna sañjalpa saṁmiśrāt vyāpāra*, *bāhyata vyāpārāt*, by external *vyāpāra* (external actions) and *dhyāna* (contemplation), he has to contemplate according to this *saṁkalpa*, to this desire. According to this desire, he has to contemplate.

JOHN: And the desire is to make this man . . .

SWAMIJI: Fat, strong.

SCHOLAR: So, he says that this *dhyāna* arises from that *saṁvid devī–tayoditāt*.

SWAMIJI: Yes. Which *saṁvid devī*?

SCHOLAR: And that it is involved . . .

SWAMIJI: Which *saṁvid devī*?

SCHOLAR: *Saṁvid devī–"asya syāt puṣṭir."*

SWAMIJI: Yes, this *saṁvid devī*.

JOHN: Making the man [fat and strong].

SWAMIJI: And *vyāpārāt cāpi bāhyataḥ*, and external actions also. External actions also he has to [perform] there. External actions: that those words must be uttered so that . . . not harsh words. In all that *dīkṣā* (initiation), harsh words are not to be used; [only] soft words, protecting words, mild words.

SCHOLAR: '*Sauḥ*', '*vaṣaṭ*'.[292]

SWAMIJI: Yes, all these. That is *bāhi vyāpāra*. By that, . . .

Audio 4 - 35:48

स्फुटीभूता सती भाति तस्य तादृक्फलप्रदा।
पुष्टिः शुष्कस्य सरसीभावो जलमतः सितम्॥ ११७॥

sphuṭībhūtā satī bhāti tasya tādṛkphalapradā /
puṣṭiḥ śuṣkasya sarasībhāvo jalamataḥ sitam //117//
[not recited in full]

292 The emphasis here is on soft *mantras* like '*sauḥ*' and '*vaṣaṭ*' because they are dental/labial (i.e., *dantoṣṭham*), which are said to increase *rasa* in the body.

. . . *sphuṭībhūtā satī saṁvit*, when this consciousness of that desire gets its ripe formation, is ripened, *bhāti tasya tādṛk phalapradā bhāti*, [that internal *saṁvit*] exactly puts that fruit in that *sādhaka*.

SCHOLAR: *Tādṛk yatheṣṭam*.

SWAMIJI: *Yatheṣṭam*.[293]

JOHN: Now, is this *sādhaka* speaking for himself [saying], "I need more meat on my bones" or is this for some other person?

SWAMIJI: No, the master. The master has to do this for the *sādhaka*, for his disciple. If his disciple is very weak, skinny, and reduces his weight day-by-day, for him, he does this kind of [act] according to the *saṁvit devī*–[the master] has to put this desire in his [own] consciousness first, and then, from that consciousness, he has to create *dhyāna* and *sañjalpa*, and external words, sounds, etc.

JOHN: So, *dhyāna* would be holding that awareness in your mind.

SWAMIJI: Yes.

JOHN: What is this other one, this external action?

SWAMIJI: *Sañjalpa*. *Sañjalpa* means, *mantra japa*.

JOHN: External repetition of *mantra*s.

SWAMIJI: Yes.

JOHN: Pleasurable *mantra*s.

SWAMIJI: And *vyāpāra* (action) also, [but] not crude ways of action. *Puṣṭi śuṣkasya sarasī bhāvaḥ*, because protection, *puṣṭi*, fattening one man, means to put *rasa* in him, liquid, . . .

SCHOLAR: Vital liquid.

SWAMIJI: . . . vital liquid in him. It is why *jalamataḥ sitam*, it is why [it is to be conceived as] water [which] is shining in a white way (water is white; *sitam* means, white).

SCHOLAR: Aha, so it's not *jalamataḥ sitam anugamya*?[294]

293 According to wish or inclination.
294 *Anugamya*, lit., to be followed or imitated.

SWAMIJI: No (agreement), *jalam ataḥ sitam.*[295]

Audio 4 - 37:58

अनुगम्य ततो ध्यानं तत्प्रधानं प्रतन्यते।
ये च स्वभवतो वर्णा रसनिःष्यन्दिनो यथा॥ ११८॥

anugamya tato dhyānaṁ tatpradhānaṁ pratanyate /
ye ca svabhāvato varṇā rasaniḥṣyandino yathā //118//
[not recited]

Tato dhyānaṁ anugamya, in this way, [the master] has to create, contemplate, on water. He has to contemplate on water and adjust that contemplation of water with the *sādhaka* so that that watery substance is inserted in the *sādhaka.*

JOHN: In other words, the *sādhaka* would drink that, is it?

SWAMIJI: No, it is only contemplation, through meditation. [The master] inserts that meditation, and adjusts that meditation, with the *sādhaka* so that the *sādhaka* is refined with that *jala* (water) and dryness is removed [from] his system. And *tatpradhānam pratanyate*, *jalapradhānam dhyānam pratanyate*, and then the master contemplates on that *dhyāna* which is filled with water (*jala pradhāna*).

SCHOLAR: Can you explain "*anugamya*" again? *Anugamya*–how do you take "*anugamya*" here?

SWAMIJI: *Anugam-*, *jalam ataḥ sitam*. After understanding this, after understanding that *jala* is white, so he contemplates according to the whiteness, not blackness, not redness. Redness will suck *rasa* from the *sādhaka*.

SCHOLAR: This is *sākāra dhyāna*.

SWAMIJI: Yes, it is *sākāra dhyāna.*[296] And not only *dhyāna*, he has to recite *mantra*s also accordingly, *mantra*s also which are soft, which create *rasa*.

---

295 This (*ataḥ*) *rasa* is to be conceived as white/pure (*sita*) water (*jala*).

296 Meditation (*dhyāna*) on a form, shape, or figure (*sākāra*).

Audio 4 - 39:48

दन्त्यौष्ठ्यदन्त्यप्रायास्ते कैश्चिद्वर्णैः कृताः सह।

dantyauṣṭhyadantyaprāyāstekaiścidvarṇaiḥ kṛtāḥ saha / 119a [not recited]

That is *dantyauṣṭhya*[297] *dantyaprāyā*, those [words which] are recited through the teeth, those words, those *mantra*s, which are recited through teeth, or which are recited by the teeth and the lips simultaneously, together.

JOHN: Can you give some examples of those?

SWAMIJI: '*Vaṁ*', '*laṁ*', [but] not '*raṁ*'.

JOHN: Not '*raṁ*'.

SWAMIJI: No, '*raṁ*' is [sounded] from the head. The head is hot, so this will produce heat in the *sādhaka*. '*Vaṁ*' because there is a connection of the teeth in that [sound], so it will produce *rasa*. The teeth produce *rasa*, the teeth always produce *rasa*. There must not be *oṣṭhya*[298] alone.

JOHN: Then the most essential one will be '*va*'.

SWAMIJI: '*Va*', yes.

SCHOLAR: '*Vaṣaṭ*', '*vauṣaṭ*', is that . . . ?

SWAMIJI: '*Vauṣaṭ*', yes.

JOHN: Because '*va*' uses both teeth and lips together.

SWAMIJI: Teeth and lips, yes. And *danta* also is '*sa*', '*la*'. *Kaiścit varṇaiḥ kṛtā saha*, it is not only '*vaṁ*' or '*saṁ*'. You can adjust some more *mantra*s with it, but the beginning must be with '*va*' or with '*sa*'–*dantya*.

Audio 4 - 41:12

तं बीजभावमागत्य संविदं स्फुटयन्ति ताम्॥ ११९॥

297 *Dantyauṣṭhya* means, pronounced using both the teeth (*danta*) and lips (*oṣṭha*)."

298 Labial.

taṁ bījabhāvamāgatya saṁvidaṁ sphuṭayanti tām //119b//

Then, *bījabhāvam* means, *mantra bhāvam*, the state of *mantra*. When that is produced, when that is uttered by the master for that *sādhaka*, *tām saṁvidaṁ sphuṭayanti*, that *saṁvida* gets its real position.

SCHOLAR: That awareness, "Let him have *puṣṭi*," becomes fully expanded.

SWAMIJI: (agreement)

Audio 4 - 41:42

पुष्टिं कुरु रसेनैनमाप्यायय तरामिति।
संजल्पोऽपि विकल्पात्मा किं तामेव न पूरयेत्॥ १२० ॥

puṣṭiṁ kuru rasenainamāpyāyaya tarāmiti /
sañjalpo'pi vikalpātmā kiṁ tāmeva na pūrayet //120//
[not recited]

"*Puṣṭiṁ kuru*"–now this is the *sañjalpa*[299]–"O Lord, protect him, give him fat, give him strength (*puṣṭim kuru*). *Rasena enam āpyāyaya tarām*, put fullness in him by *rasa*." This *sañjalpa* also, although it is with *vikalpa*, this also fulfils his ambition.

SCHOLAR: Although it involves discrete thoughts (*vikalpa*).

SWAMIJI: Yes.

Audio 4 - 42:17

अमृतेयमिदं क्षीरमिदं सर्पिर्बलावहम्।
तेनास्य बीजं पुष्णीयामित्येनां पूरयेत्क्रियाम्॥ १२१ ॥

amṛteyamidaṁ kṣīramidaṁ sarpirbalāvaham /
tenāsya bījaṁ puṣṇīyāmityenāṁ pūrayetkriyām //121//
[not recited]

299 *Mantra, japa.*

Amṛtaiyam, this is *amṛta*. *Amṛta* is some herb. It is called *śākhā gluvi* in Kashmiri.[300] It is not the only [use of] *śākhā gluvi*. You can put it in *sāmagrī* also,[301] in the oblation in a [sacrificial] fire (*havan*). In a *havan* with the *sāmagrī*, you mix that *śākhā gluvi*. Because, in the end, [the master] has to [perform] the ceremony of *havan* also for his [disciple's attainment of] fullness. [The master must say]: "*Amṛteyam* (this is *amṛta*), *idam kṣīram* (this is milk), *idam sarpi* (this is *ghee*), *balāvaham* (this is [the substance] which puts strength in the body)." *Tenāsya bījam puṣṇīyam*, by this way, this *bīja*, this *mantra bhāva*, this state of *mantra*, the recitation of *mantra*, *puṣṇīyam ityenāṁ pūrayet kriyām*, puts strength in that [sacrificial substance] and [the disciple] gets the fullness of that fruit.

SCHOLAR: This *kṣīram* is *dadhi* here.[302]

SWAMIJI: *Kṣīram* is *dadhi*–"*dadhi homāt parā puṣṭiḥ.*"[303]

SCHOLAR: By sacrificing curds . . .

SWAMIJI: Curds in the fire.

SCHOLAR: . . . gives the highest *puṣṭi*.

SWAMIJI: Highest *puṣṭi*.

SCHOLAR: Highest nourishment.

SWAMIJI: Nourishment.

JOHN: Now, one twenty-two.

SWAMIJI:

Audio 4 - 43:49

तस्माद्विश्वेश्वरो बोधभैरवः समुपास्यते।
अवच्छेदानवच्छिद्भ्यां भोगमोक्षार्थिभिरक्रमात॥ १२२॥

---

300 *Śākhā gluvi* is an herb prescribed by Ayurvedic doctors for subsiding bodily heat.

301 A mixture of natural substances (e.g., rice, barley, etc.) used as offerings in a *havan* ceremony.

302 Curd (yogurt).

303 Jayaratha's commentary.

tasmādviśveśvaro bodhabhairavaḥ samupāsyate /
avacchedānavacchidbhyāṁ bhogamokṣārthibhir kramāt //
122//

SCHOLAR: *Kramāt*?

SWAMIJI: Not "*janaiḥ*." *Bhoga mokṣārthibhir kramāt.*

SCHOLAR: *Kramāt* (respectively).

SWAMIJI: Yes. "*Janaiḥ*" is incorrect, "*janaiḥ*" is not the real reading of Abhinavagupta.

SCHOLAR: You remember this from Swami Maheśvara's manuscript.[304]

SWAMIJI: Yes.

Tasmāt, so, this Lord of the universe, who is *bodha*-Bhairava,[305] He is worshipped (*samupāsyate*, worshipped) by those who need *bhoga* (enjoyment) and by those who need liberation (*mokṣa*)–the *bhoga* of *saṁsāra* (the enjoyment of the world) and the liberation from the world. Those who desire for enjoyment of the world, they also worship this *viśveśvaraḥ*,[306] *bodha*-Bhairava, and those who desire for liberation, [for] getting liberated from this world, they also worship *bodha*-Bhairava. And *avaccheda anavat chidbyām*, in succession, *avacchedena anavacchedena ca*, those who desire for worldly enjoyments and worship Lord Śiva, they worship Lord Śiva in a limited way. Those who worship for liberation, they worship Lord Śiva in an unlimited way.

SCHOLAR: *Bodha*-Bhairava is "awareness-Bhairava," that Bhairava with awareness.

SWAMIJI: Bhairava filled with awareness. In the next *śloka*, he gives the reference of the *Bhagavad Gītā*:

Audio 4 - 45:42

304 Pandit Maheśvara Razdan was Swamiji's Sanskrit teacher and his teacher in Shaiva *āgama*, scriptures of Kashmir Shaivism.
305 Swamiji will explain that "*bodha*-Bhairava is Bhairava [who is] filled with consciousness and awareness."
306 Lord of the universe.

यऽप्यन्यदेवताभक्ता इत्यतो गुरुरादिशत्।

ye'pyanyadevatābhaktā ityato gururādiśat / *123a*

Our master, our ancient master, Lord Kṛṣṇa, also said the same thing in His *Bhagavad Gītā* in this verse: *Ye'pyanya devatā bhaktā*, those who worship other *devatās* (gods) also, they also come to Me in the end–that worship reaches Me in the end. Although that worship is indirect worship–it is not direct worship because they worship Brahmā, or they worship Indra, or they worship Viṣṇu–but that action of worship also comes to Me in the end because I am the fruit-giver of everything, [for] everyone.

So, in the next *śloka*, he explains the verse of the *Bhagavad Gītā*:

Audio 4 - 46:52

ye'pyanyadevatābhaktā yajante śraddhayānivitāḥ /
te'pi māmeva kaunteya yajantyavidhipūrvakam //*9.24*//

Those devotees who are devoted to other *devatās* also, and they worship [them] with great devotion, those also worship Me, O Arjuna, but they worship Me indirectly, not directly.

Audio 4 - 47:20

ये बोधाद्व्यतिरिक्तं हि किंचिद्याज्यतया विदुः ॥ १२३ ॥
तेऽपि वेद्यं विविञ्चाना बोधाभेदेन मन्वते।

ye bodhādvyatiriktaṁ hi kiñcidyājyatayā viduḥ //*123b*//
te'pi vedyaṁ viviñcānā bodhābhedena manvate / *124a*

Those worshippers who confirm that this worshipped deity is absolutely different from one's own *bodha*, one's own consciousness, . . .*

SCHOLAR: They take something else other than consciousness as the object of their awareness.

SWAMIJI: Yes, they worship the Lord as other than

consciousness.

*. . . *te api vedyam viviñcānā*, those also, those worshippers also, if they go to the depth of this action, . . .*

That means, if they confirm and analyze the object of their worship, what is the object of their worship. The "object" means, the worshipped being, [which] is the object of their worship, e.g., lord Indra, lord Viṣṇu, lord Brahmā, or something else.

*. . . if they go to the depth of this thinking, *bodhābhedena manvate*, they will ultimately come to this understanding that it is one with consciousness, one's own consciousness. Lord Indra is nothing [other] than one's own consciousness. [The same holds true for] Brahmā, or Viṣṇu, or other deities.

Audio 4 - 48:55

तेनाविच्छिन्नतामर्शरूपाहन्ताप्रथात्मनः ॥ १२४ ॥
स्वयं-प्रथस्य न विधिः सृष्ट्यात्मास्य च पूर्वगः ।
वेद्या हि देवतासृष्टिः शक्तेर्हेतोः समुत्थिता ॥ १२५ ॥
अहंरूपा तु संवित्तिर्नित्या स्वप्रथनात्मिका ।

tenāvicchinnatāmarśarūpāhantāprathātmanaḥ //124b//
svayaṁprathasya na vidhiḥ sṛṣṭyātmāsya ca pūrvagaḥ /
vedyā hi devatāsṛṣṭiḥ śakterhetoḥ samutthitā //125//
ahaṁrūpā tu saṁvittirnityā svaprathanātmikā /

He discriminates now here in these *śloka*s [between] That consciousness, the real Deity of consciousness, one's own consciousness, and the deity of those differentiated deities, *devatās*, lords, e.g., Indra, Brahmā, Viṣṇu, etc., and he differentiates that.

Tena avicchinnatāmarśa rūpa ahantā prathātmanaḥ svayaṁ prathasya na vidhiḥ, the one who is *svayaṁ prathā*, who is shining of His own accord (*svayaṁ prathā*),[307] who is not being shined by others, who shines by Himself, . . .

SCHOLAR: [Who is] not being illumined by others.

SWAMIJI: . . . *svayam prathasya*, the one who shines by Himself (that is, one's own consciousness, that conscious Being) is *avicchinnatāmarśa rūpa ahantā prathātmanaḥ*, shines in the unlimited way of I-ness, I-consciousness (*avicchinnatāmarśa* means, unlimited).

SCHOLAR: *Āmarśa*, awareness.

SWAMIJI: *Āmarśa* means, awareness, awareness of I-ness.[308] That I-ness is found in that *svayam prathā*, *svayam prathaysa devasya*.[309] *Śivasya na vidhi*, for Him there is no way, there is no particular way, how to do it.[310] You can do it in a temple, you can meditate on Him in a temple, or you can meditate on Him in a butcher's house. There is no *vidhi*[311] for Him, because *vidhi* is *sṛṣṭyātmā*, it is created by people, the way is created by people.

SCHOLAR: *Apravṛttapravartaka*.

SWAMIJI: *Apravṛttapravartaka*.[312] And [*vidhi*] is *pūrvagaḥ* (*asya ca pūrvagaḥ*); *pūrvagaḥ*, it is done in the beginning, it is not done in Its nature. It cannot be implied in His being.

SCHOLAR: [It cannot be] proceeded by any created . . . any action.

---

307 Lit., spreading out or extending (*prathā*) of one's own accord (*svayam*).

308 That is, Self-awareness.

309 That is, unlimited Self-awareness is found in He who is self-luminous.

310 That is, to be Self-aware.

311 A rule, formula, injunction, ordinance, statute, precept, law, direction (especially for the performance of a rite as given in the Brahmaṇa portion of the Veda). See commentary on verse 133a below.

312 From Jayaratha's commentary. One who is not inclined (*apravṛtta*) is impelled (*pravartaka*) by injunctions (*vidhi*) to act. This will be discussed in verse 126 below.

SWAMIJI: Because *vedyā hi devatā sṛṣṭi*, the creation of *devatā* is *vedyā*, objective. And this creation of deities (Indra, Brahmā, etc.) has risen by the cause of one's own [limited] energy, but the formation of the universal-I of consciousness is eternal and is shining in Its own way, in His own way.

SCHOLAR: It is Self-revelation (*svaprathanātmaka*).

SWAMIJI: Yes.

Audio 4 - 52:25

विधिर्नियोगस्त्र्यंशा च भावना चोदनात्मिका ॥ १२६ ॥

vidhirniyogastryaṁśā ca bhāvanā codanātmikā //126//

One is *vidhi*, one is *niyoga*, and one is *bhāvanā*. *Vidhi* is *apravṛtta pravartaka*, just to make him tread on the path [that] he is not inclined to [tread]. That is *vidhi*. *Vidhi* makes you to tread on that path. That is *apravṛtta pravartaka*.

Na punar, *ajñātajñāpakaḥ* is not *vidhi*.[313] If it is not known, the master makes it in such a way that you understand it. [*Vidhi*] is not understanding, it is just to make you tread on the path [that] you are not inclined to tread. For that [end] is [the purpose of] *vidhi*.

SCHOLAR: It covers new ground–*apravṛtta pravartaka*.

SWAMIJI: Yes. And *niyoga*[314] is also the same, in the same field.

SCHOLAR: *Vidhi* is *niyoga* and it is *bhāvanā*. That's the *vidhyanuvādabhāva*.

SWAMIJI: Yes, and that is *bhāvanā*, and that *bhāvanā* is threefold (*bhāvanā*, the inclination in your mind): 1. What you are going to do with this [command]? 2. *Kim kena*, by which way, what are the means for doing this? 3. And what is the agency to do it? These are adjusted in this *vidhi*.

313 Nor again (*na punar*) does an injunction (*vidhi*) cause one to know (*jñāpakaḥ*) what is not known (*ajñāta*).
314 Order, command.

SCHOLAR: So it has three aspects–*bhāvanā*.

SWAMIJI: Three aspects–*bhāvanā*.

Audio 4 - 54:03

तदेकसिद्धा इन्द्राद्या विधिपूर्वा हि देवताः।

tadekasiddhā indrādyā vidhipūrvā hi devatāḥ / 127a

So, these Indra, etc., these deities, live in *vidhi*.

SCHOLAR: They are established by that alone.

SWAMIJI: Yes, they follow *vidhi*.

SCHOLAR: As their only evidence.

SWAMIJI: Yes.

Audio 4 - 54:21

ahaṁbodhastu na tathā, ... //127b//
[not recited]

But *ahaṁ bodha*, this consciousness of I, I-consciousness, is not given to that *vidhi*. *Ahaṁ bodha* is away from that *vidhi*.

Bas, [after] "*ahaṁ bodhastu na tathā*," you must put a comma there.

Audio 4 - 54:40

अहंबोधस्तु न तथा ते तु संवेद्यरूपताम्॥ १२७॥
उन्मग्नामेव पश्यन्तस्तं विदन्तोऽपि नो विदुः।

[ahaṁbodhastu na tathā], te tu saṁvedyarūpatām //127b//
unmagnāmeva paśyantastaṁ vidanto'pi no viduḥ / 128a

Those worshipers of Indra, etc. (*te tu* means, the worshipers of Indra, etc.), *saṁvedya rūpatām unmagnām eva paśyantaḥ*, they only realize that *saṁvedya* is there, not *saṁvedaka*; [they only realize that] the object is there, not the subject. Their consciousness is inserted in objectivity, their consciousness is not inserted in subjectivity, subjective consciousness.

SCHOLAR: They worship Indra or Śiva as external.

SWAMIJI: Yes. So that *saṁvedya rūpatām unmagnām eva paśyanta*, that objective awareness has risen in them, in their consciousness (*unmagnām eva paśyantaḥ*). *Tām vedanto'pi*, in fact, although they understand and they live in that universal I-consciousness, *no viduḥ*, they don't understand It.

Audio 4 - 55:41

तदुक्तं न विदुर्मां तु तत्त्वेनातश्चलन्ति ते ॥ १२८ ॥

taduktaṁ na vidurmāṁ tu tattvenātaścalanti te //128b//
[not recited]

Taduktam, this is well-explained in the *Bhagavad Gītā* [that], *na viduḥ*, when they have not understood Me–actually, when they have not understood Me–*ataścalanti*, so they are removed from that I-consciousness, I-God consciousness. They are being kept away from I-God consciousness. Although they are living in that God consciousness, . . .

SCHOLAR: Because It's everywhere.

SWAMIJI: . . . but they do not understand. If they don't understand, so they are removed from that God consciousness forever.

Audio 4 - 56:15

चलनं तु व्यवच्छिन्नरूपतापत्तिरेव या।

calanaṁ tu vyavacchinnarūpatāpattireva yā /129a
[not recited]

Because, *calanam*, the removal [from God consciousness] is *vyavacchinna rūpatāpattireva*, to leave that universal consciousness and adjust one's self in individual consciousness. That is *calanam*, that is moving [away from God consciousness].

End of Audio 4 - 56:34

Audio 5 - 00:00

देवान्देवयजो यान्तीत्यादि तेन न्यरूप्यत ॥ १२९ ॥

devāndevayajo yāntītyādi tena nyarūpyata //129b//

It is why . . .*

[*Tena* means] "it is why." *Tena* means not "by Lord Kṛṣṇa." *Tena* means "it is why" (*tasmāt*)–*tena* [*iti*] *vyavacchinna rūpatāpatti lakṣaṇena hetunā* (comm.).[315]

*. . . He, Lord Kṛṣṇa, has explained in His *Bhagavad Gītā* [that], *devān devayajo yānti*, those who worship deities, lords, *devas*, they go to [those] *devas*, they don't come to Me.[316]

Now, he explains in this next *śloka*, one hundred and thirtieth:

Audio 5 - 00:47

निमज्ज्य वेद्यतां ये तु तत्र संविन्मयीं स्थितिम्।
विदुस्ते ह्यनवच्छिन्नं तद्भक्ता अपि यान्ति माम्॥ १३० ॥

nimajjya vedyatāṁ ye tu tatra saṁvinmayīṁ sthitim /
viduste hyanavacchinnaṁ tadbhaktā api yānti mām //130//
[not recited in full]

Tatra, although they are worshipping lord Indra, lord Viṣṇu, and other lords (Brahmā, etc.), if, while worshipping Brahmā, etc., they understand and come to this understanding that lord Brahmā is one with God consciousness [or that] lord Indra is one with God consciousness, I-consciousness, and *saṁvit mayīm sthitim viduḥ*, and understand the nature of consciousness there also, in that worship also, in worshipping lord Indra (*tatra saṁvinmayīm sthitim viduḥ*), *te tadbhaktā api*, those, *tad bhaktā api*, although they are devoted to Indra, etc., other lords, but *anavacchinnaṁ mām yānti*, they get entry in

315 Jayaratha's commentary: The sign or characteristic of individual consciousness (*rūpatāpatti lakṣaṇa*) is the reason/cause (*hetunā*) for being separated (*vyavacchinna*) from God consciousness.
316 See the *Bhagavad Gītā*, 9.26.

My universal nature in the end. They don't go to lord Indra, or Brahmā, or Viṣṇu, they get entry in Me–*anava-cchinnaṁ mām yānti*.[317]

Audio 5 - 02:01

सर्वत्रात्र ह्यहंशब्दो बोधमात्रैकवाचकः।
स भोक्तृप्रभुशब्दाभ्यां याज्ययष्टृतयोदितः॥ १३१॥

sarvatrātra hyahaṁśabdo bodhamātraikavācakaḥ /
sa bhoktṛprabhuśabdābhyāṁ yājyayaṣṭṭatayoditaḥ //131//

In this *Bhagavad Gītā*, this *ahaṁ śabda*, this word "I," which has been utilized by Lord Kṛṣṇa in so many places, in so many *śloka*s in the *Bhagavad Gītā*–*aham*, *aham*–it does not imply the physical frame of Lord Kṛṣṇa, it implies the universal consciousness.

DEVOTEE: *Bodhamātraika.*

SWAMIJI: *Bodhamātraika vācakaḥ*. And that *bodha*[318] has become *yājya* and *yaṣṭṭa* (*yājya* means, that which is worshipped by the *sādhaka*; *yaṣṭṭa* means, the worshipper), the worshipper and the worshipped. The state of the worshipped and the state of the worshipper is the formation of Lord Śiva Himself, because *ahaṁ hi sarvayajñānāṁ bhoktā ca prabhureva ca* (comm.), Lord Kṛṣṇa reveals in His *Bhagavad Gītā* to Arjuna that, "I am *bhoktā* and I am *prabhuḥ*, I am the enjoyer of the fruit of that action of a *havan*,[319] I am the enjoyer, and I am the giver, I am the bestower, of that fruit. I

317 "Because He pervades in each and every aspect of the world. He is everywhere. It is His kingdom. He is shining everywhere. He is shining in good and bad, right and wrong. If you worship in a wrong way, you are worshiping Lord Śiva. If you worship in the right way, you are worshiping Lord Śiva. But you must understand that, then there is no worry." *Bhagavadgītārthasaṁgraha* of Abhinavagupta, translation and commentary by Swami Lakshmanjoo (original audio recording, LJA archives, Los Angeles, 1978), 9.26.

318 That Being which is universal consciousness.

319 Sacrificial fire ceremony.

bestow that fruit and I am the enjoyer also." "Enjoyer" means, the *sādhaka*. The *sādhaka* enjoys the fruit.

There must be some misunderstanding in you for this *śloka*.

SCHOLAR: Yes, there was–many times (laughs).

SWAMIJI: The enjoyer is the *sādhaka* (*bhoktā* is the *sādhaka*). *Prabhu* is the giver, the bestower of the fruit. [Lord Kṛṣṇa says], "I am the bestower of the fruit and I am the enjoyer of the fruit!" Lord Kṛṣṇa's way of explanation is that, that the fruit giver is also universal consciousness and the fruit enjoyer also is universal consciousness–they are not separated. The *sādhaka* is one with that *sādhya*.[320]

Audio 5 - 04:33

याजमानी संविदेव याज्या नान्येति चोदितम्।
न त्वाकृतिः कुतोऽप्यन्या देवता न हि सोचिता॥ १३२॥

yājamānī saṁvideva yājyā nānyeti coditam /
nānyākṛtiḥ kuto'pyanyā devatā na hi socitā //132//

"*Nānyākṛtiḥ*" is [to be placed] there [instead of] "*na tvākṛtiḥ.*"

Yājamānī saṁvit eva, one's own consciousness is *yājamānī* (the one who worships). *Yājamānī saṁvit* means, that consciousness which is residing in the field of worshipping and that consciousness which is residing in the field of the worshipped, i.e., worshipped and worshipping. Worshipping-consciousness resides in the consciousness of the *sādhaka* and worshipped-consciousness is residing in the field of the *sādhya* (that one who is to be worshipped). *Yājyā*[321] is also *nānyā*, is not separate from one's own consciousness. *Iti ca uditam*, this we have explained previously (*iti ca uditam*, comma). *Nānyākṛtiḥ*, there is no other formation anywhere existing except your own consciousness. The formation of the worshipper and

320 The contemplator (*sādhaka*) is one with the contemplated (*sādhya*).

321 That which is worshipped by the *sādhaka*.

the formation of the worshipped is one. *Kuto apyanayā devatā*, so where lies the question of other deities? Other deities are not existing at all! Lord Śiva has taken the formation of Brahmā, Viṣṇu, Nārāyaṇa, and all others. *Na hi socitā*, that possessing of other formations [to worship] is not worthwhile.

Audio 5 - 06:24

विधिश्च नोक्तः कोऽप्यत्र मन्त्रादि वृत्तिधाम वा।

vidhiśca noktaḥ ko'pyatra mantrādi vṛttidhāma vā /*133a*
[not recited]

So for this state of consciousness, there is no need of *vidhi* (you know, *vidhi* is a sacred command or performance) and nor is there the need of *mantra vākya*[322] because *mantra vākya*s are also resting in *vidhi*.

SCHOLAR: *Mantra* here is Vedic.[323]

SWAMIJI: Vedic, yes.

JOHN: *Saṁhitā*.

SCHOLAR: The *Ṛg Veda* and the *Sāma* [*Veda*].

SWAMIJI: Yes. First, the Vedas are classified in two sections: one is of those *mantra*s, the other is of the Brāhmaṇas,[324] and the Brāhmaṇas are also divided in three sections. *Mantra* is meant for meditation (*mantra vākya* is meant for meditation) and Brāhmaṇa *vākya* is meant for the outward circle.

JOHN: *Yajñopavīta*.[325]

SWAMIJI: *Yajñopavīta*, etc., and all those performances. And those *brāhmaṇa vākya*s are divided into three classes: one class is of *vidhi*, the other is *arthavāda*, and the third one is *nāmadheya vākyam*. *Nāmadheya vākyam* is that performance in which you give a name to a child–that is *nāmadheya*

322 The utterance of *mantra*.
323 Of or pertaining to the Vedas.
324 Ancient commentaries on the four Vedas.
325 The sacred thread ceremony.

vākya. *Arthavada vākya* is just to make you believe that this is to be done, [that] you must do it, [that] you must do according to *vidhi vākya*. So, all these three are found in Brāhmaṇa *vākya*. Neither Brāhmaṇa *vākya* is concerned with that universal consciousness, the state of universal consciousness, nor is *mantra vākya*.

Audio 5 - 08:27

सोऽयमात्मानमावृत्य स्थितो जडपदं गतः ॥ १३३ ॥
आवृतानावृतात्मा तु देवादिस्थावरान्तगः ।
जडाजडस्याप्येतस्य द्वैरूप्यस्यास्ति चित्रता ॥ १३४ ॥

so'yamātmānamāvṛtyasthito jaḍapadaṁ gataḥ //133b//
āvṛtānāvṛtātmā tu devādisthāvarāntagaḥ /
jaḍājaḍasyāpyetasya dvairūpyasyāsti citratā //134//

And this state of consciousness, by Its sweet will, the sweet will of independence, has covered His own [nature]. When He covers His own nature, He becomes *jaḍa*.[326] And when He partly covers and partly reveals His nature, He becomes *āvṛta anāvṛta*, i.e., partly *āvṛta* (covered), partly revealed (*anāvṛta*). That is the creation of the *devatā*s, the lords (Viṣṇu, Brahmā, etc).

SCHOLAR: *Sthāvara*.

SWAMIJI: Up to *sthāvara*,[327] yes. *Devādisthāvara*, so, it is from *deva* to *sthāvara*. In *sthāvara*, He has become *jaḍa*. In *deva*, He has become *āvṛta* and *anāvṛta*, both. And you will find variations in these two classes also, in the classes of *jaḍa* and in the classes of *ajaḍa*.[328] And this is according to the *svātantra bhāva*[329] of Lord Śiva.

326 Inert or insentient.
327 Non-moving beings, viz., *jaḍa*.
328 Not inanimate, i.e., sentient.
329 State of independence.

Audio 5 - 09:54

तस्य स्वतन्त्रभावो हि किं किं यन्न विचित्रयेत् ।

tasya svatantrabhāvo hi kiṁ kiṁ yanna vicitrayet / 135a

"Vicintayet" is not [correct]. [It should read] *"vicitrayet."* *Tasya svatantrabhāvo hi kiṁ kiṁ yatna vicitrayet.* His *svatantra bhāva*, His state of independence, can [variegate][330] everything! What is that which is not [variegated] by His independent energy?

Audio 5 - 10:22

तदुक्तं त्रिशिरःशास्त्रे सम्बुद्ध इति वेत्ति यः ॥ १३५ ॥

taduktaṁ triśiraḥśāstre sambuddha iti vetti yaḥ //135b//
[not recited]

Taduktam triśiraḥ śāstre, it is said in the *Triśirobhairava* [*śastra* that], *yaḥ iti vetti*, the one who perceives this, in this way, is really enlightened; *yaḥ iti vetti*, the one who perceives in this way is *sambuddha*, is enlightened.

Audio 5 - 10:44

ज्ञेयभावो हि चिद्धर्मस्तच्छायाच्छादयेन्न ताम् ॥ १३६ ॥

jñeyabhāvo hi ciddharmastacchāyācchādayenna tām //136//

Objective perception is also connected with the aspect of consciousness. Objective perception is also connected with That consciousness.

SCHOLAR: It is a quality, an attribute of.

SWAMIJI: Yes. *Tacchāyācchdayet na tām*, so, Its *chāyā*, Its reflection, does not cover that supreme consciousness (*jñeyasya chāyā cid-dharmaṁ na chādayet*).

330 Differentiate.

Audio 5 - 11:27

तेनाजडस्य भागस्य पुद्गलाण्वादिसंज्ञिनः।
अनावरणभागांशे वैचित्र्यं बहुधा स्थितम्॥ १३६॥

tenājaḍasya bhāgasya pudgalāṇvādisañjñinaḥ /
anāvaraṇabhāgāṁśe vaicitryaṁ bahudhā sthitam //136//

So there is *āvaraṇa bhāgāṁśa*: One is that section of this universe which is covered, already covered, where there is no possibility of the revealing of your own nature. That is *āvaraṇa bhāgāṁśa. Āvaraṇa bhāgāṁśa* will be perceived in those who are ignorant persons and in all of this objective world. This is *āvaraṇa bhāgāṁśa*, not *an-āvar*[*aṇabhāgāṁśa*]. [This section is] *āvaraṇa bhāgāṁśa. Anāvaraṇa bhāgāṁśa* is [found] in *yogi*s, in those who recognize their real nature of Being. That is *anāvaraṇa bhāgāṁśa.*

Now he explains with reference to *anāvaraṇa bhāgāṁśa.*

Anāvaraṇa bhāgāṁśa is when God is revealed, where God is revealed, where God shines properly. *Ajaḍasya bhāgasya*, that *ajaḍa bhāga*, in that section of *ajaḍa*,[331] *pudgala aṇvādi-saṁjñinaḥ*, he may be "*pudgala*,"[332] he may be "*aṇu*"[333]–nominated [as such]. "*Pudgala*" is also a limited soul. "*Aṇu*" is he who has come from the unlimited state to limitation and here tries again to liberate himself, to get the realization of his real Being. *Anāvaraṇa bhāgāṁśa*, that is *anāvaraṇa bhāg-āṁśa*, the section of the revealing section. In the world of the revealing world, *vaicitryam bahudhā sthitam*, there is also variation in the state of revealing.

JOHN: Different kinds of people.

SWAMIJI: Different kinds of people realize God in different ways.

331 Not inanimate, i.e., sentient.
332 The soul, personal entity; the ego or individual. In Jaina philosophy, *pudgala* is "matter."
333 Lit., atom, but frequently used in Shaivism to mean, the limited individual.

Audio 5 - 13:28

संविद्रूपे न भेदोऽस्ति वास्तवो यद्यपि ध्रुवे।
तथाप्यावृतिनिर्ह्रासतारतम्यात्स लक्ष्यते॥ १३७॥

saṁvidrūpe na bhedo'sti vāstavo yadyapi dhruve /
tathāpyāvṛtinirhrāsatāratamyātsa lakṣyate //137//

Although (*yadyapi*, although) in that eternal *saṁvidrūpe*,[334] *dhruve saṁvidrūpe na bhedo asti*, there is no differentiation of Its appearing, of Its appearance (the appearance is the same), although the appearance of *saṁvidrūpa* is the same, but *āvṛti nirhrāsa tāratamya*, when *āvṛti nirhrāsa* is to be done, . . .*

You see, when you want to make yourself revealed, when you want to make yourself recognized, you have to *nirhrāsa āvṛti*, you have to remove *āvṛti*, you have to remove these coverings.

*. . . the state of removal of coverings also takes place in various ways.[335] *Āvṛti nirhrāsa tāratamya* (*tāratamya* means, digression), that is, [here in *sakala*], only *āṇavamala*, *kārmamala*, and *māyīyamala* is there, [they] persist. Here [in *pralayākala*[336]] is *āṇavamala* and *māyīyamala*, *kārmamala* is gone. That is *āvṛti hrāsa tāratamya*.[337]

SCHOLAR: Depending on the degree to which . . .

SWAMIJI: So, in consideration of that [gradation] of that uncovering, that differentiation appears, the differentiation of Its being revealed appears. So, you reveal your nature this way, and the other person reveals his nature in a better way, and the third person reveals his nature, recognizes his nature, in the best way.

---

334 The formation (*rūpa*) of consciousness (*saṁvit*).

335 Swamiji noted that Abhinavagupta is saying that the removal of coverings takes place "in various ways" (*tāratamya*), not "successively." *Tantrāloka* 1, additional audio (LJA archives).

336 See Appendix 10 (p394) for an explanation of *sakala*, *pralayākala* and the seven perceivers.

337 A gradational (*tāratamya*) decrease (*hrāsa*) of impurity (*āvṛti*).

SCHOLAR: But this is really only in *kalpita*[338]–this differentiation. That is why he says "*lakṣa*"[339] here.

SWAMIJI: That is *mala hrāsa*[340] . . . yes?

SCHOLAR: *Na tu sākṣāt sambhavati.*

SWAMIJI: *Na tu sākṣāt sambhavati.*[341] Otherwise, if It is revealed or if It is not revealed, It is there!

SCHOLAR: So, he says "*lakṣyate*" to indicate that it is secondary.[342]

SWAMIJI:

Audio 5 - 15:58

atha sthite sarvadikke śivatattve'dhunocyate /
tasmiñjñāte'thavājñāte śivatvamanivāritam //[343]

If you know It, It is there. If you do not know It, It is there. There is no need to recognize It [because] It is already there! So, this is the reality of Its being. But we want to perceive It through *sādhanā*.[344] So, as long as *sādhanā* is concerned, there is *tāratamya*,[345] there is *tāratamya* of Its being recognized.

JOHN: Some more revealed and some less revealed.

SWAMIJI: And this *tāratamya* . . .

---

338 Lit: made, fabricated, artificial; composed, invented.

339 Seems or appears.

340 The decrease (*hrāsa*) of impurity (*mala*).

341 Jayaratha's commentary: Though (*tu*) this conceived (*saṁbhavati*) gradation is not directly seen (*na sākṣāt*).

342 That is, the gradations of revelation are a secondary consideration.

343 Verse 1 from chapter 7 of Somānanda's *Śivadṛṣṭi*. "In the *Śivadṛṣṭi*, Somānanda has explained, *atha sthite sarvadikke śivatattve* [*vyvasthite*]. Now, I will explain to you Śiva, who is existing everywhere, within and without. *Tasmin jñāyte tava jñāyte*, if you know Him, well and good. *Atava ajñāyte*, if you don't know Him, well and good. *Śivatvam*, He is Śiva. If you know Him, He is there. If you don't know Him, He is still there. Don't worry about it." *Special Verses on Practice*, (LJA archives), verse 57.

344 Contemplative practice, meditation.

345 Gradations, variations.

Audio 5 - 16:33

तद्विस्तरेण वक्ष्यामः शक्तिपातविनिर्णये।

tadvistareṇa vakṣyāmaḥ śaktipātavinirṇaye / 138a

. . . this will be explained in the *nirṇaya* of *śaktipāta*.[346]

समाप्य परतां स्थौल्यप्रसङ्गे चर्चयिष्यते॥ १३८॥

samāpya paratāṁ staulyaprasaṅge carcayiṣyate //138//
[not recited]

I think–"*samāpya paratāṁ staulya prasaṅge carcayiṣyate*"–"*samāpya paratāṁ*" would be better [read as] "*paratām samāpya*" because, here, in this first *āhnika*, it is *paratā* here (*paratā* means, *uddeśa rūpa*[347]). That, after having ended the *uddeśa* [in this first *āhnika*, then] in the *sthūla prasaṅga*, this will be explained–*lakṣaṇa* and *parīkṣa*.[348]

JOHN: But what's the difference between this . . . ?

SWAMIJI: I had explained it as *samā api*, *samā api paratā*, but it is not *samā api paratā*, [it is] *paratām samāpya*. Here, [in this first *āhnika*], we will end only in *paratā*, the *paratā* of this *śāstra*, and this differentiation of, variation of, *śaktipāta* will be explained in *sthaulya prasaṅga*, in *sthūla prasaṅga*, in its *lakṣaṇa* and *parīkṣā*.

SCHOLAR: When it is dealt with at length (*sthaulya prasaṅge*). So there's the suspicion that the text is corrupt here somewhere, is it, Sir?

SWAMIJI: It is not . . . yes (agreement).

---

346 The complete ascertainment (*nirṇaya*) of grace (*śaktipāta*) will be the subject-matter of the thirteenth *āhnika* of the *Tantrāloka*. See Appendix 22 (p414) for a brief explanation of *śaktipāta*.

347 The act of pointing to or at; a brief statement.

348 *Lakṣaṇa*: indicating, expressing indirectly; *parīkṣā*: inspection, investigation, examination.

JOHN: Is this in the thirteenth *āhnika*? This is . . . ?

SWAMIJI: In the thirteenth *āhnika*, yes. This is the [subject of the] thirteenth *āhnika–śaktipāta*.

INTRODUCTION TO THE MEANS (UPĀYAS) (139-165)

Audio 5 - 17:54

अतः कञ्चित्प्रमातारं प्रति प्रथयते विभुः।
पूर्णमेव निजं रूपं कञ्चिदंशांशिकाक्रमात्॥ १३९ ॥

ataḥ kañcitpramātāraṁ prati prathayate vibhuḥ /
pūrṇameva nijaṁ rūpaṁ kañcidaṁśāṁśikākramāt //139//

SWAMIJI: So, this is the section of *mala nirhrāsa*, that your nature is revealed, [that] your nature is revealed [in this or] that way.

JOHN: This section we are coming on to now.

SWAMIJI: Yes. *Ataḥ kañcit pramātāraṁ prati prathayate vibhuḥ*, this all-pervading Lord reveals His nature to that person, to some person, to some fortunate person, in Its [fullness]. *Kañcit*, for some fortunate [person], who has got *tīvra tīvra tīvra śaktipāta*,[349] *pūrṇameva nijaṁ rūpaṁ*, He reveals His nature in Its fullness, without any *nyūnatā*, without any deficiency. *Kañcit*, and for those who are unfortunate, *kañcit aṁśāśākā kramāt*, He reveals His nature by-and-by, by parts.

Audio 5 - 19:08

विश्वभावैकभावात्मस्वरूपप्रथनं हि यत्।
अणूनां तत्परं ज्ञानं तदन्यदपरं बहु॥ १४० ॥

349 Lit., supreme, supreme, supreme grace, i.e., the highest grace. See Appendix 22 (p414).

viśvabhāvaikabhāvātmasvarūpaprathanaṁ hi yat /
aṇūnāṁ tatparaṁ jñānaṁ tadanyadaparaṁ bahu //140//

So, the revealing of His nature in Its fullness and the revealing of His nature partly are these two knowledges: One is supreme knowledge and one is inferior knowledge. Supreme knowledge is only one because where *svarūpa*[350] is found as one with the universe, It is universal, universal Being. The universal state of *svarūpa* is pure knowledge, full knowledge, real knowledge. That is *tatparam jñānam*, *tatpūrṇam jñānam*. *Tadanyat*, the other [knowledge] is where you don't perceive your nature as one with the universe. You perceive your nature as your own Self as in *samādhi*, [but] not in *samādhi* and *vyutthāna* the same.[351] That is *apara jñāna* (*tadanyat aparam*). And that knowledge is *bahu*, you will get so many variations in that knowledge.

SCHOLAR: Manifold.

SWAMIJI: Manifold.

JOHN: This manifoldness of knowledge is to explain many different kinds of scriptures?

SWAMIJI: Many different kinds of *upāyas*.[352] There are so many *upāyas*. And Its appearance also varies, varies from one to another. And that full knowledge does not vary, it is only one. *Viśva bhāvaika bhāvātma svarūpa prathanaṁ hi yat, aṇūnāṁ tatparaṁ jñānaṁ*. *Tat jñānam ekam*, it is understood [that] that [supreme] knowledge is only one, but the other knowledge where you don't feel, you don't perceive, your nature as one with the universe, that knowledge is many.

JOHN: Like in *āṇavopāya*, etc.

SWAMIJI: Yes.

---

350 One's own nature. See Appendix 24 (p417).

351 This is the state of inferior knowledge where one perceives the nature of the Self in *samādhi* only and not in the external world (*vyutthāna*). See Appendix 23 (p416) for explanation of *samādhi* in Kashmir Shaivism.

352 Means, ways, practices.

SCHOLAR: So, this higher knowledge is . . .

SWAMIJI: One.

SCHOLAR: . . . *svarūpa prathanam*; *viśvaika bhāvātma svarūpa prathanam.*

SWAMIJI: *Viśva bhāva eka bhāvātma*, it is one with the universe.

SCHOLAR: The revelation of one's own nature as absolutely one with the universe.

SWAMIJI: One with the universe, yes.

Audio 5 - 21:36

तच्च साक्षादुपायेन तदुपायादिनापि च।
प्रथमानं विचित्राभिर्भङ्गीभिरिह भिद्यते॥ १४१ ॥

tacca sākṣādupāyena tadupāyādināpi vā [353] /
prathamānaṁ vicitrābhirbhaṅgībhiriha bhidyate //141//

Now [Abhinavagupta] handles this *aparā jñāna*, the inferior knowledge.

And that inferior knowledge, that *apara jñāna*, *prathamānam* (appears) *vicitrābhir bhaṅgībhir*, in manifold ways–maybe in the direct way of holding the means or the indirect way of holding the means. When you hold your means directly, It appears in Its fullness, [but] not as full as It was in that supreme *jñāna* (knowledge), but with consideration to inferior knowledge, It is full.

JOHN: What does it mean to "hold the means directly"?

SWAMIJI: *Śāmbhavopāya*. *Tadupāyādināpi vā*, or, take hold of *śāktopāya* for holding *śāmbhavopāya,* or take hold of *āṇavopaya* for holding *śāmbhavopāya*. And so, these means seem to be many, *iha bhidyāte*, and they get variations in their states.

353 Swamiji here says "*vā*" although the *Kashmir Series of Text and Studies* has "*ca*."

Audio 5 - 23:05

तत्रापि स्वपरद्वारद्वारित्वात्सर्वशोंशशः ।
व्यवधानाव्यवधिना भूयान्भेदः प्रवर्तते ॥ १४२ ॥

tatrāpi svaparadvāradvāritvātsarvaśoṁśaśaḥ /
vyavadhānāvyavadhinā bhūyānbhedaḥ pravartate //142

In that also, in that variation also, there is *svadvāra* and *paradvāra*,[354] entrance through one's own nature and entrance through another agency, [respectively]. You enter in your own nature through the main entrance or you enter in your own nature through a sub-entrance (another agency). For instance, [when] you try to contemplate on Lord Śiva and be one-pointed with That, that is entry in its real entrance. [When] you recite *mantra*, that is entry in its unreal way. When there is *śāmbhavopāya*, it is the real entry. When there is *śāktopāya*, it is not so real an entry. When there is *āṇavopāya*, it is not the real entry [because] it is through some other agent, but it will carry you to That point, to the same point. That is *svapara-dvāra*. *Svadvāra* is *śāmbhavena śāmbhavam*, by holding inferior *śāmbhava* and [getting] entry in superior *śāmbhava*–that is *svadvāra*.[355] *Paradvāra* is to get entry in [inferior] *śāmbhava* by holding supreme *śāktopāya*. When you hold supreme *śāktopāya*, you get entry in inferior *śāmbhavopāya*.

Do you understand?

JOHN: Yes.

SWAMIJI: When you hold supreme *śāktopāya*, by holding supreme *śāktopāya*, you get entry in inferior *śāmbhavopāya*. By holding superior/supreme *āṇavopāya*, you'll get entry in inferior *śāktopāya*. That is it. That is what he says here. That is [the meaning of] "*svaparadvāra*"–*svadvāra* and *para-*

354 *Dvāra* means, an opening, a door or an entry way.

355 In the same way, by holding inferior *śāktopāya* and getting entry in superior *śāktopāya*, and by holding inferior *āṇavopāya* and getting entry in superior *āṇavopāya*.

dvāra.[356] *Dvāritvāt svavaśaḥ aṁśāśaḥ*, and there also there is variation, wholly or partly.[357] So there are so many means. The means are innumerable, numberless, in this inferior state of being.[358] And there is *vyavadhāna* and *avyavadhāna*.[359] [For example], when there is *śāmbhavopāya*, you hold inferior *śāmbhavopāya* to get entry in superior *śāmbhavopāya*, and that inferior *śāmbhavopāya* has got some defect, it is a defective inferior *śāmbhavopāya*. And sometimes that inferior *śāmbhavopāya* is without any defect, without any other defect.

JOHN: What could be the defect in *śāmbhavopāya*?

SWAMIJI: A leakage of *śāktopāya* therein or a leakage of *āṇavopāya* therein. That is a defective *śāmbhavopāya* when there is the leakage of *śāktopāya* also.[360]

JOHN: In that *śāmbhavopāya*.

SWAMIJI: So, there are many ways! *Bhūyān bhedaḥ pravartate*, so, this differentiation (*bheda*, differentiation) is many, many, many ways.

---

356 In his commentary, Jayaratha notes that these amount to six different means (*upāyas*).

357 "Jayaratha has said that knowledge is twofold: one is complete and one is incomplete. Complete knowledge is *śāmbhava* and incomplete knowledge is *śākta* and *āṇavopāya*. It is the general information for the means. "*Param*" is *śāmbhavopāya*. "*Aparam*" is *śāktopāya* and *āṇavopāya*." *Tantrāloka* 1, additional audio (LJA archive).

358 In his commentary, Jayaratha notes that these amount to twelve different means.

359 *Vyavadhāna*: with obstruction or interruption. *Avyavādhana*: without interruption, contiguity.

360 In his commentary, Jayaratha notes that these amount to twenty-four different means.

THE SUCCESSIVE WAY OF UPĀYAS (143-165)

Now here, from here, from the 143rd *śloka*, he will explain now in a successive way.

JOHN: These different *upāya*s.

SWAMIJI: Yes. First is the position of *śāmbhavopāya*.

JOHN: He doesn't talk about *anupāya*.[361]

SWAMIJI: No, first *śāmbhavopāya*. *Pradhane hi kṛto yatnaḥ*,[362] if you die, you must die before the greatest master. If you live, you must live for the best thing, the best portion of life. So, this is the way of Shaivism that you must hold first the best thing. If you cannot hold it, then try the inferior one. So, [Abhinavagupta] starts with *śāmbhavopāya* first.

Audio 5 - 27:48

ज्ञानस्य चाभ्युपायो यो न तदज्ञानमुच्यते।
ज्ञानमेव तु तत्सूक्ष्मं परं त्विच्छात्मकं मतम्॥ १४३ ॥

jñānasya cābhyupāyo yo na tadajñānamucyate /
jñāmeva tu [hi] tatsūkṣmaṁ paraṁ tvicchātmakaṁ matam //143//

The means to perceive knowledge or achieve knowledge (the real knowledge of the Self) is not ignorance and is not the absence of ignorance. The *upāya* is *jñāna*.[363]

---

361 *Anupāya* (lit., "no means") will be discussed in the second *āhnika* of the *Tantrāloka*.

362 From Jayaratha's commentary on verse 19.

363 In this verse, Abhinavagupta is clarifying what was stated earlier in verses 26 and 27, that differentiated knowledge is ignorance and the absence of undifferentiated knowledge is also ignorance. Here, the means (*upāya*) is real knowledge (*jñāna*).

SCHOLAR: Absence of knowledge.

SWAMIJI: The absence of knowledge is not the means for achieving [real] knowledge. The means is knowledge itself for [achieving] that knowledge. And that is the subtlest state of knowledge, which is called *icchā*, which resides in the field, in the world, of *icchā*, not *jñāna*, not *kriyā*.[364] It is only *icchā*. That is, the first start, the first starting point of perception,[365] is the means.

JOHN: What is this thing about ignorance?

SWAMIJI: Ignorance is not . . . by rejecting knowledge, differentiated knowledge, you cannot get entry in that supreme knowledge.

SCHOLAR: The objector is saying that the means and the end must be different. So if the end is knowledge, what is the nature of the means? Is it non-knowledge? And so [Abhinavagupta] answers here that . . .

SWAMIJI: It is not non-knowledge, it cannot be non-knowledge.

SCHOLAR: . . . the relation between the means and the end is secondary.

SWAMIJI: It is knowledge, but it is subtle knowledge.

JOHN: A special kind of knowledge.

SWAMIJI: Yes, a special kind of knowledge, and it will be attached to *icchā*, *icchā* in the supreme way, because it is *śāmbhavopāya*.[366]

Audio 5 - 29:38

उपायोपेयभावस्तु ज्ञानस्य स्थौल्यविभ्रमः।
एषैव च क्रियाशक्तिर्बन्धमोक्षैककारणम्॥ १४४॥

upāyopeyabhāvastu jñānasya sthaulyavibhramaḥ /
eṣaiva ca kriyāśaktirbandhamokṣaikakāraṇam //144//

---

364 *Icchā* (will), *jñāna* (knowledge), *kriyā* (action).
365 *Prathama ābhāsa*.
366 *Śāmbhavopāya* is also nominated as *icchopāya*.

This state of *upāya* and *upeya*, this state of being *upāya* and *upeya* (*upāya* means, the means, *upeya* is the object which is got by the means), is *sthaulya vibhramaḥ*, this is the *vibhrama*, this is the *vikāsa* (expansion) of its grossness.[367]

JOHN: This duality.

SWAMIJI: No, the duality of knowledge and the known, the means and the meant. *Eṣa eva ca kriyā śaktir bandha mokṣaika kāraṇam*, it is said in the *Spanda śāstra*[368] that this *kriyā śakti*, this energy of action, is explained to bind your nature and is explained to reveal your nature–the energy of action. The energy of action will reveal your nature and bind your nature, both. This state of the means and the meant is only the expansion of [*icchā sakti*s] *sthūlatā* (grossness). Otherwise, the means and the meant is nothing, because *eṣaiva ca kriyā śaktir bandha mokṣaika kāraṇam*, this energy of action is said to be binding you when it is not known. When it is known, it will liberate you. *Bas*.

Audio 5 - 31:41

तत्राद्ये स्वपरामर्शे निर्विकल्पैकधामनि।
यत्स्फुरेत्प्रकटं साक्षात्तदिच्छाख्यं प्रकीर्तितम्॥ १४५॥

tatrādye svaparāmarśe nirvikalpaikadhāmani /
yatsphuretprakaṭaṁ sākṣāttadicchākhyaṁ
prakīrttitam //145 [not recited]

That which appears in feeling in the first start of *svātma parāmarśa*, the first start which is the abode of the *nirvikalpa* state,[369] that, in reality, is called the means pertaining to will (*śāmbhavopāya*, that is *śāmbhavopāya*)–when that *sphuraṇa* takes place in the first start of any movement.

JOHN: This vibration, this beginning. "*Sphuraṇa*" means?

---

367 The conceived distinction between the means (*upāya*) and the meant (*upeya*) is the expansion of the gross state of *icchā śakti* (subtle knowledge), that is, *kriyā śakti* (the energy of action).
368 The *Spanda Kārikā*, 3.16, (LJA).
369 The thought-less state.

SWAMIJI: *Sphuraṇa*,[370] the first start (*prathamikālocana*).[371] For that, he gives a reference:

Audio 5 - 32:36

यथा विस्फुरितदृशामनुसन्धिं विनाप्यलम्।
भाति भावः स्फुटस्तद्वत्केषामपि शिवात्मता॥ १४६॥

yathā visphuritadṛśāmanusandhiṁ vināpyalam
bhāti bhāvaḥ sphuṭastadvatkeṣāmapi śivātmatā //146//

Just as those who have clear vision, whose eyesight is quite fit, they perceive any object without putting any mental force on it to perceive it, . . .*

Without putting any mental force: For instance, what is this?[372] You have to put force if you are ignorant. If you are residing in ignorance, then you have to put force and proofs also to see what it really is. But for those who have got *visphurita dṛśā*, whose eyesight, or power of perceiving, is absolutely clear . . .

SCHOLAR: It doesn't mean those who suddenly . . . when one suddenly opens the eyes.

SWAMIJI: No, not suddenly. [*Visphurita dṛśā* means], those who have clear vision. For instance, you have to concentrate between the two breaths, in the junction [between two breaths, and] if that junction is clear to you.

JOHN: While maintaining awareness.

SWAMIJI: While maintaining awareness. It is not clear; for many *sādhaka*s, it does not get clearance.

JOHN: No, no, it is not clear.

SWAMIJI: You can't find it, you can't realize it, you can't

370 *Sphuraṇa* (viz., *spanda*) literally means, glittering; the act of trembling, throbbing, vibration, pulsation; springing or breaking forth, starting into view, expansion, manifestation.

371 The first start of perception, without any attribution of impressions (*vikalpas*).

372 Swamiji is referring to an object in the room.

perceive it properly. But there are some *sādhaka*s who can perceive it at once, what it really is.

JOHN: With awareness.

SWAMIJI: Awareness is there for both classes.[373] But *visphurita dṛśā*s are those *sādhaka*s who have got the mental capability of [clearly] seeing and perceiving the object. They have not to put *anusandhi* (*anusandhi*[374] means, e.g., recitation of *mantra*, holding of breath, and keeping away from other senses)–this they have not to do. They just go and catch it, hold it.

*. . . in the same way, *keṣāmapi śivātmatā*, there are some *sādhaka*s who can perceive the state of Śiva in an instant. This is the capability of staying in *śāmbhavopāya*. Those are *śāmbhava sādhaka*s.

JOHN: 147.

SWAMIJI: Now, [*śloka*] 147 is for those who are capable of *śāktopāya*:

Audio 5 - 35:49

भूयो भूयो विकल्पांशनिश्चयक्रमचर्चनात्।
यत्परामर्शमभ्येति ज्ञानोपायं तु तद्विदुः ॥ १४७ ॥

bhūyo bhūyo vikalpāṁśaniścayakramacarcanāt /
yatparāmarśamabhyeti jñānopāya tu tadviduḥ //147//
[not recited in full]

Those who again and again perceive [an object] just to clarify the object again and again, *niścaya krama carcanāt*, by the succession of putting intellectual force on it, *yat mabhyeti*, that *parāmarśa*[375] which takes place to them is called *jñānopāya*, is pertaining to the [means] of knowledge, and that is *śāktopāya*.

---

373 That is, for those who cannot see clearly and for those who see clearly (*visphurita dṛśā*s).

374 Lit., to explore, ascertain, inspect, plan, arrange; to aim at.

375 Lit., Reflection, consideration, inference, conclusion, drawing conclusions from analogy or experience.

And the next [*upāya*]:

Audio 5 - 36:25

यत्तु तत्कल्पनाक्लृप्तबहिर्भूतार्थसाधनम्।
क्रियोपायं तदाम्नातं भेदो नात्रापवर्गगः ॥ १४८ ॥

yattu tatkalpanāklṛptabahirbhūtārthasādhanam /
kriyopāyaṁ tadāmnātaṁ bhedo nātrāpavargagaḥ //148//

And that object which takes place by adjusting external means also–those external means which are meant, which are clarified, which are explained, by Lord Śiva Himself–those means are called *kriyopāya*, pertaining to *kriyā śakti*.[376]

SCHOLAR: How are you taking "*tatkalpanāklṛpta*"?

SWAMIJI: From Lord Śiva's will. *Tatkalpanāklṛpta bahir bhūtārtha sādhanam*, Lord Śiva has adjusted the *kalpanā*[377] of holding the support of external aspects.

SCHOLAR: So, "*tat*" is "*tasya*," not "*tābhiḥ*."[378]

SWAMIJI: "*Tasya*." Actually, it is the *kalpanā* of Lord Śiva. *Tasya kalpanā klṛpta bahirbhūta sādhanam*, it is His will that He has created external means also for perceiving His nature. That is *kriyopāya* [as it is] said in the *tantra*s, explained in the *tantra*s. But, [although the means are many], there is no differentiation in its meant, in its . . .

JOHN: Meant.

SCHOLAR: Goal, its object.

SWAMIJI: . . . goal, object. The object is one, the *upeya* is one.

Audio 5 - 38:24

यतो नान्या क्रिया नाम ज्ञानमेव हि तत्तथा।
रूढेर्योगान्ततां प्राप्तमिति श्रीगमशासने॥ १४९ ॥

---

376 *Kriyopāya* is another name for *āṇavopāya*, which pertains to *kriyā śakti*, the energy of action.

377 Lit., forming, fashioning, making, performing; forming in the imagination, inventing.

378 *Tasya* (genitive singular), not *tābhiḥ* (instrumental plural).

yato nānyā kriyā nāma jñānameva hi tattathā /
rūḍheryogāntatāṁ prāptamiti śrīgamaśāsane //149//

It is explained in the *Gama tantra* that the energy of action is not separate from the energy of knowledge. In fact, the energy of knowledge has become the energy of action when that energy of knowledge has got entry in *yoga*, in the supreme limit of *yoga*, because *yoga* is action.[379]

Yoga is pertaining to the energy of action, *jñāna* is pertaining to the energy of knowledge, and *icchā* is pertaining to the energy of that reality of the point. *Icchā* is the start, knowledge is the center, and *kriyā* is the external limit.

SCHOLAR: So, what exactly does he mean by "*yoga*" here?

SWAMIJI: *Yoga* means, *yogāntatām*, when that knowledge has got entry in *yoga*. *Yoga* means, to extract your mind from external objects and divert it towards internal objects.[380] That is *yoga*, and that is action. [*Yoga*] is action, though this action is an absolutely pure action, away from differentiated action.

SCHOLAR: But then why does he say "*yogāntatām*"?

SWAMIJI: *Yogasya antatām–parākāṣṭha.*[381]

SCHOLAR: *Parākāṣṭhām* . . . ?

SWAMIJI: *Parākāṣṭhām, antimam avasthām*,[382] the last state of *yoga*.

SCHOLAR: And why is it *kriyā* only when it is at the last stage of *yoga*?

SWAMIJI: That is *kriyā* because *yoga* is the last state of *kriyā*. [It is] "last" in the sense of when *yoga* is in its full bloom. When there is only a touch of *yoga*, that is not the last state of *yoga*. You have got some touches of *yoga* in *śāktopāya* also. You have got some touches of *yoga* in *āṇavopāya*. In the

---

379 "[*Yoga* is the] unification of action along with God consciousness." *Bhagavad Gītā* (LJA audio archive, 1978).

380 Viz., *yogaś-citta-vṛtti-nirodhaḥ*, Patañjali's *Yoga Sūtras*, 1.2.

381 *Yoga* is the highest summit or culmination (*antatām/parākāṣṭha*) of *kriyā* (action).

382 Abiding (*avasthā*) in the ultimate (*antima*).

subtle sphere of *āṇavopāya*, you have got subtle touches of *yoga*, but in gross *āṇavopāya*, you have got gross touches of *yoga*, for instance, there is *mantra* also going, *japa* also going. That is *yogasya antatām*,[383] and that is *kriyā*. So, in fact, *kriyā* has come out from the energy of knowledge, it is no other than knowledge (*yato nānyā kriyā nāma*, *kriyā* is not separate from knowledge). *Jñānameva hi tat*, that knowledge has become *kriyā* when it has entered in the uppermost limit of *yoga*. Knowledge has become *kriyā*.

SCHOLAR: You say, "uppermost limit of knowledge"?[384]

SWAMIJI: Uppermost, topmost.

SCHOLAR: But you said before (inaudible) the lowest limit.

SWAMIJI: [For example], a topmost thief. First, when you are going on the path of theft, you are a very weak thief; you get afraid just in an instant. When you are a topmost thief, you don't care. That is *antatām*, *yogāntatām*. In this sense you should take it. And that is *kriyā*, because *kriyā* is an external thing. When [knowledge] goes to the topmost action, then it is *kriyā*. When [knowledge] goes to [its] weak [i.e., subtle] state, it is not exactly *kriyā* [because] it is just attached with knowledge also, in the beginning.

JOHN: So then the topmost state would be those grossest in terms of *yajña*s, *pūjā*s, where action is being . . . ?

SWAMIJI: Yes, that is *kriyā*.

SCHOLAR: That is *yogāntatāḥ*.

SWAMIJI: Yes, *yogāntatāḥ*.[385]

Yogo nānyaḥ . . . he reads now [from the] *Gama tantra* in the next [verse], the 150th *śloka*:

383 Of or belonging to *yoga* (*yogasya*), the last stage (*antatām*) of *kriyā*.

384 Swamiji actually said, "the uppermost limit of *yoga* [viz., *kriyā*]," not "the uppermost limit of knowledge."

385 *Yajña*s, *pūjā*s, etc., are *yogasya antatām* (of or belonging to *yoga*, the last stage of *kriyā*). The maintenance of *yoga* while engaged in differentiated activity is *yogāntatāḥ* (the summit of *yoga*/action).

Audio 5 - 43:14

योगो नान्यः क्रिया नान्या तत्त्वारूढा हि या मतिः ।
स्वचित्तवासनाशान्तौ सा क्रियेत्यभिधीयते ॥ १५० ॥

yogo nānyaḥ kriyā nānyā tattvārūḍhā hi yā matiḥ /
svacittavāsanāśāntau sā kriyetyabhidhīyate //150//

Yoga is not separate from *kriyā*, and *kriyā* is not separate from *yoga*. And that knowledge (*yā matiḥ*, that knowledge), which is established on the essence of reality (*tattvārūḍhā hi yā matiḥ*, which has been established in the reality of nature) for the purpose of removing the various impressions in your mind (the various impressions of objects, objective impressions), that is *kriyā*. So, that *kriyā* is meant for removing those bad impressions in your mind. Those impressions are removed by *yoga*, and that is *kriyā*.

JOHN: This topmost *yoga*, *yogānta-*, . . .

SWAMIJI: *Yogāntataḥ* is the topmost [action].

JOHN: Yes, that is really the lowest.

SWAMIJI: Lowest, yes. The topmost is the lowest (laughs).[386]

SCHOLAR: So, *yajña* will purify the mind.

SWAMIJI: *Yajña* purifies, yes. This [purification] is the topmost *yoga*.

JOHN: Or the bottom-most.

SWAMIJI: Yes. Now he translates this *śloka* of the *tantra* to which he has referred here [from the] *Gama śāstra*, and this *Gama śāstra* is explained in the following *śloka*s:

JOHN: One fifty-one.

SWAMIJI: One fifty-one and one fifty-two (two *śloka*s).

---

386 The topmost action (*kriyā*) is lowest among the three energies: *icchā*, *jñāna*, and *kriyā*.

Audio 5 - 45:13

स्वचित्ते वासनाः कर्ममलमायाप्रसूतयः ।
तासां शान्तिनिमित्तं या मतिः संवित्स्वभाविका ॥ १५१ ॥
सा देहारम्भिबाह्यस्थतत्त्वव्रताधिशायिनी ।
क्रिया सैव च योगः स्यात्तत्त्वानां चिल्लयीकृतौ ॥ १५२ ॥

svacitte vāsanāḥ karmamalamāyāprasūtayaḥ /
tāsāṁ śāntinimittaṁ yā matiḥ saṁvitsvabhāvikā //151//
sā dehārambhibāhyasthatattvavrātādhiśāyinī /
kriyā saiva ca yogaḥ syāttattvānāṁ cillayīkṛtau //152//

There is one word in the *Gama śāstra*: "*svacittavāsanā-śāntau.*" What is "*svacitta*"? The impressions pertaining to your own mind. "Impressions pertaining to your own mind," what does that mean? He explains, Abhinavagupta explains, in his *śloka* now.

Svacitte vāsanā, the impressions remaining in your mind are *kārmamalamāyā prasūtaya*, the expansion of *kārmamala*, the expansion of *āṇavamala*, and the expansion of *māyīya-mala*. These are the impressions that remain in your mind–*kārmamala*, *āṇavamala*, and *māyīyamala*. *Śāntau* (*śāntau* is *saptamī*, but it must be explained in the *nimitta* way)[387] . . .

SCHOLAR: Locative.

SWAMIJI: Locative.

. . . *tāsām śāntinimittam*, for the removal of these three *mala*s is *śāntau*, is the meaning of *śāntau* (*śāntau* means, for the removal of these three *mala*s–*āṇavamala*, *māyīyamala*, and *kārmamala*). But the removal aspect is *matiḥ* (knowledge). You can't remove [the *mala*s] without knowledge, without awareness. Awareness removes these triple *mala*s; *yā saṁvit svabhāvikā matiḥ*, that knowledge which is *saṁvit svabhāvikā*, filled with awareness. And that knowledge (*sā*), *deha ārambhibāhyastha-tattva-vrātādhiśāyinī*, when that knowledge gets entry in the topmost *kriyā*–that is, by *yajña*,

387 Causal (*nimitta*) locative (*saptamī*).

pūjā (worship), all these things–that is *kriyā*, that is actually [what is] meant by "action." *Saiva ca yogaḥ syāt*, that is also *yoga* because *tattvānām cit layīkṛtau*, in that *kriyā*, all the gross elements get entry in the subtle elements. For instance, the gross elements begin from *pṛthvī* to *māyā*. These collective gross elements get entry in Śuddhavidyā, and [Śuddhavidyā] gets entry in Īśvara, [and Īśvara] gets entry [in Sadāśiva]. That is *tattvānām cit layīkṛtau*.[388]

SCHOLAR: So in *ṣaḍadhva śodhana*[389] or any of these things.

SWAMIJI: Yes, that is *śodhana*. And it is not only *śodhana*; [it is] *śodhana*, *bodhana*, *praveśana*, and *yojana*.

SCHOLAR: Four stages in *dīkṣā* (initiation).

SWAMIJI: Four stages in *dīkṣā*. First is *śodhana*, just to purify it, purify these gross elements; then *bodhana*, just to make the *sādhaka* [intellectually] understand what really is meant by the Self (that is *bodhana*); then *praveśana*, then you make the *sādhaka* enter in that real Self; and *yojana*, then you unite the *sādhaka* with that Lord Śiva. So, these are the fourfold ways of initiation.[390]

JOHN: But they don't happen simultaneously.

SWAMIJI: Not simultaneously, in succession: first *śodhana*, then *bodhana*, then *praveśana*, and then *yojana*.

JOHN: But there may be a big gap between.

---

388 The action (*kṛta*) of dissolving (*cit laya*) the elements (*tattvas*) in one another.

389 The process of purifying (*śodhana*) the six-fold orbits of the universe (*ṣaḍadhva*). See *Kashmir Shaivism–The Secret Supreme*, "The Sixfold Path of the Universe (*Ṣaḍadhvan*)."

390 "*Śodhana-bodhana-praveśana-yojanarūpe*. So this *svādhyā yajñe* is *śodhana,* first purifying; *bodhana* is just giving enlightenment to the mind of his disciple; and *praveśana,* just to pushing him inside God consciousness; *praveśana-yojana*, and unifying him with God consciousness in the end. This is the actual way of *svādhyā yajña* from the Shaiva point of view." *Bhagavad Gītā* (LJA audio archive), 4.29 commentary.

SWAMIJI: Not a gap.

JOHN: One and the next.

SWAMIJI: (inaudible) This is *kriyā dīkṣā*, topmost *kriyā dīkṣā*–gross!

SCHOLAR: But doesn't that *yojana*[391] take place in *ṣaḍadhva śodhana*? Doesn't he lift up to the state of Śiva?

SWAMIJI: Yes, yes.

SCHOLAR: Through his *kuṇḍalinī*?

SWAMIJI: Not *kuṇḍalinī*.

SCHOLAR: *Guru*s.

SWAMIJI: By *mantra*s. This is only the world of *mantra*s that takes place in [gross] *kriyā*. Because we are concerned with [the topmost] *kriyā* here, not with *mantra*s. That [*kuṇḍalinī*] *śodhana*[392] is meant in *śāktopāya*.[393] That [explanation] you will get in the twenty-ninth *āhnika*.[394] These things will shine there.

Now he gives an outward example:

Audio 5 - 50:12

लोकेऽपि किल गच्छामीत्येवमन्तः स्फुरैव या ।
सा देहं देशमक्षांश्चाप्याविशन्ती गतिक्रिया ॥ १५३ ॥

loke'pi kila gacchāmītyevamantaḥ sphuraiva yā /
sā dehaṁ deśamakṣāṁścāpyāviśantī gatikriyā //153//

---

391 Union, viz., *yoga*.

392 Process of purification.

393 "The rise of *kuṇḍalinī* is the state of *śāktopāya*." *Interview on Kashmir Shaivism,* Swami Lakshmanjoo with John Hughes and Alexis Sanderson (original audio recordings, LJA archives, Los Angeles 1980).

394 This initiation which purifies (*śodhana*) the sixfold path (*ṣaḍadhva*) of the disciple, which then results in the rise of *prāṇa kuṇḍalinī*, is given in the 29th *āhnika* of the *Tantrāloka* in the section on the initiation of piercing (*vedha dīkṣā*). See Appendix 12 (p398) and also *Kashmir Shaivism–The Secret Supreme*, chapter 18, "Variations in the Rise of Prāṇa Kuṇḍalinī."

In this world also, in the outward sphere of the world also, you will understand how knowledge becomes action. For instance, *loke'pi*, in this outward field of the universe, *gacchāmī*, that *sphuraṇa,*[395] that impression, that rises in your mind that, "I will go to Amirakadal"[396] ("I will go to Amirakadal," it is in your mind now), or this sensation [that], "I will go to Mr. Watal's" (it is only in the mind), that is *sphuraṇa*, that is knowledge. That is knowledge [that] you know that, "I will go to . . . ." Then what happens next? Your mind begins to move, your hand begins to move, your feet begin to move, and your body is just making arrangements for standing, and you just stand. This is *kriyā*, this is action. So that *sphuraṇa* has entered in the sphere of action. *Iti evam antaḥ sphuraiva yā*, *sā*, that knowledge, that intensity of knowledge, *āviśantī*, enters–in what?–first in the body (in his personal body); then *deśa*, that place (because, unless there is that place in your mind, you won't get up from your room)–*deśam*; *akṣāṁśca*, and your organs, your collective organs, are diverted towards that place. *Akṣāṁśca āviśantī*, when they enter in that, *gati-kriyā*, you begin to walk, you begin to enter in the car and *khrrrrrrrr*.[397]

DEVOTEES: (laughter)

SWAMIJI: *Loke'pi kila gacchāmī tyevamantaḥ sphuraiva yā, sā dehaṁ deśamakṣāṁścāpyāviśantī, gatikriyā bhavati*, when [knowledge] enters in these things, *bas*, this is what is meant by the action of going.

Tasmāt . . . he concludes now what has come in conclusion now:

Audio 5 - 52:52

तस्मात्क्रियापि या नाम ज्ञानमेव हि सा ततः ।
ज्ञानमेव विमोक्षाय युक्तं चैतदुदाहृतम् ॥ १५४॥

395 *Sphuraṇa* (viz., *spanda*) literally means, glittering; the act of trembling, throbbing, vibration, pulsation; springing or breaking forth, starting into view, expansion, manifestation.

396 A place in the city of Srinagar.

397 Swamiji imitates the sound of a car engine.

tasmātkriyāpi yā nāma jñānameva hi sā tataḥ /
jñānameva vimokṣāya yuktaṁ caitadudāhṛtam //154//

Hence, this action, the energy of action, is not separate from the energy of knowledge. It is well-said previously, in the beginning of this *śāstra*, that knowledge is the means to get liberated from repeated births and deaths.[398]

SCHOLAR: Only knowledge.

SWAMIJI: Only knowledge. Because that knowledge is another formation of action. It is knowledge that travels all around, in and out. When knowledge travels inside, it is knowledge and will, [and when knowledge travels outside], it is action. So this is knowledge that does everything, inside and outside; inside it is knowledge (*jñāna*) and will (*icchā*), and outside it is action (*kriyā*)–outside it is action!

Audio 5 - 53:53

मोक्षो हि नाम नैवानयः स्वरूपप्रथनं हि सः ।
स्वरूपं चात्मनः संविन्नान्यत्तत्र तु याः पुनः ॥ १५५ ॥
क्रियादिकाः शक्तयस्ताः संविद्रूपाधिका नहि ।
असंविद्रूपतायोगाद्धर्मिणश्चानिरूपणात् ॥ १५६ ॥

mokṣo hi nāma naivānyaḥ svarūpaprathanaṁ hi saḥ /
svarūpaṁ cātmanaḥ saṁvitnānyattatra tu yāḥ punaḥ //155
kriyādikāḥ śaktayastāḥ saṁvidrūpādhikā nahi /
asaṁvidrūpatāyogāddharmiṇaścānirūpaṇāt //156//

What is liberation? *Mokṣo hi nāma naivānyat*, nothing [other] than perceiving your own nature. That is liberation. *Mokṣa hi nāma prathanaṁ hi saḥ*, *svarūpa prathanaṁ* is liberation. To realize your own nature, that is liberation. And

398 In verse 23 it is said: "In this world of spirituality, everywhere, in each and every *śāstra*, it is sung that ignorance is the cause of repeated births and deaths and knowledge is the cause of liberation from it."

what is your nature? Your nature is your own consciousness (*svarūpam ca atmanaḥ saṁvit*), nothing else. Your own consciousness is your *svarūpa*. But, in the state of that consciousness, one's own consciousness, you will, you know, and you act. How do these three aspects come out from that consciousness if it is only one consciousness? The revealing of your own nature is liberation, nothing else. What is your nature? [Your] nature is your own consciousness, but in that consciousness, in your nature which is one with that consciousness, there are three aspects: *icchā*, *jñāna*, and *kriyā* (*kriyādikā śaktaya*). *Tāḥ saṁvit rūpādhikā*, those also, those energies, those three energies, triple energies, are not separate from that consciousness, from the state of consciousness, because *asaṁvit rūpatā-yogāt*, these–the energy of action (*kriyā śakti*), the energy of knowledge (*jñāna śakti*), and the energy of will (*icchā śakti*)–cannot exist without knowledge, without consciousness. So they are filled with the state of consciousness. And *dharmiṇa-ścānirūpaṇāt*, in this philosophy of Shaivism, we have not understood, we have not recognized, the aspects as separate from the aspect-holder; the aspect-holder is not separate from his aspects. You know?

JOHN: Yes.

SWAMIJI: *Dharmiṇaca anirūpaṇāt*, the aspect-holder is not separately explained in this Shaivism. The aspect-holder is one with his aspects [just] as fire is one with that burning aspect, [just as] fire is one with that lightening aspect. Fire has got [the capacity for] producing light also, this aspect, but that producing of light, this aspect, is not separate from fire, you see. And the heating aspect is not separate from fire, the burning aspect is not separate from fire. So, all these aspects are one with the aspect-holder. So, this is our Shaivism!

There are some philosophical schools of thought, they hold that the aspects are separate from the aspect-holder.

Audio 5 - 57:17

परमेश्वरशास्त्रे हि न च काणाददृष्टिवत् ।

parameśvaraśāstre hi na ca kāṇādadṛṣṭivat /157a
[not recited]

In this *Parameśvara śāstra*,[399] in this school of Shaivism, it is not meant as it is meant by the Kāṇāda *śāstra*, the Kāṇāda school of thought.

SCHOLAR: Vaiśeṣika.

SWAMIJI: Vaiśeṣika.[400]

Audio 5 - 57:34

शक्तीनां धर्मरूपाणामाश्रयः कोऽपि कथ्यते ॥ १५७ ॥

śaktīnāṁ dharmarūpāṇāmāśrayaḥ ko'pi kathyate //157//

[According to Kashmir Shaivism], it is not the truth that there is *āśrayaḥ*,[401] [that] *āśrayaḥ* is God and all His aspects are kept in Him–*āśrayaḥ*.

SCHOLAR: Basis, ground.

SWAMIJI: Basis, ground. [According to Vaiśeṣika], the ground is Lord Śiva and all these aspects are grounded in Lord Śiva. But it is not our system! We don't recognize this kind of thought. We recognize that all these aspects are one with that aspect-holder. "Ground" and "grounded" are not two things–they are already there.

---

399 Scripture of thc supreme Lord.

400 Kāṇāda was the sage who is credited as the founder of the school of Vaiśeṣika, the second of the six classical systems of Indian philosophy. It analyses the special qualities that distinguish one object from another. The Kāṇāda school maintains that the aspects and the aspect-holders are separate.

401 That to which anything is annexed or with which anything is closely connected or on which anything depends or rests.

Audio 5 - 58:22

ततश्च दृक्क्रियेच्छाद्या भिन्नाश्चेच्छक्तयस्तथा ।
एकः शिव इतीयं वाग्वस्तुशून्यैव जायते ॥ १५८॥

tataśca dṛkkriyecchādyā bhinnāścecchaktayastathā /
ekaḥ śiva itīyaṁ vāgvastuśūnyaiva jāyate //158//
[not recited]

Tataśca dṛkkriyecchādyā, if we would accept this kind of school, this kind of thought of Kāṇāda, then what would happen to us? *Tataśca dṛk kriyā icchādyā bhinnāścet śaktaya*, if these (the energy of knowledge, the energy of action, and the energy of will) would remain separated from the holder, from the energy of the energy-holder, *ekaḥ śiva itīyam vāk vastu śūnya*, then [the theory that] "Lord Śiva is only existing as one," it would be destroyed in one moment, this theory wouldn't exist at all. This theory would vanish in one second because . . .

JOHN: There would be no oneness.

SWAMIJI: . . . there would be no oneness. So it is not accepted in our system.

Audio 6 - 00:00

तस्मात्संवित्त्वमेवैतत्स्वातन्त्र्यं तत्तदप्यलम् ।
विविच्यमानं बह्वीषु पर्यवस्यपि शक्तिषु ॥ १५९॥

tasmātsaṁvittvamevaitatsvātantryaṁ yattadapyalam /
vivicyamānaṁ bahvīṣu paryavasyati śaktiṣu //159//

So, *tasmāt saṁvittvam evaitat svātantryam*, this state of consciousness is not separate from *svātantrya*.[402] *Svātantrya* is the state of consciousness, and that *svātantrya*, if it is analyzed, parsed, well-parsed, when you parse *svātantrya*, . . .*

You know "parsing"?

402 Lord Śiva's absolute independent freedom.

JOHN: Taking apart the word.

SWAMIJI: Taking apart what it really means.

*. . . and then you will see numberless energies remaining in that *svātantrya*. *Vivicyamānam*, when it is parsed, well analyzed, then *bahvīṣu śaktiṣu paryavasyati*, this *svātantrya* will end in numberless energies. You will see that numberless energies are there in *svātantrya śakti*.

Do you understand?

SCHOLAR: Yes.

SWAMIJI: *Yataścātmaprathā mokṣa* . . . next, the 160th *śloka*:

Audio 6 - 01:29

यतश्चात्मप्रथा मोक्षस्तन्नेहाशङ्क्यमीदृशम् ।
नावश्यं कारणात्कार्यं तज्ज्ञान्यपि न मुच्यते ॥१६०॥

yataścātmaprathā mokṣastatnehāśaṅkyamīdṛśam /
nāvaśyaṁ kāraṇātkāryaṁ tajjñānyapi na mucyate //160//

As it is decided, as this is the correct truth, that *ātmaprathā mokṣa*, liberation is realizing your own nature (liberation means, realizing your own nature), then, if this is so, then *na iha āśaṅkyam īdṛśam*, this doubt you should not put within you that *nāvaśyam kāraṇāt kāryam*.[403] There are two aspects. One is the cause and one is the effect. What is the cause of liberation? Knowledge (*jñānameva vimokṣāya*). What is the effect?

JOHN: Knowledge.

SWAMIJI: No, the effect is liberation. The cause is knowledge and the effect is liberation (*jñānam mokṣāya kāraṇām*). *Jñānam* . . .

JOHN: The cause is *jñānam* and the effect is *mokṣa*.

SWAMIJI: And the effect is *mokṣa*. But, you should not put this kind of doubt in it, in this theory, because it is not the

403 That it is not certain (*nāvaśya*) that from the cause (*kāraṇāt*) an effect will be produced (*kāryām*).

theory of cause and effect, really. In the real sense, it is not cause and effect, the theory of cause and effect, that knowledge is the cause of liberation. It is something else. That we will explain just now.

So, you should not put this kind of doubt in the way that, "It does not always happen that the cause will get its effect, always. Sometimes you put a seed in the ground and it does not get a sprout–the effect is nowhere. [Sometimes] you don't get the effect from the cause." So, you must not put this doubt on this subject: if knowledge is the cause of liberation. [You must not say], "Suppose this knowledge will act just like that seed without getting its sprout. For instance, if you have got knowledge, it is not cent-per-cent[404] sure that you will get liberation because, if you have got a seed, it is not cent-per-cent sure that you will get a sprout out of it when you sow it in the ground. It may fail. It may fail to get a sprout." So, you should not put this kind of doubt in this theory [that], "If knowledge is the cause of liberation, sometimes knowledge fails to get its effect. So, if you possess knowledge, [it is possible that] you won't posses liberation, [that] you won't achieve liberation, sometimes. Sometimes, it is possible, it may happen, [that] you won't get liberation." But this kind of doubt you should not put in this [theory] because this theory that knowledge is the cause of liberation is not actually the theory of cause and effect.

Yataścātmaprathā mokṣa, knowledge [itself] is liberation! *Yataścātmaprathā mokṣa*, actually, knowledge is liberation, knowledge is not the "cause" of liberation; when this theory stands that "knowledge is liberation," not this theory that "knowledge is the cause of liberation." [If the latter], then it would happen that knowledge wouldn't get its effect sometimes. But the theory is actually, "knowledge is liberation." So, this kind of doubt should not be put here. [If it is], then what would happen? *Tat jñānyapi na mucyate*, then the one who is experienced in his own nature (the *jñāni*), then the one who possesses knowledge, would not get liberation. He would be

404 One hundred percent.

just like us. *Tad jñāni api na mucyate*, but the possessor of knowledge is absolutely liberated, it is cent-per-cent sure, there is no question. This question will never arise that, "The possessor of knowledge will not be liberated." It is sure that he will be liberated. He is liberated.

Audio 6 - 06:13

यतो ज्ञानेन मोक्षस्य या हेतुफलतोदिता ।
न सा मुख्या, ततो नायं प्रसङ्ग इति निश्चितम् ॥ १६१ ॥

yato jñānena mokṣasya yā hetuphalatoditā /
na sā mukhyā, tato nāyaṁ prasaṅga iti niścitam //161//
[not recited in full]

[Objection:] But you have put already, "*jñānameva vimokṣāya*?"[405] [So,] in this previous *śloka, jñānameva vimokṣāya*, in this *śloka*, it seems that *jñānameva vimokṣāya* [means] knowledge is the cause of liberation, i.e., knowledge is the *hetu* (cause) and its [*phala*] fruit is liberation.

For that, [Abhinavagupta] puts this doubt aside.

Yato jñānena mokṣasya yā hetuphalatoditā, this *hetutā* and *phalatā*, this [knowledge] being a cause and [liberation] being an effect (what is already explained in the previous *śloka*), *na sā mokṣa*, it is not real. It is just to make you understand that knowledge is the cause of liberation. Actually, knowledge is not the "cause" of liberation, knowledge *is* liberation! Knowledge is itself liberation. *Tato nāyaṁ prasaṅga*, so this kind of doubt won't exist here in our theory. *Iti niścitam*, this is our *siddhānta*, this is our establishment of thought.

Audio 6 - 07:36

एवं ज्ञानस्वभावैव क्रिया स्थुलत्वमात्मनि ।
यतो वहति तेनास्यां चित्रता दृश्यतां किल ॥ १६२ ॥

evaṁ jñānasvabhāvaiva kriyā sthūlatvamātmani /
yato vahati tenāsyāṁ citratā dṛśyatāṁ kila //162//

405 Verse 154.

Thus, *jñāna svabhāvaiva kriyā*, this energy of action is *jñāna svabhāva*, is one with the energy of knowledge, it is not separate from the energy of knowledge. And when this energy of knowledge takes the formation of grossness, then it becomes *kriyā*, then it becomes the energy of action. This energy of knowledge, when it takes the state of grossness, then it is nominated as the energy of action, and, in that energy of action, there is *citratā*, there are variations, variations of formations. In knowledge there is no variation, knowledge is only one, and knowledge becomes many when it enters in the grossness of its being, that is, *kriyā*.

Audio 6 - 08:45

क्रियोपायेऽभ्युपायानां ग्राह्यबाह्यविभेदिनाम् ।
भेदोपभेदवैविध्यान्निःसंस्व्यत्वमवान्तरात् ॥ १६३ ॥

kriyopāye'bhyupāyānāṁ grāhyabāhyavibhedinām /
bhedopabhedavaicidhyānniḥsaṁkhyatvamavāntarāt //163//

In this world of action, in this world of the means of action (*kriyopāye*–the *upāya*; *upāya* means, the means), in the world of means pertaining to action (that is, *kriyopāya*, *āṇavopāya*), there is *upāyānāṁ niḥsaṁkhyatvam*, the means here are existing in numberless ways, because some means are pertaining to *grāhya* (some means are pertaining to the external world), some means are pertaining to the mind, some means are pertaining to external objects, and *bheda upabheda vaicitriyāt*, and there is also differentiation between them, too, also. So, the means are here *niḥsaṁkhyatvam*, numberless.

Audio 6 - 10:00

अनेन चैतत्प्रध्वस्तं यत्केचन शशङ्किरे ।
उपायभेदान्मोक्षेऽपि भेदः स्यादिति सूरयः ॥ १६४ ॥

anena caitatpradhvastaṁ yatkecana śaśaṅkire /
upāyabhedānmokṣe'pi bhedaḥ syāditi sūrayaḥ //164//

By this, this [following] theory is destroyed. This theory is destroyed, [this theory of] those "experienced souls" (*sūraya* means, those *paṇḍits*, those experienced souls), who have put this doubt in our theory that, *upāyabhedāt mokṣe'pi bhedaḥ syāt*, when the means are many, the meant must also be many. But the meant is only one. So, [our] theory has destroyed their theory–our theory that knowledge is not separate from *kriyā*. So, knowledge (the means) is only one, so the meant is also one. [Although] knowledge has taken the formation of *kriyā* and become many, but in fact it is only one. So, if the means are one, the meant is also one. So, that theory of those *paṇḍits* is no more existing.

Audio 6 - 11:36

मलतच्छक्तिविध्वंसतिरोभूच्युतिमध्यतः ।
हेतुभेदेऽपि नो भिन्ना घटध्वंसादिवृत्तिवत् ॥ १६५ ॥

malatacchaktividhvaṁsatirobhūcyutimadhyataḥ /
hetubhede'pi no bhinnā ghaṭadhaṁsādivṛttivat //165//

Now he keeps this example here: *mala tat śakti vidhvaṁsa*, when you have, just say, *mala tat śakti vidhvaṁsa*, the destruction of the *mala*s (impurities) along with their energies, the destruction of the impurities along with their energies, or *tirobhū*, concealing these impurities [along] with their energies, or *cyuti*, removing away the impurities along with their energies–these are three ways–in fact, [these are] one and the same act, but it appears as three; because destruction is always the same, concealing is also the same (gets the same [result]), and removing away is also the same. It is *hetu bhede api*. [Although] there are *hetu bheda*, [although] there are differentiated means also for the meant, for achieving the meant, but *no bhinnā*, actually these means are not separated, these are one. *Ghaṭadhvaṁsādivṛtti vat*, because, [for example], the meant is to destroy a pot, an earthen pot. You can destroy it by crashing it, smashing it, along with another pot–it will be destroyed. You can destroy it with a hammer. You can destroy it with a fist, with a blow of a fist. [Although] these means are many, but the meant is only one. You can destroy it [in many ways]–*ghaṭadhvaṁsādi vṛttivat*. So, [although] there are many means, the meant is only one.

Bas, the *prakaraṇa* (topic) is over. Now he will begin with the *prakaraṇa* of the *Mālinīvijaya* [*tantra*]. He will give references of *Mālinīvijaya* for *śāmbhavopāya*, *śāktopāya*, *āṇavopāya*, and *anupāya*.

ŚĀMBHAVA-ŚĀKTA-ĀṆAVOPĀYA IN THE MĀLINĪVIJAYA TANTRA (166-169)

Audio 6 -15:45

तदेतत्त्रिविधत्वं हि शास्त्रे श्रीपूर्वनामनि ।
आदेशि परमेशित्रा समावेशविनिर्णये ॥ १६६ ॥

tadetattrividhatvaṁ hi śāstre śrīpūrvanāmani /
ādeśi parameśitrā samāveśavinirṇaye //166//

In the subject of *samāveśa*[406] in the *Mālinīvijaya*, these threefold means are explained by Lord Śiva with authority (*ādeśi* means, to explain with authority–*ādeśi*). *Tat trayameva granthaṁ pāṭhati* (comm.), now, he reads those *śloka*s:

Audio 6 - 14:40

अकिञ्चिच्चिन्तकस्यैव गुरुणा प्रतिबोधतः ।
उत्पद्यते य आवेशः शाम्भवोऽसावुदीरितः ॥ १६७ ॥

406 Trance, absorption, or entry. "*Samāveśa* means, *bas*, the state of appeasement, when you are absolutely free from any thought." *Tantrāloka* 3.170 (LJA archive). See commentary on verses 179b and 180a below.

akiñciccintakasyaiva guruṇā pratibodhataḥ /
utpadyate ya āveśaḥ śāmbhavo'sāvudīritaḥ //167//[407]

That trance[408] which takes place to that *sādhaka* who does not adopt any thought or any *mantra* or anything else, just by the grace of his master, that entry is called the *śāmbhava* entry.[409]

Uccārarahitaṁ vastu . . . the next [*śloka*]:

Audio 6 - 15:16

उच्चाररहितं वस्तु चेतसैव विचिन्तयन् ।
यं समावेशमाप्नोति शाक्तः सोऽत्राभिधीयते ॥१६८॥

uccārarahitaṁ vastu cetasaiva vicintayan /
yaṁ samāveśamāpnoti śāktaḥ so'trābhidhīyate //168//[410]

When, in your mind only, that object which cannot be uttered or recited, that object is contemplated through the mind only, through thought only, and that trance which takes place by that is called *śākta samāveśa*, is the trance pertaining to *śāktopāya*.

---

407 *Mālinīvijaya Tantra* 2.23.

408 *Pratibodhata*, lit., awaking, perception, knowledge.

409 According to the *Mālinīvijaya tantra*, "This is *śāmbhava samāveśa* when one is capable of keeping away all the thoughts, *akiñcit cintaka saiva*, and impressions, by the elevating infusion of your master (*guruṇā pratibodhata*), because he infuses this power in you. *Svasmāt gurutaḥ pratibodhata*, when you are capable yourself, then your master will carry you there, otherwise not, otherwise your master will also be not successful in carrying you there. It means, you must be capable of digesting this kind of awareness in your mind, in your thought. This is the meaning of the *śloka* which is explained by our masters." *Shiva Sūtras–The Supreme Awakening* 1.5 commentary.

410 *Mālinīvijaya Tantra* 2.22.

Audio 6 - 15:52

उच्चारकरणध्यानवर्णस्थानप्रकल्पनैः ।
यो भवेत्स समावेशः सम्यगाणव उच्यते ॥ १६९ ॥

uccārakaraṇadhyānavarṇasthānaprakalpanaiḥ /
yo bhavetsa samāveśaḥ samyagāṇava ucyate //169//[411]

And that trance that takes place by adopting the recitation of breath,[412] and *karaṇa* (the organic way of meditation),[413] and contemplation (*dhyāna*), and reciting of *varṇa*s (special *varṇa*s), . . .*

JOHN: What are *varṇa*s?

SWAMIJI: *Varṇa*s? Some words.[414]

JOHN: Not the same as *mantra*s? Or the same as *mantra*s?

SWAMIJI: No. "*Varṇa*" is [here referring to] that *varṇa* which takes place automatically, just like *anāhatā*,[415] e.g., "*oooooooom̐*," and that ending sound is called "*varṇa*."

*. . . and *sthāna kalpanā* is meditating on that point, a particular point (e.g., *bhrumadhya*,[416] heart, etc.), that *samāveśa* is here called *āṇava samāveśa*.[417] But in the *Mālinīvijaya*, you see, the reading is not in this way. The reading is from *āṇavopāya* to *śāktopāya* and then *śāmbhavopāya* in the end (in the *Mālinīvijaya*, the reading of Lord Śiva). But Abhinavagupta has found it necessary that he should read it from the top so that any *sādhaka* (aspirant), who may be capable of the top knowledge, he would get entry in *śāmbhavopāya* first–why to bother for *śāktopāya* and *āṇavopāya*? So he has put the reading in the reverse way. But the reading of

411 *Mālinīvijaya Tantra* 2.21.
412 "The word "*uccāra*" means "breathing," actual concentration on the breath." *Kashmir Shaivism–The Secret Supreme*, 5.37.
413 *Karaṇa*: through the organs of cognition and action.
414 Lit., letter, sound, vowel, syllable, word.
415 Un-pronounced, un-struck sound.
416 Between the two eyebrows.
417 The trance or absorption of *āṇavopāya*.

Lord Siva is not in this way; it is from *āṇavopāya* to *śāktopāya* and then *śāmbhavopāya*. That is *vyatyāsapāṭhe.*[418]

Tadeva krameṇa [*vyācaṣṭe*].[419] Now he explains this first *śloka* of *śāmbhavopāya*.

JOHN: This is one seventy.

SWAMIJI: It is one seventy:

THE MEANS PERTAINING TO ŚĀMBHAVOPĀYA (170-212)

Audio 6 - 18:16

अकिंचिच्चिन्तकस्येति विकल्पानुपयोगिता ।
तया च झटिति ज्ञेय समापत्तिर्निरूप्यते ॥ १७० ॥

akiñciccintakasyeti vikalpānupayogitā /
tayā ca jhaṭiti jñeyasamāpattirnirūpyate //170//

Now there is the first word, "*akiñcit cintakasya*" (without adopting any thought). What does that mean? Now Abhinavagupta explains what is "*akiñcit* [*cintakasya*], not adopting any thought." What does that mean? That means, *vikalpa anupayogitā*, discard all thoughts, discard all attributions of meditating points (all those aspects of meditating points are discarded). That is *akiñcit cintakasya*, not adopting any thought. *Tayā*, and by that, *jñeya samāpattiḥ nirūpyate*, it is explained that you get the achievement of that object which is to be known, Lord Śiva. You get [that] achieve-ment, not in succession, but in an instant, instantaneously. This is the meaning of "*akiñcit cintakasya*" in the text of the *Mālinīvijaya*.

JOHN: Now, one seventy-one.

418 Jayaratha's commentary: a reading (*pāṭha*) in an inverted order (*vyatyās*).
419 The three *upāya*s will be explained in due succession.

SWAMIJI: One seventy-one:

Audio 6 - 19:34

सा कथं भवतीत्याह गुरुणातिगरीयसा ।
ज्ञेयाभिमुखबोधेन द्राक्प्ररूढत्वशालिना ॥५७१॥

sā kathaṁ bhavatītyāha guruṇātigarīyasā /
jñeyābhimukhabodhena drākprarūḍhatvaśālinā //171//
[not recited]

Now, there is another word: "*guruṇā pratibodhataḥ.*"[420] "*Guruṇā*" is in the instrumental case and "*pratibodhataḥ*" is *pañcamī.*[421] What is that called?

SCHOLAR: Ablative.

SWAMIJI: Ablative case –"*pratibodhataḥ.*"

[Question:] *Sā kathaṁ*, that discarding away of all thoughts, [discarding the] adoption of all thoughts, how can that be possible?

JOHN: Discarding of all thoughts.

SWAMIJI: Yes. To that, [Lord Śiva] explains "*guruṇā pratibodhataḥ,*" what "*guruṇā*" means–"by the master."[422] [Here], the meaning of *guruṇā* is not "by the master, through the master, by the master's grace"–it does not mean that. It means, *guruṇā*, by the subtlest way of understanding–*guruṇā*.

SCHOLAR: Perhaps "intense"? Would "intense" be the right word?

SWAMIJI: Intense–*ati garīyasā*.

JOHN: Most intense understanding.

SWAMIJI: Yes.

SCHOLAR: Most intense realization.

SWAMIJI: Yes. *Jñeya abhimukhena bodhena*, just to divert

420 From Jayaratha's commentary on verse 167.
421 The fifth case.
422 The literal meaning of "*guruṇā.*"

your attention towards that object, *jñeya abhimukhena*, and that knowledge.

JOHN: Which object?

SWAMIJI: The object, Lord Śiva. And *drākprarūḍhatvaśālinā*, "*guruṇā*" is not only "intense," but that intensity where *drākprarūḍhatvaśālinaḥ*, you are established in one moment, you establish your consciousness there in one second.

JOHN: One second.

SWAMIJI: Yes.

SCHOLAR: So, "intense awareness directed towards the object of knowledge, obtaining completion in an instant."

SWAMIJI: In an instant, yes.

JOHN: There is no succession in this.

SWAMIJI: There is no succession, no (affirmative).

JOHN: So this "*guruṇā*" does not mean "*guru*."

SWAMIJI: "*Guruṇā*" doesn't mean "*guru*." This is the first meaning. *Ati garīyasā*, "*guruṇā pratibodhataḥ*" was in the ablative case but he says why [he has] translated it in the instrumental case:

Audio 6 - 21:48

तृतीयार्थे तसि व्याख्या वा वैयधिकरण्यतः ।

tṛtīyārthe tasi vyākhyā vā vaiyadhikaraṇyataḥ / 172a
[not recited in full]

Actually, "*guruṇā pratibodhataḥ*" is *tṛtīya*, the instrumental case.

SCHOLAR: In sense.

SWAMIJI: *Guruṇā pratibodhataḥ* is "*pratibodhena*," the affix ["*tas*"]. It is put in each and every *vibhakti*, in each and every case–*tasil*.[423]

SCHOLAR: *Itarābhyo'pi tasil.*

423 Consequently, "*pratibodhataḥ*" can have a variety of meanings.

SWAMIJI: *Tasil*, yes. So, I [Abhinavagupta] have translated it in this way. Or (*vā*) *vaiyadhikaraṇyataḥ*, or you may put "*guruṇā*" in the instrumental case and "*pratibodhata*" in the ablative case. That way, the explanation is something else: *guruṇā* means, *guruṇā kṛto yaḥ bodhaḥ tataḥ,*[424] by the insertion of knowledge of your master. By the insert-ment, insertion, when your master inserts his knowledge in you, by that [initiation], you are established in that consciousness of Lord Śiva in an instant.

SCHOLAR: This is the meaning of *śāmbhavī dīkṣā*.

SWAMIJI: Yes, it is *śāmbhavī dīkṣā*.[425] Now, there is another word, another important word, in the text of *Mālinīvijaya*: "*āveśa*." What is *āveśa*? What is trance?[426]

Audio 6 - 23:16

आवेशश्चास्वतन्त्रस्य स्वतद्रूपनिमज्जनात् ॥ १७२ ॥
परतद्रूपता शम्भो राद्याच्छक्त्यविभागिनः ।

āveśaścāsvatantrasya svatadrūpanimajjanāt //172b//
paratadrūpatā śambhorādyācchaktyavibhāginaḥ /173a

What does "*āveśa*" mean? *Āveśa* means, when your dependent nature is subsided (*svatad rūpa nimajjanāt*, you subside your dependent nature of your being) and *paratad rūpatā*, you are united with the nature of Lord Śiva. That is *āveśa*. Just as

424 From Jayaratha's commentary.

425 *Śāmbhavopāya* initiation (*dīkṣā*). "The penetrative state of the trance is called *śāmbhava samāveśa*. The penetrative state of the trance is that when once it shines before you, there is no way to escape from this, you are gone in it, you are diluted in it. This trance has digested you, I mean, your individual being. This is *śāmbhava samāveśa* when one is capable of keeping away all the thoughts, *akiñcit cintaka saiva*, and impressions, by the elevating infusion of your master (*guruṇā pratibodhataḥ*), because he infuses this power in you." *Shiva Sutras*, 1.5 commentary, (LJA archive).

426 *Āveśa* literally means, joining one's self; entering, entrance, taking possession of.

a ghost enters in somebody [and his] nature is subsided and the nature of that ghost remains there, shining, that is *āveśa*. And the union [with] Śambho,[427] who is *ādyāt* (eternal, ancient) and *śakti avibhāgina* (one with *svātantrya śakti*), you get entry in That.

Audio 6 - 24:31

तेनायमत्र वाक्यार्थो विज्ञेयं प्रोन्मिषत्स्वयम् ॥ १७३ ॥

tenāyamatra vākyārtho vijñeyaṁ pronmiṣatsvayam //173b//

Now, this is the meaning of this text of the *Mālinīvijaya* in substance (*vākyārtha*).

Vijñeyam pronmiṣat svayam āsate, *vijñeyam*, the object which is to be known (that is, Lord Śiva, the state of Lord Śiva), *svayam pronmiṣat āsate*, shines by Itself without doing any effort of *sādhanā*.

SCHOLAR: *Pronmiṣat.*

SWAMIJI: *Pronmiṣat.*

SCHOLAR: Unfolding.

SWAMIJI: *Unmiṣat*, blooms out, opens, blooms. [The state of Lord Śiva] blooms, blooms out, *svayam*, without any adoption of any effort, . . .*

SCHOLAR: Spontaneously.

SWAMIJI:

Audio 6 - 25:26

विनापि निश्चयेन द्राक् मातृदर्पणबिम्बितम ।
मातारामधरीकुर्वत् स्वां विभूतिं प्रदर्शयत् ॥ १७४ ॥
आस्ते हृदयनैर्मल्यातिशये तारतम्यतः ।

vināpi niścayena drāk mātṛdarpaṇabimbitam /
mātāramadharīkurvat svāṁ vibhūtiṁ pradarśayat //174//
āste hṛdayanairmalyātiśaye tāratamyataḥ / 175a

[not recited]

427 An appellation of Lord Śiva, which means, auspicious one.

*. . . *vināpi niścayena*, without putting your awareness, and in an instant (*drāk*). And how? *Mātṛ darpaṇa bimbitam, mātāram adharīkurvat*, at the same time, simultaneously, when your individual state of the intellect is subsided totally, *mātṛ darpaṇa bimbitam, buddhi darpaṇa bimbitam* (*mātṛ* means there "intellect"), in the mirror of the individual intellect, that which has been . . .

What is *pratibimbitam*?

SCHOLAR: Reflected.

SWAMIJI: . . . reflected, your individuality which is reflected in the limited intellectual field of being, that is subsided instantaneously, and, at the same time–not only subsided only–*svām vibhūtim pradarśayat*, when, at the same time, simultaneously, side-by-side, your glory of all-knowledge and all-action shines forth (*svāṁ vibhūtim pradarśayat*; *vibhūtim* means, knowledge and action), the energy of knowledge and energy of action shines forth, and in this way, that object which is to be perceived is being established there *tāratamyataḥ*.

Tāratamyataḥ means, without any interruption of any other foreign matter. *Tāratamyata* means, when there is no foreign matter in-between. For instance, you recite a *mantra*. "*Oṁ śiva, oṁ śiva, oṁ śiva, oṁ śiva*, this is Denise, this Shanna, *oṁ śiva, oṁ śiva, oṁ śiva*," this kind of meditation is not *tāratamyata*. [When you recite], "*oṁ śiva, oṁ śiva, oṁ śiva, oṁ śiva*," no "Shanna," no "Denise," nothing [besides "*oṁ śiva*"], . . .

SCHOLAR: More and more intense.

SWAMIJI: . . . intense, then that is *tāratamyataḥ*, a spontaneous way of meditation, without any interruption of foreign thoughts.

SCHOLAR: So, the basic meaning of the word ["*tāratamyata*"] is "getting more and more," isn't it?

SWAMIJI: More and more, yes–*tāratamyataḥ*.

SCHOLAR: It also implies that, because there is no interruption, it gets more and more intense.

JOHN: Absolutely spontaneous.

SWAMIJI: Spontaneous.

JOHN: What is this "without awareness" (*vināpi*)?

SCHOLAR: Without *vikalpa*.

SWAMIJI: *Vināpi*, without *vikalpa*.

JOHN: Just awareness of . . .

SCHOLAR: It really means, judgement.

SWAMIJI: This is not *krama* (successive). When [you think], "This book is here, this book is here, this book is here, this book is here" [continuously], this is *tāratamya*. When [you think], "This book is here, a *kongari*[428] is here," then, "This book is here, this book is here, this book is here, . . ."

JOHN: "Microphone is there."

SWAMIJI: " . . . a microphone is there," this is not *tāratamya*. [*Tāratamya* is] when there is no other foreign matter in-between.

JOHN: No break of . . .

SWAMIJI: No break.

SCHOLAR: Unimpeded expansion.

SWAMIJI: Yes, that is *tāratamya*.

DENISE: No obstacle.

SWAMIJI: No obstacles.

JOHN: But this speaks of meditation. I mean, you can also have *tāratamya* in *āṇavopāya*.

SWAMIJI: Yes, *āṇavopāya*, *śāktopāya*, too.

JOHN: In fact, the ideal state is to have *tāratamya*.

SWAMIJI: *Tāratamya*, yes.

JOHN: Not this thinking about breakfast, thinking about lunch.

SWAMIJI: Without any interruption.

428 A small fire pot used by Kashmiris to keep their bodies warm during the winter.

Audio 6 - 29:08

ज्ञेयं द्विधा च चिन्मात्रं जडं चाद्यं च कल्पितम् ॥ १७५॥
इतरत्तु तथा सत्यं तद्विभागोऽयमीदृशः ।
जडेन यः समावेशः स प्रतिच्छन्दकाकृतिः ॥ १७६ ॥

jñeyaṁ dvidhā ca cinmātraṁ jaḍaṁ cādyaṁ ca kalpitam //175b//
itarattu tathā satyaṁ tadvibhāgo'yamīdṛśaḥ /
jaḍena yaḥ samāveśaḥ sa praticchandakākṛtiḥ //176//

It is not "*sapraticchandakākṛtiḥ*." You must correct it [to read] "*sa*" as separate–"*sa praticchandakākṛtiḥ*."

SCHOLAR: Yes, yes, much better.

SWAMIJI: Yes.

Audio 6 - 29:32

चैतन्येन समावेश स्तादात्म्यं नापरं किल ।

caitanyena samāveśastādātmyaṁ nāparaṁ kila / 177a

Now, he removes this objection because he has put Lord Śiva as an object,[429] he has nominated Lord Śiva as the object of understanding–you have to understand [that] He has become the object. The object is *jñeya*,[430] but actually there are two classes of objects: one state of an object is *cinmātra* (filled with consciousness), the other is deprived of consciousness. *Jñeyam dvidhā*, the object is twofold: *cinmātram jaḍam ca*, one is *cinmātra* (filled with consciousness), the other object is *jaḍa*.[431] *Itarattu tathā satyam, ādyam ca kalpitam*, the first *cinmātra* object is [nominated as an object] just to make you understand

429 Anticipating Abhinavagupta's clarification of the difference between the entrances (*aveśa*) of sentient and insentient objects into consciousness, Jayaratha objects that since insentient objects enter consciousness, how can it be said that a sentient object enters consciousness (*bodhātmaiva samāveśa*)?
430 The object of knowledge.
431 Insentient, inert.

that It is the object, It is to be known, but actually It is not the object, It is the subject. What?

JOHN: This *cinmātra* object.

SWAMIJI: *Cinmātra* object. The *cinmātra* object is actually subjective, It is not objective. It is just to make you understand; *kalpitam*[432] means, just to make you understand that it is to be known. *Itarattu*, the second one, the second object, the second who is *jaḍa*, is *tathā satyam*; *tathā jñeyatvena satyam bhavati*, that is an actual object.

SCHOLAR: As it is.

SWAMIJI: As it is. *Tat vibhāgo ayam īdṛśaḥ*, now, he [explains] the differentiation of these *samāveśa*s: the entry in *jaḍa* and the entry in consciousness. *Jaḍena yaḥ samāveśa*, when you enter in *jaḍa*, [when] you get entry in *jaḍa*, *sa praticchandakākṛtiḥ*, it is only a reflection, it is not real. It is only a reflection. *Caitanyena samāveśa*, when you get entry in consciousness, *tādātmyaṁ*, that is an actual union with That consciousness, *na param kila*, it is nothing else than that.

Audio 6 - 31:54

तेनाविकल्पा संवित्तिरभावनाद्यनपेक्षिणी ॥ १७७ ॥
शिवतादात्म्यमापन्ना समावेशोऽत्र शांभवः ।

tenāvikalpā saṁvittirbhāvanādyanapekṣiṇī //177b//
śivatādātmyamāpannā samāveśo'tra śāṁbhavaḥ / 178a

So, here in the text of the *Mālinīvijaya,*[433] the concluded meaning is: when *avikalpā saṁvitti*, your consciousness which is *nirvikalpa*, which is without any attribution of any thoughts, any impressions, any moods, and *bhāvanādi anapekṣiṇī*, where you don't need the support of *bhāvanā*, *dhyāna*, *dhāraṇā*, etc., *mantra*, *japa*, and *śivatādātmyam-*

432 The conception (*kalpitam*) of Lord Śiva (*cinmātra*) as an object.
433 Referring to the previous verse (167) from the *Mālinīvijaya Tantra* concerning the topic of *śāmbhava samāveśa*.

āpannā, and your consciousness is united with the oneness of Lord Śiva, that, in the real sense, is called *śāmbhava samāveśa* in this text of the *Mālinīvijaya*.

Audio 6 - 32:52

तत्प्रसादात्पुनः पश्चा द्भाविनोऽत्र विनिश्चयाः ॥१७८॥
सन्तु तादात्म्यमापान्ना न तु तेषामुपायता ।

tatprasādātpunaḥ paścādbhāvino'tra viniścayāḥ //178b//
santu tādātmyamāpannā na tu teṣāmupāyatā / 179a

By the grace of Lord Śiva, by the grace of this trance, this *śāmbhava samāveśa* (*śāmbhava* trance), when afterwards, after getting establishment in this trance of *śāmbhava*, *bhāvino'tra viniścayā*, all these rules and all these regulations of *śāktopāya* and *āṇavopāya*, if they exist for him, *santu*, let them exist, [because] *tādātmyamāpannā*, they are one, they have become one, with that *śāmbhava samāveśa*. If he is given to the recitation of *mantra* afterwards, after getting the trance of *śāmbhava samāveśa*, if he recites *mantra*, if he is doing *japa*, if he is doing meditation, if he is doing *pūjā*, *havana*, worship, everything, let it remain there for him, [because] *śivatādātmyam*, it has become *śāmbhavopāya* for him everywhere; everywhere he experiences the *śāmbhava* state. *Na tu teṣām upāyatā*, they[434] are not means (*upāya*s) for him afresh, they are not afresh means for him.

SCHOLAR: If he experiences the *śāmbhavopāya* . . . ?

SWAMIJI: *Sāmbhavopāya* once, if he experiences the *śāmbhavopāya* [state] once, he can attribute *śāktopāya* afterwards also in the same level.

SCHOLAR: Once that *samāveśa* has taken place.

SWAMIJI: [Once] *śāmbhava samāveśa* has taken place, *śākta samāveśa* will shine as *śāmbhava samāveśa* and *āṇava samāveśa* will shine as *śāmbhava samāveśa* for him because *śivatādātmyamāpannā*, all these means have become, are

434 *Mantra*, *pūjā*, etc.

united with, that *śivatādātmya*. So they are not afresh means for him.[435]

JOHN: But to gain this original *samāveśa* in *śāmbhavopāya*, he must practice some other . . .

SWAMIJI: He must practice *śāmbhava samāveśa* first. When he is established in that *śāmbhavopāya* [state], he can practice any degraded *mantra* and that will become *śāmbhavopāya* for him, for you.

SCHOLAR: And when that *śāmbhavopāya* is penetrating everything, that becomes *anupāya*.

SWAMIJI: No, the final establishment of *śāmbhavopāya* is *anupāya*. *Anupāya* is "no means." Actually, *anupāya* is no means, it is no *upāya*.

SCHOLAR: So, that would come when there was no falling from the *śāmbhava* state.

SWAMIJI: Yes, that is *anupāya*. He is established.

SCHOLAR: No *vyutthāna*[436] at all.

SWAMIJI: No *vyutthāna* . . . *vyutthāna* yes, but not in that sense.

JOHN: But no individual sense.

SWAMIJI: Yes.

SCHOLAR: It is always *unmīlanā samādhi* for him.[437]

SWAMIJI: Yes.

---

435 "Because," as Swamiji will explain (184b-185), "when you once enter in *śāmbhava samāveśa*, [then] if you enter in *śākta samāveśa*, that will also become *śāmbhava samāveśa*, and if you enter in *āṇava* [*samāveśa*], that will also be, for you, *śāmbhava samāveśa*."

436 External, differentiated worldly experience.

437 "*Unmīlanā samādhi* is experienced in *turyātītā* and *nimīlanā samādhi* is experienced in *turya*. This is the difference between *turya* and *turyātītā*. *Nimīlanā samādhi* means, absorption of universal consciousness. When universal consciousness is absorbed in your nature, that is *turya*. When universal consciousness is expanded everywhere, that is *turyātītā* [viz., *unmīlanā samādhi*]." *Tantrāloka* 10.288. See Appendix 14, p401 for explanation of *turya* and *turyātītā*.

Audio 6 - 35:54

विकल्पापेक्षया मान मविकल्पमिति ब्रुवन् ॥ १७९ ॥
प्रत्युक्त एव सिद्धं हि विकल्पेनानुगम्यते ।

vikalpāpekṣeyā mānamavikalpamiti bruvan //179b//
pratyukta eva siddhaṁ hi vikalpenānugamyate /180a

Now, he removes this doubt from other schools of thought, some schools who explain that *nirvikalpa* (thought-lessness), the state of *nirvikalpa*, is only established by the help of *vikalpa* (thought); *vikalpa apekṣayā avikalpam mānam bruvan*, *avikalpa* (thought-lessness)[438] is only established by the help of *vikalpa*.

JOHN: *Nirvikalpa*. So this *nirvikalpa*, some schools are holding that the *nirvikalpa* state is attained through *vikalpa*.

SWAMIJI: Some say.

JOHN: Which schools are these?

SWAMIJI: These are Dvaitavādins.[439]

JOHN: Not Vedāntins.

SCHOLAR: These Theravādins[440] also believe, and these Vaibhāśikas.[441]

SWAMIJI: Vaibhāśikas also.

JOHN: "Through *vikapla*" means?

SWAMIJI: "Through *vikalpa*" means, through the adoption of aspects. When you put [forth] aspects that this is . . . . What is this? This is specs.[442] How this is specs? Because this has got the shape of specs and it can be used as specs. This is *vikalpa*. So, this specs is established [when you confirm that], "This is specs," then you are in *nirvikalpa*, then you get entry in

438 *Avikalpa* and *nirvikalpa* are synonymous.
439 Dualistic schools.
440 Theravāda is said to be the oldest surviving school of Buddhism.
441 Vaibhāśika is an early Buddhist school.
442 A pair of spectacles.

nirvikalpa.[443]

SCHOLAR: Like *maṇijñānī*.[444]

SWAMIJI: *Maṇijñānī.*

JOHN: So how do they do it? I mean, what is the practice for those . . . ?

SCHOLAR: They are referring, aren't they, to the meditation?

SWAMIJI: When [the value of] some jewel is to be found out–that [question of], "What is the cost of this jewel? What should be the cost of this jewel?–[then the jeweler] puts some of these [tests] for getting the complete ascertainment for how much it costs, this is *vikalpa*. And afterwards, when he has come to the understanding that this is a jewel worth five *lakhs* of rupees, then he will enter in *nirvikalpa*. This is their way of understanding.

SCHOLAR: It is also the nature of the practice.

SWAMIJI: But, our way of understanding is not that.

JOHN: So, this is practice for them.

SWAMIJI: Yes, this is practice for them.[445]

JOHN: So they use . . . what is the object of this *vikalpa*?

SWAMIJI: [Other Schools say:] First, you have to practice, like *āṇavopāya*, *śāktopāya*, and then you will enter in the *śāmbhavopāya* in the end. *Nirvikalpa* comes in the end. But, the Shaivite does not understand that, recognize that. The Shaivite recognizes that *nirvikalpa* is first and then *vikalpa* takes place. Unless there is *nirvikalpa*, [*vikalpa*] does not exist, it won't exist afterwards. *Nirvikalpa* will give it life.

---

443 "When you are satisfied [that], "I have known it, I know what it is," that is [the object's] *saṁhṛti* (destruction), because there is no curiosity to see it again and again." *Tantrāloka* 4.145 (LJA archive).

444 A jeweler; literally, a knower of jewels. The analogy of a jeweler (*maṇijñānī*) will be discussed in *śloka*s 183b, 184a, 228, and their commentaries.

445 For the achievement of *nirvikalpa*. Every school of spirituality agrees that thought-lessness is the door to the Absolute.

SCHOLAR: Among the Buddhists, only the Yogācāras[446] believe that *nirvikalpa* precedes *vikalpa*. Others think that there is *anādi avidyā*, . . .

SWAMIJI: Yes.

SCHOLAR: . . . beginning-less ignorance . . .

SWAMIJI: That is what he says here: *vikalpa apekṣayā avikalpa mānam bruvan*, those who say that *avikalpa* is only established by the support of *vikalpa* first, [that] you have to take the support of *vikalpa* first for realizing the state of *nirvikalpa*, those who say like this, *pratyukta eva*, they are answered by the Shaivites that it is not this way! Because, *siddham hi vikalpenānygamyate*, that object,[447] [only when it] is already established in the *nirvikalpa* state, then you can attribute *vikalpa*s on it afterwards. *Vikalpa*s will be attributed afterwards, after it is established in the *nirvikalpa* state. So the *nirvikalpa* state is the life of the object.

SCHOLAR: Yes.

SWAMIJI: For instance, I want to see Denise. Before that, I see only a phantom figure of Denise; and before that, I see only the seeing force; and before that, I see only myself, and that is *nirvikalpa*. So, after that *nirvikalpa*, Denise appears in the end.

JOHN: So they are just having it backwards. They are saying the first thing that you have is the *vikalpa* state–these schools.

SWAMIJI: [They say that] the *vikalpa* state [occurs first] and then you will come to *nirvikalpa*. But that is not the real theory.

SCHOLAR: [They say that *nirvikalpa* is achieved] through purification of the mind, through *bhāvanā*, etc.

SWAMIJI: Yes, *bhāvanā*, *dhyāna*, *dhāraṇā*, etcetera, everything.

SCHOLAR: *Vitarka*, *vicāra*, that they call.

446 An influential Buddhist school, literally meaning "*yoga* practice."
447 Any object, be it *jaḍa* (insentient) or *ajaḍa* (sentient).

SWAMIJI: Yes.

JOHN: So the purpose in their practice, I'm trying to understand, is to take *vikalpa*, and discard *vikalpa*, and arrive at *nirvikalpa*.

SWAMIJI: Afterwards, in the end, and enter in *nirvikalpa*. It is their theory, but our theory is not like this. Our theory is, first *nirvikalpa*; *nirvikalpa* is the life, first.

JOHN: So we don't hold then that you discard *vikalpa* to gain *nirvikalpa* in this sense.

SWAMIJI: No (affirmative). For the *śāmbhava sādhaka*, you have to catch hold of *nirvikalpa* without [utilizing] any other aspects that reside lower [than] that.

JOHN: How about *āṇavopāya*?

SWAMIJI: *Āṇavopāya* is *vikalpa*.

JOHN: It has *vikalpa*.

SWAMIJI: It is only *vikalpa*.

DEVOTEE: But *ādhāra*[448] is *nirvikalpa*.

SWAMIJI: But *nirvikalpa* is the life, *śāmbhava* is the life, *śāmbhava* is the reality of *samāveśa*. *Samāveśa* of *āṇavopāya* and *samāveśa* of *śāktopāya* are only imitations of *samāveśa*, they are not actual *samāveśa*s.

JOHN: Not completely full.

SWAMIJI: Because they are just like this: you have to rise to the *nirvikalpa* state through *vikalpa* in *āṇavopāya* and in *śāktopāya*. But in *śāmbhavopāya*, you have not to rise [to *nirvikalpa* through *vikalpa*]. You have to get establishment in [*nirvikalpa* in] an instant with awareness, with awareness of the *śāmbhava* state, and that is the real *samāveśa*.

DENISE: Swamiji, what does "*samāveśa*" mean?

SWAMIJI: Trance, entry, entry in your nature.

Gṛhītamiti suspaṣṭā . . . the 180th *śloka*:

448 The ground, basis, foundation. That is, the ground of perception.

Audio 6 - 42:36

गृहीतमिति सुस्पष्टा निश्चयस्य यतः प्रथा ॥ १८० ॥
गृह्णामीत्यविकल्पैक्यबलात्तु प्रतिपद्यते।

gṛhītamiti suspaṣṭā niścayasya yataḥ prathā //180b//
gṛhṇāmītyavikalpaikyabalāttu pratipadyate / 181a

Just take, *gṛhītam gṛhṇāmi,*[449] just take, "I understand this *kongari.*[450] This is a *kongari.*" This is already understood in *nirvikalpa* first, and then afterwards, in the aspects of *vikalpas*, you understand that, "I *gṛhṇāmi* [understand] this is [*kongari*]." But the *gṛhītam*[451] in *nirvikalpa*, through *nirvikalpa*, which is already held in consciousness, *gṛhṇāmi,*[452] that is held afterwards in/through *vikalpa–gṛhītam gṛhṇāmi. Gṛhītam nirvikalpena, gṛhṇāmi vikalpa rūpatāya*, this kind of perception, "*gṛhṇāmi*," the perception that, "I understand this is a *kongari*," this *kongari* also, this aspect of the *vikalpa* [thought] also, will shine only by the force of *nirvikalpa*. This is the force of *nirvikalpa* that makes you understand that this is a *kongari* in the *vikalpa* state. So, the state of *vikalpas* also exist in the basis of *nirvikalpa*.

Audio 6 - 44:18

अविकल्पात्मसंवित्तौ या स्फुरत्तैव वस्तुनः ॥ १८१ ॥
सा सिद्धिर्न विकल्पात्तु वस्त्वपेक्षाविवर्जितात् ।

avikalpātmasaṁvittau yā sphurattaiva vastunaḥ //181//
sā siddhirna vikalpāttu vastvapekṣāvivarjitāt / 182a

But what is the *siddhi*? What is the proof of becoming [established], the establishment of some object? The establishment of an object is not, "This is a *kongari*." The *siddhi* of this

449 The understanding (*gṛhītam*) that "I have understood" (*gṛhṇāmi*).
450 A Kashmiri fire pot.
451 The understanding.
452 The thought that "I have understood."

kongari is only when you see this *kongari* in the *nirvikalpa* state, in *prathamikābhāsa*; *prathamikābhāsa prathamālocana*, the first start of perception, without any attributions of *vikalpas*, is the establishment of this object.

SCHOLAR: The word in English is, "without predication."

SWAMIJI: Without predication. *Avikalpātma saṁvittau yā sphurattaiva vastunaḥ*, that object which gets forth, which gets in your consciousness in the *nirvikalpa* state, that is *siddhi* (*sā siddhir*), that is called the *siddhi* of that object, that is the establishment of that object. *Na vikalpāttu vastu apekṣāvivarjitāt*, *vikalpa* cannot prove this object, only *nirvikalpa* can prove this object. But where *vikalpas* are held? Where *vikalpas* are not held? For instance, in the *śāmbhava* state, *vikalpas* are not held, *vikalpas* don't give any support. In *śāktopāya* and in *āṇavopāya*, yes, they will give support (that is *vikalpa sāpekṣatā*[453] there). [It is] *vikalpa nirapekṣatā*[454] in the *śāmbhava* state.

Audio 6 - 46:12

केवलं संविदः सोऽयं नैर्मल्येतरविभ्रमः ॥१८२॥

kevalaṁ saṁvidaḥ so'yaṁ nairmalyetaravibhramaḥ //182b

Where *vikalpas* protect you, give you support, there you must come to this understanding that your state of awareness is not quite pure. Where your state of awareness is not pure, then you need the support of *vikalpas*; you need the support of *mantras*, *japa*, *dhyāna*, meditation, all these things. Where your consciousness is pure, then you don't need any support there; then you have to enter in the *śāmbhava* state in the beginning, first.[455] *Kevalaṁ saṁvidaḥ*[456] (*saṁvidaḥ* means,

453 Dependent (*sāpekṣa*) on thought (*vikalpa*).

454 Not dependent (*nirapekṣa*) on thought (*vikalpa*).

455 At the first start of perception (*prathamālocana*).

456 There is only this difference (*kevalam*) concerning the consciousness of the means (*saṁvida*).

upāyānām):[457] *upāyānām so'yam nairmalyetara vibhramaḥ*, this is the *nairmalya* and *anairmalya vibhrama*, the expansion of purity and impurity.

JOHN: *Vikalpa* and *nirvikalpa*.

SWAMIJI: *Vikalpa* and *nirvikalpa*.

Audio 6 - 47:21

यद्विकल्पानपेक्षत्वसापेक्षत्वे निजात्मनि ।

yadvikalpānapekṣatvasāpekṣatve nijātmani / 183a
[not recited in full]

When *vikalpa* is needed and where *vikalpa* is not needed: Where *vikalpa*s are not needed, that is because your consciousness is pure. Where *vikalpa*s are needed, it means that your consciousness is impure, so you need the support of *śāktopāya*, you need the support of *āṇavopāya*. And when your consciousness of awareness is absolutely pure, you don't need *śāktopāya* or *āṇavopāya* for that–just entry and that is all.

Audio 6 - 48:02

निशीथेऽपि मणिज्ञानी विद्युत्कालप्रदर्शितान् ॥ १८३ ॥
तांस्तान्विशेषांश्चिनुते रत्नानां भूयसामपि ।

niśīthe'pi maṇijñānī vidyutkālapradarśitān //183b//
tāṁstānviśeṣāṁścinute ratnanāṁ bhūyasāmapi / 184a
[not recited]

Niśīthe'pi . . . he gives references.

SCHOLAR: Analogy.

SWAMIJI: Example. *Niśīthe'pi maṇijñānī*, that [person] who knows–the (*maṇijñānī* means,)–who knows the valuation of jewels, although you put that jewel, some particular jewel, before him at midnight (*niśīthe'pi*, at midnight also), he will at once tell you that this is worth two *lakhs*, two *lakhs* and two

457 Of or pertaining to the *upāya*s.

dollars, [that] this is worth such and such money–at midnight also.[458] But the one who is the aspirant of *śāktopāya* and *āṇavopāya*, he won't be able, and his calculations will be wrong with torches also. [Even] if he [uses] a torch and lights also, and sees and analyzes that jewel, that calculation won't be exact. But for that *maṇijñānī*, for that, if you put before him that jewel at midnight also, without any light, he will tell you [its precise value].

SCHOLAR: But it says here . . .

SWAMIJI: *Vidyut kāla pradarśitān*, only just in a twinkle of an eye you will show him [the jewel] and [then] keep that jewel in your pocket.[459] At that very moment, he will [accurately] tell you that this is worth this, because he is established in the *śāmbhava* state; that is established in *vidyut kāla pradarśitam*, only by the "lightening" of that moment.

SCHOLAR: But it doesn't mean, an actual lightening. It doesn't mean, shown in the time of lightening?

SWAMIJI: No, just for a short time, a short moment. *Vidyut kāla pradarśitam tān tān viśeṣān*, those *viśeṣān*, those differences, differentiations, he can calculate only in that [brief] moment.

DEVOTEE: *Ratnānām bhūyasāmapi.*

SWAMIJI: *Bhūyasāmapi*, if you put one hundred jewels before him, one hundred and one thousand jewels before him, and tell him, "What is the cost of these jewels one-by-one? Tell me," and you collect them only after half a second and put them in [your] pocket, he will tell you, one-by-one, [the exact value of] everything, because he is established in the *śāmbhava* state–that .

458 The expert jeweler, who is likened to a person residing in the *śambhava* state, is capable of accurately determining the value of a jewel "even at midnight," i.e., even when his perception is compromised because of the lack of light, etc.

459 Shown (*pradarśita*) by shining forth (*vidyut*) in a short span of time (*kāla*).

Audio 6 - 50:33

नैर्मल्यं संविदश्चेदं पूर्वाभ्यासवशादथो ॥ १८४ ॥
अनियन्त्रेश्वरेच्छात इत्येतच्चर्चयिष्यते ।

nairmalyaṁ saṁvidaścedaṁ pūrvābhyāsavaśādatho //184b
aniyantreśvarecchāta ityetaccarcayiṣyate / 185a

This purification of your consciousness, [of the] awareness of your consciousness, takes place by your constant meditation in [your] past lives. If you [were] meditating in your past lives, so many past lives, constantly, this purification of that awareness comes in appearance. Or, that purification comes by the grace of the Lord in one instant.

JOHN: One second.

SWAMIJI: One second. *Ityetat carcayiṣyate*, this grace of the Lord will be explained in the thirteenth *āhnika*, not here.[460]

End of Audio 6 - 51:29

Śāmbhava samāveśa is not only *śāmbhava samāveśa*, it is *śākta samāveśa* also and *āṇava samāveśa* also, because when you once enter in *śāmbhava samāveśa*, [then] if you enter in *śākta samāveśa*, that will also become *śāmbhava samāveśa*, and if you enter in *āṇava* [*samāveśa*], that will also be, for you, *śāmbhava samāveśa*.

SCHOLAR: Because *śāmbhava* is universal and embraces every possible *ābhāsa* .[461]

SWAMIJI: Yes. So, this *śāmbhava samāveśa* is threefold.

JOHN: *Śāmbhava* in *śāmbhava* . . .

SWAMIJI: *Śāmbhava*, *śākta*, and *āṇava*. In that case, *śākta* is also *śāmbhava samāveśa* and *āṇava* is also *śāmbhava samāveśa*.

---

460 In the thirteenth *āhnika*, the subject of *anugraha* (grace, *śaktipāta*) is described at length. See Appendix 22 (p414) for a brief explanation of grace.

461 Lit., appearance.

Audio 7 - 00:45

पञ्चशद्विधता चास्य समावेशस्य वर्णिता ॥ १८५ ॥

pañcāśadvidhatā cāsya samāveśasya varṇitā //185b//
[not recited]

But, not only that. *Śāmbhava samāveśa* is not only threefold. Lord Śiva has explained this *samāveśa* as fiftyfold, not only threefold.

Audio 7 - 01:05

तत्त्वषड्त्रिंशकैतत्स्थस्फुटभेदाभिसन्धितः ।

tattvaṣaṭtriṁśakaitatsthasphuṭabhedābhisandhitaḥ / 186a

Because, the thirty-six elements, [those] which are the thirty-six elements, in that class of the thirty-six elements, the vividly differentiated ways of *śāmbhava* [practice] are seen there. For instance, fivefold is *bhūta samāveśa* (that is *bhauta samāveśa*;[462] fivefold because of the five elements from earth to ether), and thirtyfold is elementary *samāveśa* (*tattva samāveśa*)–*bhūta samāveśa* is fivefold, thirtyfold is *tattva samāveśa*–and *ātmā samāveśa* is threefold (*ātmā*, *vidyā*, and Śiva).

JOHN: *Ātmā*, here, in this sense is being used . . . ?

SWAMIJI: *Puruṣa–ātmā*, *jīva*, the individual.

JOHN: Using it in the individual sense.

SWAMIJI: Individual, yes. *Ātmā*, *vidyā*, and Śakti (or Śiva). That will be Śakti, not Śiva, because Śiva is *samāveśya*, not *samā*[*veśa*].[463] There is no entry in Śiva.

And *mantra samāveśa*, the *samāveśa* pertaining to *mantra*s, is tenfold, because *a-kāraśca*, *u-kāraśaca*, [etc.,] those ten states of *mantra* (*a-kāra*, *u-kāra*, *ma-kāra*, *bindu*, *ardha-*

462 The entry or trance relating to the *mahābhūta*s, the five great elements.
463 Śiva is the entered (*samāveśya*), Śakti is the entrance (*samāveśa*).

candra, *nirodhī*, *nāda*, *nādānta*, *śakti*, and *vyāpinī*).[464] These are the tenfold *samāveśa*s of *śāmbhava samāveśa*. And *śakti samāveśa*[465] is twofold: Śakti and Śiva. Śiva is Śakti there. Śakti is also Śakti there and Śiva is also Śakti there, because it is *samāveśya*, it is not *samāveśa*. Śiva is actually *samāveśya*, not *samāveśa*. We have to enter in Śiva. Śiva has not to enter in anything, in any aspect.[466]

Audio 7 - 03:33

एतत्तत्त्वान्तरे यत्पुंविद्याशक्त्यात्मकं त्रयम् ॥ १८६ ॥
अम्भोधिकाष्ठाज्वलनसंख्यैर्भेदैर्यतः क्रमात् ।

etattattvāntare yatpuṁvidyāśaktyātmakaṁ trayam //186b//
ambhodhikāṣṭhājvalanasaṁkhyairbhedairyataḥ kramāt /

In[467] these thirty-six elements, those elements which are threefold (the individual [*puruṣa*], *vidyā*,[468] and *śakti*[469]), these

464 "*A-kāra, u-kāra, ma-kāra* are the gross formation of *auṁ-kāra*. *Bindu-ardhacandra* is the subtle formation of *auṁ-kāra*. *Nirodhinī, nāda, nādānta, śakti, vyāpinī, samanā,* and *unmanā* are the subtlest formation of *auṁ-kāra*." Vijñāna Bhairava–*The Manual of Self-realization*, verse 78. *Samanā* and *unmanā* are not included among the ten states of mantra listed above, presumably because they are represented by the two-fold elements of *śakti samāveśa* (Śakti and Śiva, respectively). In the next verse, *samanā* and *unmanā* are included in the explanation of the tenfold divisions of *vidyā samāveśa*. See Appendix 17 (p405) for a detailed explanation of the divisions of the *praṇava mantra, auṁ* (*oṁ*).

465 "*Śakti samāveśa*" is not referring to the *samāveśa* of *śāktopaya*. It is referring to *śāmbhavopāya samāveśa* through Lord Śiva's immediate energy (Śakti).

466 *Bhūta samāveśa* (fivefold), *tattva samāveśa* (thirtyfold), *ātmā samāveśa* (threefold), *mantra samāveśa* (tenfold), and *śakti samāveśa* (twofold), all of which total fifty practices of *śāmbhavopāya*. See Appendix 18 (p409).

467 *Antare*, being in the interior of.

468 Knowledge.

469 Energy.

are said to be fourfold, tenfold, and threefold [respectively]. Fourfold is *puruṣa samāveśa*, tenfold is *vidyā samāveśa*, and *śakti* is threefold *samāveśa*. Fourfold is *sakala*, *pralayākala*, *vijñānākala*, and Śuddhavidyā (the individual is fourfold).[470]

SCHOLAR: It is the same as this *ātmā trividhā*. This is the same as that . . . ?

SWAMIJI: No, no, no. It is, *ātmā*, *vidyā*, and *śakti* is threefold. This is one way. And in *ātmā*[471], *ātmā* is itself fourfold because it is *sakala* (the individual is *sakala*), *pralayākala*, *vijñānākala*, and Śuddhavidyā. So, they[472] have to be carried to, they have to enter in, Śiva. They have to be entered in Śiva. So, the individual is fourfold. *Vidyā* is tenfold because, there,[473] although they are twelvefold . . . for instance, *a-kāra*, *u-kāra*, and *ma-kāra*, these are to be only [one] *varṇa*, this is to be only one word. *A-kāra*, *u-kāra*, *ma-kāra* is one word,[474] so this is onefold; *bindu* is second, *ardhacandra* is third, *nirodhī* is fourth, *nāda* is fifth, *nādānta* is sixth, *śakti* is seventh, *vyāpinī* is eighth, *samanā* is ninth, and *unmanā* is tenth. So, this is found in the world of *vidyā*. So *vidyā* is tenfold. And *śakti* is threefold because in *śakti*, [which is] in fact, *svātantrya śakti*– in fact, it is *svātantrya śakti*, but *svātantrya śakti* is threefold– there is will (*icchā*), there is knowledge (*jñāna*), and there is action (*kriyā*).[475]

Now, in the next *śloka*, he explains why only these three elements are explained separately [from the 36 elements]; why he has put [an emphasis] on these three elements: *ātmā*, *vidyā*, and *śakti*.

---

470 These are the four lower states among the seven perceivers. See verse 80.

471 The individual self (*puruṣa*).

472 Each of these four states of the individual.

473 In the phases of *mantra samāveśa* mentioned in verse 186a.

474 That is, *auṁ* (*oṁ*).

475 See Appendix 18 (p409) for details of the threefold *samāveśa* of *ātmā*, *vidyā*, and *śakti*.

Audio 7 - 06:37

पुंविद्याशक्तिसंज्ञं यत्तत्सर्वव्यापकं यतः ॥१८७॥
अव्यापकेभ्यस्तेनेदं भेदेन गणितं किल ।

pumvidyāśaktisamjñam yattatsarvavyāpakam yataḥ //187b
avyāpakebhyastenedam bhedena gaṇitam kila /188a
[not recited]

Puṁ-vidyā-śakti saṁjñaṁ yat, because these threefold elements (*puruṣa*, *vidyā*, and *śakti*) pervade all the elements, pervade the whole world of elements; because the other elements are *avyāpaka*, they don't pervade each other, but these pervade the whole. *Tenedaṁ bhedena gaṇitam*, this is why it is explained separately.

SCHOLAR: They don't pervade each other. The others do not pervade each other?

SWAMIJI: The others do not pervade each other. They pervade each and every element–these threefold [elements].

SCHOLAR: So how can the doctrine of *sarvasarvātmakata* be . . . ?[476]

SWAMIJI: That doctrine is the supreme doctrine where there is no "pervasion" and "pervaded."

SCHOLAR: Everything is everything.

SWAMIJI: That state is above. This is the state . . .

SCHOLAR: From practice point of view.

SWAMIJI: From practice.

---

476 *Sarvasarvātmakata*: one thing in all things, and all things in one. "In the practice of the Kula System, you have to realize the totality of the universe in one particle. Take one particle of anything which exists in this world. In that one particle, there is to be realized the totality of the whole universe. The totality of energy is found in one particle. Everything is full of one thing and one thing is full of all things. *Ekaikatrāpi tattve'pi ṣaṭtriṁśattattvarūpatā,* in any one element, you will find all of the thirty-six elements." *Secret Supreme*, 19.132.

Audio 7 - 07:43

अशुद्धिशुध्यमानत्वशुद्धितस्तु मिथ्योऽपि तत् ॥१८८॥

aśuddhiśuddhyamānatvaśuddhitastu mitho'pi tat //188b//

And it is also [explained that these] threefold [elements are separate from one another].[477] This threefold world of elements (*puruṣa*, *vidyā*, and *śakti*) is *aśuddhi*, *śuddhyamāna*, and *śuddhita* [respectively]. *Aśuddhi* means, absolutely impure, [which] is *puruṣa*, the individual. *Śuddhyamāna*, going to be purified, about to be purified, is *śuddhyamānatva*; it will go to *vidyā*. And *śuddhita*, already purified, [which is *śakti*]. So, they [differ from] each other by this way also. Not only because of being [pervasive] in each and every element, this way also they are excluded from the world of [the 36] elements.

Now he explains why he has explained *bhauta samāveśa*[478] separately (*bhauta samāveśa* is gross *samāveśa*).

DEVOTEE: But here it is *śāmbhavopāya*.

SWAMIJI: Yes, in [terms of] *śāmbhavopāya* he has explained *bhauta samāveśa* separately, not with the world of [the other] elements. He has excluded these fivefold *mahābhūta*s, excluded in [terms of *śāmbhava*] *samāveśa*.

SCHOLAR: Who has excluded?

SWAMIJI: In the explanation [of *śāmbhava samāveśa*, he is] explaining [the *mahābhūta*s exclusively]. [They are exclusively] explained. He has not explained *bhauta samāveśa* [together with] the world of all the [other] elements. He has excluded that from . . .

JOHN: Yes, he explained five, and then he explained thirty.

SWAMIJI: For that, he explains:

477 These threefold elements, which are explained as separate from the 36 elements, are also explained as separate from one another.

478 *Śāmbhava samāveśa* pertaining to the five great elements (*mahābhūta*s).

Audio 7 -09:31

भूतान्यध्यक्षसिद्धानि कार्यहेत्वनुमेयतः ।
तत्त्ववर्गात्पृथग्भूतसमाख्यान्यत एव हि ॥ १८९ ॥

bhūtānyadhyakṣasiddhāni kāryahetvanumayetaḥ /
tattvavargātpṛthagbhūtasamākhyānyata eva hi //189//

In fact, these five elements are proved to exist, are proved to be existing, in the way of *pratyakṣa*,[479] not in the way of *anumāna* (guessing).

SCHOLAR: Inferring.

SWAMIJI: Inferring.[480] *Pratyakṣa*?

SCHOLAR: Immediate, they are established in an immediate [way] by the senses, directly by the senses.

SWAMIJI: Directly by the senses. The *bhūta*s, the five elements, are held with your eyes. Earth you can feel, earth you can see, water you can see, fire you can see, this *vāyu* (wind) you can [feel], and sky[481] you can see, but the *tanmātrā*s[482] you cannot see, the organs you cannot see. The organs are inferred. For instance, you see that this is a *kongari* here. By this [perception], we get the inferring proof that you have got the organ of seeing. [But] these [organs of sight] aren't the *golaka*s, these [eyeballs] are not the organs.[483] The organs are inside.[484] Otherwise a dead body will also see by these *golaka*s. The organ [of sensation] is existing inside, and that is inferred, that is not seen just like the gross elements.

479 Direct perception.

480 *Anumāna*, inference.

481 *Ākāśa*.

482 The five sensations of *śabda* (sound), *sparśa* (touch), *rūpa* (form), *rasa* (taste), and *gandha* (smell).

483 By "organs" Swamiji is referring to the *jñendriya*s and *karmendriya*s, the organs of knowledge and action. See Appendix 2 (p372) for the placement of the *indriya*s in the 36 elements.

484 By "inside" Swamiji means "inside consciousness," not "inside the body."

So, as the gross elements are seen . . .*

SCHOLAR: "Seen" or "[seen] with the senses," because you can't see with . . .

SWAMIJI: *. . . with the senses, so they are *pṛthag bhūta samākhyāni*, so we have nominated them separately from the elementary world which is proved by inference, which is proved by inference only, established by inference. So, *bhauta samāveśa* is separately explained.

Audio 7 - 11:54

सर्वप्रतीतिसद्भावगोचरं भूतमेव हि।
विदुश्चतुष्टये चात्र सावकाशे तदास्थितिम् ॥ १९० ॥

sarvapratītisadbhāvagocaraṁ bhūtameva hi /
viduścatuṣṭaye cātra sāvakāśe tadāsthitim //190//

Because, *sarva pratīti sadbhāva gocaraṁ* is *bhūta*, these five elements are experienced, are seen, by each and every being (*sarva pratīti sadbhāva gocaraṁ*), and these are *sāvakāśe catuṣṭaye*, with the ether they are [five]; four with[out] ether, and with ether, so five.

SCHOLAR: *Sadbhāva* means, concrete existence.

SWAMIJI: Yes, concrete existence.

SCHOLAR: How is *ākāśa* perceived?

SWAMIJI: Because you get *avakāśa*.[485]

SCHOLAR: That's *anumāna*?

SWAMIJI: But it is seen, it is seen by . . .

SCHOLAR: That there is space between things.

SWAMIJI: That there is space, yes. There is the seeing of this space by the eyes, by your organs.

SCHOLAR: But to infer that it is something rather than a mere absence of something . . .

485 Place, space, room.

SWAMIJI: There is something [but] it is subtle, it is a bit subtle, subtler than the other four. It is why he has explained [them as] four and the fifth.[486]

SCHOLAR: For that reason, the Buddhists don't accept that fifth. They say that there are four elements only.

SWAMIJI: Yes. Now he puts a question:

Audio 7 - 13:28

रुद्रशक्तिसमावेशःपञ्चधा ननु चर्च्यते ।
कोऽवकाशो भवेत्तत्र भौतावेशादिवर्णने ॥ १९१ ॥

rudraśaktisamāveśaḥ pañcadhā nanu carcyate /
ko'vakāśo bhavettatra bhautāveśādivarṇane //191//

It is a question now, he puts the question: This *śāmbhava samāveśa* you had decided to explain fivefold, in a fivefold way, but where was the chance, where was the point, to explain *bhauta samāveśa*? *Bhauta samāveśa* is very gross *samāveśa*. How can it be adjusted with *śāmbhava samāveśa*? *Bhauta samāveśa* cannot be adjusted with *śāmbhava samāveśa*. *Bhauta samāveśa* is gross *samāveśa*.

Audio 7 - 14:22

प्रसङ्गदेतदितिचेत्समाधिः संभवन्नयम् ।
नास्माकं मानसावर्जी लोको भिन्नरुचिर्यतः ॥ १९२ ॥

prasaṅgādetaditicetsamādhiḥ saṁbhavannayam /
nāsmākaṁ mānasāvarjī loko bhinnaruciryataḥ //192//
[not recited]

If you answer to this question of mine, that, "*Bhauta samāveśa* is explained because of *prasaṅga*, because we had *prasaṅga*, not exactly because it is *śāmbhava samāveśa*–it is not by *śāmbhava samāveśa*–we have explained it because [it

486 The four elements are *pṛthvī* (earth), *jala* (water), *tejas* (fire), and *vāyu* (air, wind). The fifth is *ākāśa* (space).

is] by-the-way, . . .

SCHOLAR: By extension, by-the-way.

SWAMIJI: . . . by extension (*prasaṅga*, by extension)," if you answer in this way, but this answer of yours is not digested by us, . . .

SCHOLAR: It's inedible.

SWAMIJI: . . . *loko bhinnaruciryataḥ*, because the public residing in the world of wisdom does not accept this.

SCHOLAR: *Etasmādbhinnaruciryataḥ*.

SWAMIJI: Yes, *etasmādbhinnarucir*. Now, he replies to that in the next *śloka*, 193rd:

Audio 7 - 15:28

उच्यते द्वैतशास्त्रेषु परमेशाद्विभेदिता ।
भूतादीनां यया सात्र न तया द्वयवर्जिते ॥ १९३ ॥

ucyate dvaitaśāstreṣu parameśādvibheditā /
bhūtādīnāṁ yathā sātra na tathā dvayavarjite //193//

The answer of this is that, just as in the *dvaita śāstras*, in those schools of thought pertaining to duality, dualism, it is explained there that these five elements are separated from Lord Śiva, [that they] are not adjusted with Lord Śiva (it is explained in the *dvaita śāstras*), but in the *advaita śāstras*,[487] it is not explained this way. In the *advaita śāstras*, it is explained that they are one with Lord Śiva. So, this *samāveśa* pertaining to the fivefold elements is also pertaining to *śāmbhava samāveśa* from our point of view, because . . .

The next *śloka*:

Audio 7 - 16:35

यावान्षट्त्रिंशकः सोऽयं यदन्यदपि किंचन ।
एतावती महादेवी रुद्रशक्तिरनर्गला ॥ १९४ ॥

487 Monistic scriptures.

yāvānṣaṭtriṁśakaḥ so'yaṁ yadanyadapi kiñcana /
etāvatī mahādevī rudraśaktiranargalā //194//

This whole universe, which is consisting of thirty-six elements, or which is something else than the thirty-six elements also, which is not perceived by us also, . . .

That which is perceived by us is the thirty-six elementary world [along with] that which is not perceived also, that which is in imagination also, the negation of the thirty-six elements also–the thirty-six elements and the negation of the thirty-six elements.

SCHOLAR: It's better than Jayaratha's interpretation. Jayaratha just says, "*bhuvanādi*."[488]

SWAMIJI: No. *Yat anyat api kiñcana* [means], that which is beyond the thirty six-elements, because the thirty-six elements are consisting with the *bhuvana*s (worlds), the thirty-six elements, and the negation of the thirty-six elements, [which] is the kingdom of Lord Śiva. This is the kingdom of Lord Śiva's energy, *svātantrya śakti*. This is not other than That kingdom from our point of view. So, it can be *śāmbhava samāveśa*, this elementary *samāveśa*.

JOHN: So these dualists, these Shaiva Siddhānta dualists, these dualists, *dvaita āgama*, huh?

SWAMIJI: Yes, *dvaita āgama*.[489]

JOHN: These five *mahābhūta*s in that system bind the individual, is that . . . ?

SWAMIJI: Yes, they bind the individual, they take [the individual] away from the consciousness of God consciousness.

JOHN: So, [the *mahābhūtā*s] have no attachment to God, they are other [than God].

SWAMIJI: No (affirmative).[490]

---

488 *Tadbhedā eva bhuvanādyāḥ*, 'the differentiated worlds also'.
489 Dualistic revelation.
490 That is, according to the dualists.

Audio 7 - 18:13

तत एव द्वितीयेऽस्मिन्नधिकारे न्यरूप्यत
धरादेर्विश्वरूपत्वं पाञ्चदश्यादिभेदतः ॥ १९५ ॥

tata eva dvitīye'sminnadhikāre nyarūpyata /
dharāderviśvarūpatvaṁ pāñcadaśyādibhedataḥ //195//

It is by the same reason that in [second chapter of] the *Mālinīvijaya Tantra* it is said that, from *dhara*[491] to Śiva, He has explained the *pañcadaśavidhi*.[492]

SCHOLAR: *Pañcadaśa*, etcetera.

SWAMIJI: Fifteen-fold *vidhi*, etcetera. The fifteen-fold *vidhi*, the way of the fifteen-fold science, the way of the thirteen-fold science, the way of the elevenfold science, the ninefold science, the sevenfold science, the fivefold science, the threefold science, and the one-fold science.

JOHN: This is rising.

SWAMIJI: This is rising. When there is the fifteen-fold science, then *dhara* (earth) is included there. When there is the thirteen-fold science, *dhara* is not included there.[493]

---

491 Earth (*pṛthvī*).

492 "The fifteen-fold process (*pañcadaśavidhiḥ*) teaches us how to rise from the lowest state of objectivity and enter into subjective consciousness. This fifteen-fold process is composed of seven *pramātṛns*, seven *pramātṛ śaktis* (energies), and the fifteenth, the object (*svarūpa*)." *Kashmir Shaivism–The Secret Supreme*, 58. See also *Tantrāloka* 10 (LJA archive). See Appendix 24 (p417) for an explanation of *svarūpa*.

493 "The fifteen-fold process and the thirteen-fold process differ in that, in the fifteen-fold process, you have to rise from objectivity to Universal Being, whereas in the thirteen-fold process, you have nothing to do with the objective world. In the thirteen-fold process, you have to rise from individuality, from individual being, to Universal Being. In the fifteen-fold process, once you have attained the state of Universal Being, the process is complete and you then have to step up to the thirteen-fold process." *Kashmir Shaivism–*

SCHOLAR: And so on.

SWAMIJI: And so on.[494]

SCHOLAR: Up to Śiva-Śakti.

Audio 7 - 19:16

SWAMIJI: Up to Śiva, Śiva-Śakti. *Śiva sākṣāt na bhidyate*,[495] Śiva is not differentiated, It is one. There is no science There. Science is for understanding. There is no understanding [in the state of Śiva because] It is understood already.

SCHOLAR: But this fifteen-fold is the seven *pramātṛ*s and their [seven respective] *śakti*s, . . .[496]

SWAMIJI: Yes.

SCHOLAR: . . . and *svarūpa*, the thing itself.

SWAMIJI: In *sakala pramātṛ bhāva*, the *svarūpa* is *dhara* (earth); in *pralayākala pramātā*, the *svarūpa* is *sakala*; in *vijñānākala pramātā*, the *svarūpa* is *pralayākala*; in Śuddhavidyā *pramātā*, the *svarūpa* is *vijñānākala*; in Īśvara *pramātā*, the *svarūpa* is *mantra pramātā*;[497] and in Sadāśiva, the *svarūpa* is Īśvara *pramātā*.[498]

Secret Supreme, 61.

494 "Even though you have attained Universal Being in the fifteen-fold process of rising, you do not have the capacity to maintain that universal state. The purpose of functioning these increasingly difficult processes is to strengthen your capacity of rising so that you can maintain this capacity and never fall from the state of Universal Being." Ibid., 61. "And you have to rise, you have to make all these elements absorb in each other." *Tantrāloka* 10, Swami Lakshmanjoo, introductory commentary (LJA archives).

495 Ibid., 10.121.

496 See Appendix 10 (p394) for explanation of the seven perceivers (*pramātṛ*s). For an explanation of the seven *pramātṛ*s and their respective energies (*pramātṛ śakti*s) see *Kashmir Shaivism–Secret Supreme*, chapters 8 and 9.

497 *Mantra pramātā* is the perceiver of the state of Śuddhavidyā.

498 *Svarūpa* (lit., self-form) is the state of one's own nature, one's natural state, which changes as one rises through the seven *pramātṛ*s. See Appendix 24 (p417) for an explanation of *svarūpa* in the fifteen-fold process (*pañcadaśavidhiḥ*).

SCHOLAR: But if this is a gradual progression, how is it all in *śāmbhava samāveśa*? If this is a progression, how is it all . . . ?

SWAMIJI: It is a rise. It is a rise in the elementary world in the *śāmbhava* state.

SCHOLAR: But the *śāmbhava* state is direct.

SWAMIJI: It is direct. You have to find out that there is no way. For instance, you have to cut the way. The fifteenfold science, etcetera, is meant to cut the way. But in fact, *dharā* is nothing [other] than *sakala*; *sakala* is nothing [other] than *pralayākala*; *pralayākala* is nothing [other] than *vijñānākala*; *vijñānākala* is nothing [other] than Śuddhavidyā; Śuddhavidyā is nothing [other] than Īśvara; Īśvara is nothing [other] than Sadāśiva; Sadāśiva is nothing [other] than Śakti and Śiva.

SCHOLAR: All this is pure *upāya*.

SWAMIJI: It is pure *upāya* in the process of *śāmbhava*. This is the *śāmbhava* process. It is not the *śākta* process or it is not the process of *āṇava*.

JOHN: So this fifteen . . .

SCHOLAR: It sounds like *śākta* [*upāya*], that is why it is puzzling, because it involves realizing that . . .

SWAMIJI: But he has included *śākta samāveśa* in *śāmbhava*. He has included already *āṇava samāveśa* in *śāmbhava*. From that point of view, he explains this. When *āṇava* is also *śāmbhava* there, when *śākta* is also *śāmbhava* there, what is the difference? There is no difference!

JOHN: So, in this fifteen-fold rising, this only takes place in *śāmbhavopāya*.

SWAMIJI: Yes, from fifteen-fold to one-fold.

JOHN: That only takes place in *śāmbhavopāya*.

SWAMIJI: *Śāmbhavopāya samāveśa*.

JOHN: Not in *śāktopāya*.

SCHOLAR: It takes place successively?

SWAMIJI: It is not a successive process. It is to find out, it is to analyze, the whole elementary world.

SCHOLAR: But that analysis takes place in *śāktopāya*. This is *śāktopāya* in *śāmbhavopāya*.

Audio 7 - 22:00

SWAMIJI: For instance, you play the process of the entry of the gross element of *pṛthvī*[499] (this is the grossest element–*pṛthvī*), you play the process of *śāmbhava samāveśa* there. You have to see that that gross element is nothing [other] than Śiva, because in the gross element you have to find the fifteen-fold science, not only the one-fold science. You have to perceive that this one point of this gross element, *pṛthvī*, is nothing [other] than fifteen, it is included in the fifteen-fold science. When it is included in the fifteen-fold science, Śiva is there. Where is the succession? Where is the rise? It is no rise.

Leave that aside. Now, go to the individual state, for instance, *sakala*. *Sakala* is subtler than *pṛthvī*. Go in individual *sakala* and in *sakala* also you have to find that *sakala* is not separate from Śiva. So, you have to feel the elevenfold science in *sakala*, from *sakala* to Śiva.

SCHOLAR: But not through *vikalpa*.

SWAMIJI: Not *vikalpa*, not *mantra*s, not *uccāra*.

SCHOLAR: You just recognize That.

SWAMIJI: You have to recognize It. It is the *śāmbhava* way of recognizing.

Now, you will put a question: "Why has [the fifteen-fold science] been explained later on in the *Tantrāloka*, in [the explanation of] *āṇavopāya*?" In fact, this is residing in the *āṇava* state. From *pṛthvī* to Śiva, this is residing in the *āṇava* state, but in order to feel that this *āṇava* state also is included in *śāmbhava*, he has explained that in [terms of] *āṇava* also. It is why he has explained here also: "*Saṁvitti phalabhedo'tra na prakalpyate*, the point is one, the goal is one for all." From the *śāmbhava* point of view, nothing is excluded. In *āṇava*,

499 Earth.

śākta is excluded, *śāmbhava* is excluded. In *śākta*, *śāmbhava* is excluded, *āṇava* is included. In *āṇava*, *śākta* is excluded, *śāmbhava* is excluded. In *śākta*, *āṇava* is included, *śāmbhava* is excluded. In what? In *śāktopāya*. In *śāmbhavopāya*, *śāktopāya* is included, *āṇavopāya* is included. This is the way of this fifteen-fold science. You have to perceive, when you are established in the *śāmbhava* state, you have not to exclude anything there. You have to include *śākta* there, you have to include *āṇava* there, you have to include worship there! You have to include that gross worship, *śrāddha*,[500] everything, what[ever] is a degraded thing in this universe, you have to include in that, in the *śāmbhava* state.[501]

JOHN: So this fifteen-fold *vidhi*, . . .

SWAMIJI: This is the fifteen-fold science that teaches you that way.

JOHN: . . . this is a practice in *śāmbhavopāya*.

SWAMIJI: This is *śāmbhavopāya*.

JOHN: Also practice in *āṇavopāya*?

SWAMIJI: No, no, no. It is to perceive fifteen in one. It is to perceive thirteen in one. It is to perceive eleven in one. It is not possible in *śāktopāya* or *āṇavopāya*.

JOHN: But then why is he, in explaining this in *āṇavopāya* later, . . . ?

SWAMIJI: Because the points are residing in *āṇavopāya*. The points are residing in *āṇavopāya*, so he has to explain that in [terms of] *āṇavopāya*.

JOHN: But this is clearly *śāmbhavopāya*.

SCHOLAR: This is recognition of those.

SWAMIJI: Yes.

JOHN: This is clear *śāmbhavopāya*.

SWAMIJI: It is only recognition. It is the Pratyabhijñā

500. A *havan* for the deceased.

501 "It is "degraded" from our viewpoint. From His viewpoint, it is not degraded." *Parātriśikā Vivaraṇa* (LJA archive).

school.[502]

JOHN: This.

SWAMIJI: Yes, the fifteen-fold science.

Audio 7 - 26:37

तस्माद्यथा पुरस्थेऽर्थे गुणाद्यंशांशिकामुखात्।
निरंशभावसंबोधस्तथैवात्रापि बुध्यताम् ॥ १९६ ॥

tasmādyathā purasthe'rthe guṇādyaṁśāṁśikāmukhāt /
niraṁśabhāvasaṁbodhastathaivātrāpi buddhyatām //196//

So, he has put this reference. Not a reference, an example:

For instance, *purasthe arthe*, this [*kongari*] is an object in front of you to be perceived. When you perceive it, you perceive it partly–you perceive this, you perceive this, you perceive this beauty, you perceive this, you perceive inside this fire, separately–then you perceive that this is a *kongari*, this is a fire pot. That [perception] is *niraṁśa bhāva*,[503] that is *śāmbhava*. This [*aṁśa bhāva*] is *āṇava*, this [particular] perceiving point is *āṇava*–you perceive like this, and this, this, this, all these separately.

SCHOLAR: *Aṁśāṁśikā*.[504]

SWAMIJI: *Aṁśāṁśikā*. And *niraṁśa bhāva*, when you perceive, "This is a *kongari*," that is *śāktopāya*. When you perceive, "I have seen the *kongari*" and you don't perceive the *kongari* also there, there you are in your own Self.

SCHOLAR: *Antarmukha bhāva*.[505]

---

502 The School of Recognition (Pratyabhijñā). "The word *pratyabhijñā* means, to spontaneously once again recognize and realize your Self. Here you have only to realize, you do not have to practice. There are no *upāyas* (means) in the Pratyabhijñā system. You must simply recognize who you are." *Kashmir Shaivism–The Secret Supreme,* 130.

503 Lit., the state (*bhāva*) without degrees (*niraṁśa*).

504 Share-by-share.

505 Introverted (*antarmukha*) state (*bhāva*).

SWAMIJI: *Antarmukhī bhāva*. When you perceive a lady in front of you, you are curious to see all her limbs, that is *āṇavopāya*. [When] you have perceived all her limbs as beautiful, or ugly, or anything else, this is *śāktopāya*. [When] you are extracted [from objective perception and remain] in your own nature [because you are satisfied in knowing that], "I have perceived her," that is *śāmbhava samāveśa*. So this is the way of the fifteen-fold science. *Tathaiva atrāpi budhyatām*, so, you should know, in this fiftyfold science also, the same way.

Audio 7 - 28:36

अत एवाविकल्पत्वध्रौव्यप्राभववैभवैः ।
अन्यैर्वा शक्तिरूपत्वाद्धर्मैः स्वसमवायिभिः ॥ १९७॥
सर्वशोऽप्यथ वांशेन तं विभुं परमेश्वरम्।
उपासते विकल्पौघसंस्काराद्ये श्रुतोत्थितात् ॥ १९८॥

ata evāvikalpatvadhrauvyaprābhavavaibhavaiḥ /
anyairvā śaktirūpatvāddharmaiḥ svasamavāyibhiḥ //197//
sarvaśo'pyatha vāṁśena taṁ vibhuṁ parameśvaram /
upāsate vikalpaughasaṁskārādye śrutotthitāt //198//

Ye tam vibhum parameśvaram upāsate, *ata eva*, so, those who worship that all-pervading Lord Śiva by means of aspects, by means of meditating on aspects, [they get entry in the aspect-holder, Lord Śiva].[506] For instance, [by meditating on] *avikalpatva* (the state of thought-lessness), *dhrauvya* (the state of *dhruvatā*; *dhruvatā* means, *anuttaratā*),[507] *prābhava* (the state of glory),[508] . . .*

SCHOLAR: "*Dhrauvya*" means?

506 As per Swamiji's translation of verse 199a.
507 Lit., the condition of being chief, principal, best, or excellent, on account of being *dhruva* (lit., fixed, firm, immovable, unchangeable, constant, lasting, permanent, eternal). In his translations of other texts, Swamiji defines *anuttara* as "unparalleled," "where there is no similarity," "the supreme state."
508 Lit., lordliness.

SWAMIJI: *Dhrauvya*: *dhruvasya bhāva*.

SCHOLAR: Permanence and supremacy. Permanence.

SWAMIJI: Permanence, yes. *Prābhava* means, *prabhu*, *prabhutā*.

SCHOLAR: Lordliness.

SWAMIJI: *. . . *vaibhavaiḥ* means, *aiśvarya* (His glory–*jñāna* and *kriyā*),[509] . . .*

DEVOTEE: Is there difference between "*prābhava*" and "*vaibhava*"? *Vaibhava* is "all-pervading glory."

SWAMIJI: All-pervading glory, and *prābhava* is the *samarthatā* of Lord Śiva.

SCHOLAR: His inherent capacity.

SWAMIJI: Capacity of possessing glories–that is "*prabhu*." "*Vibhu*" is, he who has got all-pervading glory.

SCHOLAR: So, *prābhava* is more transcendent than immanent.

SWAMIJI: Yes.

*. . . *anyairvā*, or *anyairvā dharmaiḥ*, or other aspects also, holding other aspects also in view–because all these aspects, *śakti rūpatvāt*, are no other than His energies–and His energies, those [that] are *svasamavāyibhiḥ*, absolutely eternally attached to Him (all these aspects), and some *sādhaka*s find Him *sarvaśa*, filled with all these aspects, *prathamāṁśena*, and some *sādhaka*s concentrate on Him partly, . . .

SCHOLAR: Yes, through one of these.

SWAMIJI: . . . through one of these [aspects], *vikalpaugha saṁskārādye śrutotthitāt*, by their own capacity of perceiving (*vikalpaugha saṁskāra*, by the impressions of their past capacity).

SCHOLAR: This is not *vikalpa saṁskāra* in the *śāktopāya*

---

509 *Vibhu* is, who has got all-pervading glory, which is all-knowledge (*jñāna*) and all-action (*kriyā*).

sense?[510]

SWAMIJI: No, no, no, no. *Vikalpaugha saṁskārāt*, by the impressions of their *vikalpa*s, of their imaginations. They imagine that, "My Lord is always permanent, eternal," "My Lord is all-pervading and nothing else," "My Lord is *prabhu*," "My Lord is *svātantra*," and so on. That is *vikalpaugha saṁskārāt*, by their own impressions of their *vikalpa*s as they have come to know from the *śāstra*s (*śrutotthitāt*).

Audio 7 - 32:06

ते तत्तत्स्वविकल्पान्तःस्फुरत्तद्धर्मपाटवात् ।

te tattatsvavikalpāntaḥsphurattaddharmapāṭavāt / *199a*

Those *sādhaka*s also, by their own imagination of meditating on these aspects of Lord Śiva, when these aspects get their fullness in meditation, they get entry in the aspect-holder, Lord Śiva.

SCHOLAR: *Tattat svavikalpāntaḥ sphurattad.*

SWAMIJI: *Tat tat svavikalpa*, by their own imagination, by their own impressions.

SCHOLAR: Through the intensity of these aspects . . .

SWAMIJI: Of these aspects.

SCHOLAR: . . . as they appear within their respective *vikalpa*s.

SWAMIJI: Respective *vikalpa*s. And those aspects, when they achieve fullness, . . .*

For instance, I meditate on the aspect of Lord Śiva as *prakāśa*,[511] but in the beginning It is *asphuṭa*.[512] In the beginning, I don't perceive that *prakāśa* face-to-face. I have to imagine only.

---

510 *Vikalpa saṁskāra* will be discussed in the fourth *āhnika*, which is the contemplative process wherein "only one thought should get awareness in continuity." *Tantrāloka* 4.3 (LJA archive).

511 The light of consciousness.

512 Not vivid.

*. . . after that imagination goes in a dense formation and that imagination appears in form, and then, when *prakāśa* appears to me in Its full bloom, then [I] get entry in the *prakāśa*-holder, Lord Śiva.

Audio 7 - 33:29

धर्मिणं पूर्णधर्मौघमभेदेनाधिशेरते ॥ १९९ ॥

dharmiṇaṁ pūrṇadharmaughamabhedenādhiśerate //199b
[not recited in full]

And you see, and they feel, that this *dharmi*, the holder of aspects, Lord Śiva, is not the holder of only a few aspects. *Pūrṇa dharmaugham*, all aspects are residing There. And *abhedanādhiśerate*, they become one with Him, and that is the *samāsya*.[513]

JOHN: That is the end of 199.

Audio 7 - 33:54

ऊचिवानत एव श्रीविद्याधिपतिरादरात् ।

ūcivānata eva śrīvidyādhipatirādarāt /

Vidyādhipati means, Bṛhaspatipāda. Bṛhaspatipāda was the greatest philosopher and the greatest devotee of Lord Śiva–Bṛhaspatipāda.[514]

SCHOLAR: Vidyādhipati.

SWAMIJI: Vidyādhipati, that is, Bṛhaspatipāda.

SCHOLAR: But he was a dualist, wasn't he? I thought Bṛhaspatipāda is a dualist. This *vidyādhipati* . . .

SWAMIJI: Yes, a dualist, but he was devoted to Lord Śiva, entirely!

SCHOLAR: But this doesn't sound like a dualist verse. This sounds like a monistic verse.

513 All aspects are combined in a state of fullness.
514 He is also known as the *guru* of the gods.

SWAMIJI: This is a monistic verse, yes. He was not just like the [dualist] of the Paśupāta dualists.[515] He had entry in Lord Śiva, and he was a master, and he was respected by Abhinavagupta. His name was respected by Abhinavagupta.

[Bṛhaspatipāda has corroborated this view by saying the following]:

Audio 7 - 34:52

त्वत्स्वरूपमविकल्पमक्षजा
कल्पने न वषयीकरोति चेत् ।
अन्तरुल्लिखितचित्रसंविदो
नो भवेयुरनुभूतयः स्फुटाः ॥२००॥

tvatsvarūpamavikalpamakṣajā
kalpane na viṣayīkaroti cet /
antarullikhitacitrasaṁvido
no bhaveyuranubhūtayaḥ sphuṭāḥ //200//

O Lord, these *anubhūtaya*s (these perceptions, objective perceptions) lying in the field of the universe–"This is a pot," "This is [spectacles]," "This is a sheet," "This is a bed," "This is a [microphone]," "This is a book"–*anubhūtaya*, these objective perceptions would never come into existence, O Lord, these objective perceptions would never come into existence, if the energy of the organs would not *sākṣātkāra*,[516] perceive, if these organs would not perceive Your nature, Your nature which is beyond thoughts, beyond imaginations, beyond perceptions, in the first [place].

So, "This is a *kongari*" ("This is a fire pot"), this is a vivid *anubhūti* (vivid perception) of this object, . . .*

SCHOLAR: Yes, *sphuṭa*.

SWAMIJI: *. . . and before that, there is something perceived

515 The dualistic Paśupāta school of Shaivism.

516 *Sākṣātkāra* is a technical term used in Shaivism to describe direct perception, often associated with direct perception of the Self, or direct realization.

in a subtle form, and before that, there is a subtler [form], and before that, there is a subtler [form], and the first point of this flow of perception, the first point, at the first point, resides Lord Śiva. That is *avikalpa*.[517] So, that *avikalpa* state of Lord Śiva is perceived first by the organs and then you perceive this object, this gross object. This is what he says in this [verse].

SCHOLAR: If that were not the case, they wouldn't appear!

SWAMIJI: They wouldn't appear at all in the external world!

SCHOLAR: That's what he is saying.

SWAMIJI: Yes. What is the subject we are explaining? The subject is *śāmbhavopāya*. So, this is *śāmbhavopāya*. You have not to perceive this *kongari* in this [gross objective] field. You have to perceive this *kongari* at that first start of [perception] and then you will enter in the *śāmbhava* state.

SCHOLAR: So, he is saying likewise here?

SWAMIJI: Yes, all these aspects, . . .

SCHOLAR: But this is *śāktopāya*.

SWAMIJI: No, it is *prasaṅgāt*.[518]

SCHOLAR: *Prasaṅgāt śāktopāya*.

SWAMIJI: All these aspects are leading to *śāktopāya* and *āṇavopāya*.

SCHOLAR: Yes, he introduces this *prasaṅga*.

SWAMIJI: The grossest is *āṇavopāya*, subtler is *śāktopāya*, and the subtlest, that [initial] point, is the *śāmbhavopāya* state. It is why Vidyādhipati is quoted here; Vidyāpati's *śloka* that the *śāmbhava* state is the state which is held first, and then the *śākta* [state] is held afterwards, and the *āṇava* [state] is held in the end.

JOHN: Well, in this practice here, where you enter through these aspects, imagining *prakāśa* or . . .

SWAMIJI: Yes. For instance, I give you a pinch. It is pinching. You feel that. In the beginning of the pinch, it is the

517 Thought-lessness, viz., *nirvikalpa*.

518 By intimate association, by extension.

śāmbhava state; in the end of the pinch, this is the *śāmbhava* state. In the center, it is *śāktopāya*, and [the pinching] won't be *āṇavopāya* because it is felt, it is *uccāra rahita vastu*.[519]

JOHN: But how is this *śāmbhavopāya* . . . ?

SWAMIJI: This [feeling] is *uccāra rahita vastu*, it is not seen. Whatever is felt is *śāktopāya*.

SCHOLAR: Because *sparśa* (touch) is more refined.

SWAMIJI: *Sparśa* is refined, yes. *Sparśa* is only felt, it is not seen. When you are in contact with that *sparśa*, your eyes close, . . .

SCHOLAR: It is like pure *pramāṇa* (cognition).

SWAMIJI: . . . you close your eyes, you close all your organs, you are in peace (laughter).

JOHN: Well, how is this imagining entering in *śāmbhavopāya*? This imagining. In these *śloka*s, where you imagine that aspect is . . .

SWAMIJI: No, this imagination will only take place in *śāktopāya*. This is *śāmbhavopāya*: *dharmiṇam pūrṇa dharmaugham*.[520]

SCHOLAR: That is the *śāmbhava samāveśa*.

SWAMIJI: *Śāmbhava samāveśa* is here.

SCHOLAR: But he says, "Through the intensity *(pāṭavāt)*,"[521] the gradual intensity grows, . . .

SWAMIJI: Gradually, gradually, yes.

SCHOLAR: . . . and eventually that non-discursive state comes–no thought.

SWAMIJI: Yes. So, Vidyādhipati is quoted here.

---

519 The thing (*vastu*) that defies (*rahita*) utterance (*uccāra*).
520 This line is from verse 199: "And you see, and they feel, that this *dharmi*, the holder of aspects (Lord Śiva) is not the holder of only a few aspects. *Pūrṇa dharmaugham*, all aspects are residing There."
521 From verse 199a.

Audio 7 - 39:46

तदुक्तं श्रीमतङ्गादौ स्वशक्तिकिरणात्मकम् ।
अथ पत्युरधिष्ठानमित्याद्युक्तं विशेषणैः ॥२०१॥

taduktaṁ śrīmataṅgādau svaśaktikiraṇātmakam /
atha patyuradhiṣṭhānamityādyuktaṁ viśeṣaṇaiḥ //201//

In the *Mataṅga tantra* also it is said, it is explained, that the *adhiṣṭhāna* (residence) of our Master is found in the collective state of His energies–the collective state, not the [partial] state. When you are meditating on His energies partly, one-by-one, that is not the real residence of Lord Śiva. The real residence of Lord Śiva is as he has told here: *pūrṇa dharmaugham*, all aspects are shining there, not only one–numberless! Lord Śiva's aspects are numberless, you can't imagine. That is *pūrṇa dharma*,[522] that is *śāmbhava*.

SCHOLAR: So the totality is *ahaṁ*[523] and what they have in common is *prakāśa-idaṁ*.[524]

SWAMIJI: Yes, *idaṁ*. *Atha patyur adhiṣṭhānam ityād-yuktam viśeṣaṇaiḥ*, these qualities have been explained for [indicating] Him.

Audio 7 - 41:16

तस्यां दिवि सुदीप्तात्मा निष्कम्पोऽचलमूर्तिमान् ।
काष्ठ सैव परा सूक्ष्मा सर्वदिक्कामृतात्मिका ॥२०२॥
प्रध्वस्तावरणा शान्ता वस्तुमात्रातिलालसा ।
आद्यन्तोपरता साध्वी मूर्तित्वेनोपचर्यते ॥२०३॥

tasyāṁ divi sudīptātmā niṣkampo'calamūrtimān /
kāṣṭhā saiva parā sūkṣmā sarvadikkāmṛtātmikā //202//
pradhvastāvaraṇā śāntā vastumātrātilālasā /
ādyantoparatā sādhvī mūrtitvenopacaryate //203//

522 The undifferentiated totality of aspects or qualities.
523 *Ahaṁ*, I-ness.
524 The light (*prakāśa*) of *idaṁ*, this-ness.

Tasyāṁ divi, in that *divi*, *tasyāṁ alaukikāyām śaktau*, . . .

SCHOLAR: In that transcendent energy.

SWAMIJI: . . . in that transcendental energy resides that supreme [Being who is] filled with *prakāśa*–Lord Śiva (*tasyām divi sudīptātmā*). And that Lord Śiva is *niṣkampa*, without any movement; He does not get changed by the mere agitation of the energies.

SCHOLAR: He is *anacka*.[525]

SWAMIJI: *Anacka*.

Acala mūrtimān, His *mūrti*[526] is *acala*, always residing as one. *Saiva parā kāṣṭhā sūkṣmā*, that subtle state is the state of Lord Śiva, which is found *sarvadikkā* (everywhere), and which is found filled with nectar (*amṛtātmikā*). Not only that. *Pradhvastāvaraṇā*, all veils are over, all veils, all coverings, are vanished, have vanished there. *Śāntā* (appeased state), this is the most appeased state of Lord Śiva. *Vastu mātra atilālasā*, bent upon . . . This state is fond of That state (*vastu mātra atilālasā*). You are fond of John, John is fond of Denise, Denise is fond of Stephanie, I am fond of Denise or I am fond of you, but He is fond of Himself! That is *vastu mātra atilālasā*, He is very fond of Himself only (laughter).

SCHOLAR: So this energy, which is *vastu mātra atilālasā*, is like *lelihāna*,[527] . . .

SWAMIJI: *Lelihāna*, yes.

SCHOLAR: . . . Its always drawing everything into Itself.

SWAMIJI: Yes. And *ādyantoparatā*, there is no end, there is no beginning; *ādi anta uparatā*, ending and beginning is over there. And *sādhvī*, This is the embodiment of simplicity (*sādhvī* means, the embodiment of simplicity), there is no

---

525 Lit., soundless (without a vowel), "*anackaṁ*" refers to "that universal energy which is moving in such a velocity that movelessness takes place–*anackaṁ*. *Anackaṁ* means, without movement." *Vijñāna Bhairava–The Manual for Self Realization*, 9.

526 Conceived form.

527 Lit., frequently licking or darting out the tongue. *Lelihāna* denotes enjoyment by way of tasting or absorbing (viz., destruction).

crookedness, there is no fraud. It is *sādhu*. *Sadhu* means, . . .

SCHOLAR: Innocent.

SWAMIJI: Not "innocent." Simple. There is no crack. There is no . . .

SCHOLAR: Pure.

SWAMIJI: Pure! Absolutely pure. And this is the *mūrtitvena upacaryate*, this is the *mūrti* of Lord Śiva. This is said to be the *mūrti* of Lord Śiva.

SCHOLAR: This is "conceived as" (*upacaryate*).

SWAMIJI: Yes, "conceived."

Audio 7 - 44:24

तथोपचारस्यात्रैतन्निमित्तं सप्रयोजनम् ।

tathopacārasyātraitatnimitaṁ saprayojanam /204a

This is only *upacāra*,[528] an *upacāra* with some purpose. The purpose is Lord Śiva, the achievement of Lord Śiva. Perceiving Lord Śiva is the purpose. The *upacāra* is His energies. It is *upacāra*. For instance, *mukhyārtha bādha*.[529] Take one *upacāra* [such as] *mukhyārtha bādha*: "*Gaṅgāyām ghoṣaḥ*, there is a house in the Gaṅgā."[530] But in the Gaṅgā you can't construct a house. [The house] must be on the shore. So *mukhyārtha* is condemned there. In the same way, [His] energies are only to be condemned in the long run. The energy-holder is to be possessed. You have to perceive [His] energies with this purpose–not with this purpose that you will perceive [His] energies–you have to perceive [His] energies with this purpose that you will perceive the energy-holder.

SCHOLAR: That you will be That.

528 An approach; usage, manner of speech; metaphor or figurative application.

529 From Jayaratha's commentary. *Mukhyārtha bādha* is an apparent contradiction or absurdity (*bādha*) with respect to the primary meaning or sense of a word (*mukhyārtha*).

530 The Ganges river.

SWAMIJI: Yes, you will be one with That, yes.

Audio 7 - 45:48

तन्मुखा स्फुटता धर्मिण्याशु तन्मयतास्थितिः ॥२०४॥

tanmukhā sphuṭatā dharmiṇyāśu tanmayatāsthitiḥ //204b//

Because, by those energies, by the energies only, you get entry in the energy-holder, and in a very short period.

SCHOLAR: They become your energies.

SWAMIJI: Yes.

Audio 7 - 46:09
Audio 8 - 00:00

त एव धर्माः शक्त्याख्यास्तैस्तैरुचितरूपकैः ।
आकारैः पर्युपास्यन्ते तन्मयीभावसिद्धये ॥२०५॥

ta eva dharmāḥ śaktyākhyāstaistairucitarūpakaiḥ /
ākāraiḥ paryupāsyante tanmayībhāvasiddhaye //205//

This is the 205th [*śloka*].

All those aspects, which are no other than His energies, are worshipped or meditated on with many forms, with many various forms. The purpose of worshipping them is just to become one with Lord Śiva. This is why [His] energies are being worshipped.

Audio 8 - 00:44

तत्र काचित्पुनः शक्तिरनन्ता वा मिताश्च वा ।
आक्षिपेद्धवतासत्त्वन्यायाद्दूरान्तिकत्वतः ॥२०६॥

tatra kācitpunaḥ śaktiranantā vā mitāśca vā /
ākṣipeddhavatāsattvanyāyāddūrāntikatvataḥ //206//

These energies sometimes are meditated [upon] collectively and sometimes are meditated [upon] one-by-one. And these energies, in the end, *ākṣipet*, carry you to that point which is near Lord Siva or which is just away from Lord Siva, by the *sāmānya sattva* and *viśeṣa sattva* [respectively].[531] *Sāmānya sattva* is all-pervading *sattva*.

SCHOLAR: Universal Being.

SWAMIJI: Universal.

> For instance, *bukharis* (stoves). By this [word] "stoves" you hold all these stoves existing in this universe–when you say "stove." Or "heater," when you say "heater," by this word you hold all the heaters existing in this universe. If you say "cow" you hold all the cows. But, by this word "cow," you don't hold men, you don't hold a [microphone], you don't hold a stove–you hold only the classes of cow.

Or "It is a *dhavata*." *Dhavata* is a kind of tree (*dhavata*).

SCHOLAR: Not white, *dhava dhavatā*.

> **SWAMIJI:** *Dhavata* is a white tree. It is a particular tree. It is called "*kharakula*" in Kashmiri, the tree of *khar*. This is some particular tree. When you say "*dhavata*," you hold only those *dhava* trees, not those [trees] which are not *dhava*. For instance, you say "apple tree." By saying "apple tree" you hold all the apple trees, [but] you don't hold peaches, the tree of peaches.

When you say "existence," by this [word] "existence" (*sattva*, being), by "being," you hold everything that is existing in this universe. This is *mahā sāmānya sattva*. This is called "*mahā sāmānya sattva*."

SCHOLAR: The great universal.

SWAMIJI: Yes.

SCHOLAR: Universal of universal.

SWAMIJI: So, that universal state is [held] by that [word]

---

531 By meditating upon the universal (*sāmānya*) Being (*sattva*) or upon a particular (*viśeṣa*) being (*sattva*), respectively.

"being" and *śāktopāya* and *āṇavopāya* are [held] by this: "This is [a pair of spectacles]." "This is *my* specs," it is *āṇavopāya*. "This is specs," it is *śāktopāya*.

JOHN: This is existing.

SWAMIJI: "Existing" is *śāmbhavopāya*, because that "existence" is in this also, in this also, in this also, in this–everywhere! Existence is everywhere found. It is the *śāmbhava* state. The *śāmbhava* state is a collective perception, *śākta* is a partly-collective perception, and *āṇava* is a perception through parts.

SCHOLAR: "*Sattva*"[532] tells you nothing about things.

SWAMIJI: Only existence. And *dūrāntikatvataḥ*, *ākṣipet dhavatā sattva nyāyāt*, by the *nyāya* (by the conception) of "*dhavata*"and "*sattva*,"[533] . . .*

SCHOLAR: "Analogy."

SWAMIJI: Yes, "analogy."[534]

*. . . *dūrāntikatvataḥ*, those are far away from the perception of Lord Śiva, . . .

What?

SCHOLAR: Like those attributed to "*dhavata*."

SWAMIJI: Like "*dhavata*."

*. . . and "*sattva*" is very near to the state of Lord Śiva. And if you meditate on *icchā śakti*, *jñāna śakti*, *kriyā śakti*, you are meditating in the field of *śāktopāya*. If you meditate only in *kriyā śakti*, you are meditating in *āṇavopāya*. If you meditate on *svātantrya*, [you are meditating in *śāmbhavopāya*]. *Svātantryā* is found everywhere! *Svātantrya* is not only in [the energy of] will; it is in will, it is in knowledge, [it is] in action. In each and every object of the universe, *svātantrya* exists.

SCHOLAR: So there he transcends *upāya*.

SWAMIJI: Yes.

---

532 The word "existence" or "being."

533 Viz., *viśeṣa sattva* and *sāmānya sattva*.

534 Referring to the meaning of "*nyāya*."

SCHOLAR: Nothing to be achieved there.

SWAMIJI: Yes (agreement).

Audio 8 - 05:32

तेन पूर्णस्वभावत्वं प्रकाशत्वं चिदात्मता ।
भैरवत्वं विश्वशक्तीराक्षिपेद्व्यापकत्वतः ॥ २०७ ॥

tena pūrṇasvabhāvatvaṁ prakāśatvaṁ cidātmatā /
bhairavatvaṁ viśvaśaktīrākṣipedvyāpakatvataḥ //207//

So, what is the conclusion of all this discussion?

"*Pūrṇa svabhāvatva*" is *cidrūpatva.*[535] *Pūrṇa svabhāvatva*, which is *prakāśa rūpatva*[536] and *cid rūpatva* (filled with consciousness), and which is *bhairavatva*,[537] and [that] *bhairavatva, viśva śaktir ākṣipet*, consumes all the energies existing in the universe, digests [them] in Its own nature, because *vyāpakatvataḥ*,[538] because all energies . . .*

If they are partly, by parts, meditated [upon], that will go to *āṇavopāya*. If they are [meditated upon] partly-collectively and partly in parts, that is *śāktopāya*. If they are meditated [upon] collectively in *svātantrya*, that is *śāmbhavopāya*.

*. . . and that Bhairava *rūpatva*–It is only one–*pūrṇa svabhāvatvam*, *prakāśatvam*, *cidātmatva*, *bhairavatva*, the state of Bhairava, which is filled with *prakāśa*, which is filled with consciousness, which is filled with fullness, that state of *prakāśa*, *ākṣipet*, consumes or implies all the energies existing in this universe because [of His] being pervading everywhere–Lord Śiva.

Audio 8 - 07:07

सदाशिवादयस्तूर्ध्वव्याप्त्यभावादधोजुषः ।
शक्तोः समाक्षिपेयुस्तदुपासान्तिकदूरतः ॥ २०८ ॥

535 The fullness of Self (*pūrṇa svabhāvatva*) is the state of having the form of consciousness (*cidrūpatva*).

536 The state of having the form of the light of consciousness.

537 Inherent to the state of Bhairava.

538 That state, i.e., of Bhairava, is all-pervading (*vyāpakatva*).

sadāśivādayastūrdhvavyāptyabhāvādadhojuṣaḥ /
śaktīḥ samākṣipeyustadupāsāntikadūrataḥ //208//

But the *deva*s (gods), which are Sadāśiva, Īśvara, Śuddhavidyā (*mantra pramātā*), all these energies, *ūrdhva vyāpti abhāvāt*, they have not [the capacity] for *ūrdhva vyāpti*, they can't pervade above their state of being. They can pervade those [elements] which are below them. So, *ūrdhva vyāpti* is not there existing. *Ūrdhva vyāpti* lies only in Lord Śiva; *ūrdhva vyāpti*, pervasion [upward].

SCHOLAR: Because He is at the top.

SWAMIJI: Yes, He is the "topest" top. So, *adhojuṣaḥ śaktīḥ samākṣipeyuḥ*, those [lower] energies are held by these beings (Sadāśiva, Īśvara, and Śuddhavidyā); those energies are held which lie only in the lower state.[539] And *tat upāsa*, so, the meditation (*upāsanā*, the means of meditation) is *antika dūrataḥ*, some are near and some are away from [the state of Lord Śiva]. *Tat upāsa*, so, *upāsanā* is *antika* (near) and *dūrata* (away). And those *upāsanā*s done in *śāktopāya* and *āṇavopāya* are away from this existence of Lord Śiva, and the *upāsanā*s done in the *śāmbhava* state are near.

Audio 8 - 09:01

इत्थं-भावे च शाक्ताख्यो वैकल्पिकपथक्रमः ।
इह तूक्तो यतस्तस्मात् प्रतियोग्यविकल्पकम् ॥२०९॥

itthaṁ bhāve ca śāktākhyo vaikalpikapathakramaḥ /
iha tūkto yatastasmāt pratiyogyavikalpakam //209//

But, the readers must be wonderstruck [as to] why, in the subject of the *śāmbhava* state, I have explained the energies which exist in *śākta*, *śāktopāya*. Why have I explained the energies that are to be explained in *śāktopāya* [here]? In [my

539 Inferior (*adhojuṣa*) *śakti*s. See Appendix 2 (p372) on the 36 *tattva*s for explanation of the energies, or elements, below Sadāśiva, Īśvara, and Śuddhavidyā.

explanation of] *śāmbhavopāya*, I have explained the [lower] energies, but the [lower] energies ought not to be explained in the explanation of *śāmbhavopāya*. This *śāktopāya* is put forth in the field of *śāmbhavopāya* for this purpose that *tasmāt pratiyogya avikalpakam*, from that, one would get diverted towards that fullness of Lord Śiva and leave those [lower] energies, the state of [the lower] energies, aside. For that purpose, we have put *śāktopāya* in-between as *prasaṅga*.

JOHN: "*Prasaṅga*" means?

SWAMIJI: *Prasaṅga* means . . .

SCHOLAR: "By extension."

SWAMIJI: "By extension," when you go far [from the point] and you explain some other subjects also, you touch other subjects also. So, we have touched the subject of *śāktopāya* also in the explanation of *śāmbhava* with this purpose that that [lower energy] must be ignored there. The purpose of meditating on [the lower] energies [is that they] must be ignored. Only one energy is to be meditated upon in the *śāmbhava* state and that is *svātantrya*–that is "existence," that is not "specs."

SCHOLAR: So, the opposite is defined by its opposite?

SWAMIJI: Opposite, yes. The opposite is defined just to keep it away from your being.

Avikalpapathārūḍho yena yena pathā viśet . . . the next [*śloka*], 210th:

Audio 8 - 11:20

अविकल्पपथारूढो येन येन पथ्या विशेत् ।
धरासदाशिवान्तेन तेन तेन शिवोभवेत् ॥२१०॥

avikalpapathārūḍho yena yena pathā viśet /
dharāsadāśivāntena tena tena śivībhavet //210//[540]

The person who is established on the path of thoughtlessness (*nirvikalpa*), who is established there, well-establish-

540 See *Special Verses on Practice*, (LJA archives), verse 70.

ed, then afterwards it does not matter to him by which way he moves out. He may move through the *śāmbhava* way, he may move in the *śākta* way, he may move in the *āṇava* state, he may move from *dharā* to Sadāśiva (from earth to the Sadāśiva state), *tena tena śivībhavet*, all those ways will lead him to the *śāmbhava* state in the end. For him, everything is *śāmbhava*. It is why previously it has been explained that *śāmbhava* is threefold: *āṇava-śāmbhava*, *śākta-śāmbhava*, and *śāmbhava-śāmbhava*. *Śāmbhava* is *śāmbhava*, *śākta* is *śāmbhava*, and *āṇava* is also the *śāmbhava* state. When you go in the depth of understanding, what is actually the basis of *āṇava*, what is actually the basis of *śākta*, what is that?

JOHN: Lord Śiva.

SWAMIJI: *Śāmbhava*. *Śāmbhava* is everywhere.[541]

Nirmale . . . the next [*śloka*]:

Audio 8 - 12:57

निर्मले हृदये प्राग्र्यस्फुरद्भूम्यंशभासिनि।
प्रकाशे तन्मुखेनैव संवित्परशिवात्मता ॥२११॥

nirmale hṛdaye prāgryasphuradbhūmyaṁśabhāsini /
prakāśe tanmukhenaiva saṁvitparaśivātmatā //211//

541 Likewise, "For that *yogi* who is established in *anupāya* (lit., no means), all *upāya*s become *anupāya* for him. *Śāmbhavopāya* becomes *anupāya* for him. If he conducts with *śāmbhavopāya*, for him it is as good as *anupāya*. If he conducts *śāktopāya*, it is just like *anupāya* for him. All *upāya*s become the same, take the same position of the *upāya*s. Now, the actual position of these *upāya*s is, when you are established in *āṇavopāya*, you are always in *āṇavopāya*. If you conduct with *śāktopāya*, that will become *āṇavopāya* to you. If you think of *śāmbhavopāya* or *śāktopāya* or *anupāya*, you [may] think [of engaging in these practices], but it will be *āṇavopāya* for [you]. When you go ahead another step in *śāktopāya*, then *āṇavopāya* is *śāktopāya* for [you], *śāktopāya* is *śāktopāya* for [you], and *śāmbhavopāya* takes the position of *śāktopāya* for [you], and *anupāya* also takes the position of *śāktopāya* for [you]." Ibid., vs. 70. See Appendix 25 (p418) for explanation of *upāya*s.

When your heart and mind are purified, and when your heart[542] is residing *prāgrya sphurat bhūmya*, residing on the top of each and every movement [of perception] or on the first start of each and every movement [of perception], when your heart is residing on the top, . . .*

For instance, you perceive these specs. Don't go ahead. Go back. Go back to your perception abode, and you will only see, [but] you won't see any thing. There will be only the force of seeing, and that force of seeing is the *śāmbhava* state. Just see, [but] don't see any thing.[543]

JOHN: What *mudrā* is this?

DENISE: *Khecarī*?

SWAMIJI: It is just like *khecarī*[544]–the *bhairavī mudrā*.[545]

---

542 "The "heart" does not means this [physical] heart. The "heart" means, the energy of consciousness (*saṁvit śakti*)." *Parātriśikā Laghuvṛtti* (LJA archives).

543 "For instance, I want to see Denise. Before that, I see only a phantom figure of Denise, and before that, I see only the seeing force, and before that, I see only my Self, and that is *nirvikalpa*." Swamiji's commentary from verse 180.

544 "What is real *khecarī mudrā*? When you are treading the way of totality (*kulamārgeṇa*), you must see the totality in a piece of the totality. Take one part of the universe and see the whole universe existing there. That is the way of totality. You must understand that everything is filled with completion. If only one individual being is there, you must understand and you must feel that in that one individual being, all individuals exist. Take, for example, one grain of rice. See the power that exists in that grain of rice. This one grain of rice has the power of producing not only a hundred plants, but thousands, millions, billions of plants. Innumerable plants exist in that one grain of rice. So, one part of the world is complete in itself. You must, when treading the way of totality, feel the voidness of differentiated perceptions in each and every being. This, in the real sense, is *khecarī*. It is this *khecarī mudrā* that is to be practiced. So, the reality of this *khecarī mudrā* is just as it is explained in the *Tantrasadbhāva*: "becoming one with supreme consciousness." *Shiva Sutras–The Supreme Awakening*, 2.5.

545 "You will find Her as one with Bhairava by keeping your organs

. . . nirmale hṛdaye . . .

That is what he says: *prāgryasphuradbhūmyaṁśabhāsini*, that which is residing on the *prāgrya bhūmi*, the first state [of perception], the first state of movement (*prāgrya* means, the [topmost] force).

SCHOLAR: But also the first in the sense of *śāmbhavopāya*, that first moment (*ādya parāmarśa*).

SWAMIJI: The first moment, *ādya parāmarśa*, that is *prāgrya*.

. . . nirmale hṛdaye prāgrya sphurad bhūmi aṁśa bhāsini prakāśe, and that is *prakāśa*,[546] *tanmukhenaiva saṁvit para-śivātmatā*, and by that means[547] you get entry in that supreme state of Lord Śiva, which is only knowledge.

JOHN: Only knowledge.

SWAMIJI: No, It is knowledge. Only Being, the Being of knowledge–*saṁvit*.

JOHN: *Saṁvit*.

SWAMIJI: *Saṁvit*.

Audio 8 - 14:58

एवं परेच्छाशक्त्यंशसदुपायमिमं विदुः ।
शाम्भवाख्यं समावेशं सुमत्यन्तेनिवासिनः ॥२१२॥

---

in action, and then by establishing your self inside, observing the action within. This is Bhairava *mudrā*." Ibid. 1.6 "Just keep your eyes wide open and your breath in a fix, "Should I move it out or should I take it in?"–not going out, not coming in. That you will come to know, this state of *mudrā* you will come to know, in *cakita mudrā*. *Cakita mudrā* is the "pose of astonishment." Actually, this is Bhairava *mudra*, because you do not breathe in and out. This is Bhairava *mudrā*. Your eyes are wide open. Your mouth is open. You don't breathe." *Vijñāna Bhairava–The Manual for Self-Realization*, verse 77, Dhāraṇa 52.

546 The light of God-consciousness.

547 By the means of maintaining awareness on the initial movement of any perception (*ādya parāmarśa, prāgrya, prakāśa*) with a purified heart and mind (*nirmale hṛdaye*).

evaṁ parecchāśaktyaṁśasadupāyamimaṁ viduḥ /
śāmbhavākhyaṁ samāveśaṁ sumatyantenivāsinaḥ //212//

So, thus, all the disciples of Sumatinātha explain . . .*
In fact, Sumatinātha was not [Abhinavagupta's] immediate master. Śambhunātha was his immediate master.

JOHN: Yes, in the Kula system–Śambhunātha.

SWAMIJI: Śambhunātha was his immediate master in this system, in the Kula system, and Śambhunātha's immediate master was Somadeva, and Somadeva's immediate master was Sumatinātha. So, Sumatinātha was the great-grandmaster of Abhinavagupta.[548]

SCHOLAR: And his [master] was someone . . . was Bhairava.

SWAMIJI: Yes, Bhairava.

SCHOLAR: But [Jayaratha] says, *"kaścid śrīmān vibhur bhairava." Kaścit*, so he means, some person.

SWAMIJI: Some person.

SCHOLAR: Like maybe called Bhairavānanda or something.

SWAMIJI: Yes, yes.

*. . . thus: *parecchāśaktyaṁśa sat upāyam*, this [*upāya* is] *sat upāyam* (*sat upāyam* means, nice means, best means, true means, and delicious means; *sat* means "delicious" also, "which is beautiful"), this is the delicious and beautiful means. What is the delicious means?

JOHN: *Śāmbhava.*

---

548 The Kula System was introduced in Kashmir in the beginning of the 5th century A.D. by Śrī Macchandanātha. Later, in the 9th century, because its teachings had become distorted, it was reintroduced by Sumatinātha. In the line of masters that followed from Sumatinātha, Somanātha was his disciple. Śambhunātha was the disciple of Somanātha, and the great Abhinavagupta was the disciple of Śambhunātha. See *Kashmir Shaivism–The Secret Supreme*, 19.133 See verse 7 for Abhinavagupta's invocation to Macchandanātha as head/founder of the Kula System.

SWAMIJI: *Sāmbhava*. So this way, that supreme-delicious means, which is the best means, is explained by the disciples of Sumatinātha as *śāmbhava*, *śāmbhava samāveśa*. And the history [of the line of masters] I have given you already.[549] Why has [Abhinavagupta] put "*sumati ante nivāsinaḥ*"?[550] [Because] Sumati[nātha] was the chief, the great-grandmaster, of the Kula system, of Abhinavagupta.[551]

THE MEANS PERTAINING TO ŚĀKTOPĀYA (213-219)

Audio 8 - 17:20

शाक्तोऽथ भण्यते चेतोधी-मनोहंकृति स्फुटम ।
सविकल्पतया मायामयमिच्छादि वस्तुतः ॥२१३॥

śākto'tha bhaṇyate cetodhī-manohaṁkṛti sphuṭam /
savikalpatayā māyāmayamicchādi vastutaḥ //213//
[incomplete audio]

Now we will explain the means of *śāktopāya*. Here, you find the functioning of *citta*, intellect, mind, and ego.

JOHN: *Citta* here means "individualized consciousness," is it?

SWAMIJI: Individual consciousness, yes. It is just like *smṛti* (memory, remembrance). Remembrance is functioning there, intellect is functioning, mind is functioning, and *ahaṁkāra* is functioning, in *śāktopāya*.

SCHOLAR: This "*ceta*" is not a separate word in "*ceto dhī*

549 See *Kashmir Shaivism–The Secret Supreme* 19, "The Schools of Kashmir Shaivism."

550 Among (*ante*) Sumati's disciples (*nivāsinaḥ*).

551 Here, Abhinvagupta is also referring to his own master, Śambhunātha, as a disciple of Sumatinātha, and therefore directly related to the Kula *saṁpradāya* (lineage).

manohaṁkṛti sphuṭam." *Citta* in "*cetasaiva vicintayan.*"[552]

SWAMIJI: No, "*ceta*" is a separate word.

SCHOLAR: Yes, yes. So this is misprinted in the text because they have a hyphen here after *ceto*.

SWAMIJI: No, it is a compound word: *cetodhī-manohaṁkṛti*. There is also, after *dhī*, there is also a dash.

SCHOLAR: Yes.

SWAMIJI: It can go like this. This is a compound word: *cetodhī-manohaṁkṛti*. [It is a] *dvanda* [compound].[553]

SCHOLAR: Yes. But what is the difference between *ceta* and *mana* here?

SWAMIJI: That is what I [will] tell you. *Ceta* means "memory, remembrance," *dhī* is "intellect," *mana* is "mind," *ahaṁkṛti* is "ego." These are functioning in *śāktopāya*. So it is vividly residing in the field of *māyā*, because there you find *vikalpa*s, all-round *vikalpa*s. In memory there is *vikalpa*, [as well as] in the intellect, in the mind, and in *ahaṁkāra*. *Vikalpa*s are all-round functioning there [in *śāktopāya*].

JOHN: So, what is the best way to translate "*vikalpa*" here in terms of these four: memory, intellect, mind, and . . . ?

SWAMIJI: Various perceptions, differentiated perception. Differentiated perception of thought is functioning there. Although it is *māyāmayi*[554] because of that, but the goal is *śāmbhava* for this [*upāya*] also; *icchādi vastutaḥ*, in fact, the goal of this is *śāmbhava*.[555]

SCHOLAR: "*Ādi*" is here.

SWAMIJI: *Ādi*, the goal, the abode, the resting state, the resting place.

SCHOLAR: "*Icchādi vastutaḥ*," not "*icchādya śakti*."

---

552 Quoting a line from verse 168.

553 *Dvanda* is a compound word that refers to one or more objects that could otherwise be connected by the conjunction "and."

554 Lit., consisting of illusion.

555 That is, the state of thought-lessness supported and maintained by the means of the will (*icchā*).

SWAMIJI: Not *icchā, jñāna*, and *kriyā*–no. *Icchā ādi*–"*ādi*" is *icchā*. *Icchā śaktir eva ādir yasya*. *Cetaḥ dhī mano ahaṁkṛti, sphuṭam kṛtvā* (*kriyā viśeṣaṇa*, an adverb), *sphuṭam kṛtvā ceto dhī manohaṁkṛti bhavati, savikalpatayā māyāmayam*, because there are differentiated perceptions of the means, so it is not beyond *māyā*, [it is not] beyond illusion. But, in fact, the goal of [*śāktopāya*] also is *icchā*. The goal of this is . . . this means is also *icchā-śāmbhava*.[556]

The next [*śloka*]:

Audio 8 - 21:05

अभिमानेन संकल्पा ध्यवसायक्रमेण यः ॥
शाक्तः स मायोपायोऽपि तदन्ते निर्विकल्पकः ॥२१४॥

abhimānena saṅkalpādhyavasāyakrameṇa yaḥ /
śāktaḥ sa māyopāyo'pi tadante nirvikalpakaḥ //214//

By the functioning of the ego (*abhimān*), by the functioning of *saṅkalpa* (the mind), *adhyavasāya krameṇa*, and by the successive perception of *adhyavasāya* (the intellect, the intellectual process), . . .

SCHOLAR: Process of intellectual judgement.

SWAMIJI: . . . this *śāktopāya*, although it is *māyopāya*, although it is residing in the field of *māyā*, but in the end is *nirvikalpa*.[557] In the end, this also, this means is also, *nirvikalpa*, one with *śāmbhava*.

Audio 8 - 21:54

पशोर्वै याविकल्पा भूर्दशा सा शाम्भवी परम् ।
अपूर्णा मातृदौरात्म्यात्तदपाये विकस्वरा ॥२५५॥

paśorvai yāvikalpā bhūrdaśā sā śāmbhavī param /
apūrṇā mātṛdaurātmyāttadapāye vikasvarā //215//

---

556 *Icchopāya* (the means of the will) is another name for *śāmbhavopāya*.
557 The state of thought-lessness.

In the state of *paśudaśā*, at the state of *paśu*, at the state of limited individuality, there is also the state of *nirvikalpa*. At the individual state also, there is the state of *nirvikalpa* existing. Although It is existing, the *nirvikalpa* state [is existing] at that state also (*sā śāmbhavī*, that is *śāmbhavī*, that is one with Śiva, that is one with *śāmbhavopāya*), *param apūrṇa*, because, as there is *mātṛdaurātmya*, the functioning of the individual being is there, the individual being is functioning there, the universal Being is not functioning there–there also, in that *nirvikalpa* state.

For instance, when you pass from wakefulness to the dreaming state, in the center there is the *nirvikalpa* state. Although that *nirvikalpa* state is concerned with Śiva, but there is *mātṛdaurātmya*[558] because you are functioning it, the individual being is functioning that state, so that state, although it is Śiva, the state of Śiva, it is not complete, it is *apūrṇa*.

JOHN: *Apūrṇa*.

SCHOLAR: *Daurātmya*,[559] opposite of *mahātmya*.[560]

SWAMIJI: Yes, *daurātmya*, opposite to *mahātmya*.

JOHN: Is that because *tirodhāna śakti* is playing there?[561]

SWAMIJI: *Tirodhāna śakti* is, *māyā śakti* is, playing there.[562] And *tadapāye*, when that *daurātmatā*, when that is removed, *vikasvarā*, then it shines just like the *śāmbhava* state.

---

558 The condition of limited (*daurātmya*) knowership (*mātṛ*).

559 Lit., bad-heartedness, wickedness, depravity.

560 Lit., magnanimity, high-mindedness; exalted state or position, majesty, dignity.

561 Concealment (*tirodhāna*) is one of the five great acts of Lord Śiva. *Tirodhāna śakti* is "taking you, absolutely carrying you, away from That light. It is *tirodhāna śakti* that makes [people] become atheists. [But] this is the real indication of *tirodhāna śakti*: showing signs of being elevated and internally not [being] elevated." *Tantrāloka* 14.16 (LJA archive).

562 "*Māyā* is not limited. *Māyā* can conceal and reveal also. *Tirodhāna śakti* will conceal only. For those who are elevated souls, *māyā* is just *svātantrya śakti* for them." Ibid., 9.155.

SCHOLAR: By means of a trick.

SWAMIJI: Yes, a trick. Yes, a trick (laughter).

JOHN: A trick of awareness. So this *māyā śakti*, or *tirodhāna śakti*, is what makes this gap, this center, non-full.

SWAMIJI: That gap is the point, but it is shrunk. It does not pervade forward and backward. It is [at a] standstill there because of *mātṛdaurātmya*, so it is incomplete.

SCHOLAR: There is no power of awareness.

SWAMIJI: It has not power of awareness.

JOHN: So then *māyā śakti* makes that . . .

SWAMIJI: When *māyā śakti* is removed there, it becomes *vikasvarā*, it blooms forth in the center, backward and forward.

SCHOLAR: Perhaps we can translate *daurātmya* as "impotence."

SWAMIJI: Impotence, impotence of awareness.

Audio 8 - 25:00

एवं वैकल्पिकी भूमिः शाक्ते कर्तृत्ववेदने ।
यस्यां स्फुटे परं त्वस्यां संकोचः पूर्वनीतितः ॥२१६॥
तथा संकोचसंभारविलायनपरस्य तु ।
सा यथेष्टान्तराभासकारिणी शक्तिरुज्ज्वला ॥२१७॥

evaṁ vaikalpikī bhūmiḥ śākte, kartṛtvavedane /
yasyāṁ sphuṭe paraṁ tvasyāṁ saṁkocaḥ pūrvanītitaḥ 216
tathā saṁkocasaṁbhāravilāyanaparasya tu /
sā yatheṣṭāntarābhāsakāriṇī śaktirujjvalā //217//

So, he concludes the substance of this *śāktopāya* now.

Evaṁ vaikalpikī bhūmi śākte, in this state of *śāktopāya* (this is a state concerned with perceptions, differentiated perceptions, *vikalpas*), *śākte* (you should put a comma there [after] *evaṁ vaikalpikī bhūmiḥ śākte*), *yasyāṁ*, *kartṛtva vedane sphuṭe*, in which *śāktopāya* this knowledge and action is vividly found there–the power of knowledge (the energy of knowledge) and the energy of action are found there, are already there (*yasyāṁ sphuṭe*)–*param tu*, but (*param tu* means "but") *asyām pūrva nītitaḥ saṁkocaḥ*, but it is shrunk. That power of knowledge and the power of action are shrunk there.

SCHOLAR: So this "*vaikalpikī bhūmi*" is as . . .

SWAMIJI: It is *śāktopāya*.

SCHOLAR: . . . *śāktopāya* when, say, he is taking, for example, wine and he thinks, "This is not gross wine, but [rather] *ānanda* Bhairava."[563]

SWAMIJI: For instance, "I am Lord Śiva! I am Lord Śiva!" This is *vikalpa bhūmi*, this is *śuddha vikalpa bhūmi*.[564]

SCHOLAR: And in *kriyā*, too?

SWAMIJI: Yes, in *kriyā*, too, yes.

SCHOLAR: So when, for example, he is taking that *surā*,[565] he thinks, "This is *ānanda* Bhairava, . . . "

SWAMIJI: Yes.

SCHOLAR: ". . . not the juice of grapes," that's *vikalpa*, too.

SWAMIJI: Yes, but these are *vikalpa*s there. So, in fact, that *śāmbhava* state is not vividly found there, it is shrunk because of these adjustments, because *śāktopāya* won't be adjusted without *vikalpa*, without *ceta* (without mind), without the function of all these. You have to adjust them on that path, on the path of *śāktopāya*. In *śāmbhavopāya*, no adjustment is there.

JOHN: So what was that example you were just going to give? You just said, "I am Lord Śiva!" and you were going to give . . .

SWAMIJI: Yes, this is also *vikalpa*: "I am Śiva. This whole universe is My own glory."

SCHOLAR: "*Sarvo mamāyam eva.*"

---

563 The bliss of Bhairava.

564 The state of pure *vikalpa*.

565 Wine.

SWAMIJI: Yes, *"sarvo mamāyam vibhava."* So these are shrunk; these two, actions and knowledge, are shrunk there in *śāktopāya*. So when–the next [*śloka*]–*tathā saṁkocasaṁbhāra vilāyana*, so when a *sādhaka* is bent upon removing all these shrinking states, shrunken states, . . .

SCHOLAR: Contracted, shrunken.

SWAMIJI: . . . *sa yatheṣṭāntarābhāsakāriṇi*, that supreme energy blooms forth, that internal supreme energy blooms forth all-round, and you find the state of *śāmbhava* existing in full glory (*sā yatehṣṭāntarābhāsa kāriṇī śaktirujjvalā*).

Nanu . . . this is a question:

Audio 8 - 28:52

ननु वैकल्पिकी किं धीराणवे नास्ति तत्र सा ।
अन्योपायात्र तूच्चाररहितत्वं न्यरूपयत् ॥२१८॥

nanu vaikalpikī kiṁ dhīrāṇave nāsti tatra sā /
anyopāyātra tūccārarahitatvaṁ nyarūpayat //218//

Now he puts the question: This adjustment of differentiated perceptions is also found in *āṇavopāya*. What is the difference between *āṇavopāya* and *śāktopāya* then?

JOHN: Right.

SWAMIJI: There is no difference between *śāktopāya* and *āṇavopāya*. *Āṇavopāya* is the same as *śāktopāya*. In *āṇavopāya* you find differentiated perception functioning. In *śāktopāya*, differentiated perception [is also functioning as] you told just now. *Nanu vaikalpikī dhī kim āṇave nāsti*?

SCHOLAR: "Is it not also . . . ?"

SWAMIJI: "Is it also not found in *āṇavopāya*?" It is! There you must put a note of interrogation. For that, he answers now: *Tatra sā anyopāyā*, in *āṇavopāya*, . . .*

It is the answer. From "*tatra*," it is the answer.

SCHOLAR: *Samādhi*.

SWAMIJI: *Samādhi*.[566]

*. . . *tatra sā anyopāya*, *tatra*, in *āṇavopāya*, that intellectual adjustment is *anyopāyā*, takes place along with other agents, along with other agencies, along with the agency of *mantra*s, *uccāra*s, breath, *sthāna*, *kalpanā*, everything (*anyopāya* means, there are other adjustments also found). *Atra tu*, in *śāktopāya* (*atra tu*, in *śāktopāya*), *uccāra rahitatvaṁ*, Lord Śiva has explained [that] there is no *uccāra*.[567]

JOHN: "*Uccāra*" means?

SWAMIJI: There is no recitation of breath. There is no reciting of breath or reciting of *mantra*s or . . .

SCHOLAR: Etcetera.

SWAMIJI: Etcetera.

SCHOLAR: So, you said that when you are in *śāmbhavopāya*, you adjust all the other *upāya*s in *śāmbhavopāya*. When you are in *śāktopāya*, *āṇavopaya* is adjusted. Is that right? When you are in *śāktopāya*, *āṇavopāya* can be embraced within that. So, even if that *sādhaka* is using those other methods, say, in *bahir arcana*[568] or something, he maintains that *śākta* awareness.

SWAMIJI: No, no.

JOHN: Didn't you say one time that a *sādhaka* who has passed through *āṇavopāya* and has reached the stage of *śāktopāya*, . . .

SWAMIJI: *Śāktopāya*, yes.

JOHN: . . . he can also practice practices in *āṇavopāya* still?

SWAMIJI: [He can practice] *āṇavopāya* and be in the *śākta* state. That I have told, yes. That is absolutely correct.

SCHOLAR: So that explains how you can have these outer rituals in *śāktopāya*.

SWAMIJI: Yes.

---

566 The justification of a statement.
567 *Uccāra* literally means "utterance."
568 External (*bahir*) worship (*arcana*).

SCHOLAR: In the twenty-ninth and twenty-eighth [*āhnikas*], there are rituals to do because . . .

SWAMIJI: Yes, yes. That is quite true. There is no . . .

SCHOLAR: There is no contradiction.

SWAMIJI: *Atra tu uccāra rahitatvaṁ nyarūpayat*, in *śāktopāya*, Lord Śiva has explained that there is no *uccāra*.

JOHN: Just thought.

SWAMIJI: Just thought.

SCHOLAR: No awareness in breath.

SWAMIJI: "*Uccāra*" is the word there in the *Mālinīvijaya Tantra*,[569] but you must not [take it as] "*uccāreṇa rahitam.*" It is not "*uccāreṇa rahitam.*"[570]

SCHOLAR: "*Uccāraiḥ.*"

SWAMIJI: "*Uccāraiḥ rahitam*"[571] must be the *vigraha* there.[572] There is not only *uccāra* avoided [in *śāktopāya*]. There is *mantra* avoided, there is . . . everything is avoided there.

SCHOLAR: So it is *upalakṣaṇam*.[573]

SWAMIJI: Yes.

JOHN: One for everything.

SCHOLAR: Yes.

SWAMIJI:

Audio 8 - 32:31

उच्चारशब्देनात्रोक्ता बह्वन्तेन तदादयः ।
शक्त्युपाये न सन्त्येते भेदाभेदौ हि शक्तिता ॥२१९॥

uccāraśabdenātrokta bahvantena tadādayaḥ /
śaktyupāye na santyete bhedābhedau hi śaktitā //219//

569 See verse 168 which is taken from *Mālinīvijaya tantra*, 2.22.
570 Instrumental singular (*uccāreṇa*).
571 Instrumental plural (*uccāraiḥ*).
572 The resolution of a compound word into its constituent parts.
573 The act of implying something that has not been expressed, implying any analogous object where only one is specified.

This word "*uccāra*" here in "*uccāra rahitam*" does not mean "*uccāreṇa rahitam.*" Only *uccāra* is not excluded because *bahvantena–katham bhūtena uccāra śabdena bahvantena*–it is *bahu vacana.*[574] "*Uccāraiḥ rahitam*" means "*uccāra rahitam.*" It is not "*uccāreṇa rahitam.*" You must not explain it as "*uccāreṇa rahitam*" (in the singular case). No, [you must explain it] in the plural case. "*Uccāraiḥ rahitam*" [is the meaning of] "*uccāra rahitam.*" So, *uccāra*, *karaṇa*, *dhyāna*, *varṇa*, all of these are excluded there [in *śāktopāya*].

Bahvantena tadādayaḥ; *tadādaya*, all those [practices] which are functioning in *āṇavopāya*, *uccārādayaḥ śaktyupāye na santi*, *ete tadādayaḥ*, all these are not found in *śāktopāya* (*śaktyupāye na santi*), *hi*, because (*hi* means, because) *śaktitā bhedābhedau*, there is dualistic functioning and non-dualistic functioning also in *śāktopāya*.

JOHN: What is non-dualistic functioning in *śāktopāya*?

SWAMIJI: Because it is only thought. [It is the] process of thought. It is not an objective process.

JOHN: But isn't thought *bheda*?[575] Thought is *vikalpa*.

SWAMIJI: No, it is not *vikalpa* there [in the state of *śāktopāya*][576] because you have not to take the support of *vikalpas*.[577] Only [one] thought with awareness, that is *śāktopāya*.[578] For instance, "I am Lord Śiva," this thought [in continuity], this is no *vikalpa*. *Ahaṁpratyavamarśo yaḥ prakāśātmāpi vāgvapuḥ nāsau vikalpaḥ*,[579] this is not *vikalpa*.

SCHOLAR: When it becomes intense, then it's not *vikalpa*.

SWAMIJI: Intense with universality, universal thought, it is

574 Plural number.

575 Dualistic.

576 As opposed to the practice of *śāktopāya* in which thoughts (*vikalpas*) are functioning.

577 "Differentiated thought must not leak there, they should not come, otherwise [the state of] *śāktopāya* won't exist." *Tantrāloka* 5.5 (LJA archive).

578 "Just [one] thought, one-pointedness of one thought, any thought." Ibid. In the 4th *āhnika*, this is called *vikalpa saṁskāra*.

579 From Jayaratha's commentary on *Tantrāloka* 3.25.

not *vikalpa*.

JOHN: It is not.

SWAMIJI: It is not *vikalpa*.

JOHN: So then which aspect of this . . . ?

SWAMIJI: It is decided in Shaivism that *aham vimarśa*[580] is not *vikalpa*. Where there is "I" and "this" opposite, when there is the functioning of "I"-*vimarśa* with the opposite of "this," that is *vikalpa*. When there is no opposition, that is *nirvikalpa*.

SCHOLAR: So, Swamiji, when you are centering in *śāktopāya*, at first that is *vikalpa* because it is outside, but when that is real *draṣṭṛtvam*[581] . . .

SWAMIJI: Yes, because you have to take the support [of *vikalpa*] first just for entry.

JOHN: So that's the *bheda*[582] aspect.

SWAMIJI: That is *bheda*.

JOHN: And then when you enter, that's *abheda*.

SWAMIJI: That is *abheda*.[583]

SCHOLAR: When that center is inside, . . .

SWAMIJI: That is *abheda*.

SCHOLAR: . . . *svasthāne vartanam*.[584]

SWAMIJI: *Svasthāne vartanam*, yes. Look at this, look at this–this is *bheda*.

JOHN: *Bheda*, these two things.

SWAMIJI: And observe the center–that is *abheda*.

JOHN: *Abheda*.

580 Self-awareness.
581 The subjective state.
582 Dualistic, differentiated.
583 Non-dual, monistic, undifferentiated, viz., *nirvikalpa*,
584 Lit., standing in or occupying one's own condition.

THE MEANS PERTAINING TO ĀṆAVOPĀYA (220-232)

SWAMIJI:

Audio 8 - 35:51

अणुर्नाम स्फुटो भेदस्तदुपाय इहाणवः ।
विकल्पनिश्चयात्मैव पर्यन्ते निर्विकल्पकः ॥२२०॥

aṇurnāma sphuṭo bhedastadupāya ihāṇavaḥ /
vikalpaniścayātmaiva paryante nirvikalpakaḥ //220//

This "*aṇu*" (the individual) means that it is vividly residing in the differentiated world, differentiatedness, and the means functioning there is called *āṇavopāya*. *Vikalpaniścayātmaiva*, and there is the functioning of *vikalpa* and *niścaya*; this is the intellectual field and differentiated perception (the field of differentiated perception).[585] What? *Āṇavopāya*.

JOHN: *Āṇavopāya*.

SWAMIJI: But in the end, *paryante*, this *āṇavopāya*, too, is *nirvikalpakaḥ*, it is carried to *śāmbhavopāya*.[586]

Now a question. Next, [*śloka*] 221:

Audio 8 - 36:52

ननु धी-मानसाहंकृत्पुमांसो व्याप्नुयुः शिवम् ।
नाधोवर्तितया तेन कथितं कथमीदृशम् ॥२२१॥

nanu dhī mānasāhaṁkṛtpumāṁso vyāpnuyuḥ śivam /
nādhovartitayā tena kathitaṁ kathamīdṛśam //221//

585 *Niścaya*: the intellectual field; *vikalpa*: differentiated perception.
586 The thought-less (*nirvikalpa*) condition of the *śāmbhavopāya* state.

This is a question now. He puts a question.

Intellectual functioning, the functioning of the mind, and the functioning of *ahaṁkāra*, *śivam pumāṁso na vyāpnuyu*, *pumāṁsa dhī mānasāhaṁkṛt*, intellectual functioning, the functioning of the mind, and the functioning of *ahaṁkāra*, that are pertaining to *puruṣa*, the individual being, cannot pervade this state of Śiva because of its residing in the lower field (*na adho vartitayā*).

SCHOLAR: *Na vyāpnuyu.*

SWAMIJI: [They] cannot pervade the state of Śiva. Where there is the functioning of the intellect, the functioning of the mind, and the functioning of *ahaṁkāra*, to that individual being, how can those things pervade the state of Śiva? Because they reside below Śiva, below the state of Śiva (*adhovartitayā*). *Tena kathitam kathamīdṛśam*, so how have you dared to say that *paryante nirvikalpakaḥ*, [that] *āṇavopāya* also, in the end, carries you to the *śāmbhava* state? It is absolutely incorrect. This is the question. Now the answer.

Ucyate . . . [now the] *samādhi*:[587]

Audio 8 - 38:39

उच्यते वस्तुतोऽस्माकं शिव एव तथाविधः ।
स्वरूपगोपनं कृत्वा स्वप्रकाशः पुनस्तथा ॥२२२॥

ucyate vastuto'smākaṁ śiva eva tathāvidhaḥ /
svarūpagopanaṁ kṛtvā svaprakāśaḥ punastathā //222//

The answer for this question is that, for us who are Shaivites (*asmākaṁ*), *śiva eva tathāvidhaḥ*, this is the state of Śiva that pervades in *śāktopāya*, that pervades in *āṇavopāya*. Śiva has become Śakti, and Śiva has become the individual being, *śiva eva tathāvidhaḥ svarūpa gopanam kṛtvā*, just to conceal His own nature. Just to conceal His own nature, He has become an individual being. In fact, *svaprakāśaḥ punastathā*, He reveals again His own nature according to His

587 Justification of a statement.

independent will (*svātantrya śakti*). He conceals and reveals. *Asmākaṁ*, this is our theory. *Śiva eva gṛhīta paśubhāva*,[588] the individual being is not other than Śiva. Śiva has become the individual being.

It is not only said in our monistic school of thought, but in the dualistic school of thought of Shaivism, this is also said:

Audio 8 - 40:13

द्वैतशास्त्रे मतङ्गादौ चाप्येतत्सुनिरूपितम ।
अधोव्याप्तुः शिवस्यैव स प्रकाशो व्यवस्थितः ॥२२३॥
येन बुद्धि-मनोभूमावपि भाति परं पदम् ॥२२४॥

dvaitaśāstre mataṅgādau cāpyetatsunirūpitam /
adhovyāptuḥ śivasyaiva sa prakāśo vyavasthitaḥ //223//
yena buddhi manobhūmāvapi bhāti paraṁ padam //224//

In the *Mataṅga śāstra*, which is an absolutely dualistic thought of Shaivism, in that *Mataṅga śāstra* also it is explained that, when Śiva resides in the lower states, the lower field of individuality, in that lower field also, His real nature of consciousness is existing unharmed. It is why (*yena*, it is why) *buddhi manobhūmāvapi*, in *samādhi*[589] also, [which takes place in] the state of the intellect [and in] the state of the mind, . . .

> Do you know the state of the intellect and the state of the mind when I go into *samādhi*? In this body, I am in this body, [I am an] individual being, and I go in *samādhi*, I enter in my *samādhi* (trance), and I realize the state of God, but that realization is incorrect realization. Is it not? Because it is realized in individuality. It is realized in the

588 Jayaratha references this quote from the 5th verse of the *Paramārthasāra*.
589 Intense absorption or a kind of trance; the state of profound meditation. See Appendix 23 (p416) for an explanation of *samādhi* in Kashmir Shaivism.

state of *manobuddhi bhūmi.*[590] This is the intellectual state of the individual and the thought-full state of the individual. It is not the thought-full state of Śiva and the intellectual state of Śiva because intellectual thought cannot exist There.

. . . but *paraṁ padam*, that supreme state shines there also! Where?

JOHN: In that *samādhi.*

SWAMIJI: In that *samādhi*, which is residing in individuality, not in the universal state.[591] What is the cause of that? The cause of that is that in the individual state also, that supreme consciousness is residing.

JOHN: So does this mean that individual *samādhi* is limited?

SWAMIJI: Individual *samādhi* is incorrect *samādhi*. How can it be possible? How can it take place?

JOHN: Is this in all *upāya*s, *śāmbhavopāya* also, or just in *āṇavopāya*, in limited *aṇu*?

SWAMIJI: In *āṇavopāya* and in *śāktopāya*.

JOHN: Not *śāmbhavopāya*.

SWAMIJI: *Śāmbhavopāya* is not *samādhi*, there is not *samādhi*. *Śāmbhavopāya* is, you only [maintain] awareness, in and out. In the *śāmbhava* state, you don't "enter." There is no entry. That is *vikāsa*.

JOHN: Expansion.

SCHOLAR: That's why Shaivism is different.

SWAMIJI: Yes (laughs).

---

590 In the field (*bhūmi*) of the mind, intellect.

591 Individual *samādhi* takes place in the state of *sakala*, *pralayā-'kala*, and *vijñānākala*. Universal *samādhi* begins from the state of *śuddhavidyā*. See Appendix 23 (p416) for *samādhi* and Appendix 10 (p394) for the Seven Perceivers. See also *Kashmir Shaivism–The Secret Supreme*, "The Seven States of the Seven Perceivers (*Pramātṛns*)."

JOHN: So, in *śāmbhavopāya*, this is the expansion of your nature into everything.

SWAMIJI: Yes, everything.

JOHN: So *śāktopāya* and *āṇavopāya* . . .

SWAMIJI: . . . *āṇavopāya* is limited.

JOHN: Those are the only places where you have *samādhi*.

SWAMIJI: And it is incorrect *samādhi*. It is incorrect *samādhi* but, when it is incorrect *samādhi*, should we take it for granted that the perception there is also incorrect? No, the perception is correct! The perception of Lord Śiva, Śiva's existence, there is correct, because actually Lord Śiva is residing everywhere, in *samādhi* and out.

SCHOLAR: But this is *dvaita śāstra*.[592]

SWAMIJI: *Dvaita śāstra* also explains this. *Dvaita śāstra* also, not only we.

SCHOLAR: Yes, but it puzzles me how a dualist can say that something can be somewhere without being there. I mean, if Śiva is in the mind, how can He not be that?

SWAMIJI: *Yena buddhi manobhūmā*, the state of the mind and the state of the intellect is a limited state. In that limited state also that Śiva appears.

SCHOLAR: How do they see that? How do the dualists see that? From a Shaivite point of view . . .

SWAMIJI: In *samādhi*.

SCHOLAR: But how do they understand that philosophically? From a Trika point of view, it is absolutely clear, but from a dualist's point of view . . .

SWAMIJI: No, they perceive the state of *samādhi*, that intense bliss, intense *ānanda*.

SCHOLAR: Śiva appears there by His grace for them.

SWAMIJI: Yes.

JOHN: So they see Śiva as completely other. They under-

592 Dualistic texts.

stand Siva as being completely other, the dualists, . . .

SWAMIJI: Yes, other.

JOHN: . . . yet He penetrates their own awareness.

SWAMIJI: Yes.

SCHOLAR: But He is *adhovyā*, yes, He's *adhovyā vyāptaḥ* . . .

SWAMIJI: *Adhovyāptuḥ śivasyaiva sa prakāśe vyavasthitaḥ*, when Śiva is *adhovyāpti*,[593] when Śiva pervades in the limited state of the universe, the limited state of being–what is that limited state of being? The limited state of being is *samādhi*–but that *prakāśa*[594] is existing there also.

SCHOLAR: So they don't believe that Śiva is *adhovyāpta* all the time? Do they believe that Śiva is pervading what is below Him all the time or only in the moments of grace when He reveals Himself?

SWAMIJI: Only these two lines [from verse 223] are from the *Mataṅga* [*śāstra*], not this [line from verse 224]. This is our conclusion of this. The *Mataṅga śāstra* says that, "*adhovyāpti* [*śivasyaiva sa prakāśe vyavasthitaḥ*]," Śiva does not remove His *prakāśa*; although Śiva is residing in the lower states also, but that *svaprakāśa*, His real nature of being, is existing there also. The conclusion of the Shaivite is, "*yena buddhi manobhūmāvapi bhāti paraṁ padam*," when we enter in *samādhi*, that *paraṁ pada*[595] is shining there.

JOHN: Even though it's limited; even though we are limited.

SWAMIJI: Even though [that *samādhi*] is not correct. It can't be! How can that supreme state of Lord Śiva appear in your heart, only in this much place? It is universal!

Audio 8 - 46:35

द्वावप्येतौ समावेशौ निर्विकल्पार्णवं प्रति ।
प्रयात एव तद्रूढिं विना नैव हि किंचन ॥२२५॥

593 Pervading (*vyāpti*) what is below (*adhaḥ*).
594 The light of God consciousness.
595 The supreme abode.

dvāvapyetau samāveśau nirvikalpārṇavaṁ prati /
prayāta eva tadrūḍhiṁ vinā naiva hi kiṁcana //225//

So, the conclusion of this is that these two *samāveśās* (these two, *āṇava* and *śākta*, *āṇavopāya* and *śāktopāya*), *nirvikalpa araṇavaṁ prati prayāta eva*, are already established in the ocean of *nirvikalpa*, in the ocean of *śāmbhava*. Their existence is established in the ocean of *śāmbhava*.

SCHOLAR: Not "they lead towards" (*prayātaya*).[596] Not *prayāta*, "they lead towards that, they end up in that."

SWAMIJI: *Nirvikalpārṇavaṁ prati prayātaḥ.*

SCHOLAR: They move towards that.

SWAMIJI: Yes. They have entered there (*prayātaḥ*)

SCHOLAR: *Pratiḥ*,[597] *ābhi mukhye.*[598]

SWAMIJI: *Ābhi mukhye*,[599] yes.

SCHOLAR: In the sense that they end up in that. Finally they lead in . . .

SWAMIJI: Finally, yes, because *tadrūḍhiṁ vinā naiva hi kiñcana*, that which is not established there is not existing, cannot exist.

SCHOLAR: So *śāmbhavopāya* is both the goal of those *upāya*s and it's also the *garbha*,[600] the . . .

SWAMIJI: Abode.

SCHOLAR: Yes, that which enables them to . . .

SWAMIJI: Yes. Now he gives a reference of the *Mālinīvijaya* [*tantra*]:

Audio 8 - 48:07

संवित्तिफलभिच्चात्र न प्रकल्प्येत्यतोऽब्रवीत् ।
कल्पनायाश्च मुख्यत्वमत्रैव किल सूचितम् ॥२२६॥

596 Arrived at, come to.
597 Towards, near to.
598 Jayaratha's commentary.
599 Turned towards, facing; going near, approaching.
600 Lit., womb.

saṁvittiphalabhiccātra na prakalpyetyato'bravīt /[601]
kalpanāyāśca mukhyatvamatraiva kila sūcitam //226//

The fruit of these *upāyas*, the fruits are not differentiated. The means are differentiated (*saṁvitti* means, the means). The means are differentiated but the meant is not differentiated. *Ityata abravīt*, it is not explained by me [Abhinavagupta], it is explained by Lord Śiva in the *Mālinīvijaya* [*tantra*]. And *kalpanāyāśca mukyatvam atraiva kila sūcitam*, this *kalpanā*[602] that you should not take this [notion] that there is differentiated fruit from these differentiated means, *atraiva kila sūcitam*, it is pointed out in the *Mālinīvijaya tantra*. *Kalpanāyaḥ mukhyatvam na prakalpya*; *kalpanāyaśca mukhyatvam* means, not suggesting, not suggesting differentiated fruit. He has given stress to it.

SCHOLAR: He has stressed this . . . ?

SWAMIJI: He has stressed this point. On this point he has stressed.

SCHOLAR: This fact of *kalpanā*.

SWAMIJI: [That this] *kalpanā* should not be adjusted. This [state of the meant] is *mukhyatā*. That is *amukhyatā*, the differentiated means is *amukhya*, it is not predominant. Predominance is one-pointed, the one-pointed goal of all these *upāyas*.

SCHOLAR: Why does he say "*kalpanāyaśca mukhyatvam*"?

SWAMIJI: *Kalpanāyaśca*, this *kalpanā*, this *kalpanā* that, "There are differentiated means [and that] there are differentiated goals also of these differentiated means."

SCHOLAR: That is *mukhya*? You said that conception that there are different is . . . that is *amukhya*.

SWAMIJI: *Na prakalpya*. *Na prakalpya iti kalpanāyāḥ*.

SCHOLAR: Ah, right.

---

601 "*Saṁvittiphalabhedo'tra na prakalpyo . . .*," *Mālinīvijaya tantra* 2.25a.

602 Notion, idea.

SWAMIJI: *Na prakalpya iti kalpanāyāḥ*, not this *kalpanā* (*na prakalpya*). He has given stress to "*na kalpanā*": you should never think of that! Because [Jayaratha] has put *saṁvittīphalabhedo'tra na prakalpyo manīṣibhiḥ*, those who are *manīṣa*, those who are *yogi*s, they should not adjust this thought in their mind that, "From these various means, you get various fruits." One fruit will be achieved and that is the state of Śiva.

Audio 8 - 50:49

विकल्पापेक्षया योऽपि प्रामाण्यं प्राह तन्मते ॥
तद्विकल्पक्रमोपात्तनिर्विकल्पप्रमाणता ॥२२७॥

vikalpāpekṣayā yo'pi prāmāṇyaṁ prāha tanmate /
tadvikalpakramopāttanirvikalpapramāṇatā //227//

There is another section of philosophers. They say that you have to adjust *vikalpa*s first, then you'll get entry in the *nirvikalpa* state. But Shaivites do not adjust like that.

JOHN: What does that mean, "adjust *vikalpa*s"?

SWAMIJI: For instance, you know *paḍtāl.*[603] "Two plus two is equal to four." This is one *kalpanā*. This is correct. This is *nirvikalpa*. Two plus two is four. Is it not four?

SCHOLAR: Yes, when you realize that, that's . . .

SWAMIJI: That is *nirvikalpa*.

SCHOLAR: Yes.

JOHN: Why is that . . . ?

SWAMIJI: But how? How two plus two is four? So we–just give me a pencil–we say, "This is one, this is one (adjust), this is one, this is one–one, two, three, four–this is four." So this is *kalpanā*. This [investigation] is *āṇavopāya* and *śāktopāya*. This *kalpanā* is *āṇavopāya* and *śāktopāya*. [The conclusion that] two plus two is four is *śāmbhavopāya*. It is granted [that] two

603 From the Hindi expression *jāñca paḍtāl,* i.e., to investigate, analyse, inquire, etc.

plus two is four. But how?

DEVOTEE: One, one, one, one.

SWAMIJI: But how?

JOHN: One, one, one, one.

SWAMIJI: This is *āṇavopāya*. This is the way of *āṇavopāya* and *śāktopāya*.

SCHOLAR: And *śāmbhavopāya* is *maṇijñānīvat*.

SWAMIJI: *Maṇijñānīvat*, yes.[604]

JOHN: So this *vikalpa* then, other systems say to adjust *vikalpa* . . .

SWAMIJI: No, they say that you can't say, "two plus two is four," unless you do like this first: one, one, . . . [First] you enter in *āṇavopāya*, you enter in *śāktopāya*, and then you can enter in the *śāmbhava* state in the end.

JOHN: In the end. In other words, the end of these states is not . . .

SWAMIJI: But we do not accept that! This is not our way of perception. Our way of perception is, first entry in *śāmbhava*[605] and then entry in *śākta* and *āṇava*[606] afterwards.

SCHOLAR: From the real point of view.

SWAMIJI: Yes, from our point of view. This is what he says. *Vikalpāpekṣayā yo'pi prāmāṇyaṁ*, that person also, that philosopher also, who says, who proves, that an object can be proved by adjusting *vikalpa*s, and that the object will reside in the end and get entry in *nirvikalpa*,[607] . . .

> For instance, "What is this? What is this? What is this? What is this? What is this? What is this? What is this? Oh, this is a cat." "What is this? What is this?," all this adjustment is *ānavopāya* and *śāktopāya*, and in the end you perceive it is

604 Like (*vat*) the condition of a *maṇijñānī* (knower of jewels). See also commentary on *śloka*s 179b and 180a above and *śloka* 228 below.

605 Viz., *nirvikalpa* (thought-lessness).

606 Viz., *vikalpa* (differentiated thought).

607 Viz. the *śāmbhava* state.

a cat (this is *śāmbhavopāya*).

SCHOLAR: That's what they believe.

SWAMIJI: That is what they believe. We don't believe that. We believe that, first the cat [is perceived],[608] and then all these limbs and all those functions [of the cat are perceived].

SCHOLAR: They think you can get the whole by adding the parts.

SWAMIJI: Yes, by adding parts. They think that.

SCHOLAR: It is not possible.

SWAMIJI: . . . *vikalpa apekṣayā yo'pi prāmāṇyaṁ prāha*, that person also, that philosopher also, who proves that by adjusting *vikalpa*s you'll get entry in the *nirvikalpa* state, *tanmate api*, in his theory also, *vikalpa krama upatta nirvikalpa pramāṇatā*, in his theory also, this is accepted. In that theory also, that after functioning in *vikalpa*s, you get entry, in the end, in *nirvikalpa*. So *nirvikalpa* is the goal. From their point of view also, *nirvikalpa* is the goal. So, from our point [of view], it is the goal [that is] already there.

Audio 8 - 55:04
Audio 9 - 00:00

रत्नतत्त्वमविद्वान्प्राङ्-निश्चयोपायचर्चनात् ।
अनुपायाविकल्पाप्तौ रत्नज्ञ इति भण्यते ॥२२८॥

ratnatattvamavidvānprāṅniścayopāyacarcanāt /
anupāyāvikalpāptau ratnajña iti bhaṇyate //228//

In the beginning, the jeweler who is an incomplete, who is not a trained, how can he be[come] a trained? *Niścaya upāya carcanāt*, that observing the valuation of jewels, . . .

JOHN: The evaluation?

SWAMIJI: . . . the valuation of jewels, he has to confirm

608 Viz., in the *nirvikalpa* state.

through tests, through various tests of jewels. And his master infuses in his thought that, "You must test like this, you must test like this, and then you will come to know that this costs this much, the value of this jewel is this much." So, [these tests are] for [one who] is ignorant in the beginning, [for] that who is ignorant in the beginning. *Ratna tattvam avidvānprāg*, in the beginning, he does not know the valuation of that jewelry, jewels, so he has to put tests, various tests, for confirmation. *Niścaya upāya carcanāt*, when he confirms in the end, and he becomes a master on that confirmation, *anupāya avikalpa-aptau*, then he gets entry in the *nirvikalpa* state (or *śāmbhava* or *anupāya*). And then, when a particular jewel is to be tested, there is no need for him to test. Just one glance will do, and he will say, "This costs two *lakhs* rupees" or "This costs one *lakh* rupees."[609] But the one who is ignorant in the beginning, he has to produce tests. He can't say like this. The one who says like this is residing in the *śāmbhava* state. The one who says by tests resides in *śāktopāya* and *āṇavopāya*. This is the difference.

SCHOLAR: Or like *sahṛdaya*, it goes straight to *rasa*.[610]

SWAMIJI: Straight to *rasa*, yes.[611]

---

609 See also commentaries on *śloka*s 179b and 180a, and *śloka*s 183b and 184a and their commentaries.

610 *Sahṛdaya*: lit., with the heart [of awareness]; *rasa*: the best or finest or prime part of anything, essence; the taste or character of a work, the feeling or sentiment prevailing in it. Abhinavagupta has given importance to *sahṛdaya* in his writings on aesthetic experience (*Dhyanāloka locaṇa*). Swamiji says that, "*Sahṛdaya* is that person whose heart is enhanced with joy and glamour and excitement. He is fortunate whose heart is like that." *Parātriśikā Vivaraṇa* (LJA archive)

611 "When there is beautiful music going on, or some soft or beautiful touch of some beautiful object, or some smell of the fragrance of some scent, and when you are absolutely attentive to it with awareness, then you feel the expansion of excitement in your heart. And that expansion of excitement in your heart is called the energy of *ānanda* (bliss) of Lord Śiva. And by that energy, one gets strengthened, one's heart gets strengthened. For instance, one becomes "full of

JOHN: So then in Shaivism, only the master can exist. You are not a master until you are in *śāmbhavopāya*.[612]

SWAMIJI: Yes, that is quite true. This is the meaning of this *śloka*: *ratna tattvam avidvānprāk*, first he does not know the valuation of *ratna* (a jewel). *Niścaya upāya carcanāt*, when he goes through all these tests, *anupāya avikalpāptau*, and in the end, he gets establishment in the *nirvikalpa* state of *anupāya*, [then] *ratnajña iti bhaṇyate*, it is said that he is a real, he knows jewelry.

SCHOLAR: He knows what that jewel is.

SWAMIJI: Yes. So, for him, there is no need to try, there is no trial. He can say like this.

Audio 9 - 03:08

अभेदोपायमत्रोक्तं शाम्भवं शाक्तमुच्यते ।
भेदाभेदात्मकोपायं भेदोपायं तदाणवम् ॥२२९॥

abhedopāyamatroktaṁ śāmbhavaṁ śāktamucyate /
bhedā bhedātmakopāyaṁ bhedopāyaṁ tadāṇavam //229//

So, in this field of the means, in this field of the world of the means, *abhedopāya*[613] is called *śāmbhava* (*abhedopāyaṁ atra śāmbhavaṁ uktam*), and *śāktopāya* is *bhedābhedopāya* (this is partly dualistic, partly non-dualistic), *bhedopāyaṁ tadāṇavam*, and *āṇavopaya* is absolutely dualistic.

JOHN: Isn't there a point in *āṇavopāya* which is non-dualistic? After your explanation, I see how in *śāktopāya* there is *bheda-abheda*, but why in *āṇavopāya* is there no *abheda*? I mean, you enter into that awareness at some point through God's grace.

---

heart" (*sahṛdaya*). When there is no heart, then you do not get any feeling in music or in touch or in scent, smell, good smell. When there is heart, then you can feel that fragrance, the excitement of a fragrance, or the excitement of touch, or excitement in music." *Tantrāloka* 3.209-210 (LJA archives).

612 This comment will be verified in verse 234.

613 Lit., non-dual or monistic means.

SWAMIJI: But then you enter in the *śāmbhava* state. Then you are not in *āṇavopāya*; the residence in *āṇavopāya* is over.

SCHOLAR: The *samāveśa* is . . .

SWAMIJI: Yes, "*samāveśa*" is the word.

SCHOLAR: *Upāya* and *samāveśa* are different slightly there.

SWAMIJI: Yes, *āṇavopāya* is something and the *samāveśa* is something [else]. *Samāveśa* is one in each and every *upāya*–*samāveśa*–and the means are different.

SCHOLAR: *Upāya* in Shaivism is not different from *upeya*.[614] That is why these two words are used.

Audio 9 - 04:30

अन्ते ज्ञानेऽत्र सोपाये समस्तः कर्मविस्तरः ।
प्रस्फुटेनैव रूपेण भावी सोऽन्तर्भविष्यति ॥२३०॥

ante jñāne'tra sopaye samastaḥ karmavistaraḥ /
prasphutenaiva rūpeṇa bhāvī so'ntarbhaviṣyati //230//

In the last perception of the means, which is adjustable with all its other classes, other agencies, which gets perception along with other agencies (that is, *āṇavopāya*), in that *āṇavopāya*, all of the fields, all of the world of worship, all of the fields of *kriyā śakti*, will be explained in *bhāvī*, . . .

SCHOLAR: Below.

SWAMIJI: . . . in the body of the *Tantrāloka*, onwards.[615]

Audio 9 - 05:30

क्रिया हि नाम विज्ञानान्नान्यद्वस्तु क्रमात्मताम् ।
उपायवशतः प्राप्तं तत्क्रियेति पुरोदितम् ॥२३१॥

kriyā hi nāma vijñānannānyadvastu kramātmatām /
upāyavaśataḥ prāptaṁ tatkriyeti puroditam //231//

614 The means (*upāya*) are not different from the meant (*upeya*).
615 From the fifth *āhnika* onwards.

This *kriyopāya*,[616] which is called *āṇavopāya*, which is one with *āṇavopāya*, is not other than *vijñānopāya*.[617] This *upāya*, this means, is also residing in the field of knowledge; this means of action is also residing in the field of knowledge. This is also one with *vijñāna* (*nānyat vastu*). *Kramātmatam upāyavaśataḥ prāptaṁ*, knowledge residing in the field of succession is called *jñāna śakti*. Knowledge residing above the field of succession is called *icchā śakti*. Knowledge residing below the field of succession is called *kriyā śakti*. Knowledge is the thing. Knowledge is upwards and downwards. Knowledge residing above the field of succession, . . .

JOHN: That's in *icchā śakti*.

SWAMIJI: . . . that is *icchā śakti*.

JOHN: Then knowledge residing in succession . . .

SWAMIJI: In succession is *jñāna śakti*. Knowledge residing below succession [is *kriyā śakti*].

JOHN: But what is "below succession"? What does it mean, "below succession"?

SWAMIJI: When there is no touch of knowledge in action.

JOHN: When it is just action.

SWAMIJI: When it is just action–*pūjā*, worship, [when there is] no awareness.

SCHOLAR: *Yogāntatām*.

SWAMIJI: *Yogāntatām*, *prāptaṁ tatkriyeti puroditam*,[618] that is *kriyā śakti*.

DEVOTEE: (inaudible) *pāyavaśataḥ prāptaṁ tat kriya*.

SWAMIJI: That is *kriyā*. So, in fact, *kriyā*, *jñāna*, and *icchā* are one.

SCHOLAR: *Triśūla*.

616 The means (*upāya*) pertaining to action (*kriyā*).

617 The means pertaining to knowledge (*vijñāna*).

618 Up to the supreme limit of *yoga* (*yogāntatām*), which has been explained in verse 149.

SWAMIJI:

Audio 9 - 07:22

सम्यग्ज्ञानं च मुक्त्येककारणं स्वपरस्थितम् ।
यतो हि कल्पनामात्रं स्वपरादिविभूतयः ॥२३२॥

samyagjñānaṁ ca muktyekakāraṇaṁ svaparasthitam /
yato hi kalpanāmātraṁ svaparādivibhutayaḥ //232//

The cause of liberation, the cause of getting liberation, is not the master, is not the effort of the disciple, is not the effort of the master. The real cause of liberation is just where there is knowledge. Where there is knowledge, the appearance of knowledge, [that] is the cause of liberation. *Svaparasthitam*, it may reside in the master, it may be residing in the disciple, we don't stress on that, we stress on knowledge. That perfect knowledge of Self is the cause of liberation. It may be residing in the master or it may be residing in the disciple. *Yato hi kalpanāmātraṁ svaparādi vibhūtayaḥ*, "This is the master," "This is the disciple," what does that [matter]? There is no difference! You may perceive that supreme knowledge in your master, [then] you are liberated! It doesn't matter if [supreme knowledge] is not residing in you! Wherever it is residing, you are liberated. It may reside in the master, it may reside in you (in the disciple). Because, *yato hi kalpanāmātraṁ svaparādo vibhūtayaḥ*, "This is the master," "This is the disciple," this is all the ignorant way of understanding, the incorrect way of understanding. The correct way of understanding is, wherever there is knowledge, that is liberation. It may be residing in Lord Śiva, it may be residing in you. If you once perceive that it is residing in Lord Śiva, you are liberated. You may not perceive that it is residing in me.[619] So there is faith: if you believe that your master is filled with the glory of awareness, [then] *you* are filled with the glory of awareness. It is not only the master who is filled with the glory.

619 Swamiji is referring to himself.

Here we end.

DEVOTEES: (laughter)

SWAMIJI: (laughs) Yes, there is some other *prakaraṇa*.[620] *Yato hi kalpanāmātraṁ svaparādi*, if the disciple gets awareness, if the disciple knows that, "The real knowledge is existing in my master," it does not mean that it is existing in his master. It is existing in his awareness! In whose awareness?

DEVOTEES: In the disciple's.

SWAMIJI: The disciple's awareness, so he is liberated. He has perceived that [knowledge]. "There" and "here," it is only *kalpanā*.[621]

SCHOLAR: Recognition (*pratyabhijñā*).

SWAMIJI: It is recognition, wherever it is. You may recognize it from the *guru*, you may recognize it from your own nature.

SCHOLAR: Because it is *sparśa*,[622] it is like . . .

SWAMIJI: Yes.

SCHOLAR: Is that right?

SWAMIJI: Cent-per-cent correct.[623]

In the previous *śloka*, he has explained that complete knowledge is the cause of liberation. [Complete knowledge] may be residing in the master or in the disciple. The division of the master and the disciple is an incorrect division. The master is the disciple and the disciple is the master. There is no difference between the master and the disciple.

---

620 Subject, topic.

621 A creation of the mind.

622 Lit., touch or contact.

623 Swamiji is confirming the scholar's suggestion that the recognition of supreme knowledge can be likened to the sensation of *sparśa* (touch), which resides exactly within consciousness.

MASTER AND DISCIPLE (233-237)

Audio 9 - 11:10

तुल्ये काल्पनिकत्वे च यदैक्यस्फुरणात्मकः ।
गुरुः स तावदेकात्मा सिद्धो मुक्तश्च भण्यते ॥२३३॥

tulye kālpanikatve ca yadaikyasphuraṇātmakaḥ /
guruḥ sa tāvadekātmā siddho muktaśca bhaṇyate //233//

The master possesses the fullness of knowledge, and that fullness of knowledge, wherever it pervades, is only the master. You should not think that it pervades in the disciple. It is the expansion of his glory. The master is expanding in the brain of the disciple also. So it is only the master that expands. *Guruḥ sa tāvat ekātmā*, and that master is one, and although he has entered in the memory of the disciple,[624] but he is one and he is a *siddha*[625] and he is *muktaḥ*.[626] There is no difference between the master and the disciple.

SCHOLAR: *Tulye kālpanikatve.*

SWAMIJI: *Tulye kālpanikatve*, the *kalpanā* is the same in the master and in the disciple. [The notion] that "he is the master" or "he is the disciple," it is incorrect, an incorrect theory. It is only one Lord who transforms in disciples in His own form. He is only one!

Audio 9 - 12:52

यावानस्य हि संतानो गुरुस्तावान्स कीर्तितः ।
सम्यग्ज्ञानमयश्चेति स्वात्मना मुच्यते ततः ॥२३४॥

624 As a thought or notion (*kalpanā*).
625 An accomplished or perfected being.
626 Liberated.

yāvānasya hi saṁtāno gurustāvānsa kīrtitaḥ /

It is "*tāvān*."[627]

samyagjñānamayaśceti svātmanā mucyate tataḥ //234//

The chain of master and disciples, the complete chain of master and disciples, is the chain of masters, it is not the chain of master and disciples. *Gurustāvān sa kīrtitaḥ*, this is the journey of the master only, from himself to the disciple, from the disciple to another disciple, from the disciple to another disciple. It is only one chain of the master. *Samyag jñāna mayaśceti*, when [the master] is complete, when [the master] completely possesses knowledge, when there is knowledge in the master only and not in the disciple, that knowledge is not complete of the master.[628] It will be completed only when it is complete in the disciple also.

JOHN: Why is this? Why is knowledge said not to be complete in the master if it is not complete in the disciple?

SWAMIJI: The master is incomplete unless his disciple is also complete. His disciple must be complete in knowledge and then the master is complete in knowledge, because this is the expansion of his own nature in the disciples. He has expanded [his nature in his] disciples, so as long as the disciples are ignorant, the master is ignorant. You should not say, "The disciple is ignorant. The disciple has not achieved anything." The master has not achieved that [completion]. So it is the duty of the master that the complete achievement should be made in all the chain of disciples.

JOHN: In all disciples.

SWAMIJI: Yes, all disciples. As long as it is not done, the master is not freed, the master is not liberated. He'll be liberated only when his disciples will be liberated. This is the

627 Swamiji corrected "*tāvat*," which appears in the text in which he is working, to read "*tāvān*."

628 That is, the master's knowledge is not complete.

theory of the *Tantrāloka*. *Svātmanā mucyate tadaḥ*, so he does not liberate his disciples, he liberates his own self. As long as it is that he liberates his disciples, in fact, he liberates his own self.

JOHN: So, what this is also saying is that there is, in Shaivism, a much closer relationship between the disciple and the master.

SWAMIJI: Not "close."

JOHN: Absolutely one.

SWAMIJI: It is only one, yes.

Audio 9 - 15:30

तत एव स्वसंतानं ज्ञानी तारयतीत्यदः ।
युक्त्यागमाभ्यां संसिद्धं तावानेको यतो मुनिः ॥२३५॥

tata eva svasaṁtānaṁ jñānī tārayatītyadaḥ /
yuktyāgamābhyāṁ saṁsiddhaṁ tāvāneko yato muniḥ //235
[not recited in full]

It is why this experienced and fully [knowledgeable] master makes all his disciples filled with his knowledge, *yuktyāgamābhyām*, by *yukti*s, by *śāstrā*s,[629] by experiences, and *āgamābhyāṁ* (by *śāstra*s). *Tāvānekoyatomuniḥ*, in fact, the master is one, traveling in each and every chain of his disciples.

SCHOLAR: Instrumental dual.[630]

SWAMIJI: *Yukti* means, the tricks of the master, how to get liberation.

SCHOLAR: Doesn't it also mean "logic"?

SWAMIJI: Logic, yes.

JOHN: Reasoning.

SWAMIJI: Reasoning, spiritual reasoning.

629 Scripture.
630 The scholar is referring to the grammatical case of the word "*yuktyāgamābhyām.*"

JOHN: Same as *tarka*?[631]

SWAMIJI: *Tarka*, yes, *satarka*.[632]

Audio 9 - 16:38

तेनात्र ये चोदयन्ति ननु ज्ञानाद्विमुक्तता ।
दीक्षादिका क्रिया चेयं सा कथं मुक्तये भवेत् ॥२३६॥
ज्ञानात्मा सेति चेज्ज्ञानं यत्रस्थं तं विमोचयेत् ।
अन्यस्य मोचने वापि भवेत्किं नासमञ्जसम् ।
इति ते मूलतः क्षिप्ता यत्त्वत्रान्यैः समर्थितम् ॥२३७॥

tenātra ye codayanti nanu jñānādvimuktatā /
dīkṣādikā kriyā ceyaṁ sā kathaṁ muktaye bhavet //236//
jñānātmā seti cejjñānaṁ yatrasthaṁ taṁ vimocayet /
anyasya mocane vāpi bhavetkiṁ nāsamañjasam /
iti te mūlataḥ kṣiptā yattvatrānyaiḥ samarthitam //237//

So [there are] those *puṇḍit*s, those masters, who put this question on this subject that, [since] the cause of liberation is knowledge, complete knowledge, and that [with consideration of] the tradition of initiation (*dīkṣā*), which is done in a sacrificial fire and *mantra*s and all this, how can that [initiation] liberate his disciple? [Those masters say], "It won't have that power to liberate him! The power of liberation is only found in knowledge, not in *kriyā*, not in *dīkṣā*. [Even] if one says that, '*Dīkṣā* is also one with knowledge', but that knowledge of reality, wherever it resides, it will liberate him only. So that knowledge will liberate the master only, not the disciple, because if the master is filled with knowledge and the disciple is not filled with knowledge, how can the master liberate his disciple with his knowledge?"

[Śaiva answer:] All these points are cleared by this point of ours that there is no difference between the master and the

631 "Transcendental discriminating logic." *Tantrāloka* 4.40 (LJA archive).

632 Lit., having argument or reasoning, skilled in speculation.

disciple. If the master is liberated, the disciple is absolutely liberated, because they are one. Those masters [who pose the objection above] don't know that they are one, [that] there is no difference between the master and the disciple. Once the master is liberated, the disciple is liberated. It is an admitted fact.

SCHOLAR: But the objector can still ask, "How is it that that identity takes place?"

SWAMIJI: [They object that], "When knowledge is residing in the master, in the master's memory, in the master's self, and ignorance is in the disciples," but this theory will be, this objection will stand, only when you'll perceive that the master and the disciples are two. When we have admitted that the master and the disciple are one . . .

SCHOLAR: Through *dīkṣā*.

SWAMIJI: No, without *dīkṣā*! If the master has admitted [someone] to be his disciple, if he is ignorant, if the disciple is ignorant, you must conclude that the master is ignorant, [that] the master is to be completed now, because ignorance is peeping in the disciple. Because the master and the disciples are one from our theory.

JOHN: So this objection . . .

SWAMIJI: But this objection does not stand. How can it stand? It will stand only when the master and the disciple would be separate.

JOHN: This transferring of knowledge.

SWAMIJI: Yes.

JOHN: That you can transfer knowledge . . .

SWAMIJI: You can't transfer knowledge from the master to the disciple from their theory. From our theory it can be because the master and the disciples are one.[633]

Now next, he puts the next subject:

---

633 In his commentary, Jayaratha observes that knowledge and action are also considered to be one.

THE THEORY OF MALAS[634]-IMPURITIES (238-239)

Audio 9 - 20:57

मलो नाम किल द्रव्यं चक्षुःस्थपटलादिवत ।
तद्विहन्त्री क्रिया दीक्षा त्वञ्जनादिककर्मवत् ॥२३८॥
तत्पुरस्तान्निषेत्स्यामो युक्त्यागमविगर्हितम् ।
मलमायाकर्मणां च दर्शयिष्यामहे स्थितिम् ॥२३९॥

malo nāma kīla dravyaṁ cakṣuḥsthapaṭalādivat /
tadvihantri kriyā dīkṣā tvañjanādikakarmavat //238//
tatpurastānniṣetsyāmo yuktyāgamavigarhitam /
malamāyākarmaṇāṁ ca darśayiṣyāmahe sthitim //239//

And there is another point to be discussed regarding *mala* (impurity). Some masters say that *mala* is *dravya*, *mala* is some substantial thing, [that] it is not ignorance, it is *dravya*, and just like *cakṣuḥstha paṭalādivat*, when there is cataract in your eyes, . . .

JOHN: Some real thing, some real covering.

SWAMIJI: Some covering.

. . . *tat vīhantrī kriyā dīkṣā*, and that covering is removed by the action of *dīkṣā*, *tvañjanādikakarma*, just like that *añjana* (*añjana* means, that collyrium that is put in the eyes, that black powder which is applied), it is just like that, that black powder [that] removes the cataract. In the same way, *dīkṣā* removes that *mala* from the knowledge of the disciples. *Tatpurastat nisetsyāmo*, this also we will . . . this theory of these masters we will *niṣetsyāma*, . . .

634 See Appendix 6 (p385) for details of the *mala*s. See also *Kashmir Shaivism–Secret Supreme*, chapter 7, "The Three Impurities (*mala*s)."

SCHOLAR: Deny.

SWAMIJI: . . . we will disprove, disagree, *yukti āgama vigarhitam*, because it is against the theory of *yukti* and against the theory of the *śāstra*s (against the theory of the tricks of masters and against the theory of the *śāstra*s).

SCHOLAR: "Tricks of masters."

SWAMIJI: *Yukti* is the tricks of masters, how to get entry–*yukti*. *Yukti* means, just a trick how to enter. Don't you agree with it?

SCHOLAR: *Yukti* always seems to be used in the sense of logical argument as opposed to scriptural argument.

SWAMIJI: *Āgama* is that.

SCHOLAR: Scriptural argument.

SWAMIJI: Yes, scriptural argument. *Yukti* is spiritual argument, and that is a trick (*yukti āgama vigarhitam*). *Mala-māyākarmaṇāṁ ca darśayiṣyāmahe*, and we will clarify the substance of *mala*, *māyā*, and *karma* (*āṇavamala*, *māyīya-mala*, and *kārmamala*) vividly.[635]

Next, 240.

JOHN: So he doesn't say here why [the Shaivites] object to that.

SCHOLAR: Later.

JOHN: He says, "Later we'll explain why."

SWAMIJI: Later on in the ninth *āhnika*, the ninth chapter, of the *Tāntrāloka*.

635 See Appendix 6 (p385) for an explanation of the *mala*s.

THE FOURFOLD MEANS OF LIBERATION (240-244)

Audio 9 - 23:48

एवं शक्तित्रयोपायं यज्ज्ञानं तत्र पश्चिमम् ।
मूलं तदुत्तरं मध्यमुत्तरोत्तरमादिमम् ॥२४०॥

evaṁ śakti trayopāyaṁ yajjñānaṁ tatra paścimam /
mūlaṁ taduttaraṁ madhyamuttarottaramādimam //240//

So, this way, where these three means are laid down, *śakti traya upāya*, the *upāya*s of the three energies (that is, the means regarding action [*kriyā*], the means regarding knowledge [*jñāna*], and the means regarding *icchā*[636]), *tat jñānaṁ tatra paścimam*, the last knowledge, the last means, is *mūla*.

DEVOTEE: "*Mūlaṁ*" means?

SWAMIJI: *Mūla* is *āṇavopāya*, the "root." The root of the means is *āṇavopāya*–inferior. *Taduttaraṁ madhyamaṁ*, *madhyam*, the central *upāya* is above that.

DEVOTEE: *Śāktopāya*.

SWAMIJI: *Uttarottaram*, and above that is *ādimam*, the first *upāya*, *śāmbhavopāya*.

Audio 9 - 25:03

ततोऽपि परमं ज्ञानमुपायादिविवर्जितम् ।
आनन्दशक्तिविश्रान्तमनुत्तरमिहोच्यते ॥२४१॥

tato'pi paramaṁ jñānamupāyādivivarjitam /
ānandaśaktiviśrāntamanuttaramihocyate //241//

---

636 Will.

Above these three means also, there is another supreme means where there is no need of holding any means (*upāyādi vivarjitam*), and it is residing in the energy of *ānanda* (bliss). It is not residing in the energy of will or knowledge or action. It is residing in the energy of *ānanda* (bliss). *Anuttaram ihocate*, and this is the most supreme means.

Audio 9 - 25:45

तत्स्वप्रकाशं विज्ञानं विद्याविद्येश्वरादिभिः ।
अपि दुर्लभसद्भावं श्रीसिद्धातन्त्र उच्यते ॥२४२॥

tatsvaprakāśaṁ vijñānaṁ vidyāvidyeśvaradhibhiḥ /
api durlabhasadbhāvaṁ śrī siddhātantra ucyate //242//

In the *Śrī Siddha tantra*, it is defined that that complete knowledge of *anupāya* is very difficult to be achieved by *vidyā* and *vidyeśvara* also, by those who are residing in Śuddhavidyā and [those] who are residing in Īśvara and *mantramaheśvara* (Sadāśiva). Those also cannot achieve this *upāya* [easily]. *Api durlabha sadbhāvaṁ śrī siddhātantra ucyate.*

SCHOLAR: Hard to realize (*durlabha sadbhava*).

SWAMIJI: Hard to realize.

Audio 9 - 26:31

मालिन्यां सूचितं चैतत्पटलेऽष्टादशे स्फुटम् ।
न चैतदप्रसन्नेन शंकरेणोपादिश्यते ॥२४३॥
इत्यनेनैव पाठेन मालिनीविजयोत्तरे ।

mālinyāṁ sūcitaṁ caitatpatala'ṣṭādaśe sphuṭam /
na caitadaprasannena śaṁkarenopadiśyate //243//
ityanenaiva pāṭhena mālinīvijayottare /

In the *Mālinīvijayottara* also, in the eighteenth chapter there, it is explained that this knowledge of *anupāya* was explained to Pārvatī by Lord Śiva only when He was extremely satisfied with Her, extremely joyful with Her. *Na ca etad aprasannena*, forcefully He has not related this *upāya* to Her. Who?

JOHN: This Pārvatī.

SCHOLAR: *Śivatā pārvatī.*

SWAMIJI: Yes.

SCHOLAR: You said "*upadiśyate*" but my text has "*eti vākyataḥ.*"

SWAMIJI: "*Iti vākyataḥ,*" yes. "*Upadiśyate*"[637] is the reading in the *Mālinīvijaya*. "*Iti vākyataḥ*"[638] is of Abhinavagupta.

Ītyanenaiva pāṭhena mālinīvijayottare, it is said there [in the *Mālinīvijaya Tantra*], the next line is there:

Audio 9 - 27:51

kathañcidupadiṣṭe'pi vāsanā na prajāyate //[639]

With great effort, if you achieve that, if you reach near the line of that *anupāya*, but you can't hold it.

SCHOLAR: *Na vāsanā.*[640]

SWAMIJI: [*Na*] *vāsanā*, you can't insert that fragrance in your consciousness, that fragrance of *anupāya*. That fragrance of *anupāya* cannot be inserted easily because it is not very easy to satisfy Lord Śiva. Pārvatī had, with great effort, satisfied Lord Śiva and then He explained this *anupāya* to Her. So, *anupāya* is so difficult that, although it has reached near to you, but you can't hold it, you can't hold it easily, you can't grasp it, you can't observe it. This is *anupāya*.

637 The original text reads शंकरेणेति वाक्यतः. *Upadiśyate* means indicating or teaching.

638 Thus (*iti*) it is said (*vākyataḥ*).

639 Jayaratha references this line from the *Mālinīvijaya tantra* in his commentary for verse 244. Swamiji recites "*kathañcidupadiṣṭe'pi*" instead of "*kathañcidupalabdhe'pi.*" *Upadiṣṭa* means "taught" and *upalabdha* means "learnt."

640 No (*na*) impression (*vāsanā*).

Audio 9 - 29:04

इति ज्ञानचतुष्कं यत्सिद्धिमुक्तिमहोदयम् ।
तन्मया तन्त्र्यते तन्त्रालोकनाम्न्यत्र शासने ॥२४४॥

iti jñānacatuṣkaṁ yatsiddhimuktimahodayam /
tanmayā tantryate tantrālokanamnyatra śāsane //244//

So this way, these fourfold ways of means, which are the bestowers of power and liberation, all *siddhis* (all powers) and liberation, *tanmayā*, those fourfold means will be explained, *tantryate*, explained . . .

SCHOLAR: Successively.

SWAMIJI: . . . successively, *tantrāloka nāmnyatra śāsane*, in the *Tantrāloka śāstra*. In the *Tantrāloka śāstra*, we'll discuss these fourfold means.

Now, 245. This is another subject now.

Naming (uddeśa)
Definition (lakṣaṇa)
Investigation (parīkṣā) (245-269)

Verses 245–260 explain how perception of the objective world takes place in three phases: 1) *uddeśa* (nomination), the naming of an object; 2) *lakṣaṇa* (definition), describing an object by: a) *uttara* (answer), b) *nirṇaya* (explanation); and 3) *parīkṣā* (complete investigation), the complete ascertainment of the object.[641]

641 This is in keeping with *Nyāya* (the science of reasoning/logic), the first of the six classical systems of Indian philosophy expounded by the sage Gautama.

Verses 261–269 explain how *uddeśa*, *lakṣaṇa*, and *parīkṣā* are always found in the four *pramāṇas*:[642] *dṛṣṭa* (direct perception), *anumāna* (inference), *aupamya* (by similarity or comparison), and *āptavacana* (statements of authority).

Verses 270–271 explain *uddeśa*, *lakṣaṇa*, and *parīkṣā* in relation to the three levels of speech (*paśyantī*, *madhyamā*, and *vaikarī*), and the three energies of *parā*, *parāparā*, and *aparā*, respectively.

SWAMIJI: Now, for whom this theory of the four means is being explained? For [that person who is] fully elevated or [for that person who is] not elevated at all? Or for that person who has got doubts, who has got the desire to be elevated, for him, is the *Tantrāloka* meant for him? Or for those who are already elevated? Or [for those] who are not elevated at all? So, there are three sections of people: one section is fully elevated (filled with knowledge), one section is filled with ignorance (absolute ignorance), one section is those who desire to get, to achieve, knowledge.

Audio 9 - 30:58

तत्रेह यद्यदन्तर्वा बहिर्वा परिमृश्यते ।
अनुद्घाटितरूपं तत्पूर्वमेव प्रकाशते ॥२४५॥

tatreha yadyadantarvā bahirvā parimṛśyate /
anudghāṭitarūpaṁ tatpūrvameva prakāśate //245//

In this universe, or in this world of the theory of Shaivism, *yadyadantarvā bahirvā parimṛśyate*, whatever you perceive in your inner consciousness or in outer consciousness, *anudghātitaṁ rūpaṁ tatpūrvameva prakāśate*, first you'll perceive that it is not vividly perceived. At the first point [of perception], it is not vividly perceived. If you perceive this inkpot, if you are going to perceive this inkpot, at first you won't perceive it

642 The reliable means of obtaining knowledge.

vividly. After investigation,[643] you perceive that this is an inkpot. Before investigation, you perceive that this is something, something black, but afterwards, when you investigate it fully, then you come to know that it is an inkpot. So, *pūrvameva tat anudghāṭitaṁ rūpaṁ prakāśyate*, first it appears to you *anudghātita* (*anudghātita* means, not vividly).

Audio 9 - 32:19

तथानुद्धाटिताकारा निर्वाच्येनात्मना प्रथा ।
संशयः कुत्रचिद्रूपे निश्चिते सति नान्यथा ॥२४६॥

tathānudghāṭitākārā nirvācyenātmanā prathā /
saṁśayaḥ kutracidrūpe niścite sati nānyathā //246//

And that flux of knowledge, in that way, that flux of knowledge, *anudghāṭita* (not vividly), not the vivid flux of knowledge, . . .*

Because you perceive only that it is something black. You don't perceive that this is an inkpot. That is *anughāṭita ākāra anirivācyenātmanā prathā*. And you cannot conclude what it actually is at that point.

*. . . and that flux of knowledge, that way, is called "doubt," and that doubt exists only when there is some undoubted realization also side-by-side.

SCHOLAR: *Kutra cidrūpe.*

JOHN: If somebody were to say, "This is an ink pot for sure" . . .

SWAMIJI: No, no, no, this is not an inkpot, not an inkpot. The [perception of the] inkpot has not risen yet. "What is this?" [has risen].

JOHN: The question.

SWAMIJI: "What is this?" So, "this" is something. "This" is something and he wants to know what "this" actually is. So, *kutracid rūpe niścite*, he has concluded that there is some-

643 *Parīkṣā,* analyzing, investigating.

thing–"It is something." So that "something" is understood.

SCHOLAR: It is not completely formless.

SWAMIJI: It is not completely formless, but what it is [is yet to be known]. He is desirous to know what it is. That is *saṁśaya*, that is the explanation of "doubt." This is actually doubt. Doubt is not [existing] if you have no curiosity to know anything. If you have no curiosity to know, for instance, that this is a stand–you have no curiosity in your mind that this is a stand, [that] this is the seat of this *bukhari*,[644] [that] this is the seat of this stove–if, for understanding this seat, you have no curiosity, it is not *saṁśaya*. *Saṁśaya* is there when there is desire to know it. There must be the desire to know it. For those, the *Tantrāloka* is meant–[for those] who have the desire to know it. [For those] who have no desire to know it, for those it is not meant [because] they have no doubt. Absolutely ignorant persons have no doubt. Absolutely elevated persons have no doubt. Only those who have the desire to know, who want to know, that is "doubt." That is what he says: *kutra cidrūpe niścetī sati*, some points are understood by him, for this point [that], "There is something."

JOHN: He agrees that there is something.

SWAMIJI: He agrees there is something. That is *saṁśaya*. Not otherwise–*saṁśaya* won't exist otherwise.

Audio 9 - 35:55

एतत्किमिति मुख्येऽस्मिन्नेतदंशः सुनिश्चितः ।
संशयोऽस्तित्वनास्त्यादिधर्मानुद्घाटितात्मकः ॥ २४७ ॥

etatkimiti mukhye'śminnetadaṁśaḥ suniścitaḥ /
saṁśayo'stitvanāstyādidharmānudghāṭitātmakaḥ //247//
[not recited]

Etatkim iti mukhye'śmin, now, this *saṁśaya* is classified in two ways: one is predominant doubt and the other is not-predominant doubt. For instance, "What is this?" "What is

644 A wood-burning stove.

this?" This is a predominant doubt. "What is this there? What is lying there?" "This" is predominant there. He has not concluded that "this" must be an inkpot or [that] "this" must be some bowl. He has not concluded that. And another doubt is, "Is it a log or is it a man?" For instance, there is a log lying in your garden and there is not complete light there, [there is] a bit of darkness also, and you perceive [something] just like a man standing (actually it is a log), and you say, you ask, when you investigate, "Is this a log or a man?" But these two things you have realized.[645] In this doubt, in this theory of doubt, you have realized that this is not a pot. [You know that] this must be either a log or a man. [You know that] this is not a dog, this is not a jug, this is not an inkpot, this is not [anything else]. All those are excluded. Only there is the desire of knowing if it is, whether it is, a log or a man. So it is *amukhya saṁśayaḥ*[646] because it is not complete doubt. The complete section of doubt is only [when you ask], "What is this?" It can be a dog, it can be a log, it can be a pot, it can be anything; it can be a stove, it can be a man, it can be a king, it can be anything. In that predominant theory of doubt, it can be anything, but this is *apradhāna* [*saṁśayaḥ*]:[647] "Is this a log or a man?" Others are granted, that this is not a pot, [that] this is not anything [else]. Only there is the doubt of these two, only in these two: if it is a log or a man.

Etat kim iti mukhye'śmin, so, in this *mukhya* [*saṁśayaḥ*],[648] . . .*

Because *saṁśayo astitvanāsti ādidharmānudghāṭita*, the reality of doubt is [that] some points are understood and some points are not understood in that [perceived] thing (*astitva nāstyādi dharma anudghāṭitātmakaḥ*).

*. . . so, this predominant doubt–"What is this?"–in this doubt, what is understood? Nothing is understood there. But [Abhinavagupta] says [that] there is [something] understood:

645 You already know what a log is and you know what a man is.

646 A non-predominant (*amukhya*) doubt (*saṁśaya*).

647 A secondary (*apradhāna*) doubt (*saṁśaya*).

648 Predominant (*mukhya*) doubt (*saṁśaya*).

"*Etat,*" "What is this?" "This" he has understood. "This" is something. So, there are two: one is understood and one is not understood–"This" and "What is this?" "What is" is not understood. "This" is understood, this point is understood. *Etat kim iti mukhye aśminnetat aṁśaḥ suniścitaḥ*, "*etat*" is understood–"this." Because, the theory of *saṁśayaḥ* is, where there is something understood and some point is not understood.

Audio 9 - 39:53

किमित्येतस्य शब्दस्य नाधिकोऽर्थः प्रकाशते ।

kimityetasya śabdasya nādhiko'rthaḥ prakāśate /

"*Kim*" [means] "what." "What," it leads to *saṁśayaḥ*.

Audio 9 - 40:04

किं त्वनुन्मुदिताकारं वस्त्वेवाभिदधात्ययम् ॥ २४८ ॥

kiṁ tvanunmudritākāraṁ vastvevābhidadhātyayam //248//

It explains to you–the next two lines–it explains to you that *anunmudritākāraṁ vastu*, there is something which is not vividly seen, what it actually is. That is doubt.

Audio 9 - 40:28

स्थाणुर्वा पुरुषो वेति न मुख्योऽस्त्येष संशयः ।
भूयःस्थधर्मजातेषु निश्चयोत्पाद एव हि ॥ २४९ ॥

sthāṇurvā puruṣo veti na mukhyo'styeṣa saṁśayaḥ /
bhūyaḥsthadharmajāteṣu niścayotpāda eva hi //249//
[not recited in full]

This is another section of doubt, not-predominant [doubt].

SCHOLAR: Did you actually translate "*kimityetasya śabda-*

sya nādhiko'rthaḥ prakāśate"?[649]

SWAMIJI: Yes, yes.

SCHOLAR: Literally?

SWAMIJI: Yes. The word "*kiṁ*"[650] does not explain to you anything else, anything more than "not-vividness."

SCHOLAR: Unlike the other case. "*Amukhya*" does tell you more.

SWAMIJI: Yes. *Sthāṇur vā puruṣo veti*, and in this other section of doubt, "Is this a log or is this a man?," *na mukhyo astyeṣa saṁśayaḥ*, this is not a predominant doubt, this is an *apradhāna* doubt, because *bhūyaḥsthadharmajāteṣu niścayotpāda eva hi*, he has concluded all other aspects, he has understood all other aspects. For instance, only two aspects are not understood yet. Spectacles are understood, a pot is understood, a *bukharī* is understood (a stove is understood), [but] a man is not understood, a log is not understood. A log and a man are not understood.[651] Other things are understood, that those things are not "this."

SCHOLAR: And in this context, everything is understood that those two things have in common, . . .

SWAMIJI: Yes.

SCHOLAR: . . . but not the one factor which would differentiate them.

SWAMIJI: Yes. Other things are understood, the negation of other things.

SCHOLAR: That this is tall, this has so much width.

SWAMIJI: No, no, other things, I mean other things than [a log or a man]. *Etat kim*, in this first predominant doubt, nothing is understood–it can be a pot, it can be anything–but *sthāṇur vā puruṣo*,[652] in this not-predominant doubt, every-

649 Verse 248a.
650 The question, "What?"
651 Although he knows what a log and a man are, he does not know if the object that he is perceiving is a log or a man.
652 "Is it a log or a man?"

thing else is understood, only two things are to be understood now. Which two things?

SCHOLAR: Is it a man or is it a pole?

SWAMIJI: Yes. Other things are understood [insofar as those] other things are not there.

Audio 9 - 42:36

आमर्शनीयद्वैरूप्यानुद्घाटनवशात्पुनः ।
संशयः स किमित्यंशे विकल्पस्त्वन्यथा स्फुटः ॥२५०॥

āmarśanīyadvairūpyānudghāṭana vaśātpunaḥ /
saṁśayaḥ sa kimityaṁśe vikalpastvanyathā sphuṭaḥ //250//

Now he discards the objection, the objection [that] may arise in this theory, that it may be a *vikalpa*.[653] Why not call it a *vikalpa*? Why call it *saṁśayaḥ*? Because *vikalpa* also has two things to be understood: "*udite hotavyaṁ*" and "*anudite hotavyaṁ*", ("when the sun rises, you must worship" and "when the sun has not risen, you must worship"). So it is *vikalpa*. You can worship before sunrise or after sunrise.

SCHOLAR: For example.

SWAMIJI: So, this is *vikalpa*. This is not *saṁśaya*, this is not doubt. Why not call this also *vikalpa*, not doubt–*sthāṇur vā puruṣo*? In the [instance] of *sthāṇur vā puruṣo* (this can be a log or this can be a man), if this can be a log or this can be a man also, why not call it *vikalpa*? Why call it doubt?

SCHOLAR: *Vā vikalpe.* Yes.

SWAMIJI: When there is *vā* (or)–if it is a log "or" a man–when there is "or," when there are two things, why not call it *vikalpa*? Why bother about doubt, the theory of doubt? [Abhinavagupta] says, "No, this is the theory of doubt, this is not the theory of *vikalpa*." *Āmarśanīya dvairūpya anudghāṭana vaśāt punaḥ saṁśayaḥ*, it is doubt because these two things are not understood properly. In *vikalpa*, two things are

653 An alternative or an option among certain possibilities.

understood; in the theory of *vikalpa*, two things are understood. In the theory of doubt, two things are not understood–*sthāṇuḥ* (a log) is not understood, a man is not understood.[654] So, he is in a fix what to call it, if it is a log or if it is a man. But in *vikalpa*, both things are understood.

Audio 9 - 44:53

तेनानुद्घाटितात्मत्वभावप्रथानमेव यत्
प्रथमं स इहोद्देशः प्रश्नः संशय एव च ॥२५१॥

tenānudgāṭitātmatvabhāvaprathanameva yat /
prathamaṁ sa ihoddeśaḥ praśnaḥ saṁśayaḥ eva ca //251//

So, the [initial] appearance of that object which is not completely vivid, the appearance of an object which is not completely vivid, is first called *uddeśa*, *praśna*, and *saṁśaya*. It is called *uddeśa*, it is *praśna*, it is *saṁsāya*. *Uddeśa* means, just to nominate. In the first *āhnika* of the *Tantrāloka*, he has nominated what it is to be explained. So there is doubt. So the doubt appears in the readers [with respect to] what it could be in the following chapters of the *Tantrāloka*. So there is curiosity in the readers to know. So, this *Tantrāloka*, the first *āhnika*, is *uddeśa*. *Uddeśa* means, nomination, the first nomination: "I'll explain to you the way you'll tread."

JOHN: Like an index.

SWAMIJI: Index. And it is *praśna*, it is a question, because in your field of consciousness, a question arises–at once a question rises there. And it is *saṁśaya*, it is doubt. So, doubt, question, and *uddeśa* are the same. *Uddeśa*, *praśna*, and *saṁśaya*, these three are one. *Uddeśa* is the same, *praśna* is the same, and the *saṁśaya* is the samc the nomination, questioning, and doubt.

654 Again, although he knows what a log and a man are, it is not clear to him as to which one he is perceiving.

Audio 9 - 47:03

तथानुद्घाटिताकारभावप्रसरवर्त्मना ।
प्रसरन्ती स्वसंवित्तोः प्रष्ट्री शिष्यात्मतां गता ॥२५२॥

tathānudghāṭitākārabhāvaprasaravartmanā /
prasarantī svasaṁvittiḥ praṣṭrī śiṣyātmatāṁ gatā //252//

And that consciousness of one's self, when that consciousness travels on the path without knowing how it is traveling, how that consciousness is traveling (*anudghāṭitākāra*, that traveling on the path without knowing [the path] on which it travels), and that consciousness is called *praṣṭrī* (*praṣṭrī* means, always questioning), and that consciousness is called "always questioning." He resides in the field of questioning, and that consciousness, in other words, would be called *śiṣya* (disciple).

JOHN: What is the exact meaning of "*śiṣya*"?

SWAMIJI: *Śiṣya* means, *śāsu anuśiṣṭau.*

SCHOLAR: To be taught.

SWAMIJI: To be taught.

JOHN: To be taught, or he who questions.

SWAMIJI: Yes. As long as he is questioning on the path on which he treads, or she treads, without knowing what is the path, that is [the condition of being a] *śiṣya*. That consciousness of your self has become a *śiṣya* (*śiṣya* has come from the verbal root *śāsu*).[655]

Audio 9 - 48:48

तथान्तरपरामर्शनिश्चयात्मतिरोहितेः ।
प्रसरानन्तरोद्भूतसंहारोदयभागपि ॥२५३॥
यावत्येव भवेद्बाह्यप्रसरे प्रस्फुटात्मनि ।
अनुन्मीलितरूपा सा प्रष्ट्री तावति भण्यते ॥२५४॥

655 The verbal root *śās* means "to teach, instruct, inform."

tathantaraparāmarśaniścayātmatirohiteḥ /
prasaranāntarodbhūtasaṁharodayabhāgapi //253//
yāvatyeva bhavedbāhyaprasare prasphuṭātmani /
anunmīlitarūpā sā praṣṭrī tāvati bhaṇyate //254//

And that consciousness of your self, where that consciousness has absolutely forgotten the complete *niścaya*, the complete perception [of any given object], *niścaya ātma tirohite*, when that *niścaya* is not yet done to [i.e., held by] that consciousness of one's self, and it is treading on the path to know, to understand, and *saṁhāra udayabhāgapi*, and that *niścaya* [once held] sometimes dissolves and sometimes appears, reappears, and, in this way, as long as one's consciousness flows on the path completely unaware of the point to be understood, that is the theory, that is the state, of *praṣṭrī*, that is the state of that person who puts a question (*praṣṭrī tāvati bhaṇyate*).

JOHN: What is this *niścaya*, coming and going?

SWAMIJI: Sometimes that consciousness concludes that, "This is the point." Just after another second she understands, "No, this is not the point. There must be something else."

SCHOLAR: I know too well.

DEVOTEES: (laughter)

SWAMIJI: "Oh, I understood this is the point!" Just [after another second], "Oh, this is not the point!" This is *sṛṣṭi* . . .

DEVOTEE: *Sṛṣṭi-saṁhāra.*[656]

SWAMIJI: Yes. And that is the path on which that *praṣṭrī* treads–*praṣṭrī*.

JOHN: Questioner.

SWAMIJI: *Praṣṭrī*, the questioner, consciousness-questioner.

JOHN: Consciousness-questioner.

SWAMIJI: Consciousness is the questioner.

656 Creation, destruction.

Audio 9 - 50:54

स्वयमेवं विबोधश्च तथा प्रश्नोत्तरात्मकः ।
गुरुशिष्यपदेऽप्येष देहभेदो ह्यतात्त्विकः ॥२५५॥

svayamevaṁ vibodhaśca tathā praśnottarātmakaḥ /
guruśiṣyapade'pyeṣa dehabhedo hyatāttvikaḥ //255//

This is your own consciousness who puts the question and who puts the answer also, who gets the answer also. The questioner and the person who gives the answer to that question is your own consciousness established in the state of [both] master and disciple. So this is one's own consciousness that puts a question and it is one's own consciousness that gets its reply in the state of the master and the disciple. And the state of the master and the disciple, too, are incorrect states, because *dehabhedo hyatāttvikaḥ*, the [distinction between the] body of the master and the body of the disciple is not real.

SCHOLAR: Not really separate.

SWAMIJI: No, the body, [that] the body [of the master and the body of the disciple are] separate, . . .

SCHOLAR: *Dehabhedaḥ*?

SWAMIJI: . . . *dehabhedo hyatāttvikaḥ*, it is not true.

SCHOLAR: The distinction of bodies (*dehabheda*).

SWAMIJI: The distinction of the body [of the master and the disciple] is not true. You should not put, "The distinction of the body in the master and the disciple." You must put, "The distinction of consciousness"! [But even] if consciousness is distinct, it is not distinct. Consciousness is one in the master and the same is in the disciple.

JOHN: What about the condition where the disciple, he experiences consciousness to be distinct [while] the master doesn't experience consciousness to be distinct? So, from one point of view, the consciousness is distinct, . . .

SWAMIJI: But this is the master only that travels from

distinction and non-distinction–this is the traveling of the master.

JOHN: So that is why you said earlier [that] it is the master who inserts and the master who . . . because the disciple is in ignorance and can't do anything.

SWAMIJI: Yes.

Audio 9 - 52:52

बोधो हि बोधरूपत्वादन्तर्नानाकृतीः स्थिताः ।
बहिराभासयत्येव द्राक्सामान्यविशेषतः ॥२५६॥

bodho hi bodharūpatvādantarnānākṛtīḥ sthitāḥ /
bahirābhāsayatyeva drāksāmānyaviśeṣataḥ //256//

This is *bodha*, this is one's own consciousness, because of its being conscious, and [this conscious being] puts forth externally various formations of ascertainments, *drāk* (instantaneously), *sāmānya viśeṣataḥ*, in the way of *sāmānya* and in the way of *viśeṣaḥ*.[657]

JOHN: Universality and individuality.

SWAMIJI: No. When there is doubt, when there is *praśna* (when there is questioning), that is *sāmānya*. When there is an answer, . . .

JOHN: That is *viśeṣa*.

SWAMIJI: . . . that is *viśeṣa*.

SCHOLAR: Because before *viśeṣa* there is universality in the sense that it might be anything.

SWAMIJI: Yes. The state of being the questioner is *sāmānya*. *Viśeṣa* is when the answer grows.

Audio 9 - 54:02

स्रक्ष्यमाणोविशेषांशाकांक्षायोग्यस्य कस्यचित् ।
धर्मस्य सृष्टिः सामान्यसृष्टिः सा संशयात्मिका ॥२५७॥

657 In the way of non-specific (*sāmānya*) and specific (*viśeṣa*) ascertainments.

srakṣyamāṇaviśeṣāṁśākāṁkṣāyogyasya kasyacit /
dharmasya sṛṣṭiḥ sāmānyasṛṣṭiḥ sā saṁśayātmikā //257//

That *sāmānya sṛṣṭi*, the creation of that *sāmānya*, is called doubt, and that doubt is only fulfilled by *viśeṣa sṛṣṭi*, by the particular flow of the answer, the particular flow [of the answer] that suits that *praṣṭrī*, that suits that [questioning-]consciousness residing in the field of doubt. Because, when you are residing in the field of doubt and you put your question before me, before some master, and I explain [the answer of] that question to you, if you are not satisfied, you say, "I am not satisfied, sir. This is not the real answer I would like to know." You don't appreciate that answer. So it seems that your consciousness is [already] filled with that answer. You know in the background what is the answer. It is why you don't accept my answer if it is not fitting you. That is what he says here: *srakṣyamāṇa viśeṣāṁśa akaṁkṣāyogyasya*, he is desirous of knowing the answer that is residing in the background of his [own] consciousness, in the consciousness of the disciple.

SCHOLAR: So you don't ask anything which you don't really know the answer to.

SWAMIJI: Yes. *Dharmasya sṛṣṭiḥ sāmānya sṛṣṭiḥ sā saṁśayātmikā*, that is *saṁśayaḥ*, that is the state of being a disciple. So, it is concluded there that the questioner knows the answer. This theory would be understood when you read that *Parātriṁśikā Vivaraṇa*.[658]

658 "As long as Bhairava is concerned, Bhairava goes on speaking and speaking and speaking and answering Her questions, [but] unless Bhairavī is satisfied, the answer is not complete and fit. So the answer must be according to the reality of Devī. Devī must accept that [answer]. So it means that *Devī* knows, in the background of Her consciousness, what the answer is. But She does not know actually what is the answer, but when Bhairava speaks, She can recollect that, "This is the real answer [that] I have to accept." *Parātriśikā Vivaraṇa*, verse 1, commentary, (LJA archive, 1983). "Abhinavagupta has changed the name to *Parātriśikā*. *Parātriśikā* is

SCHOLAR: He explains that in great detail.

SWAMIJI: Yes, he explains that.

Audio 9 - 56:07

स्रक्ष्यमाणो विशेषांशो यदा तूपरमेत्तदा ।
निर्णयो मातृरुचितो नान्यथा कल्पकोटिभिः ॥२५८॥

srakṣyamāṇo viśeṣāṁśo yadā tūparamettadā /
nirṇayo mātṛrucito nānyathā kalpakoṭibhiḥ //258 /

And when this *viśeṣāṁśa* (the answer) is *srakṣyamāṇa*, is being created, [when it] comes on the path of creation, and that *viśeṣāṁśa*, *yadā tū uparamet*, when it is over,[659] *nirṇaya*, and that is *nirṇaya*, that is called *nirṇaya,*[660] and that *nirṇaya*, that explanation of that doubt, is *mātṛ rucitā*, is dependent upon the will of the *mātā*,[661] upon the will of the disciple. If the disciple is satisfied, then he has got the answer of the question. If he is not satisfied, he says, "No, sir, I am not yet satisfied. By this answer, I am not satisfied. Tell me something else." But he does not say what to tell. He knows what is to be told–in the background of his consciousness he knows what is to be told–because as soon as that [answer] comes out from the lips of his master, he is satisfied. He says, "Now I am satisfied." *Nānyathā kalpakoṭibhiḥ*, not unless he will [accept the answer], it may take ages for the master to explain to him if he is not satisfied. If the disciple is not satisfied, it may take so many centuries to explain to him, but [still] he won't be satisfied. He will be satisfied only when he is told [an answer] according to [what already exists in] the background of his

---

the supreme energy which is the Kingdom of three energies, the explanation of three energies: *parā*, *parāparā*, and *aparā*. This is the kingdom of three energies here. So you should put "*Parātriśikā*" when you add [the title]. In its edition, you should put *Parātriśikā*, not *Parātriṁśikā*." Ibid.

659 When the answer is given and accepted *in toto*.

660 A complete ascertainment.

661 From the root *mātṛ*, which means "measurer" or "knower."

consciousness [where] that is residing.

Audio 9 - 58:05
Audio 10 - 00:00

तस्याथ वस्तुनः स्वात्मवीर्याक्रमणपाटवात्।
उन्मुद्रणं तयाकृत्या लक्षणोत्तरनिर्णयाः ॥२५९॥

tasyātha vastunaḥ svātmavīryākramaṇapāṭavāt /
unmudraṇaṁ tayākrityā lakṣaṇottaranirṇayāḥ //259//

When that object, when you put your own power of consciousness on that object, just to clarify that object which is nominated in *uddeśa*, and you clarify it, there you will find *lakṣaṇa*, *uttara*, and *nirṇaya*. That is, when you get the clearance of that object, that is *lakṣaṇa*, that is *uttara*, that is *nirṇaya*–that is *lakṣaṇa* (definition), that is *uttara* (answer), and that is *nirṇaya* (explanation)–in [the perception of] each and every object, whatever it may be.

The next [*śloka*]:

Audio 10 - 01:02

निर्णीततावद्धर्मांशपृष्ठपातितया पुनः ।
भूयो भूयः समुद्देश लक्षणात्मपरीक्षणम् ॥२६०॥

nirṇītatāvaddharmāṁśapṛṣṭhapātitayā punaḥ /
bhūyo bhūyaḥ samuddeśalakṣaṇātmaparīkṣaṇam //260//

And *parīkṣā*[662] is [pertaining to] the object which is already explained. And [with respect] to that object, when you repeatedly explain it, repeatedly clarify it, that is *parīkṣā*.

SCHOLAR: So he has explained three levels.

SWAMIJI: Yes, *uddeśa*, *lakṣaṇa*, and *parīkṣā*.

SCHOLAR: *Uddeśa* (the mentioned), *lakṣaṇa* (definition), and *parīkṣā* (complete investigation).

---

662 Inspection, investigation, examination, test.

SWAMIJI: [*Lakṣaṇa* is the] definition and *parīkṣā* is the complete investigation, yes. "Complete investigation" is quite the exact word. And this *uddeśa*, *lakṣaṇa*, and *parīkṣā* are found in each and every object, in the perception of each and every object. For that, he puts another *śloka*, 261:

Audio 10 - 02:02

दृष्टानुमानौपम्याप्तवचनादिषु सर्वतः ।
उद्देशलक्षणावेक्षात्रितयं प्राणिनां स्फुरेत् ॥२६१॥

dṛṣṭānumānaupamyāptavacanādiṣu sarvataḥ /
uddeśalakṣaṇāvekṣātritayaṁ prāṇināṁ sphuret //261//

Dṛṣṭa is *pratyakṣa*,[663] *anumāna* is inference (by inference), *aupamya* (by similarity), and *āptavacana* (the sayings of that man with authority), and in these four sections, always you will find *uddeśa*, *lakṣaṇa*, and *parīkṣā*.[664]

etadeva krameṇa darśayati[665]

Audio 10 - 02:38

निर्विकल्पितमुद्देशो विकल्पो लक्षणं पुनः ।
परीक्षणं तथाध्यक्षे विकल्पानां परम्परा ॥२६२॥

nirvikalpitamuddeśo vikalpo lakṣaṇaṁ punaḥ /
parīkṣaṇaṁ tathādhyakṣe vikalpānāṁ paramparā //262//

Uddeśa is always *nirvikalpa* (without any thought). *Vikalpo lakṣaṇaṁ*, *lakṣaṇa* is always with thought [because] you attribute *lakṣaṇa*.[666] *Parīkṣā* is *tathā adhyakṣe vikalpānāṁ*

663 Seeing (*dṛṣṭa*) means, direct perception (*pratyakṣa*).
664 The nomination (*uddeśa*), the definition (*lakṣaṇa*), and the confirmation (*parīkṣā*).
665 Jayaratha's introductory commentary for verse 262: "These will be explained in succession."
666 Give it definition, lit., a mark, sign, symbol, token, characteristic, attribute, quality.

paramparā, when you put thoughts to refer to it repeatedly, that is *parīkṣā*.

SCHOLAR: These four–*dṛṣṭa*, *anumāna*, *aupamya*, and *āptavacana*–are the four *pramāṇa*s[667] of Naiyāyika.

SWAMIJI: Naiyāyika, yes.[668]

SCHOLAR: . . . not of Shaivite philosophy.[669]

SWAMIJI: No, no (affirmative).

Audio 10 - 03:27

नगोऽयमिति चोद्देशो धूमित्वादग्निमानिति ।
लक्ष्यं व्याप्त्यादिविज्ञानजालं त्वत्र परीक्षणम् ॥२६३॥

nago'yamiti coddeśo dhūmitvādagnimāniti /
lakṣyaṁ vyāptyādivijñānajālaṁ tvatra parīkṣaṇam //263//

First, it is *anumāna*.[670] First, he will refer to *anumāna pramāṇa*, proof.

"On the peak of the mountain, there is a fire." Although you don't see a fire, it is not *pratyakṣa*,[671] you say, "There is fire on the peak of the mountain." This is *uddeśa*. This point is *uddeśa*, this saying only. *Dhūmitvāt agnimān iti lakṣyam*, this is *lakṣyaṁ*: "*Dhūmitvat*, because there is smoke."

SCHOLAR: Surely *uddeśa* is just the statement, "This is a mountain (*nago'yam*)."

SWAMIJI: "This is a mountain."

SCHOLAR: "This is a mountain." *Agnimān* is *lakṣaṇaṁ*.

SWAMIJI: *Dhūmitvāt*. "*Dhūmitvāt agnimān*, there is a fire

---

667 The reliable means of obtaining knowledge.
668 *Nyāya*, the first of the classical systems of Indian philosophy, expounded by the sage Gautama, is the science of reasoning. *Nyāya* delineates sixteen points to test the procedure of gaining knowledge.
669 The Shaivite position will be methodically revealed throughout the text by Abhinavagupta's employment of the dialectical method.
670 Inference.
671 Direct perception.

because there is smoke." *Vyāptyādi vijñāna jālam*, and the inference of *vyāpti*[672] to prove it: "Because in our kitchen we see like that. In our kitchen, [when] there is smoke, [then] there is fire also."

SCHOLAR: This word "*vyāpti*" is translated as "invariable concomitance"[673] [as in], "Wherever there is smoke, there is fire."

SWAMIJI: Yes, "Wherever there is smoke, there is fire," because in the kitchen you can see that. It is *parīkṣā*.[674] So it is with *anumāna*.[675] Now he will refer to *upamāna*. *Pratyakṣa* is already there. *Anumāna* he has explained. Now he will explain *upamāna* (*upamāna* means, similarity). By [invoking a] similarity, you confirm that this is that thing.

Audio 10 - 05:30

उद्देशोऽयमिति प्राच्यो गोतुल्यो गवयाभिधः ।
इति वा लक्षणं शेषः परीक्षोपमितौ भवेत् ॥२६४॥

uddeśo'yamiti prācyo gotulyo gavayābhidhaḥ /
iti vā lakṣaṇaṁ śeṣaḥ parīkṣopamitau bhavet //264//
[not recited]

"*Ayam*"–*ayam iti uddeśa*, "this," it is the *uddeśa* there. "*Gotulyo gavayābhidhaḥ*"–*iti vā lakṣaṇaṁ*, and *lakṣaṇa* is the definition; the *lakṣaṇa* is, "This *gavayā* (buffalo) is just like a cow, just like a bull." *Iti vā lakṣaṇaṁ*, this is *lakṣaṇaṁ*. *Śeṣaḥ parīkṣopamitau bhavet*, [then there are] other things which are attributed to that afterwards for confirmation. For instance, because [this buffalo] has got this *sāsanā*, . . .

SCHOLAR: Dewlap.

SWAMIJI: . . . that *sāsanā*, and in a cow also there is a *sāsanā*, so it is like a cow.

672 Universal rule without an exception.
673 An unchanging co-existence.
674 A confirmation.
675 An inference.

DENISE: Similar characteristics.

SWAMIJI: Similar characteristics. And those horns also are found.

SCHOLAR: That is *parīkṣā*.

SWAMIJI: That is *parīkṣā* (complete investigation). Now, *āptavacana*, now he will put the proof of *āptavacana*. *Āptavacana* is that person who is an authority, who says that, [for example], "If you [perform] a sacrificial fire in a particular way, you will attain heaven." In that, what is the *uddeśa*, what is the *lakṣaṇa*, and what is the *parīkṣā*?

Audio 10 - 07:59

स्वःकाम ईदृगुद्देशो यजेतेत्यस्य लक्षणम ।
अग्निष्टोमादिनेत्येषा परीक्षा शेषवर्तिनी ॥२६५॥

svaḥkāma īdṛguddeśo yajetetyasya lakṣaṇam /
agniṣṭomādinetyeṣā parīkṣā śeṣavartinī //265// [not recited]

"*Svaḥ kāma*, he who has got the desire to achieve heaven," this is the *uddeśa*. "Must perform oblations of fire," this is the *lakṣaṇa*. "*Agniṣṭomādinā*, by the way of *agniṣṭoma*,"[676] it is *parīkṣā*.

SCHOLAR: Etcetera.

SWAMIJI: Etcetera.[677] So *uddeśa*, *lakṣaṇa*, and *parīkṣā* you will find in each and every proof (in *pratyakṣa*, in *anumāna*, in *upamāna*, and in *āptavacana*). These are the four . . .

SCHOLAR: Means of knowledge.

SWAMIJI: . . . means of proof; knowledge also.

SCHOLAR: Usually in the West, they are translated as "the means of knowledge."

SWAMIJI: The means of knowledge, yes.

JOHN: *Pramāṇa*.

---

676 The praise of Agni.
677 By way of *agniṣṭoma*, etcetera.

Audio 10 - 07:50

विकल्पस्त्रक्ष्यमाणान्यरुचितांशसहिष्णुनः ।
वस्तुनो या तथात्वेन सृष्टिः सोद्देशसंज्ञिता ॥ २६६ ॥

vikalpasrakṣyamāṇānyarucitāṁśasahiṣṇunaḥ /
vastuno yā tathātvena sṛṣṭiḥ soddeśasaṁjñitā //266//

Vikalpa srakṣyamaṇa anyarucitāṁśa sahiṣṇunaḥ, vastunaḥ yā tathātvena sṛṣṭi. Vikalpa srakṣyamāṇa anya, etc., by *vikalpas*,[678] which are created by your own imaginations and by other means also, those points which are attributed to the aspects of that object, it is *uddeśa*, that is *uddeśa. Anya*–[*ye*] *sāmānya vyatiriktāḥ pramātuḥ saṁtoṣādāyakatvācca, rucitāḥ*, because you accept that, you accept those points, which are in you in the background.[679] That is *uddeśa. Uddeśa* is not that kind of flux of proof which you don't accept. You must accept that! That is *uddeśa*.

SCHOLAR: That is why he says "*rucitā*."[680]

SWAMIJI: *Rucitāṁ śasahiṣṇunaḥ.*

SCHOLAR: *Mātra rucitā.*

SWAMIJI: What is the reason of that, that in ignorance also, you know that, what is to happen, in the background?[681] You can't explain it at that time but you know that in the background of your consciousness.

Audio 10 - 09:31

तदैव संविच्चिनुते यावतः स्त्रक्ष्यमाणता ।
यतो ह्यकालकलिता संधत्ते सार्वकालिकम् ॥२६७॥

678 Thoughts.
679 From Jayaratha's commentary.
680 Agreeable.
681 In other words, how does one intuitively know the suitability of the definitions that are attributed to their object of inquiry? How does one intuitively know the answer to their own question?

tadaiva saṁviccinute yāvataḥ srakṣyamāṇatā /
yato hyakālakalitāsaṁdhatte sārvakālikam //267//
[not recited in full]

Because this consciousness is *akāla kalita*, is beyond the sphere of time, and She conceives, She perceives, the state of all the times.[682]

SCHOLAR: Could we say "*saṁdhatte* (synthesizes)"?

SWAMIJI: Synthesizes, yes.

SCHOLAR: "Draws together" (*saṁdhatte*).

SWAMIJI: Yes. *Tadaiva saṁviccinute yāvataḥ srakṣyamāṇatā*, there and then, at the time of *uddeśa*, one's consciousness accepts that, that this will come out of it. For instance, [he knows] this answer will come out of it [because] that answer, in the background, is [already] there.

SCHOLAR: It synthesizes as much as it will . . .

SWAMIJI: Yes, [the answer] will come like that. And when you get an answer from your master, if you accept that, well and good, [but] if you don't accept it, [then] that is not the real answer, because you know that answer in the background of your consciousness. Because, *akālakalitā saṁvit sārvakālikam saṁdhatte*, *akālakalita*, that *saṁvit* which is not bound, which is not bound by time (timeless, which is timeless), She knows, that consciousness knows, what will happen, what is existing now and what will happen afterwards in the field of the answer.

Audio 10 - 11:15

स्रक्ष्यमाणस्य या सृष्टिः प्राक्सृष्टांशस्य संहृतिः ।
अनूद्यमाने धर्मे सा संविल्लक्षणमुच्यते ॥२६८॥

srakṣyamāṇasya yā sṛṣṭiḥ prāksṛṣṭāṁśasya saṁhṛtiḥ /
anūdyamāne dharme sā saṁvillakṣaṇamucyate //268//

Srakṣyamāṇasya yā sṛṣṭiḥ prāk sṛṣṭāṁśasya saṁhṛti. "Etat

682 *Saṁvit devī* (the Goddess of consciousness).

kiṁ," for instance, "What is this?" "What is this?" It is *prāk sṛṣṭāṁśa*. The first point, it has been created in this way: "What is it? What can it be?" When that [initial] creation is destroyed–at the time of the answer, that [initial] creation is destroyed–and *srakṣyamāṇasya yā sṛṣṭi, srakṣyamāṇa*, what is to happen next: "Is it a log or is it a man? Is it a man or is it a log?" That is *srakṣyamāṇa*. That will come now in the next moment. [In the] next moment, you'll know if it is a log or if it is a man. When that is created, and when the previous consciousness is destroyed (the previous consciousness: "What is it?"), *anūdyamāne dharme sā*, when you put aspects of proofs again and again on that subject, . . .*

[For example], "This is a man because this is moving, this is in movement, so this is not a log." Or, "This is a log because this is not [moving]. And that hollow is [there but] it is [just] a hollow, it is not a mouth. This is another portion of a branch. It is not an arm. So it is a log. It is not a man."

*. . . *anūdyamāne dharme*, when you repeatedly [ascribe and] investigate aspects of a log, not aspects of a man, in that object, that is *lakṣaṇa*.[683]

SCHOLAR: *Sā saṁvit*?

SWAMIJI: *Sā saṁvit lakṣaṇam ucyate*, that consciousness is called *lakṣaṇa*.

Audio 10 - 13:27

तत्पृष्ठपातिभूयोंशसृष्टिसंहारविभ्रमाः ।
परीक्षा कथ्यते मातृरुचिता कल्पितावधिः ॥२६९॥

tatpṛṣṭhapātibhūyoṁśasṛṣṭi saṁhāravibhramāḥ /
parīkṣā kathyate mātṛrucitā kalpitāvadhiḥ //269//

And then after that, on that object, when you put . . . just imagine [that] it is a man, it is not a log. Just for the time being, we will accept that this is a man, this is not a log. *Tat*

683 Definition.

pṛṣṭhapāti bhūyoṁśa sṛṣṭi saṁhāra, that is *sṛṣṭi saṁhāra vibhramāḥ*, the expansion of creating and destroying, of creating that man and destroying that man and putting there the consciousness of a log only, and then again creating a man: "But this is a man. Why not call it a man? It must be a man. It is not a log." Then, again, with more aspects, put more aspects in that, and conclude that it is a log, it is not a man. That is *sṛṣṭi saṁhāra vibhramāḥ*. *Parīkṣā kathyate*, that is *parīkṣā*, that is called *parīkṣā*.[684] That is not *lakṣaṇa*. That is *parīkṣā* and it is [the result of] this creation and destruction, the creation of the log and the destruction of the log, the creation of a man and the destruction of a man. Do it again and again, again and again, [until] you get the full confirmation that it is a log, it is not a man.

DEVOTEE: *Mātṛ rucitā.*

SWAMIJI: And it is *mātṛ rucitā*: when the seer is satisfied himself, that is the end, that is the end of doubt.

SCHOLAR: *Kalpita avadhi.*[685]

SWAMIJI: That is the end of . . . *kalpita avadhi*. This *avadhi*, this is the limit, this is the limit of perception.

SCHOLAR: This is to answer the objection that there would be no end to *parīkṣā*.[686]

SWAMIJI: Otherwise there would be no end. But the end is there when the seer will be satisfied that it is a log.

---

684 Confirmation.

685 The limit, conclusion, or termination (*avadhi*) of conception (*kalpita*).

686 As introduced by Jayaratha in his introductory commentary for this verse.

THE THREE LEVELS OF SPEECH
PAŚYANTĪ-MADHYAMĀ-VAIKHARĪ (270-271)

Audio 10 - 15:33

प्राक्पश्यन्त्यथ मध्यान्या वैखरी चेति ता इमाः ।
परा परापरा देवी चरमा त्वपरात्मिका ॥२७०॥

prākpaśyantyatha madhyānyā vaikharī ceti tā imāḥ /
parā parāparā devī caramā tvaparātmikā //270//

It is the same thing as [when] first you get *paśyantī vāṇī*, then *madhyamā*, then *vaikharī*.[687] These three are [the goddesses], *parā*, *parāparā*, and *aparā*, in other words. First, *uddeśa* is *paśyantī*, *madhyamā* is *lakṣaṇa*, *vaikharī* is *parīkṣā*. *Uddeśa* is *parā*, *lakṣaṇa* is *parāparā*, *parīkṣā* is *aparā*.

Audio 10 - 16:15

इच्छादि शक्तित्रितयमिदमेव निगद्यते ।

icchādi śaktitritayamidameva nigadyate /271a
[not recited in full]

And this is the energy of will, the energy of knowledge, and the energy of action. It will go with that because . . .

Audio 10 - 16:27

एतत्प्राणित एवायं व्यवहारः प्रतायते ॥२७१॥

etat prāṇita evāyaṁ vyavahāraḥ pratāyate //271b//

687 For an explanation of the levels of speech (*vāṇī* or *vāk*), see *Kashmir Shaivism–The Secret Supreme*, 6.41.

. . . this whole *hanādanādi vyavahāraḥ*, this whole worldly movement, is done by the insertion of this life.

SCHOLAR: *Pratāyate pratanyate.*

SWAMIJI: *Pratanyate*, gets expanded in the universe.

THE FIVEFOLD CONTACT OF MASTERS (272-276)

Audio 10 - 16:50

एतत्प्रश्नोत्तरात्मत्वे पारमेश्वरशासने ।
परसंबन्धरूपत्वमभिसंबन्धपञ्चके ॥ २७२ ॥

etatpraśnottarātmatve pārameśvaraśāsane /
parasaṁbandharūpatvamabhisaṁbandhapañcake //272//

And there are the fivefold contacts, the fivefold contacts of master and disciple,[688] in this Shaivism, in the Trika system, where there is *praśna* and *uttara. Praśna* (a question) is put by the disciple and the answer comes from the lips of the master. In this theory of Trika, *para saṁbandhatva rūpatvam*, you find the supreme *saṁbandha* (supreme contact) in all these five contacts.

SCHOLAR: But the five contacts themselves are not only in Trika.

SWAMIJI: Yes, they are in Trika.

SCHOLAR: But not only.

SWAMIJI: Not only.

SCHOLAR: This doctrine that the *parasaṁbandha rūpatvam*[689] is in five, that is . . .

---

688 See *Kashmir Shaivism–The Secret Supreme*, 12, "The Fivefold Contacts of Masters and Disciples."
689 The formation (*rūpa*) of the supreme contact (*para saṁbandha*).

SWAMIJI: Yes, that is Trika.

SCHOLAR: Because it is found in the *Ratnamālā*, which is a Kula text.

SWAMIJI: Yes. And *para saṁbandha*, this [supreme] *saṁbandha*, is *mahān*, *avāntara*, *divya*, *divyādivya*, and *adivya*.[690]

Audio 10 - 18:20

यथोक्तं रत्नमालायां सर्वः परकलात्मकः ।
महानवान्तरो दिव्यो मिश्रोऽन्योऽन्यस्तु पञ्चमः ॥२७३॥

yathoktaṁ ratnamālāyāṁ sarvaḥ parakalātmakaḥ /
mahānavāntaro divyo miśro'nyo'nyastu pañcamaḥ //273//

This is also explained in the *Ratnamālā śāstra* that everything is *parakala*, everything is inserted in *para saṁbandha* (divine contact), [that] all contacts are inserted, all contacts are seen, in *para saṁbandha–mahā saṁbandha* also, *avāntara saṁbandha* also, *divya saṁbandha* also, *divyādivya saṁbandha* also, and *adivya saṁbandha*, the divine [contact] is all-pervading in them. For instance, *mahān saṁbandha* is the first *saṁbandha*, the first contact of master and disciple. When the master resides in the state of Śiva and the disciple resides in the state of Sadāśiva,[691] that contact is called *mahān saṁbandha*. This is the first contact.

JOHN: You mean, the highest.

SWAMIJI: Highest. And *avāntara* is when the master resides in the state of Sadāśiva and the disciple resides in the state of Anantabhaṭṭāraka. This is *avāntara saṁbandha*. And the third contact of master and disciple is when the master resides in the state of Anantabhaṭṭāraka and the disciple

690 Supreme (*mahān*), intermediate (*avāntara*), divine (*divya*), partly divine and partly not divine (*divyādivya*), and not divine (*adivya*).

691 *Sadāśiva* resides at the level of the 34th *tattva*. See Appendix 2 (p372) for explanation of the 36 *tattvas* (elements).

resides in the state of Srīkaṇṭhanātha.[692]

DEVOTEE: *Śrīkaṇṭha nandikumārādī.*[693]

SCHOLAR: Nandikumāra? Nandikeśvara.[694]

SWAMIJI: Nandikeśvara, yes.

JOHN: What is the state of this Anantabhaṭṭāraka? Is this in the same way . . . ?

SWAMIJI: Anantabhaṭṭāraka is between *mantramaheśvara* and *mantreśvara*.[695]

SCHOLAR: What is the nature of his awareness? What is the nature of that awareness, the awareness of Anantabhaṭṭāraka, which we call Anantabhaṭṭāraka?

SWAMIJI: Anantabhaṭṭāraka is the immediate agent of Lord Śiva for creating, for governing, this universal field. This is the immediate agent–Anantabhaṭṭāraka. Sadāśiva won't bother for that.[696]

SCHOLAR: Because his awareness is . . .

SWAMIJI: Īśvara would bother but Īśvara has not that power as Anantabhaṭṭāraka has.

JOHN: This is having more *kriyā* . . .

SWAMIJI: Yes, *kriyā*.

JOHN: . . . because he is between this Śuddhavidyā and this . . . ?

SWAMIJI: Yes, Anantabhaṭṭāraka is the handler [of the

---

692 Śrīkaṇṭhanātha resides between the states of *vijñānākala* and Śuddhavidyā.

693 From Jayaratha's commentary.

694 Nandi is traditionally the name for Lord Śiva's bull, but here Nandikumāra, or Nandikeśvara, is considered to be an incarnation of Śrīkaṇṭhanātha.

695 Between Sadāśiva and Īśvara *tattva*, respectively.

696 "Anantabhaṭṭāraka, also known as Aghoranātha, is the immediate assistant of Lord Śiva. He is the agent for creation, protection, and destruction, and Lord Śiva himself conducts only revealing and the concealing." Paraphrase from *Tantrāloka* 6.172-174 (LJA archive).

universe]. Sadāśiva is not the handler; He resides in His own nature.

SCHOLAR: So when the *guru* is in that state of awareness, . . .

SWAMIJI: Yes.

SCHOLAR: . . . this is in what? We are now in *divya* (divine contact).

SWAMIJI: Yes.

JOHN: Then you said there was Anantabhaṭṭāraka, then the next was?

SCHOLAR: Śrīkaṇṭha.

SWAMIJI: Śrīkaṇṭha.[697]

JOHN: He exists where? Between *mahāmāyā* and . . . ?

SWAMIJI: No, not *mahāmāyā*, above *mahāmāyā*.

JOHN: Above. Between *vijñānākala* and Śuddhavidyā?

SWAMIJI: Yes, between *vijñānākala* and Śuddhavidyā.[698]

Audio 10 - 21:37

And then, *ṛṣīṇāṁ ca samāsena nandinā pratipāditam*,[699] when that Nandikeśvara or Śrīkaṇṭhanātha's place is taken by the master and the disciple resides in the state of *ṛṣis*,[700] that is *divyādivya* (partly divine) *saṁbandha* (contact). This is the

697 The ancient master, Śrīkaṇṭhanātha, who appeared to Durvāsa at the beginning of Kali Yuga, "is another formation of Lord Śiva. Śrīkaṇṭhanātha handles the whole universe, the remaining whole universe." Ibid., 12.13. For a detailed explanation of the lineage of Masters of Kashmir Shaivism, see *Kashmir Shaivism–Secret Supreme*, "Birth of the Tantras," 13.90.

698 In the *Parātriśikā Vivaraṇa* (LJA archive), Abhinavagupta explains that *mahāmāya*, which is not listed among the elements, is the seat of *vijñānākala pramātṛ*. See Appendix 2 (p372) for complete list of 36 *tattvas*.

699 This line appears in a verse from the *Ratnamālā śāstra*, which is referenced by Jayaratha in his commentary.

700 Sage, saint, or seer.

fourth contact of master and disciple. And the fifth contact of master and disciple is when, in a *vidyāpīṭha*,[701] a master exists by explaining *śāstra*s, the theory of the *śāstra*s, and [there exists the] *śiṣya* and the *ācārya*, the master and the disciple.

SCHOLAR: What does he mean by "*vidyāpīṭha prapūjane*"?

SWAMIJI: *Vidyāpīṭha*. There are four *pīṭha*s:[702] Kāmarūpā, Jālandhara, Uḍḍayana, and Medhāpīṭha (that is Pūrṇagiri; Pūrṇagiri is Medhāpīṭha). Medhāpīṭha, where there is full knowledge (*medha* is "knowledge").

SCHOLAR: "*Vidyāpīṭha*" is?

SWAMIJI: All these. *Vidyāpīṭha* is all of these four *pīṭha*s.

SCHOLAR: But he says, "*vidyāpīṭha prapūjane*."

SWAMIJI: Yes, for worshipping, for respecting, that *vidyāpīṭha*. *Prapūjane* is "respect" (*ādara*). This [fifth contact] is *adivya saṁbandha*. There the master is also *adivya* and the disciple is also *adivya*.[703]

JOHN: Where is the disciple residing in this *adivya* (not divine) *saṁbandha*?

SWAMIJI: As a human being, and the master as a *ṛṣi* (and that also as a human being).

JOHN: "*Ṛṣi*" they are defining as what?

SWAMIJI: *Ṛṣi* is that [person] who is a human being, completely pure from all bad things.

JOHN: *Mala*.

SWAMIJI: *Mala*s. [He has] no *mala*s and [he is] a human being. That is a *ṛṣi*.

SWAMIJI: But from the Śaiva point of view, all these contacts must be inserted in *para saṁbandha*.

SCHOLAR: "Are inserted" or "must be inserted"?

SWAMIJI: Actually are inserted and you must perceive them as that. You must not perceive your master as a human being;

701 Lit., a seat of knowledge.
702 Lit., seats.
703 *Adivya*: not divine.

you must not perceive your master as a *ṛṣi*; you must not perceive your master as Nandikeśvara; you must not perceive your master as Sadāśiva and so on. You must perceive your master as Śiva and perceive yourself as Sadāśiva. That is *para saṁbandha*, in each and every contact of master and disciple.[704]

SCHOLAR: You have made this clear.

SWAMIJI: Yes, that is the theory of *saṁbandha*.

Audio 10 - 24:53

भिन्नयोः प्रष्टृतद्वक्त्रोश्चैकात्म्यं यत्स उच्यते ।

bhinnayoḥ praṣṭṛtadvaktroścaikātmyaṁ yatsa ucyate /274a

What is *para saṁbandha*? He clarifies what really *para saṁbandha* is. The supreme contact of master and disciple is when *praṣṭrā* and *vaktrā*, . . .*

Praṣṭrā means, that [person] who puts a question (that is a disciple). *Vaktrā* means, that [person] who makes the answer (that is the master).

704 "Although our Kashmir Śaivism recognizes these fivefold contacts of masters and disciples, yet it explains that only that initiation is a real initiation where the contact of the master and the disciple takes place in such a way that, at the time of initiation, the master is united with the disciple and the disciple is united with the master. In this real initiation, the master becomes one with the disciple and the disciple becomes one with the master. You should understand, however, that for this supreme contact to take place, the disciple should never find any fault in his master or his master's activity. If he does, then he is lost. This kind of initiation can take place in any state of these five contacts. It is the real supreme contact. It is even above *mahān saṁbandhaḥ* (the great contact) and is called *para saṁbandhaḥ* (the supreme contact). It is that contact by which all contacts become divine. The real theory of our Śaivism is that this contact, which is the supreme contact, must take place between each and every master and each and every disciple. When this occurs, then that initiation is a real initiation." *Kashmir Shaivism–The Secret Supreme*, 86.

*. . . *caikātmyaṁ*, when this *vaktrā* and *praṣṭrā* are united in one. When *vaktrā* and *praṣṭrā* are united in one being, that is *para saṁbandha*; *sa ucyate para saṁbandha*, that is *para saṁbandha*. So you must not think anything which is not divine in the master and you should not consider anything, any action of your own person, which is not divine. You must remain as divine. You must enter in divinity all-round, then you will enter in *para saṁbandha*, then you are in *para saṁbandha*. *Para saṁbandha* is actually existing everywhere from the Śaiva point of view.

JOHN: So this *sādhaka* (aspirant) who is existing in the level of Sadāśiva would be in *śāmbhavopāya*.

SWAMIJI: Yes, in *śāmbhavopāya*.

Audio 10 - 26:14

संबन्धः परता चास्य पूर्णैकात्म्यप्रथामयी ॥ २७४ ॥

saṁbandhaḥ paratā cāsya pūrṇaikātmyaprathāmayī //
274b//

And this, this is *saṁbandha* (*ayam saṁbandhaḥ*): *asya paratā kā*, *pūrṇa ekātmya prathāmayī paratā*, and this supremacy of this *saṁbandha* is the fullness of the union with master and disciple.

Audio 10 - 26:43

अनेनैव नयेन स्यात्संबन्धान्तरमप्यलम् ।
शास्त्रवाच्यं फलादीनां परिपूर्णत्वयोगतः ॥ २७५ ॥

anenaiva nayena syātsaṁbandhāntaramapyalam /
śāstravācyaṁ phalādīnāṁ paripūrṇatvayogataḥ //275//

In this very line,[705] you must make, tread, all these *saṁbandhas*, . . .*

Although you may be a human being, what of that? You must become as divine as Sadāśiva.

705 Of the fullness of the union with master and disciple.

*. . . *saṁbandhāntaramapyalam śāstravācyam*, which are to be explained in *śāstra*, *phalādīnām paripūrṇatva yogataḥ*, because the fruit [that] he will obtain [will be the] completely full fruit from that contact. No matter if you are human being and your master is a *ṛṣi* (a pure human being), if you insert that kind of perception in this contact that, "I am situated in the seat of Sadāśiva and he is Śiva Himself," then you will get the fruit like that.

Audio 10 - 27:56

इत्थं संविदियं देवी स्वभावादेव सर्वदा ।
उद्देशादित्रयप्राणा सर्वशास्त्रस्वरूपिणी ॥ २७६ ॥

itthaṁ saṁvidiyaṁ devī svabhāvādeva sarvadā /
uddeśāditrayaprāṇā sarvaśāstrasvarūpiṇī //276//

In this way, this Deity of consciousness is always, in an eternal way, one with *śāstra*, one with the tradition of all this philosophy of *śāstra*s, and She is given life,[706] She is given life by *uddeśa*, *lakṣaṇa*, and *parīkṣā*.[707]

CONTENTS OF TANTRĀLOKA IN BRIEF
PŪRVAJA UDDEŚA (277-285A)

Audio 10 - 28:32

तत्रोच्यते पुरोद्देशः पूर्वजानुजभेदवान् ।

tatrocyate puroddeśaḥ pūrvajānujabhedavān /277a

So, first we will explain the *uddeśa* for the *Tantrāloka*, what

706 *Prāṇa*.
707 As was said earlier in verse 270, *uddeśa* (nomination), *lakṣaṇa* (definition) and *parīkṣā* (investigation) are the three goddesses: *parā*, *parāparā*, and *aparā*.

is the *uddeśa*, and then we will explain the *lakṣaṇa*, and then we will explain the *parīkṣā*–for the *Tantrāloka*. And first we have to put here the *uddeśa* for the *Tantrāloka*. But *uddeśa* is twofold: *pūrvaja uddeśa* and *anuja uddeśa*. *Pūrvaja* means "that [which] has appeared first" and *anuja* is "that which has appeared afterwards, after confirmation" (that is *anuja uddeśa*).

Now he puts the *pūrvaja uddeśa* first, of the *Tantrāloka*:

Audio 10 - 29:29

विज्ञानभिद्गतोपायः परोपायस्तृतीयकः ॥ २७७ ॥

vijñānabhidgatopāyaḥ paropāyastṛtīyakaḥ //277b//
[not recited]

1. *Vijñānabhit*, first; *vijñānabhit*, where you get the differentiated complete knowledge of all the means. That is *vijñānabhit* (*vijñāna* means, *upāya*; *bhit* means, *bheda*). The differentiated perception of all the means is done in the first *āhnika*.

SCHOLAR: *Vijñāna* here is *vijñāna catuṣka bheda*.

SWAMIJI: *Vijñāna catuṣka bheda*,[708] yes.

2. *Gatopāya*,[709] where there is no means, where there is no necessity of means, it is the second *āhnika*.[710]

3. *Paropāya*, the supreme means (that is *śāmbhavopāya*), the third *āhnika*. *Paropāya* is *tṛtīyakaḥ*, the third.[711]

Audio 10 - 30:12

शाक्तोपायो नरोपायः कालोपायोऽथ सप्तमः ।
चक्रोदयोऽथ देशाध्वा तत्त्वाध्वा तत्त्वभेदनम् ॥ २७८ ॥

---

708 The differentiated (*bheda*) knowledge (*vijñāna*) of the four (*catuṣka*) means.

709 *Anupāya*.

710 See *Kashmir Shaivism–The Secret Supreme*, chapter 5.

711 Ibid., chapters 3, 4 and 6.

śāktopāyo naropāyaḥ kālopāyo'tha saptamaḥ /
cakrodayo'tha deśādhvā tattvādhvā tattvabhedanam //278//
[not recited]

4. *Śāktopāya* is the fourth [*āhnika*].
5. *Naropāya* (*āṇavopāya*) is the fifth [*āhnika*].[712]
6. *Kālopāya*, the means how to cross the boundary of time. That is *kālopāya*.[713]

JOHN: This differs from *āṇava, śākta*, or *śāmbhava*.

SWAMIJI: This is *āṇava*.[714]

SCHOLAR: All *āṇava*.

JOHN: This is more *āṇava*.

SWAMIJI: This is more *āṇava*, yes. *Kālopāya*, where you cross the surface of time. That is *kālopāya*.

7. Then *saptama* (the seventh *āhnika*) is *cakrodaya*. *Cakrodaya* is the seventh *āhnika*. What you already do–*cakrodaya*.[715] It is explained there in the seventh *āhnika*.
8. Then *deśādhva*. *Deśādhva* is the eighth *āhnika*. The explanation of all worlds, one hundred and eighteen worlds, that is *deśādhva*. It is the eighth *āhnika*.
9. *Tattvādhva*, the explanation of the thirty-six elements. That is the ninth *āhnika*.[716]
10. *Tattvabhedanam*, the differentiated perceptions of the elements. That is *tattvabhednam*. That is the tenth *āhnika*.[717]

---

712 Ibid., chapter 5.

713 Ibid., chapter 6.

714 Chapter 6 to chapter 37 of the *Tantrāloka* is all *āṇavopāya* discussion.

715 "The rise of *cakras* will be explained, which is most secret in our system–the rise of wheels in your body. *Cakrodaya* means, the rise of wheels, the various wheels, in your body." *Tantrāloka* 7.1, (LJA archive). The practice of *cakrodaya* is explained in *Self Realization in Kashmir Shaivism–The Oral Teachings* of Swami Lakshmanjoo, ed. John Hughes (State University of New York Press, Albany, 1995), chpt 2, "Talks on Practice."

716 See *Kashmir Shaivism–The Secret Supreme,* chapters 1 and 7.

717 Ibid., chapters 8 and 9.

JOHN: How does that differ from the ninth (*tattvādhva*) and this . . . ?

SCHOLAR: Different *pramātṛ*s.

SWAMIJI: That is the different *pramātṛ*s. He has put *sakala*, *pralayākala*, *vijñānākala*, Śuddhavidyā, Īśvara, Sadāśiva, all that, all these *pramātṛ*s he has inserted in the thirty-six elements.

JOHN: In the tenth book.

SWAMIJI: Yes, that is *tattva bhedanam*.

Audio 10 - 32:02

कलाद्यध्वाध्वोपयोगः शक्तिपाततिरोहिती ।
दीक्षोपक्रमणं दीक्षा सामयी पौत्रिके विधौ ॥ २७९ ॥

kalādyadhvādhvopayogaḥ śaktipātatirohitī /
dīkṣopakramaṇaṁ dīkṣā sāmayī pautrike vidhau //279//
[not recited]

11. *Kalādyadhva* is the differentiated explanation of the five circles (*nivṛtti kalā, pratiṣṭhā kalā*, *vidyā kalā*, *śāntā kalā*, and *śāntātītā kalā*). The differentiated explanation of those is explained in eleventh [*āhnika*].[718]

12. *Adhva upayogaḥ*, in the twelfth [*āhnika*], what is the main object to be held in crossing, on the journey of treading, on these elements–*adhva upayoga* (*adhva* means, all these elements, the elementary world). When you tread on the elementary world, on the path of the elementary world, what do you need, that is explained in that twelfth *āhnika*. In the twelfth *āhnika* is explained that, what you need. I will explain to you what you need. You need doubtlessness in the master and in his words. If you have the slightest point of doubt in his words–gone!–you won't achieve anything. That is *adhva upayoga*. That is explained in the twelfth *āhnika*.[719]

718 Ibid., chapter 2.
719 Ibid.

13. Then *śaktipāta*, the grace, the explanation of the grace of the Lord–the thirteenth *āhnika*.[720]

DEVOTEE: *Tirohitī*.

SWAMIJI: 14. *Tirohitī*, the explanation of the concealing power of your master, Lord Śiva, how He conceals His nature, that is the fourteenth [*āhnika*].

15. *Dīkṣopakramaṇam*, the beginning of initiation, that formal initiation.

JOHN: That's what, the fifteenth?

SWAMIJI: Yes, it is the fifteenth. And *dīkṣa upakramaṇam*[721] and *sāmayī dīkṣā*, these two things. *Sāmayī dīkṣā*, this is the initiation of discipline, how to maintain discipline on that path. *Bas*!

16. *Pautrike vidhau*, how to become a *putraka* of your master. *Putraka* means, when you are likely to have his property, that is *putraka*, because he nominates you as his son, as his son on this path, so you have authority on each and every property of your master–not material property, spiritual property.

JOHN: One *kongari*, one glasses case (laughter).

SWAMIJI: (laughter) *Pautrike*, this is the sixteenth *āhnika*.

Audio 10 - 35:22

प्रमेयप्रक्रिया सूक्ष्मा दीक्षा सद्यःसमुत्क्रमः ।
तुलादीक्षाथ पारोक्षी लिङ्गोद्धरोऽभिषेचनम् ॥२८०॥

prameyaprakriyā sūkṣmā dīkṣā sadyaḥsamutkramaḥ /
tulādīkṣātha pārokṣī liṅgoddhāro'bhiṣecanam //280//
[not recited]

17. *Prameyaprakriyā*, the seventeenth *āhnika*.

18. *Sūkṣmā dīkṣā*, subtle initiation, this is the eighteenth *āhnika*.

720 Ibid., chapter 10.
721 The introduction of *dīkṣa*, outward initiation.

JOHN: So this *prameya prakriyā* is about the objective world?

SWAMIJI: *Prameya* is not objective. *Prameya* is the way how to act on *dīkṣā* (initiation)–*prameya prakriyā*.

JOHN: How to act as the initiator or the initiate?

SWAMIJI: Both. That is *prameya prakriyā*.

19. *Sadyaḥ samutkramaḥ*, how to get rid of the physical frame if it is not fit, how you can die [earlier], or if you are going to die at 10am, how you can die at 6 o'clock am and get rid of that pain.

DENISE: That's not suicide?

SWAMIJI: No, no, no, not suicide. By initiation, by initiation. Your master initiates you at that time and you get rid of that physical [body].

SCHOLAR: This is *brahmavidyā*.[722]

SWAMIJI: *Brahmavidyā*, etcetera, yes.

20. *Tulā dīkṣā*, and when there is initiation of scale.

JOHN: Of scale.

SWAMIJI: Scale.

DENISE: Oh, with flowers and the disciple . . .

SWAMIJI: Yes, twenty-seven flowers, he puts twenty-seven flowers on one scale and the disciple on one scale, and this will come in balance, level.

21. *Pārokṣī dīkṣā*, initiation which is *parokṣa*.[723] [For example], the disciple comes [and says], "Master, I am still pending, I am still hanging. I have not gained, achieved, anything." [The master says], "Wait, wait, it will come. You will achieve, you will achieve!" He gets satisfaction from his master's sayings every now and then, and he attains nothing. And, at the same time, without the knowledge of the master, he passes away in the same state, having done nothing. So he repents. Who?

---

722 This is known as *utkrānti*, the technique of how to leave the body at the time of death.

723 Lit., beyond the range of sight.

JOHN: The master.

SWAMIJI: His master [laments], "Why I did not initiate him properly so that he would have been enlightened?" And for that, he puts *parokṣa dīkṣā*. That is *parokṣa dīkṣā*. Although [the disciple] is dead, [the master] puts initiation through *mantra*s and calls him back, calls that dead person back, the dead disciple. That is *pārokṣa dīkṣā*. That *pārokṣa dīkṣā* is the twenty-first *āhnika*.

22. *Liṅgoddhāra*. *Liṅgoddhāra* is, for instance, you are a Christian. You have to shun Christianity and enter on the path of Shaivism. Or you are a Buddhist. You have to shun Buddhism and enter on the path of Shaivism. So, the master has to get him out from that *liṅga*, from that sign, of that authority, of religion. He has to get him out of that first and then initiate him. That is *liṅgoddhāra*. When you have no religion and you go to your master, there is no *liṅgoddhāra* needed, because you are pure. Shanna is pure. She has no *liṅga*. She is not initiated in Christianity nor in any other system, so she can enter on the path of Shaivism without *liṅgoddhāra*.

DENISE: Like when we first came to you and we were disciples of Maharishi.

SWAMIJI: That is *liṅgoddhāra*.

DENISE: And we waited so long to get initiation. And we kept saying, "Why? Come on! Now, now please!" But we had to wait.

SWAMIJI: For *liṅgoddhāra*, that is *liṅgoddhāra*.

23. Then *abhiṣecana* is the twenty-third *āhnika–abhiṣecana*.

JOHN: What is that?

SWAMIJI: *Abhiṣecana* is to *abhiṣeka*[724] as a *sāmayī*,[725] *abhiṣeka* as a *putraka*,[726] *abhiṣeka* as a *sādhaka*,[727] and

724 Anoint, inaugurate, consecrate.
725 A person who is placed under rules and regulations.
726 A son.
727 An aspirant.

abhiṣeka as an *ācārya.*[728] Because you are initiated to be disciplined first. You are initiated to be disciplined. That is the first *abhiṣeka.* That is *sāmayīka abhiṣeka.* The second *abhiṣeka* is *sādhaka*; you are initiated to tread on the path of spirituality and you get a *mantra, guru mantra.* That is the second initiation. And then you are initiated for achieving the inheritance of your master. The inheritance of your master, that is *putraka.* And you are initiated, in the end, to be a master, and you can initiate others. That is *ācārya dīkṣā.* That is *abhiṣecanam*–fourfold.

Audio 10 - 41:00

अन्त्येष्टिः श्राद्धक्लृप्तिश्च शेषवृत्तिनिरूपणम् ।
लिङ्गार्चा बहुभित्पर्वपवित्रादि निमित्तजम् ॥ २८१ ॥

antyeṣṭiḥ śrāddhaklṛptiśca śeṣavṛttinirūpaṇam /
liṅgārcā bahubhitparvapavitrādi nimittajam //281//

24. Then *antyeṣṭi. Antyeṣṭi* is the twenty-fourth *āhnika. Antyeṣṭiḥ karma,* how to put *antyeṣṭi karma. Antyeṣṭi* is not *śrāddha. Antyeṣṭi* is that process of action which is done at the time of death, a funeral. At the time of . . .

SCHOLAR: Of the master, the *antyeṣṭi* of the master.

SWAMIJI: Yes, the master and the disciple, both.

SCHOLAR: This *cakra pūjā* and . . .

SWAMIJI: Yes.

25. *Śrāddhaklṛptiḥ* is the next *āhnika.*

JOHN: What is this . . . ?

SWAMIJI: *Śrāddhaklṛpti–śrāddha.*

JOHN: So this *śrāddha*, death anniversary.

SWAMIJI: Yes, but this *śrāddha* is something else.

SCHOLAR: This is *tāntrik śrāddha.*

SWAMIJI: It is *tāntrik śrāddha*, yes, Shaivite *śrāddha.*

728 A spiritual guide or teacher.

26. And *śeṣavṛtti nirūpaṇam*. And *śeṣavṛtti*, how he has to act for the remaining portion of his life. If he is elevated and absolutely one with Lord Śiva, how he has to act in the remaining portion of his life.

JOHN: That is number twenty-six.

SWAMIJI: That is *śeṣavṛttiḥ*, the twenty-sixth.

27. *Liṅgārcā*, how to worship a *liṅga*, a *Śiva liṅga*. What *liṅga* is to be worshipped? Is it to be worshipped of stone, is it to be worshipped of that mud *liṅga*, or is it be worshipped that *ātmā liṅga*, the internal *liṅga* of the Self?[729] He explains that in that–which *āhnika*?–the twenty-seventh.

28. *Bahubhit parva pavitrādi nimittajam*, and all those big days, special days. The speciality of days–this is a *parva*, this is a *parva*, this is a *parva*.

SCHOLAR: The guru's birthday, the guru's (inaudible).

SWAMIJI: The guru's birthday, the guru's inspiring day, the initiation day, all that.

SCHOLAR: And one's guru-brothers and sisters?

SWAMIJI: Yes, yes, that also. The guru's brother's day, the guru's sister's day, all that.

JOHN: This is the twenty-eighth.

SWAMIJI: This is the twenty-eighth, yes.

Audio 10 - 43:19

रहस्यचर्या मन्त्रौघो मण्डलं मुद्रिकाविधिः ।
एकीकारः स्वस्वरूपे प्रवेशः शास्त्रमेलनम् ॥२८२॥
आयातिकथनं शास्त्रोपादेयत्वनिरूपणम् ।

729 *Mālinīvijaya Tantra* 18.2-3 states: "That *liṅga* which is made of mud (*mṛt*), which is made of some stone (*śaila*), or which is made of some jewels (*ratna*) or gold or silver or whatever it is, you must not worship that *liṅga*. *Yajed ādhyātmikaṁ*, you must worship that internal [*liṅga*], which is situated in your own heart, *yatra līnam carācaram*, where this whole universe is existing. You must worship that *liṅga*, that is *avyakta liṅga*." *Tantrāloka* 5.120, commentary (LJA archive).

rahasyacaryā mantraugho maṇḍalaṁ mudrikāvidhiḥ /
ekīkāraḥ svasvarūpe praveśaḥ śāstramelanam //282//
āyātikathanaṁ śāstropādeyatvanirūpaṇam /283a
[not recited]

29. *Rahasyacaryā*, secret worship, secret action.

JOHN: In the twenty-ninth.

SWAMIJI: Yes, twenty-nine.[730]

30. And *mantraugha*, the differentiation of all *mantra*s. This is the vocabulary of *mantra*s in the thirtieth *āhnika*.

31. *Maṇḍalaṁ*, all *maṇḍalas*,[731] how to put *maṇḍala*s in a *yāga*.[732] That is thirty-one.

32. *Mudrikāvidhiḥ*, and *mudrā*s (postures), what postures we need in Shaivism–*mudrā*s.

JOHN: Thirty-two.

SWAMIJI: Yes, *khecarī* [*mudrā*],[733] etc.

---

730 Though Swamiji did not translate this *āhnika*, there are frequent references to the subject of *Vedha Dīkṣā* (the initiation of piercing) in *Kashmir Shaivism–The Secret Supreme*, chpt 18, and *Self Realization in Kashmir Shaivism*, ch. 5, "The Secret Knowledge of Kuṇḍalinī" (*Kuṇḍalinī Vijñāna Rahasya*). See Appendix 12 (p398) for a brief description of *Vedha Dīkṣā*.

731 Lit., a circle, a *maṇḍala* is a spiritual and ritual symbol that represents the universe. Swamiji commented that the theory of the *maṇḍala* is no longer "understood completely." *Tantrāloka* 1, additional audio (LJA archive).

732 An offering, oblation, or sacrifice.

733 [Some *yogi*s] "cut this connection of this front of this tongue and attach the tip of tongue to that palate and they get the imagination that they are tasting that nectar. But that nectar is false nectar. There are some *haṭha yogi*s who do that, but that nectar is false, only from imagination." *Tantrāloka* 5.55 commentary. "What is the real *khecarī mudrā*? When you are treading the way of totality (*kulamārgeṇa*), you must see the totality in a piece of the totality. Take one part of the universe and see the whole universe existing there. That is the way of totality. So, just as it is said in the *Tantrasadbhāva* [*tantra*], this *khecarī mudrā* is becoming one with supreme consciousness." *Shiva Sutras–The Supreme Awakening*, 90.

33. *Ekīkāraḥ*: the point is only one (*ekīkāraḥ*); *ekīkāraḥ*, oneness, union with all philosophies.

34. *Svasvarūpe praveśaḥ*, how to enter in your nature. This is the thirty-fourth.

35. *Śāstra melanam*, all *śāstra*s are united, actually.

36. *Āyātikathanaṁ*, what is the tradition of the masters and disciples–of Abhinavagupta.

37. *Śāstropādeyatvanirūpaṇam*, why you must get the help of the *śāstra*s (thirty-seventh *āhnika*).

This is the *pūrvaja uddeśa*[734] of the *Tantrāloka*.

JOHN: Which book would deal with *kuṇḍalinī*, or is that all *saṁpradāya*?

SWAMIJI: *Kuṇḍalinī* is in *śāktopāya* and in *āṇavopāya*, yes.

JOHN: I mean, but is it treated in the *Tantrāloka* or is it *saṁpradāya*. Is this *kuṇḍalinī mukhāgama* or is it in the *Tantrāloka*? *Kuṇḍalinī yoga*, this *cit*, *prāṇa*, . . .

SWAMIJI: Actually, the whole of the *Tantrāloka* is *mukhāgama*.[735] It is nothing other than *mukhāgama* because it is an actual *śāstra*. So there is no difference between this *āgama* and *mukhāgama*.

SCHOLAR: But he does explain *kuṇḍalinī* at many places–in book five and book twenty-nine, *vedha dīkṣā*.[736]

SWAMIJI: Yes.

JOHN: That's what I wanted to know.

---

734 The first nomination.

735 The revelation of masters.

736 "Whether you experience the rise of *kuṇḍalinī* as *cit kuṇḍalinī* or as *prāṇa kuṇḍalinī* depends on your attachments. If you have attachment for spirituality and also for worldly pleasures, then the rise of *kuṇḍalinī* takes place in the form of *prāṇa kuṇḍalinī*. If you do not have attachments for worldly pleasures and are only attached to spirituality, then the rise of *kuṇḍalinī* takes place in the form of *cit kuṇḍalinī*. There is nothing you can do to determine how the rise of *kuṇḍalinī* will take place. It rises in its own way, depending on your attachments." See Appendix 19 (p410) for an explanation of *kuṇḍalinī*.

SCHOLAR: But not *cit kuṇḍalinī.*

SWAMIJI: It is from mouth to ear.[737]

Audio 10 - 45:44

इति सप्ताधिकामेनां त्रिंशतं यः सदा बुधः ॥२८३॥
आह्निकानां समभयस्येत् स साक्षाद्भैरवो भवेत् ।

iti saptādhikāmenāṁ triṁśataṁ yaḥ sadā budhaḥ //283b//
āhnikānāṁ samabhyasyet sa sākṣādbhairavo bhavet /284a

So this way, that person who has read and achieved and understood the depth of these thirty-seven *āhnika*s of the *Tantrāloka*, *sa sākṣāt bhairavo bhavet*, he is no other than Bhairava. He is himself Bhairava. He becomes Bhairavanātha.

JOHN: How would you translate "*sākṣāt*"?

SWAMIJI: *Sākṣāt* [means], direct, without any agency. There is no indirect connection. Directly he is Bhairava.

SCHOLAR: What does he mean by "*sadā samabhyasyet*"? He who constantly . . .

SWAMIJI: He lives in that, lives in the *Tantrāloka.*

Audio 10 - 46:36

सप्तत्रिंशत्सु संपूर्णबोधो यद्भैरवो भवेत् ॥२८४॥

saptatriṁśatsu saṁpūrṇabodho yadbhairavo bhavet //284b
[not recited in full]

In the thirty-seven *āhnika*s, he who has got complete knowledge in the thirty-seven *āhnika*s, we have explained that he becomes Bhairava. It is not difficult for him to become Bhairava.

SCHOLAR: *Cit kiṁ citram.*

SWAMIJI: Yes.

737 Passed on through the oral tradition only.

Audio 10 - 47:01

किं चित्रमणवोऽप्यस्य दृशा भैरवतामियुः ।

kiṁ citramaṇavo'pyasya dṛśā bhairavatāmiyuḥ /285a

Everybody who comes in contact with him, [they] will become Bhairava!

SCHOLAR: By his glance.

SWAMIJI: By his glance (*dṛśā*).

Contents of Tantrāloka in detail
Anuja Uddeśa (285b-328)

Audio 10 - 47:12

इत्येष पूर्वजोद्देशः कथ्यते त्वनुजोऽधुना ॥२८५॥

ityeṣa pūrvajoddeśaḥ kathyate tvanujo'dhunā //285b//

This [was] *pūrvaja uddeśa*, now we will explain the *anuja uddeśaḥ* of the *Tantrāloka*, [which is] with explanation, more explanation.

Audio 10 - 47:28

विज्ञानभित्प्रकरणे सर्वस्योद्देशनं क्रमात् ।

vijñānabhitprakaraṇe sarvasyoddeśanaṁ kramāt /286a

This is the *anuja uddeśa*[738] of the first *āhnika*, these two lines: *vijñānabhit prakaraṇe sarvasyoddeśanaṁ kramat*, in the *prakaraṇa*,[739] in the *āhnika*, of *vijñānabheda*,[740] all subjects

738 Specific nomination.

739 Discussion.

740 Swamiji previously explained that, "*Vijñāna* means, *upāya*; *bhit*

will be nominated; all subjects that are to be explained in the *Tantrāloka*, in the body of the *Tantrāloka*, will be explained [successively in the first *āhnika*].

Audio 10 - 48:00

द्वितीयस्मिन्प्रकरणे गतोपायत्वभेदिता ॥ २८६ ॥

dvitīyasminprakaraṇe gatopāyatvabheditā //286b//

In the second *āhnika*, *gatopāyatvabheditā* will be explained; *gatopāya vabheditā*, where there is no necessity of adopting means, the means-less way.[741]

SCHOLAR: Where means are abandoned (*gata*).

SWAMIJI: Yes.

Audio 10 - 48:24

विश्वचित्प्रतिबिम्बत्वं परामर्शोदयक्रमः ।
मन्त्राद्यभिन्नरूपत्वं परोपाये विविच्यते ॥ २८७ ॥

viśvacitpratibimbatvaṁ parāmarśodayakramaḥ /
mantrādyabhinnarūpatvaṁ paropāye vivicyate //287//

This 287th *śloka* is the *anuja uddeśa* for the third *āhnika*. In the third *āhnika*, that is called *paropāya*. *Paropāya* is the *uddeśa* (nomination) of the third *āhnika*. *Vijñānabheda* is the *uddeśa* of the first *āhnika*, *gatopāya* is the *uddeśa* of the second *āhnika*, and *paropāya* is the *uddeśa* of the third *āhnika*. In that third *āhnika*, . . .*

JOHN: "*Paropāya*" means exactly?

SWAMIJI: The supreme *upāya*, the supreme means.[742]

*. . . *viśvacitpratibimbatvaṁ*, first it will be explained how this whole universe is reflected in the mirror of consciousness.

---

means, *bheda*. The differentiated perception of all the means is done in the first *āhnika*."

741 *Anupāya*.

742 *Śāmbhavopāya*.

Parāmarśodayakramaḥ, the next subject will be discussed on *parāmarśaḥ*, on the letters, what those letters indicate. *Mantra ādi abhinna rūpatvaṁ*, and the third explanation there is of *mantra ādi abhinna rūpatvam*, [how] all *mantra*s get entry in supreme I-consciousness.

JOHN: So this is all in the third *āhnika*–these three: *pratibimbavāda*, . . .

SWAMIJI: *Pratibimbavāda* and *mātṛkā cakra* and *ahaṁ parāmarśa*.[743] These three, yes.

Audio 10 - 49:56

विकल्पसंस्क्रिया तर्क तत्त्वं गुरुसतत्त्वकम ।
योगाङ्गानुपयोगित्वं कल्पितार्चाद्यनादरः ॥२८८॥
संविच्चक्रोदयो मन्त्रवीर्यं जप्यादि वास्तवम ।
निषेधविधितुल्यत्वं शाक्तोपायेऽत्र चर्च्यते ॥२८९॥

vikalpasaṁskriyā tarkatattvaṁ gurusatattvakam /
yogāṅgānupayogitvaṁ kalpitārcādyanādaraḥ //288//
saṁviccakrodayo mantravīryaṁ japyādi vāstavam /
niṣedhavidhitulyatvaṁ śāktopāye'tra carcyate //289//

These two *śloka*s are the *anuja uddeśa* for *śāktopāya*. In this [discussion of] *śāktopāya*,[744] nine subjects will be discussed. First, how this *vikalpa*[745] is to be *saṁskriyā*, is to be . . .

SCHOLAR: Purified and refined.

SWAMIJI: . . . refined; the refinement of *vikalpa*s. How *vikalpa*s are refined, from differentiated thoughts to an undifferentiated point. That is *vikalpa saṁskriyā*.

End of Audio 10 - 50:54

743 The theory of reflection, the circle of letters, and entry in supreme I-consciousness, respectively.

744 The fourth *āhnika*.

745 Differentiated thought.

Audio 11 - 00:00

This subject will be first in this [discussion of] *śāktopāya*. The second will be *tarka tattvaṁ*, what is the essence of *tarka*, what is the essence of . . .

JOHN: Intellectual reasoning?

SWAMIJI: Not intellectual. Understanding–*tarka*, *vicāra*.[746]

SCHOLAR: How to proceed to *nirvikalpa* through *vikalpa*, correct *vikalpa*.

SWAMIJI: *Tarka* is not *vikalpa*. *Tarka* is logic, pure logic–how you can get entry in God consciousness with pure logic.[747] *Gurusatattvakam*, the third subject will be discussed on the master. What is the essence of the master? What is meant by "the master"? Who is a master? Who can be a master? *Yogāṅga anupayogitvam*, the fourth subject will be discussed on that point where all these limbs of *yoga* are not attached, [where] they are not useful. *Yogāṅgānupayogitvam* means, all the limbs of *yoga*, the eight limbs of *yoga*, . . .

JOHN: These Patañjali limbs.[748]

SWAMIJI: . . . are not useful here. The fifth subject will be *kalpitā arcā anādaraḥ*, outward worship is not useful here. Outward worship is also discarded.

SCHOLAR: *Anādara*, unimportance.

SWAMIJI: Unimportance. They are not respected. Next is *saṁvit cakrodaya*, the rise of the twelve movements of Kālī. The next subject will be discussed on *mantra vīrya*, the power of all *mantras*.

JOHN: That differs from this other [discussion of] *mantra*.

SWAMIJI: Yes. *Mantra adi abhinna rūpatvam*, that is another thing in *śāmbhavopāya*, but this is *mantra vīrya*, the

746 Mode of acting or proceeding, the procedure.

747 In verse 235, Swamiji has translated *tarka* as 'spiritual reasoning', and in *Tantrāloka* 4.40 he explains *tarka* as 'transcendental discriminating logic'.

748 Patañjali, the author the *Yoga Sūtras*, which elaborates on the eight limbs of yoga (*Aṣṭaṅga Yoga*).

power of *mantra*. *Mantra vīrya* means, whatever you say, it will [come true]. It must become *mantra vīrya*.

SCHOLAR: And why is this mentioned specifically in *śāktopāya* and not *śāmbhavopāya*?

SWAMIJI: In *śāmbhavopāya*, there is only "*ahaṁ*."[749] *Mantra vīrya* cannot be [*śāmbhavopāya*]. In *mantra vīrya*, there are thoughts. It is a thought process. That [*śāmbhavopāya*] is a thought-less process.

Japyādi vāstavam, and recitation, the real recitation, what is meant by real *japa*. *Niṣedhavidhitulyatvaṁ*, nothing is right and nothing is wrong. This is the last subject here.

SCHOLAR: Which is essential to *śāktopāya*, this awareness.

SWAMIJI: Yes. *Śāktopāye'tra carcyate*.[750]

Now, the fifth *āhnika*:

Audio 11 - 03:01

बुद्धिध्यानं प्राणतत्त्वसमुच्चारश्चिदात्मता ।
उच्चार: परतत्वान्त:प्रवेशपथलक्षणम् ॥२९०॥
करणं वर्णतत्त्वं चेत्याणवे तु निरूप्यते ।

buddhidhyānaṁ prāṇatattvasamuccāraścidātmatā /
uccāraḥ paratattvāntaḥpraveśapathalakṣaṇam //290//
karaṇaṁ varṇatattvaṁ cetyāṇave tu nirūpyate /291a

One *śloka* and a half. This is the *anuja uddeśa* for *āṇavopāya*.

Buddhi dhyānaṁ, concentration with awareness, meditation with awareness, that is *buddhi dhyānam*. This is an intellectual meditation. It is not a process of meditation. One is a process of meditation, one is an intellectual meditation, when you meditate intellectually, not by a process, not by a routine-like [process]. When you meditate just like a routine-like [process], it is not [so useful], it is not so fruitful.

JOHN: What is "process/routine-like"? What is that? I'm

749 I-ness, pure supreme subjective consciousness.
750 These procedures will be discussed in the chapter on *śāktopāya*.

trying to . . .

SWAMIJI: (Swamiji mechanically breathes in and out) Like that. "*Oṁ namaḥ śivāya, oṁ namaḥ śivāya, oṁ namaḥ śivāya*," this is routine-like. When you put awareness of subjective awareness in that, that is *buddhi dhyāna*.

SCHOLAR: But it is still in *āṇavopāya*.

SWAMIJI: Yes, it is *āṇavopāya*. [*Buddhi dhyāna* is] first.

SCHOLAR: But this is not with *mantra*, this is . . . the object of *dhyāna* (*dhyeya*) is not the *mantra* here.

SWAMIJI: No, no.

SCHOLAR: It's maybe twelve *kālī*s or . . .

SWAMIJI: It is only intellectual. Not the twelve *kālī*s.

SCHOLAR: But that is also mentioned in . . .

SWAMIJI: Not *āṇavopāya*. In *śāktopāya* it is mentioned.

SCHOLAR: But even intellectual contemplation of those [*kālīs*]?

SWAMIJI: That is intellectual but it is more superior. It is intellectual but it is not meditation, it is thought.

JOHN: This?

SWAMIJI: No, this, *śāktopāya*.

JOHN: So this isn't using *mantra* or anything, this *buddhi dhyāna*? Or it is, it can be with *mantra*s or not with *mantra*s?

SWAMIJI: *Buddhi dhyāna*, no. *Buddhi dhyāna* is not with *mantra*s.

Prāṇa tattva samuccāraḥ (*prāṇa tattva* will go with *samuccāraḥ*).[751] *Prāṇa tattva samuccāra* is with *mantra*s. *Prāṇa tattva*, what is the essence of breath. What is the essence of breath? The essence of breath is the center. *Cidātmatā uccāra* is the next *prameya*, the next subject. *Cidātmatā uccāra*, how the rise of God consciousness takes place–*cidātmatā uccāraḥ*.

First is *buddhi dhyāna*, *prāṇa tattva samuccāraḥ* is next, *cidātmatā uccāra* is the third, the third subject to be discussed in *āṇavopāya*.

751 Utterance (*samuccāra*) or simply rising (*uccāra*).

Paratattvāntaḥ praveśa, how to get entry in the supreme state, the supreme essence. And *pathalakṣaṇam*, the realistic characteristic of the path.

JOHN: Of this path.

SWAMIJI: What is really the path, the spiritual path.

Karaṇam, and what is *karaṇa*, what is the *karaṇa upāsanā*.[752] *Karaṇa* is sevenfold. It will be discussed at its own place. And *varṇa tattvam*, what is the word, the supreme word. These subjects will be discussed in *āṇava* [*upāya*]–*āṇave tu nirūpyate*.

Audio 11 - 06:35

karaṇam saptadhā prāhu abhyāsam bodhapūrvakam /
guruvaktrācca bodhavyaṁ karaṇāṁ yadyapi sphuṭam //
tathāpyāgama rakṣārthaṁ tadagre varṇayiṣyate /
Tantrāloka 5.129a – 130b

Karaṇa upāsanā is sevenfold and in these sevenfold ways you will get all these explained in many places in the *Tantrāloka*, not only at one place, because Abhinavagupta's point of theory is that the most subtle thing should not be discussed in one place, it should be discussed here and there so that the *sādhaka* won't find it easily unless he puts the force of awareness, and then he will find it in the *Tantrāloka*, otherwise not. It is the sevenfold ways of *karaṇa*.[753]

JOHN: *Karaṇa* means "doing" or "acting"?

SWAMIJI: No, *karaṇaṁ* is pertaining to the organs; this meditation is pertaining to the organs. It will be discussed. This means is sevenfold (*karaṇam saptadhā prāhu*), and it is *abhyāsam bodha*, this is intellectual meditation, it is not meditation just like a routine way.

SCHOLAR: But it's not in *śāktopāya*.

SWAMIJI: It is in *āṇavopāya*.

SCHOLAR: Where it will be explained.

---

752 Meditation pertaining to the organs.

753 See *Kashmir Shaivism – The Secret Supreme*, for explanation of *karaṇa upāsana*, 5.37.

SWAMIJI: Yes, it will be explained. In *āṇavopāya* also it won't be [completely] explained.

SCHOLAR: He misses it.

SWAMIJI: No, he does not miss it. He points it out.

SCHOLAR: *Uddeśa*.

SWAMIJI: And the commentator[754] will tell you in his commentary that it will be discussed here and there, in the twentieth *āhnika*, the twenty-first *āhnika*, in the *Tantrāloka*. [It will be discussed] scatteredly so that easily you should not know it unless . . .

DENISE: Why should you easily not know it?

SWAMIJI: Any fraud-man can know then. If you are so keen to know it, then you will find it, you will search in the *Tantrāloka*. [Abhinavagupta] wants you to search, he wants us to search in the *Tantrāloka*.

DENISE: It is an adventure.

SWAMIJI: Yes. Now next, 291:

Audio 11 - 09:10

चारमानमहोरात्रसंक्रान्त्यादिविकल्पनम् ॥२९१॥
संहारचित्रता वर्णोदयः कालाध्वकल्पने ।

cāramānamahorātrasaṁkrāntyādivikalpanam //291b//
saṁhāracitratā varṇodayaḥ kālādhvakalpane /292a

Now it's in *kālādhva*,[755] in the sixth *āhnika*. What will be discussed?

Cāramānam, the measurement of breath will be explained; what is the measurement of the breath, in and out. *Ahorātra-saṁkrāntyādi-vikalpanam*, and just to put the thought in that breath, the thought of day and night, the thought of months, the thought of years, and etcetera.

SCHOLAR: *Kalpa*s.

---

754 Jayaratha.
755 The orbit or path (*adhva*) of time (*kālā*).

SWAMIJI: *Kalpas* also.[756] *Saṁhāra citratā*–and the next subject will be discussed–*saṁhāra citratā*, how *saṁhāra*[757] takes place differentiatedly. One [person] is destroyed, [but] for another person, it is a day, it is not destruction, it is only a day, it is dawn. [For example], Indra is destroyed, Indra gets *saṁhāra* (destruction), and another deity gets dawn, he gets up from his bed. And this is *saṁhāra citratā*. And [when] Lord Śiva's immediate attendant[758] is also destroyed, then only Lord Śiva remains. That is *saṁhāra citratā*, . . .

SCHOLAR: But this is on the level of *kalpanā*[759] . . .

SWAMIJI: . . . the various ways of destruction of the universe; how destruction takes place, not only once, but variously, in various ways.

SCHOLAR: But this is in the field of time, . . .

SWAMIJI: It is in the field of time.

SCHOLAR: . . . and therefore artificial.

SWAMIJI: Yes, yes. And *varṇa udayaḥ*, and then the rise of the word. The rise of the word here also. As there you had . . .

JOHN: In *āṇavopāya* we had . . . we had this here on this fourth line.

SCHOLAR: *Varṇa tattvānām*.

SWAMIJI: *Varṇa tattvānām*. *Varṇa tattva* and *varṇa udaya*, the essence of the word and the rise of the word. [*Varṇa udaya*] is explained in . . .

JOHN: Sixth?

SWAMIJI: . . . the sixth *āhnika*. Now, the seventh [*āhnika*]:

Audio 11 - 11:38

चक्रभिन्मन्त्रविद्याभिदेतच्चक्रोदये भवेत् ॥ २९२ ॥

cakrabhinmantravidyābhidetaccakrodaye bhavet //292//

756 Cycle of time.
757 Destruction.
758 Anantabhaṭṭāraka.
759 Imaginative conception.

In *cakrodaya prakaraṇa*, in the seventh *āhnika*, *cakrabhit* (the rise of the six *cakra*s, six wheels) and *mantra vidyābhit* (and *mantra bheda* and *vidyā bheda*, how *mantra bheda* and *vidyā bheda* take place).[760] These things will be discussed in *cakrodaya*.

SCHOLAR: *Cakra bhit* is the six circles?

SWAMIJI: Yes.

SCHOLAR: I thought *cakra* there was in *cakrodaya*, all those different cycles of *mantra* in breath.

SWAMIJI: Different cycles of *mantra*s, yes. Not *ṣaṭ cakra*, not the six *cakra*s.[761] For instance, one *cakra* is an ordinary *cakra*, 21,600 times, just like the ordinary course of breathing, in and out for the day and the night, twenty-four hours–21,600 times. Now you have to control that *cakra*. How can you control? By producing length in the breath, by producing length in the breath. For instance, take it double, make it double, so that in twenty-four hours, half of 21,600 times you'll breathe only; you'll breathe only half of that time, half of [21,600]. And in the end, when you breathe in and out for twenty four hours only twenty-four times, then you are a master on *cakrabhit*. It is just to get mastery on time.

SCHOLAR: So each *prāṇācāra*[762] is taking one hour?

SWAMIJI: Each *prāṇācāra* is taking one hour–so long! Because it is due to practice, by-and-by. By-and-by you have to prolong the span of time.

SCHOLAR: This doesn't involve effort?

SWAMIJI: Yes, yes, yes [it involves effort].

DEVOTEE: *Prāṇayāma*.

---

760 "*Mantra*s are pertaining to male gods, *vidyā* means those *mantra*s which are pertaining to female gods, and *cakra nāyakā*, and those *mantra*s which are the leaders of [the *cakra*s]." *Tantrāloka* 7.42 (LJA archive).

761 Referring to the classical conception of the six *cakra*s in the subtle body as depicted in various *yoga* texts like *Ṣaṭcakra Nirupāna*.

762 Movement of breath.

SWAMIJI: Because he says, in the end, "*ityeṣa sūkṣma-parimarśanaśīlanīya*,"[763] this is the most subtlest,[764] and this is called . . . this is with effort. *Ityayatnajamākhyāta yatnajaṁ tu nigadyate*,[765] that is *ayatnaja upāsanā*[766] in the sixth *āhnika*. In the seventh *āhnika*, it is *yatnaja upāsanā*, you have to put effort, prolong it.

JOHN: Is it effort like *haṭha yoga*?

SWAMIJI: It is just like *haṭha yoga* but not retention. In *haṭha yoga*, you have retention, you have to retain the breath. [Here], it is not retaining the breath. This is explained in *cakrodaya prakaraṇa*, the seventh *āhnika*.

Audio 11 - 14:48

परिमाणां पुराणां च संग्रहस्तत्त्वयोजनम् ।
एतद्देशाध्वनिर्देशे द्वयं तत्त्वाध्वनिर्णये ॥२९३॥
कार्यकारणभावश्च तत्त्वक्रमनिरूपणम् ।

parimāṇaṁ purāṇāṁ ca saṁgrahastattvayojanam /
etaddeśādhvanirdeśe dvayaṁ tattvādhvanirṇaye //293//
kāryakāraṇabhāvaśca tattvakramanirūpaṇam /294a
[not recited in full]

This will be explained, these subjects will be discussed, in the eighth *āhnika* (*deśādhva*):[767] *Parimāṇam purāṇām ca*, the measurement of all the worlds, this is the first subject. And *saṁgraha* (*saṁgraha* means, a synopsis), [a synopsis] of the *bhuvanas* (a synopsis of the worlds). And *tattva yojanā*, how the elementary world (the *tattvas*) is united with the *bhuvanas* (worlds). *Etat deśādhvanirdeśa*, this will be explained in *deśādhva*.

763 *Tantrāloka* 7.71.
764 "Which is to be attained with refined subtle understanding–*sūkṣma parimarśanaśīlanīya*." Ibid., 7.71.
765 Jayaratha's commentary for verse 7.1.
766 Effortless (*ayatna*) practice (*upāsanā*).
767 The discussion of the orbit or path (*adhva*) of space (*deśa*).

Tattvādhvan nirṇaye dvayam, in the ninth *āhnika–tattvādhva nirṇaye*[768] is the ninth *āhnika*–in the ninth *āhnika*, only two subjects will be discussed. What is that? *Kārya kāraṇa bhāvaśca*, the theory of cause and effect, and *tattva krama nirūpaṇam*, and the succession of the thirty-six elements. *Bas*, these two subjects will be discussed there in the ninth *āhnika*.

Audio 11 - 16:26

वस्तुधर्मस्तत्त्वविधिर्जाग्रदादिनिरूपणम् ॥२९४॥
प्रमातृभेद इत्येतत् तत्त्वभेदे विचार्यते ।

vastudharmastattvavidhirjāgradādinirūpaṇam //294b//
pramātṛbheda ityetat tattvabhede vicāryate /295a

In *tattvabheda prakaraṇa*,[769] in the tenth *āhnika*, this will be discussed: *Vastu dharma*[770]: Whose is this objective perception? Is objective perception [an attribute] of the object or of he who perceives it? The one who perceives this object, this objective perception, does it belong to that perceiver or to that perceived [object]? If it belongs to the perceiver, then what is the purpose of this object? If it belongs to the object (that perceiving that this is a pot or this is a packet), then what is the use of seeing it, perceiving it? Why doesn't this object appear by itself if this perceiving is connected with this object? This will be discussed in this [tenth *āhnika*]. From whom this perception comes? Does it come from . . .

JOHN: The objective side or the subjective side?

SWAMIJI: . . . the objective side or the subjective side? *Tattva vidhi,* what is the way of the elements. *Jāgrad ādi nirūpaṇam*, and the four states, the explanation of the four

768 The discussion (*nirṇaya*) of the orbit or path (*adhva*) of the elements (*tattvas*).

769 The discussion (*prakaraṇa*) of the various (*bheda*) elements (*tattva*).

770 The true nature of a thing.

states: wakefulness, dreaming, dreamless, and *turya*. And *pramātṛ bheda*, and the seven *pramātṛ*s from *sakala* to Śiva *pramātṛ*–the seven *kalā*.[771] *Ityetat tattvabheda vicāryate*, this will be explained in the tenth *āhnika*.

Audio 11 - 18:24

कलास्वरूपमेकत्रिपञ्चाद्यैस्तत्त्वकल्पनम् ॥२९५॥

kalāsvarūpamekatripañcādyaistattvakalpanam //295b//

Kalāsvarūpam, what is the reality of *kalā*, the five circles. *Ekatri pañcadyai tattva kalpanām*, and *tattva kalpanā*[772] by *eka*, *tri*, *pañca*.[773] That is the fifteenfold science. The fifteenfold science, that you have [already been taught]–*pañcadaśavidhi*. That is not only *pañcadaśavidhi*; this is the fifteenfold science, this is the thirteenfold science, the elevenfold science, the ninefold science, the sevenfold science, the fivefold science, the threefold science, and one [where] there is no science. For one, there is no science.

DEVOTEE: Śiva *sākṣāt*.[774]

JOHN: (laughs) Śiva *sākṣāt*.

SWAMIJI:

Audio 11 - 19:12

वर्णभेदक्रमः सर्वाधारशक्तिनिरूपणम् ।
कलाद्यध्वविचारान्तरेतावत्प्रविविच्यते ॥२९६॥

varṇabhedakramaḥ sarvādhāraśaktinirūpaṇam /
kalādyadhvavicārāntaretāvatpravivicyate //296//
[not recited]

771 Seven *kalā* (states) of the seven *pramātṛ*s (perceivers). See Appendix 10 (p394) for an explanation of the seven perceivers.
772 Contemplation (*kalpanā*) of the elements (*tattva*s).
773 By the onefold (*eka*) science, the threefold (*tri*) science, the fivefold (*pañca*) science, etc.
774 The direct realisation (*sākṣāt*) of Lord Śiva.

Varṇa bheda kramaḥ, and the differentiated succession of words. *Sarvādhāra śakti nirūpaṇam*, and that energy who holds the whole wheel of energies.

SCHOLAR: *Ādhāra śakti.*[775]

SWAMIJI: *Kalādyadhvavicārāntar*, in *kalādyadhva prakaraṇa*[776], the eleventh *āhnika*, *etāvat pravivicyate*, this will be explained.

Audio 11 - 19:40

अभेदभावनाकम्पह्रसौ त्वध्वोपयोजने।

abhedabhāvanākampahrāsau tvadhvopayojane /297a

Bas, only these two lines for the twelfth *āhnika*.

Adhvopayojane[777] and *abheda bhāvanā*.[778] in *abheda bhāvanā* you should explain in your mind and think–this is the thought of undifferentiatedness; the undifferentiated thought of undifferentiatedness–[you should think that] everything is the same, [that] there is no down, there is no up. That is *abheda bhāvanā*, and this will be discussed. And *kampa hrāsa*, doubts should be destroyed; no doubt should persist in your brain, in the brain of the *sādhaka*. That is *kampa hrāsa*. These two subjects will be discussed in the twelfth *āhnika*.

Audio 11 - 20:36

संख्याधिक्यं मलादीनां तत्त्वं शक्तिविचित्रता ॥२९७॥
अनपेक्षित्वसिद्धिश्च तिरोभावविचित्रता ।
शक्तिपातपरीक्षायामेतावान्वाच्यसंग्रहः ॥२९८॥

775 The power (*śakti*) of sustaining (*ādhāra*).
776 The discussion (*prakaraṇa*) of the path (*adhva*) of the five circles (*kalās*), etcetera (*ādi*). See Appendix 16 (p403) for explanation of the sixfold Path of the Universe (*Ṣaḍadhvan*).
777 The discussion (*prakaraṇa*) of the act of harnessing (*upayojana*) the aforementioned paths (*adhva*).
778 Contemplation or meditation (*bhāvanā*) upon non-duality (*abheda*).

sāṁkhyādikyaṁ malādīnāṁ tattvaṁ śaktivicitratā //297b//
anapekṣitvasiddhiśca tirobhāvavicitratā /
śaktipātaparīkṣāyāmetāvānvācyasaṁgrahaḥ //298//

In the *āhnika* of *śaktipāta* (the grace of Lord Śiva), the thirteenth *āhnika*, what will be discussed? *Sāṁkhyādhikyaṁ*, there is something more than the Sāṁkhya thought. Only Sāṁkhya thought is not the end of philosophy. There is more than that (*sāṁkhyādhikyaṁ*). *Sāṁkhyādhikya* means, there can be more than Sāṁkhyā, what Sāṁkhyā perceives.[779] *Malādīnām tattvam*, the essence of the three impurities (*āṇavamala, māyīyamala*, and *kārmamala*), what those are. *Śakti vicitratā*, and the various ways of energies. *Anapekṣitva siddhiśca*, and the *siddhi* (the completion) of your *samādhi*, the completion of your *samādhi*, when you complete your *samādhi*, the completion of *samādhi* takes place not by your effort (*anapekṣitva siddhiśca*), not by your purity, not by your treading smoothly, not by your nobility, not by all those good habits of yours. All of those have no effect for [achieving] that. This state comes only by the grace of Lord Śiva, not by your effort. Effort has no voice there. Not effort, not purifying your mind, not discipline, nothing, nothing will help except His grace. This will be discussed. That is *anapekṣitva siddhiśca*. *Tirobhāva vicitratā*, and there are various ways of how Lord Śiva conceals your nature. This nature could be concealed through various ways. For instance, if your are a [pretending to be] saint, in your hand you will put beads, you'll put beads only when people come to see you, to pay respects to you, and you will carry those beads and [say], "How are you, sir? Are you well? What are you doing?"–but [while holding] beads. These are the signs of concealment. His nature is concealed by

779 Expounded by the sage Kapila, Sāṁkhya is the third of the six classical systems of Indian philosophy. "Sāṁkhya" literally means, pertaining to numbers. Sāṁkhya proclaims the existence twenty-five *tattvas* (elements) that comprise creation in its entirety. Although accepting the existence of these twenty-five elements, Kashmir Shaivism proclaims the existence of an additional eleven elements, which seek to explain the condition of consciousness.

Lord Siva. This is *tirodhāna*,[780] this is not the grace of Lord Śiva. The grace of Lord Śiva [is demonstrated by the following example]:

There was a person here in Kashmir. He was called Zanāna Zoyi.[781] He didn't appear as a saint, but he was a perfect saint. What would he do? He would serve women only, not men. So he seemed so ignorant that women would ask him to bathe them or, [you know], anything.

DENISE: He was innocent or ignorant?

SWAMIJI: He was a servant, he was serving them, and he was called Zanāna Zoyi because he was attached to women.[782]

SCHOLAR: "Zoyi" means? Some name. Zanāna Zoyi.

SWAMIJI: Yes, insignificant. But he was, internally he was, aware. And there was another saint in those days, he was called Ṛṣīpīra, and he was told by Lord Śiva that you must see, before leaving this physical body, you must go and have *darśana*[783] of that Zanāna Zoyi, who is serving those women.

DEVOTEE: Who was world-famous.

SWAMIJI: And he was a very great, famous saint, Riṣīpīra, and he was known to kings also. And he came to that place to see, to have *darśana* of, Zanāna Zoyi. And [then] these women kicked [Zanāna Zoyi and said], "Are you so great that Ṛṣīpīra has come to see you? You bloody fool, you were serving us!"

DEVOTEES: (laughter)

SWAMIJI: But he took his blanket, there and then he took a blanket, and left his physical body. He didn't see Ṛṣipīra. He said, "No, I won't see him. Now [that] I am exposed, I

780 Concealing.

781 Also written Janāna Joyi.

782 *Zenana* (Urdu) or *janānā* (Hindi), literally meaning "of the ladies"; used to refer to the ladies' quarters in the household.

783 The sight of a deity or religious person.

won't see him, and I won't see anything now in this world. I will leave this physical frame." *Bas.* This is the way of His grace. His grace is showered secretly to those who have no sign of being a saint.

That is the *tirobhāva vicitratā*. It will be explained there in the thirteenth *āhnika*. *Śaktipāta parīkṣāyām etāvān vācya saṁgrahaḥ*, these subjects will be discussed in the *śaktipāta āhnika*, in the thirteenth *āhnika*.

Now the fourteenth [*āhnika*]:

Audio 11 - 26:34

तिरोभावव्यपगमो ज्ञानेन परिपूर्णता ।
उत्क्रान्त्यनुपयोगित्वं दीक्षोपक्रमणे स्थितम् ॥२९९॥

tirobhāvavyapagamo jñānena paripūrṇatā /
utkrāntyanupayogitvaṁ dīkṣopakramaṇe sthitam //299//

Dīkṣa upakramaṇa, the commencing point of *dīkṣā* (initiation), outward initiation, that is the fourteenth *āhnika*. In the fourteenth *āhnika*, what will be discussed? *Tirobhāva vyapagama*, what is the sign of being concealed and how you can abandon this, how you can get rid of this concealment of [your] nature. *Jñānena paripūrṇatva*, how you can be filled with real knowledge. *Utkrānti anupayogitvaṁ*, and the next subject will be discussed on *utkrānti*.[784] There is no need at the time of death to leave the physical body and enter in that blissful field.

JOHN: You are there already.

SWAMIJI: You are already there. These things will be discussed in the fourteenth *āhnika*.

JOHN: What is fourteenth *āhnika* mainly?

SWAMIJI: *Dīkṣa upakramaḥ.*

JOHN: *Dīkṣa*.

784 The procedure for leaving the body (dying). See footnote 34, 122 and 724.

SWAMIJI: *Dīkṣa upakramaḥ*, the introduction of *dīkṣā*.

Audio 11 - 27:38

शिष्यौचित्यपरीक्षादौ स्थानभित्स्थानकल्पनम् ।
सामान्यन्यासभेदोऽर्घपात्रं चैतत्प्रयोजनम् ॥ ३०० ॥
द्रव्ययोग्यत्वमर्चा च बहिर्द्वारार्चनं क्रमात् ।
प्रवेशो दिक्स्वरूपं च देहप्राणादिशोधनम् ॥ ३०१ ॥
विशेषन्यासवैचित्र्यं सविशेषार्घभाजनम् ।
देहपूजा प्राणबुद्धिचित्स्वध्वन्यासपूजने ॥ ३०२ ॥
अन्यशास्त्रगणोत्कर्षः पूजा चक्रस्य सर्वतः ।
क्षेत्रग्रहः पञ्चगव्यं पूजनं भूगणेशयोः ॥ ३०३ ॥
अस्त्रार्चा वह्निकार्यं चाप्यधिवासनमग्निगम् ।
तर्पणं चरुसंसिद्धिर्दन्तकाष्ठान्तसंस्क्रिया ॥ ३०४ ॥
शिवहस्तविधिश्चापि शय्याक्लृप्तिविचारणम् ।
स्वप्नस्य सामयं कर्म समयाश्चेति संग्रहः ॥ ३०५ ॥
समयित्वविधावस्मिन्स्यात्पञ्चदश आह्निके ।

śiṣyaucityaparīkṣādau snānabhitsnānakalpanam[785] /
sāmānyanyāsabhedo'rghapātraṁ caitatprayojanam //300//

dravyayogyatvamarcā ca bahirdvārārcanaṁ kramāt /
praveśo diksvarūpaṁ ca dehaprāṇādiśodhanam //301//

viśeṣanyāsavaicitryaṁ saviśeṣārghabhājanam /
dehapūjā prāṇabuddhicitsvadhvanyāsapūjane //302//

anyaśāstragaṇotkarṣaḥ pūjā cakrasya sarvataḥ /
kṣetragrahaḥ pañcagavyaṁ pūjanaṁ bhūgaṇeśayoḥ //303//

astrārcā vahnikāryaṁ cāpyadhivāsanamagnigam /
tarpaṇaṁ carusaṁsiddhirdantakāṣṭhāntasaṁskriyā //304//

785 In line *300ab*, Swamiji changes "*sthana*" to read "*snāna*."

śivahastavidhiścāpi śayyāklṛptivicāraṇam /
svapnasya sāmayaṁ karma samayāśceti saṁgrahaḥ //305//

samayitvavidhāvasminsyātpañcadaśa āhnike /306a

In the fifteenth *āhnika*, these subjects will be discussed.

JOHN: All these.

SWAMIJI: All these subjects. *Śiṣyaucitya*, how you can be fit to become a disciple. How the *guru* should analyze the *śiṣya*. *Sthānabhit*, the differentiated points of the way of bathing. And *snāna kalpanam*, how you should bathe.

SCHOLAR: In inferior and superior way.

SWAMIJI: Yes.

SCHOLAR: In gross and . . .

SWAMIJI: There are so many *snāna*s, so many baths. A sun bath is also a bath. And to remain in the crowd of cows also, this is a bath.[786] Remaining in a [rain]-shower when it is raining heavily, that is also a bath. These differentiated ways of bath will be discussed.

JOHN: Why would they discuss bath?

SWAMIJI: Bathing.

JOHN: Why is bathing an important point to discuss?

SWAMIJI: Not bathing with soap and water only in your bathroom.

Audio 11 - 29:39

JOHN: *Śāktopāya* bathing.

SWAMIJI: There is some more in bathing. You can bathe with *mantra* also. Some saints never bathe at all, but they bathe actually, internally.

JOHN: Like Swami Rām?[787]

SWAMIJI: Yes.

786 This is explained as bathing in the fine dust which is created by cows.
787 Swamiji's grand-master.

Sāmānya nyāsa, general *nyāsa*. Do you know *nyāsa*?

SCHOLAR: Yes.

SWAMIJI: To purify all the limbs.

SCHOLAR: With *mantra*s.

SWAMIJI: *Nyāsa bheda. Arghapātraṁ*, what is meant by *arghapātra*.[788] This will be discussed.

SCHOLAR: Chalice.

SWAMIJI: Yes. And its use (*etat prayojanam*). *Dravya yogatvam arcāca*, what things are necessary for initiations, what things you should collect for initiation, and what worship you have to do. *Bahir dvārārcanam*, and how you should enter in the hall of initiation. You have to worship the door of the hall of initiation first before entry, before entering in that initiation hall. That is *bahir dvārārcanam. Praveśa*, then entering in that initiation hall. *Diksvarūpam ca*, then purifying all ten sides.

SCHOLAR: Directions.

SWAMIJI: Ten directions. *Deha prāṇādi śodhanam*, then purifying your body, the body of the disciple, and the breath of the disciple. He has to purify that. *Viśeṣa nyāsa*, then exceptional *nyāsa*, how to produce exceptional *nyāsa*, its "various-ness." *Saviśeṣārghabhājanam*, and exceptional *arghapātra*, *arghapātra vidhi*.[789] *Dehapūjā*, then the worshipping of your own body. *Prāṇa buddhi citsu adhvanyāsa pūjane*, in *prāṇa*,[790] in *buddhi*[791] and in *cit*,[792] you have to do *nyāsa* of all

---

788 A sacrificial vessel, usually made of copper, used to contain purified offerings for worship. *Arghapātra* is also understood as the heart in internal worship. *Tantrāloka* 26.64 and 29.176.

789 The rules of how to handle the vessel (*arghapātra*) which contains special ingredients.

790 Breath.

791 The intellect.

792 *Cit* means, consciousness. In his translation of the fifteenth *āhnika*, Swamiji will explain that it refers to "the *śūnya* (void) state in that supreme awareness of God consciousness."

six *adhvas* and the worship of all six *adhvas*[793] (first *nyāsa* and then worship). *Anyaśāstra gaṇa utkarṣaḥ*, all *śāstras* are pure, all *śāstras* are divine (*utkarṣaḥ*), and other *śāstras* are not divine; *anyaśāstra gaṇa utkarṣaḥ*, this is above other *śāstras*, this theory is above other *śāstras*. *Pūjā cakrasya*, how to worship a *cakra*. *Kṣetragrahaḥ*, what is meant by entering in a *tīrtha* (in a shrine)–what is a shrine. And *pañcagavya*, what is *pañcagavyaḥ*; *pañcagavyaḥ* means, those things which are produced by cows (milk, curd, *ghee*, and dung also). That is *pañcagavyaḥ*, what is meant by that *pañcagavyaḥ*.

Audio 11 - 33:00

Pūjanam, and worship of that. And worship of *bhū-gaṇeśayoḥ*, worship of the earth [*bhū*] and Gaṇeśa. *Astrārcā*, and the worship of *astra*.[794] *Vahnikāryam ca*, and the way of *havan*.[795] *Adhivāsanam*, and *adhivāsa*,[796] while doing that *havana*, you have not to sleep in your bedroom. In the *havana śālā*,[797] before the *havana*, you have to sleep there–*adhi-vāsana*.[798]

SCHOLAR: For dream.

SWAMIJI: Yes, for dream. *Tarpaṇam*, and then what is meant by *tarpaṇa*.[799] *Carusaṁsiddhiḥ*, what is meant by *caru*, those [rice] cakes that are baked for the sacrificial fire–what is meant by that, what does that really mean. *Dantakāṣṭhānta-saṁskriyā*, and what is meant by *dantakāṣṭhā*, to cut those

793 Swamiji will explain that each *nyāsa* is done either in a sixfold way (*adhva*) or in a brief way.
794 A weapon (*astra*). "The *astrā mantra* needs to be adored. [The *mantra* is] "*astrāyaphaṭ*," [which] you will all understand by-and-by. It is only nomination here." *Tantrāloka* 1, additional audio (LJA archive).
795 Fire ceremony.
796 Lit., living in, abode, dwelling.
797 The hall (*śālā*) in which the *havana* is performed.
798 The 15th *āhnika* clarifies that for the duration of this initiation, both the master and disciple sleep in the *havan śālā*.
799 The special way of sprinkling sacrificial water.

branches for making [tooth]brushes.

SCHOLAR: Neem trees.

SWAMIJI: Neem trees–*dantakāṣṭha*. *Antasaṁskriyā*, and what is meant by *anta saṁskriyā*, the *saṁskriyā*[800] of death, the death *saṁskāra*.[801] *Śivahastavidhi*, then *śiva hasta vidhi*, how Śiva's hand will protect you. That is *śiva hasta vidhi*. *Śayyāklṛpti*, how you should produce, [how] you should conduct, bedding for the disciple and the master. *Svapnasya sāmayam*, and the way how you dream dreams, both [the master and the disciple].

SCHOLAR: *Sāmayam karma*?

SWAMIJI: No, *svapnasya*, *svapnasya karma*, *karma*, *sāmayam karma*. *Sāmayam karma*, this is *sāmayam karma*: *karma*[802] pertaining to *sāmaya*, pertaining to discipline (*sāmaya* means, discipline). And *samayā*, all disciplines, what are disciplines. *Syāt pañcadaśāhnika*, these will be explained in the fifteenth *āhnika*. This is what Abhinavagupta says in the beginning. So, in his brain, everything was moving in his brain, what he had to explain in the *Tantrāloka*.

Audio 11 - 35:38

मण्डलात्मानुसन्धानं निवेद्यपशुविस्तरः ॥३०६॥
अग्नितृप्तिः स्वस्वभावदीपनं शिष्यदेहगः ।
अध्वन्यासविधिः शोध्यशोधकादिविचित्रता ॥३०७॥
दीक्षाभेदः परो न्यासो मन्त्रसत्ताप्रयोजनम ।
भेदो योजनिकादेश्च षोडशे स्यादिहाह्निके ॥३०८॥

maṇḍalātmānusandhānaṁ nivedyapaśuvistaraḥ //306//
agnitṛptiḥ svasvabhāvadīpanaṁ śiṣyadehagaḥ /

800 Purificatory rite or consecration.
801 *Saṁskāra* means, purification. Here it refers to the *anta* (last) *saṁskriyā* of the sixteen *saṁskāras* (purifications) which take place from birth to death.
802 Activity.

adhvanyāsavidhiḥ śodhyaśodhakādivicitratā //307//

dīkṣābhedaḥ paro nyāso mantrasattāprayojanam /
bhedo yojanikādeśca ṣoḍaśe syādīhāhnike //308//

This is explained in the sixteenth *āhnika*:

Maṇḍala, to produce a *maṇḍala*.[803] And *ātmā anusandhānam*, to be aware of your Self.

SCHOLAR: Not "to be aware of the nature of *maṇḍala*"–*maṇḍalātmānusandhāna*. Or, "to be aware of the Self in a *maṇḍala*."

SWAMIJI: That also. *Nivedya paśu vistaraḥ*; *nivedyapaśu*, that *paśu*[804] who is to be offered [as a] sacrifice, how you have to produce that sheep.

SCHOLAR: How you should kill it.

SWAMIJI: How you should kill it.[805] *Agnitṛptiḥ*, how you should satisfy the fire by that, by his meat. *Svasva bhāva dīpanaṁ*, how your nature will be glorified by that. *Śiṣyādehagaḥ*, how the master enters in the body of the disciple. *Adhva nyāsa vidhiḥ*, and after entering, how [the master] purifies all the elementary world contained in the body of the disciple. *Śodhya śodhakādi vicitratā*, what is *śodhya*, what is to be purified, who is the purifier–the "various-ness" of that. *Dīkṣā bheda*, and the differentiated ways of initiations. And the supreme *nyāsa*. *Mantra sattā prayojanam*, and the characteristic of all *mantras* and its means, its purpose. *Yojanikādeśabhedaḥ*, how you are directed by your master from one world to another world, how he unites you to another world. *Ṣoḍaśe syādihāhnike*, these things will be discussed in the sixteenth *āhnika*.

---

803 Lit., a circle, a *maṇḍala* is a spiritual and ritual symbol that represents the universe. See footnote 731.

804 A beast.

805 In the 16th *āhnika*, Abhinavagupta explains in detail how only an enlightened master can perform this special type of initiation-worship whereby, at the time of sacrifice, the soul of the sheep gets liberated.

Audio 11 - 37:48

सूत्रक्लृप्तिस्तत्त्वशुद्धिः पाशदाहोऽथ योजनम् ।
अध्वभेदस्तथेत्येवं कथितं पौत्रिके विधौ ॥३०९॥

sūtraklṛptistattvaśuddhiḥ pāśadāho'tha yojanam /
adhvabhedastathetyevaṁ kathitaṁ pautrike vidhau //309//

In the seventeenth *āhnika* (this is *pautrika vidhi*),[806] these things are explained:

Sūtra klṛpti, how to make the thread, by which thread you purify all of the elementary world pertaining to the disciple.[807] *Pāśadāha*, how you produce *pāśa* (bondage) and burn it to ashes, and then unite the disciple to the world he wants to be united [with]–*yojanam*.[808] *Adhvabheda*, and the differentiated ways of this *saṁsāra*.[809] This is explained in the seventeenth *āhnika*.

Audio 11 - 38:43

जननादिविहीनत्वं मन्त्रभेदोऽथ सुस्फुटः ।
इति संक्षिप्तदीक्षाख्ये स्यादष्टादश आह्निके ॥३१०॥

jananādivihīnatvaṁ mantrabhedo'tha susphuṭaḥ /
iti saṁkṣiptadīkṣākhye syādaṣṭādaśa āhnike //310//

In the eighteenth *āhnika*, which is *saṁkṣipta dīkṣā* (*saṁkṣipta dīkṣā* means, abbreviated initiation), there it will be discussed: *jananādivihīnatvam*, how you will get rid of re-

806 Instructions (*vidhi*) for the apprentice (*putraka*).

807 *Sūtra klṛpti* means, the three threads that are utilised to tie the arms, neck, and the tuft of hair on the head of the disciple. These are symbolic of the bondage of *kārmamala*, *māyīyamala*, and *āṇavamala*, respectively.

808 The cutting and burning of the three threads (*sūtra klṛpti*) to release the disciple from the bondage of the three *mala*s.

809 The wheel of repeated births (transmigration) and deaths is *saṁsāra*.

peated births and deaths. *Mantra bheda*, and the differentiated ways of all *mantras*. Vividly, these will be discussed in the eighteenth *āhnika*.

SCHOLAR: *Mantras* for *dīkṣā, saṁkṣepa dīkṣā.*

SWAMIJI: Yes, *saṁkṣipta dīkṣā.*[810]

Audio 11 - 39:19

कलावेक्षा कृपाण्यादिन्यासश्चारः शरीरगः ।
ब्रह्मविद्याविधिश्चैवमुक्तं सद्यःसमुत्क्रमे ॥३११॥

kalāvekṣā kṛpāṇyādinyāsaścāraḥ śarīragaḥ /
brahmavidyāvidhiścaivamuktaṁ sadyaḥsamutkrame //311

In *sadyaḥ samutkrama*, the nineteenth *āhnika*, what will he explained? *Kalāvekṣā*, the *parīkṣā* of *kalā*.

DEVOTEE: *Kalā*, *vidyā*, etc.?

SWAMIJI: Yes.

SCHOLAR: The analysis of *kalā*.

JOHN: The analysis.

SWAMIJI: *Kṛpāṇyādi nyāsa*, and purifying the limbs by *kṛpā*, by a sword. You have to put a sword, the edge of a sword, on each and every limb with *mantras*. It is at the time of death. When the disciple is passing and is about to leave his physical frame, his master purifies all his limbs by a sword. That is *kṛpāṇa nyāsa*. *Brahmavidyā vidhi*, and at the point [that] he is going to throw [off] this physical frame, how to put *brahmavidyā* in his ear.[811] This is explained in *sadyaḥ samutkrama*. *Sadyaḥ samut krama* means, if he has to [remain] in

810 In this brief initiation, the highly elevated master (a *siddha*) purifies the sixfold pathway (*ṣaḍadhvan*) of the disciple through *mantras* only. Without going through any external rituals, he frees the disciple from the cycle of repeated births and deaths (*saṁsāra*) and elevates him to become one with Śiva. This is the shortest chapter of the *Tantrāloka* having only eleven verses.

811 See footnotes 32, 120 and 720.

his body for eight days with that unbearable pain, he will throw his body before eight days by this way, so he will get rid of this pain.

JOHN: This is not suicide.

SWAMIJI: This is not suicide, no, because he has to leave his body.

JOHN: Anyway.

SWAMIJI: He has to leave his body after eight days, why not leave now? Why to be the object of all of this pain?

Audio 11 - 41:11
Audio 12 - 00:00

अधिकारपरीक्षान्तःसंस्कारोऽथ तुलाविधिः।
इत्येतद्वाच्यसर्वस्वं स्याद्विंशतितमाह्निके ॥३१२॥

adhikāraparīkṣāntaḥsaṁskāro'tha tulāvidhiḥ /
ityetadvācyasarvasvaṁ syādviṁśatitamāhnike //312//

In the twentieth *āhnika*, *adhikāra parīkṣā*, who is worthy of being initiated, and how you put the *saṁskāras*[812] in him, in that worthy disciple. *Tulāvidhi*, and the way of the scale, the scaling way. I told you that[813]–the scale, the initiation of the scale.

SCHOLAR: Twenty-seven flowers.

SWAMIJI: Yes, twenty-seven flowers, and that weight will [be equal] to the [weight of the] body of the disciple. *Ityetadvācyasarvasvam syādviṁśatitamāhnike*, this will be discussed in the twentieth *āhnika*.

812 The various ways of purification.
813 See commentary on *śloka* 280 above.

Audio 12 - 00:54

मृतजीवद्विधिर्जालोपदेशः संस्क्रियागणः ।
बलाबलविचारश्चेत्येकविंशाह्निके विधिः ॥३१३॥

mṛtajīvadvidhirjālopadeśaḥ saṁskriyāgaṇaḥ /
balābalavicāraścetyekaviṁśāhnike vidhiḥ //313//

In the twenty-first *āhnika*, this is explained:

Mṛtajīvadvidhir, [when] a master's dearest disciple dies without doing anything, without attaining anything, what the master should do, what that real master does: *mṛta jīvat vidhir*, he finds [his disciple with] *jālopadeśa*, he puts that net [throughout the universe] just like a fisherman puts a net for collecting those fishes in the net. So, this is *mahājāla prayogaḥ*, how to insert *mahājāla*[814] in this whole universe, in one hundred and eighteen worlds, and [after placing that net] in one hundred and eighteen worlds, he collects his *ātmā* (soul). Whose *ātman*? [The disciple] who is dead. And then [the master makes] some body of this earth (clay), [which] is being made in that initiation sacrificial fire. And [when] that body [is made], and then, by *mantra*s, that soul gets entry in that clay body. And then, how can you know that he has come in this body, how can you know that, how [does] the master know? [Because the disciple] moves the body or puts his hand in movement. He does not talk, but he moves his body, he moves his hands.

SCHOLAR: This *puttalaka*, this image.

SWAMIJI: Yes, the image. And the master comes to know that he has come now in this body and [the master] will initiate him to get liberated from repeated births and deaths, and he initiates him. That is *mṛta jīvat vidhi jālopadeśaḥ*.

SCHOLAR: This is like *mṛta saṁjīvanī*.[815]

SWAMIJI: Yes. *Saṁskriyāgaṇaḥ*, and then [how to] put

814 A great (*mahā*) net (*jāla*).

815 A sacred knowledge which bestows immortality and can wake (*saṁjīvana*) the dead (*mṛta*).

various impressions, best spiritual impressions, in that body, in his. . . . *Balābalavicāraścet*, and he who is capable of doing that and who is not capable of doing that, this discussion will also be explained in this *āhnika*, in the twenty-first *āhnika*.

Audio 12 - 03:26

श्रवणं चाभ्यनुज्ञानं शोधनं पातकच्युतिः ।
शङ्काच्छेद इति स्पष्टं वाच्यं लिङ्गोद्धृतिक्रमे ॥ ३१४॥

śravaṇaṁ cābhyanujñānaṁ śodhanaṁ pātakacyutiḥ /
śaṅkāccheda iti spaṣṭaṁ vācyaṁ liṅgoddhṛtikrame //314

In *liṅgoddhṛtikrame*,[816] in the twenty-second *āhnika*: *Śravaṇam*, how you must hear spiritual words from [your] master. *Abhyanujñānaṁ*, how you must understand those words. *Śodhanam*, how you must be purified. *Pātakacyutiḥ*, how the master destroys [the sins of] the one who is a sinful disciple, *śaṅkāccheda*, and destroys the various doubts in the disciple. This is explained in *liṅgoddhṛtikrama*, in the twenty-second *āhnika*.

Audio 12 - 04:15

परीक्षाचार्यकरणं तद्व्रतं हरणं मतेः ।
तद्विभागः साधकत्वमभिषेकविधौ त्वियत् ॥ ३१५॥

parīkṣācāryakaraṇaṁ tadvrataṁ haraṇaṁ mateḥ /
tadvibhāgaḥ sādhakatvamabhiṣekavidhau tviyat //315//
[not recited]

In the twenty-third *āhnika*, *parīkṣācāryakaraṇaṁ*, the master must verify if his disciple–[when] he is going to initiate his disciple–if he is worthy of being initiated or not. He must verify first.

JOHN: Investigate.

---

816 The method (*krama*) of conversion (*liṅgoddhāra*).

SWAMIJI: Investigate. *Tat vratam*, if he has already investigated and, from some way or other, that investigation has not come [to verify the disciple's worthiness] in the true sense and that investigation has proved [the disciple's worth] to be incorrect and he appears in another, opposite way (the disciple), then . . .*

JOHN: "Opposite way" means?

SWAMIJI: Not attached to your master, not attached to your *mantra*, not attached to godly things. [Perhaps the disciples' intention was] just to extract the *mantra* from the master, just for curiosity, for power.

*. . . then what the master should do with him? *Tat vratam haraṇam mateḥ*, then he should extract that power of initiation from him by some particular meditation.

SCHOLAR: Takes away his awareness–*haraṇam mateḥ*.

SWAMIJI: *Mateḥ haraṇaṁ, mateḥ jñānam*, knowledge, extract his knowledge.

JOHN: But you can also take *bauddha jñāna* and *pauruṣa jñāna*,[817] both?

SWAMIJI: *Pauruṣa jñāna*.

JOHN: Not *bauddha jñāna*?

SWAMIJI: *Bauddha jñāna*, but without *pauruṣa jñāna* it is nothing.

SCHOLAR: It loses its . . .

SWAMIJI: It is useless.

SCHOLAR: It has no . . . yes.

SWAMIJI: *Bauddha jñāna* will remain, but not *pauruṣa jñāna*. *Tadvibhāga*, and that way.[818] And *sādhakatvam abhiṣeka vidhau tviyat*, this is in *abhiṣeka vidhi*,[819] in the

817 Intellectual knowledge (*bauddha jñāna*) and spiritual knowledge (*pauruṣa jñāna*).

818 *Tadvibhāga:* the way of extracting, separating (*vibhāga*) the disciples awareness (*pauruṣa jñāna*).

819 Instructions (*vidhi*) for consecration (*abhiṣeka*).

twenty-third *āhnika*, explained.

SCHOLAR: The nature of what is *sādhakatvam*.[820]

SWAMIJI: *Sādhakatvam*: how *mantra*s will be purified, because after doing this wrong thing, this master has to purify his [own] consciousness. His consciousness is not purified. His consciousness gets polluted.

DENISE: The disciple's.

JOHN: No, no, the master's.

SWAMIJI: No, the master's consciousness gets polluted by this wrath, by extracting that power from his disciple. So he has to do some *sādhanā* (meditation), *sādhanā* to get purification. This is in *abhiṣeka vidhi*. And [when he de-initiates] that *sādhaka* and then [he should] never think of that disciple in his mind, as if he is not existing at all in this world.

JOHN: Tough.

SWAMIJI: (laughs)

Audio 12 - 07:12

अधिकार्यथ संस्कारस्तत्प्रयोजनमित्यदः ।
चतुर्विंशेऽन्त्ययागाख्ये वक्तव्यं परिचर्च्यते ॥ ३१६ ॥

adhikāryatha saṁskārastatprayojanamityadaḥ /
caturviṁśe'ntyayāgākhye vaktavyaṁ paricarcyate //316//

In the twenty-fourth *āhnika*, *adhikāri*, he who is capable of this initiation, and how that purifying way is inserted in the consciousness of the disciple, and what is the purpose of that. This will be explained in the twenty-fourth *āhnika*.

Audio 12 - 07:42

प्रयोजनं भोगमोक्षदानेनात्र विधिः स्फुटः ।
पञ्चविंशाह्निके श्राद्धप्रकाशे वस्तुसंग्रहः ॥ ३९८ ॥

820 In the end, the master has to conclude what is to be done with such a disciple.

prayojanaṁ bhogamokṣadānenātra vidhiḥ sphuṭaḥ /
pañcaviṁśāhnike śrāddhaprakāśe vastusaṁgrahaḥ //317

In the twenty-fifth *āhnika*, these things will be discussed narratedly:

Bhogamokṣadānena, what is the purpose of this *dīkṣā* (initiation), and *bhoga mokṣa dānena atra vidhi*, the way how to bestow *bhoga* (*bhoga* means, enjoyment of the world) and *mokṣa* (liberation from the world). These two things, how can he bestow these two things, according to the desire of the disciple, to the disciples.[821] This will be explained in the twenty-fifth *āhnika*.

Audio 12 - 08:37

प्रयोजनं शेषवृत्तेर्नित्यार्चा स्थण्डिले परा ।
लिङ्गस्वरूपं बहुधा चाक्षसूत्रनिरूपणम् ॥३१८॥
पूजाभेद इति वाच्यं लिङ्गार्चसंप्रकाशने ।

prayojanaṁ śeṣavṛtternityārcā sthaṇḍile parā /[822]
liṅgasvarūpaṁ bahudhā cākṣasūtranirūpaṇam //318//
pūjābheda iti vācyaṁ liṅgārcāsaṁprakāśane /319a

In *liṅgārcāsaṁprakāśane*, in the twenty-seventh *āhnika*, the purpose then, after enlightenment, what is the purpose of life; *śeṣavṛtter*, *prayojanam śeṣavṛtter*, what is the purpose of the remaining portion of his life.

JOHN: After enlightenment.

SWAMIJI: After enlightenment. *Nityārcā sthaṇḍile*, how to attribute supreme worship on *sthaṇḍila* on *yāga maṇḍapa*.

JOHN: *Sthaṇḍila*?

---

821 Here, the master is not catering to the obvious desire of the disciple, but initiating according to the disciple's inherent or latent desire of which even the disciple may not be aware.

822 *Āhnika* 26 discusses the daily routine of worship (*nityārcā*), that the disciple must perform in a sacred place (*sthaṇḍila*) for the remaining period of life (*śeṣa vṛtti*).

SCHOLAR: The ground where the *maṇḍala* is drawn.

SWAMIJI: The ground, yes. *Liṅga svarūpaṁ*, and what is the reality of *liṅga*s, what *liṅga* should be worshipped. Should you worship that *liṅga* of *maṇi* (jewel), a metal *liṅga*, or of earth, or something else?

SCHOLAR: Something else.

SWAMIJI: Something else (inaudible).

DEVOTEES: (laughter)

SWAMIJI: *Akṣasūtranirūpaṇam*, what is the purpose of *japa mālā* (reciting beads), what is real *mālā* (*akṣa sūtra nirūpaṇam*). *Pūjābheda*, and the differentiated ways of [worshipping]. This is explained in the twenty-seventh *āhnika*.

Audio 12 - 10:09

नैमित्तिकविभागस्तत्प्रयोजनविधिस्ततः ॥३१९॥
पर्वभेदास्तद्विशेषश्चक्रचर्चा तदर्चनम् ।
गुर्वाद्यन्तदिनाद्यर्चाप्रयोजननिरूपणम् ॥ ३२० ॥

naimittikavibhāgastatprayojanavidhistataḥ //319b//
parvabhedāstadviśeṣaścakracarcā tadarcanam /
gurvādyantadinādyarcāprayojananirūpaṇam //320//

It is now in the twenty-eighth *āhnika*, all this, *parva bhedā*, [etc.].

It is called *nitya karma*, things adored, which is your duty to do early in the morning. And there is another *karma* (action), it is called *naimitti karma* (for some purpose); *naimitti karma*, e.g., to get rid of your enemy, to get the nearness of your master. For those there are some other things to be done. That is *naimitti karma*. How you could get the nearness of your master, there are some ways.

SCHOLAR: But this destroying your enemy, that is in *kāmya karma*.

SWAMIJI: That is *naimittika karma* also. *Naimittika* is for some purpose–all these. *Parva bhedā*, and the differentiated points of *parvās*, the big days of the year. *Tadviśeṣaścakracarcā*, and how you must adore, worship, *cakra pūjā*, on those days. *Gurvādyantadinārcā* (*guru ādi anta dinādyarcā*), the worship of your master and the worship to be done in the beginning of the day and in the end of the day.

SCHOLAR: Isn't this the birthday and the death day of the *guru*, etc.–*gurvādyantadinā*?

SWAMIJI: Yes, death and birth, yes–*adyanta dinādyarcā prayojana nirūpaṇam*. Yes, the birthday and the last day.[823]

SWAMIJI: Yes.

DEVOTEE: *Adya dinā* and *anta dinā*.[824]

SWAMIJI: *Anta dinā. Prayojana nirūpaṇam*, and its purpose.

Audio 12 - 12:19

मृतेः परीक्षा योगीशीमेलकादिविधिस्तथा ।
व्याख्याविधिः श्रुतविधिर्गुरुपूजाविधिस्त्वियत् ॥३२१॥
नैमित्तिकप्रकाशाख्येऽप्यष्टविंशाह्निके स्थितम् ।

mṛteḥ parīkṣā yogīśīmelakādividhistathā /
vyākhyāvidhiḥ śrutavidhirgurupūjāvidhistviyat //321//
naimittikeprakāśākhye'pyaṣṭāviṁśāhnike sthitam /322a
[not recited]

Mṛte parīkṣā, the investigation of the dead person.

JOHN: Is this still in the twenty-eighth?

SWAMIJI: Yes, the twenty-eighth. *Yogīśī melakādi vidhi*, and the way how you can get entry and mixed with *yoginīs*.[825]

823 This is the day the master leaves his body and attains the 'Great Liberation' (*mahāsamādhi*).

824 The first day and the last day, respectively.

825 "*Yoginī melāpa* happens when you are absolutely absorbed in the awareness of God consciousness for sometime and you are weeping inside, you are imploring, craving, doing your meditation towards Lord Śiva, and nothing happens. And sometime when this kind of

And *vyākhyā vidhi*, how the master should explain the *śāstra*s to the disciple. He should not explain in a hurried way. He should explain with love, with affection, to his disciples–all *śāstra*s (*vyākhyā vidhi*). *Śruta vidhi*, and the way how you should hear [the words of your master]. *Guru pūjā vidhi*, how you should worship your master. *Naimittika prakāśākhye'py aṣṭāviṁśa āhnike*, this will be placed in the twenty-eighth *āhnika*.

Audio 12 - 13:14

अधिकार्यात्मनो भेदः सिद्धपत्नीकुलक्रमः ॥३२२॥
अर्चाविधिर्दौतविधी रहस्योपनिषत्क्रमः ।
दीक्षाभिषेकौ बोधश्चेत्येकोनत्रिंश आह्निके ॥३२३॥

adhikāryātmano bhedaḥ siddhapatnīkulakramaḥ //322b
arcāvidhirdautavidhī rahasyopaniṣatkramaḥ /
dākṣābhiṣekau bodhaścetyekonatriṁśa āhnike //323//
[not recited]

[The twenty-ninth *āhnika*]: *Adhikāryātmano bheda*, who is worthy of being a disciple of this path.

SCHOLAR: This coming path which he is about to be explain.

SWAMIJI: This coming path. *Siddhapatnīkulakramaḥ*, what is the succession of the *yoginī* and the *siddha*s.

SCHOLAR: In *siddha cakra*.

SWAMIJI: In *siddha cakra*.[826] *Arcā vidhi*, what is the way of worship there. *Dauta vidhi*, what is the way of worshipping

action is ripened, at once your eyes are closed and you feel yourself surrounded by divine ladies and they illuminate you." Paraphrase from *Tantrāloka* 4.57-58.

826 This is a *maṇḍala* (circle) known as the *siddhacakra* (*Tantrāloka* 29.29a) that is used to worship the perfected beings (*siddha*s) and their wives and consorts (*patnī*) of the succession (*krama*) of the Kula tradition.

your *dūti.*[827] *Rahasyopaniṣat kramaḥ*, what is the secret way of *pūjā*. *Dīkṣā abhiṣekau*, what is initiation there and what is *abhiṣeka* there.[828] *Bodhaśca*, what is the knowledge there. *Ekonatriṁśa āhnike*, this will be explained in the twenty-ninth *āhnika*.

Audio 12 - 14:01

मन्त्रस्वरूपं तद्वीर्यमिति त्रिंशे निरूपितम् ।

mantrasvarūpaṁ tadvīryamiti triṁśe nirūpitam /324a

What is *mantra*, the formation of *mantra*, and the power of *mantra*, will be explained in the thirtieth *āhnika*.

Audio 12 - 14:12

शूलाब्जभेदो व्योमेशस्वस्तिकादिनिरूपणम् ॥३२४॥
विस्तरेणाभिधातव्यमित्येकत्रिंश आह्निके ।

śūlābjabhedo vyomeśasvastikādinirūpaṇam //324b//
vistareṇābhidhātavyamityekatriṁśa āhnike /325a

In the thirty-first *āhnika*, we will explain to you *śūlābja-bheda* (*triśūlabheda*).[829] *Vyomeśa svastikādinirūpaṇam*, and *khecarī*, what is *khecarī*, and what is *svastika*.[830] *Vistareṇ-*

827 Lit., a female attendant. In Kashmir Shaivism, women are held in highest esteem. In his commentary of verse 13 Jayaratha included the following *śloka*, which Swamiji translates as follows: "*yoktā saṁvatsarātsiddhir iha puṁsāṁ bhayātmanam, sā siddhistattva-niṣṭhānāṁ strīṇāṁ dvādaśabhirdinaiḥ*, that power which is achieved *yoktā saṁvatsarāt*, by the male class (men) after one year of constant practice, *sā siddhiḥ*, that very power is achieved by those divine ladies who are established in the true path of Śaivism in just twelve days." *Parātriśikā Laghu Vṛtti* (LJA archive).
828 Initiation (*dīkṣa*), special consecration (*abhiṣeka*).
829 The various (*bheda*) tridents (*triśūla*).
830 This is referring to *Tantrāloka* 31.132, which describes the construction of and elaborate *maṇḍala* of strings and boxes

ābhidhātavyamityekatriṁśa [*āhnike*], this will be explained in the thirty-first *āhnika*.

Audio 12 - 14:39

गुणप्रधानताभेदाः स्वरूपं वीर्यचर्चनम् ॥ ३२६ ॥
कलाभेद इति प्रोक्तं मुद्राणां संप्रकाशने ।

guṇapradhānatābhedāḥ svarūpaṁ vīryacarcanam //325b
kalābheda iti proktaṁ mudrāṇāṁ saṁprakāśane /326a

In the thirty-second *āhnika*, *guṇa pradhānatābhedaḥ*, what is to be subsided and what is to be predominant–these differentiations. And *vīryacarcanam*, what is the *vīrya* (power) there. *Kalābheda*, and differentiated things of *kalā*. This will be explained in *mudrā saṁprakāśanam*, the thirty-second *āhnika*.

Now he explains why *anuja uddeśa*[831] is not done for the onward *āhnika*s, for the thirty-third, thirty-four, thirty-five, thirty-six, and thirty-seven.

Audio 12 - 15:21

द्वत्रिंशतत्त्वादीशाख्यात्प्रभृति प्रस्फुटो यतः ॥ ३२६ ॥
न भेदोऽस्ति ततो नोक्तमुद्देशान्तरमत्र तत् ।

dvātriṁśatattvādīśākhyātprabhṛti prasphuṭo yataḥ //326b
na bhedo'sti tato noktamuddeśāntaramatra tat /327a

[After] the thirty-second *āhnika*, there is nothing to be discussed afresh.

SCHOLAR: Recapitulation.

---

ultimately made into the shape of a *svastika*. *Svastika* is originally a sanskrit word meaning 'good fortune' and 'well being'. It is considered to be a sacred and auspicious symbol in Hinduism, Buddhism, and Jainism and dates back at least 11,000 years.

831 Specific nomination.

SWAMIJI: Yes. It is [already] there, it is already existing in those [previous] *āhnikas*, so nothing new is to be explained there. So there is no *bheda*,[832] [just as] nothing is to be discussed above the thirty-second *tattva* (element)–[for] Īśvara, Sadāśiva, Śakti, and Śiva, there is nothing to be explained, they are fine there.

Audio 12 - 16:06

मुख्यत्वेन च वेद्यत्वादधिकारान्तरक्रमः ॥ ३२७ ॥

mukhyatvena ca vedyatvādadhikārāntarakramaḥ //327b

Because these *āhnikas* [which follow] are very predominant;[833] these *āhnikas*, these sections of the *Tantrāloka*, are very predominant, so [they constitute] another *adhikāra*.[834] It is not pertaining to the *uddeśas*.[835]

Audio 12 - 16:28

इत्युद्देशविधिः प्रोक्तः सुखसंग्रहहेतवे ।
अथास्य लक्षणावेक्षे निरूप्येते यथाक्रमम् ॥ ३२८ ॥

ityuddeśavidhiḥ proktaḥ sukhasaṁgrahahetave /
athāsya lakṣaṇāvekśe nirūpyete yathākramam //328//

These are the ways of *uddeśa* that I have explained here for collecting all the subjects of the *Tantrāloka* very easily for *sādhakas*.

Athāsya lakṣaṇāvekṣe nirūpyete yathākramam, now the *lakṣaṇa*[836] and the *parīkṣā*[837] will be done for the *Tantrāloka*, what is its *lakṣaṇa* and what is its *parīkṣā*.

832 Distinction.
833 *Mukhyatva* means, the highest rank, pre-eminent, superior, etc., which Swamiji is translating as "predominant."
834 Subject or topic.
835 Previous subjects.
836 Definition.
837 An investigation of the veracity of the definitions.

Audio 12 - 17:01

idānīmāhnikārthameva sañcinoti[838]

JOHN: This is number what?

SWAMIJI: This is number 329.

DEFINITION-LAKṢAṆA
INVESTIGATION-PARĪKṢĀ (329-332)

Audio 12 - 17:11

आत्मा संवित्प्रकाशस्थितिरनवयवा
संविदित्यात्तशक्ति-
व्रातं तस्य स्वरूपं स च निज महस-
श्छादनाद्बद्धरूपः ।
आत्मज्योतिःस्वभावप्रकटनविधिना
तस्य मोक्षः स चायं
चित्राकारस्य चित्रः प्रकटित इह य-
त्संग्रहेणार्थ एषः ॥ ३२९ ॥

ātmā saṁvitprakāśasthitiranavayavā
saṁvidityāttaśakti-
vrātaṁ tasya svarūpaṁ, sa ca nija mahasaś-
chādanādbaddharūpaḥ /
ātmajyotiḥsvabhāvaprakaṭanavidhinā
tasya mokṣaḥ sa cāyaṁ
citrākārasya citraḥ prakaṭita iha yat-
saṁgraheṇārtha eṣaḥ //329//

This is the essence of what has been said in this first *āhnika* of the *Tantrāloka*, that *ātmā saṁvit prakāśa sthiti*, the Self is

838 Jayaratha's commentary.

established in the light of consciousness and that light of consciousness is *anavayavā saṁvit*, it is *anavayavā*, without differentiated bodies.

SCHOLAR: *Ekaghana.*

SWAMIJI: *Ekaghana.*

JOHN: One mass.

SWAMIJI: One mass. *Iti*, so, *āttaśaktivrātaṁ tasya svarūpam*, the reality of the Self (that is, the reality of God consciousness) is filled with the masses of energies; *ātta śaktivrāta*, He has accepted the masses of energies in His body.

SCHOLAR: *Kroḍīkṛta.*

SWAMIJI: *Kroḍīkṛta.*[839] There you should put a comma [after "*svarūpam*"].[840] *Sa ca nija mahasaśchādanādbaddharūpaḥ*, and that *ātmā* seems to be bound when He, by His glory of *svātantrya*, conceals His light of knowledge and action (*mahasaḥ* means, the light of knowledge and action). He conceals His reality of knowledge and action and seems to be bound in this universe.

DEVOTEE: "*Maha*" in the sense of "*teja*"?

SWAMIJI: *Maha*, *teja*, yes, *teja*.[841] *Ātma jyotiḥ svabhāva prakaṭana vidhinā tasya mokṣaḥ*, and it is not only that He is bound, He again becomes liberated by revealing the nature of His Self-consciousness, His own consciousness. When He reveals His own consciousness again, by that way, He again becomes liberated and becomes *mukta*. And this liberation and being bound is the play of that Being who is *citrakāra*, who has consumed various formations of His Self. Sometimes He seems to be bound, sometimes He seems to be liberated.

JOHN: *Citrakāra* means "he assumes"?

SCHOLAR: No, "He has many" (inaudible).

---

839 He has accepted the masses of energies in His body.

840 Referring to this line in Jayaratha's commentary: *ātmanaḥ kroḍīkṛtānanta-śaktikaṁ svarūpam.*

841 Light, brilliance.

SWAMIJI: *Citrakāra*, "he has many." This is the *artha*, this is the essence, of the *Tantrāloka*, that this is only a play.

JOHN: Play of Lord Śiva.

SWAMIJI: Being bound and being liberated. Otherwise, there is nothing to be done.

JOHN: That is why you have this secret word "*rām*."

SWAMIJI: *Rām*, yes.[842]

Audio 12 - 20:46

मिथ्याज्ञानं तिमिरमसमान् दृष्टिदोषान्प्रसूते
तत्सद्भावाद्विमलमपि तद्भाति मालिन्यधाम ।
यत्तु प्रेक्ष्यं दृशि परिगतं तैमिरीं दोषमुद्रां
दूरं रुन्ध्दत्प्रभवनु कथं तस्य मालिन्यशङ्का ॥३३०॥

mithyājñānaṁ timiramasamān dṛṣṭidoṣānprasūte
tatsadbhāvādvimalamapi tadbhāti mālinyadhāma /
yattu prekṣyaṁ dṛśi parigataṁ taimirīṁ doṣamudrāṁ
dūraṁ rūnddhetprabhavatu kathaṁ tasya[843]
mālinyaśaṅkā //330//

This incorrect knowledge, when you know your Self not in the correct way, that is *mithyā jñāna*. In the differentiated state, when that knowledge is *timiram*, . . .*

JOHN: *Mithyā* means "illusory"?

SWAMIJI: Yes, illusory and not correct.

*. . . that is really the blindness or the darkness of the Self. By that blindness, you can't perceive your nature–by this *mithyā jñāna*. And that blindness creates (*prasūte*, creates) *asamāna dṛṣṭi doṣān*, many drawbacks, . . .*

Doṣa means . . .

842 See verse 85 for an explanation of the word "*rāma*."
843 Swamiji corrected "*tatra*," which appears in the text from which he was working on, to read "*tasya*."

JOHN: Defects, faults.

SWAMIJI: Defects, falsehoods of perceptions.

*. . . falsehoods of perceptions (*dṛṣṭi doṣān*) are created by that.

SCHOLAR: *Asamān*?

SWAMIJI: *Asamān*: unparalleled, great, huge. *Tat sadbhāvāt*, and by the existence of that false perception, *vimalamapi tad mālinyadhāma bhāti*, although that state of God consciousness is absolutely pure, but It seems to be impure, It appears to be impure. And when, *yattu prekṣyaṁ dṛśi parigataṁ taimirīṁ doṣamudrā dūraṁ rūnddhet*, when (*yattu-yadā*; *yattu* means, *yadā*), when *prekṣyaṁ dṛśi parigatam, prekṣyam*, that [which] is to be perceived and [which] is not existing in your own eyes, in your own sight, in your own knowledge (*dṛśi parigatam*), and because in your sight there is *taimirīṁ doṣa mudāraṁ* (there is the defect of blindness, blindness of perception), when that blindness of perception is put away, is removed away, *prabhavatu katham tatra mālinyaśaṅkā*, then there is no question of the rise of impurity in your Self. Your Self shines in glamour.

Now, in this *śloka* (331), it is *aprastutapraśaṁsa. Aprastuta praśaṁsa* [means that] the author intends to put this fact that this *Tantrāloka*, the substance of the *Tantrāloka*, is not understood by all; it won't be understood by all philosophers, all commentators, because of their defective perception.

JOHN: *Doṣa*.

SWAMIJI: *Doṣa*. And [in order] to put the falsehood of those philosophers before the readers, he puts the falsehood of other things–not those, not [the falsehood of] those philosophers. He puts the falsehood of other things, that there are some people who think that this objective world is to be avoided, is to be neglected, [that] you must neglect this objective world.

And so he [Abhinavagupta] addresses the objective world:

Audio 12 - 25:20

भावाव्रत ! हठाज्जनस्य हृदया-
न्याक्रम्य यन्नर्तयन्
भङ्गीभिर्विविधाभिरात्महृदयं
प्रच्छाद्य संक्रीडसे ।
यस्त्वामाह जडं जडः सहृदयं-
मन्यत्वदुःशिक्षितो
मन्येऽमुष्य जडात्मता स्तुतिपदं
त्वत्साम्यसंभावनात् ॥ ३३१ ॥

bhāvavrāta! haṭhājjanasya hṛdayā
nyākramya yannartayan
bhaṅgībhirvividhābhirātmahṛdayaṁ
pracchādya saṁkrīḍase /
yastvāmāha jaḍaṁ jaḍaḥ sahṛdayaṁ-
manyatvaduḥśikṣito
manye'muṣya jaḍātmatā stutipadaṁ
tvatsāmyasaṁbhāvanāt //331// [not recited]

O objective world (*bhāvavrāta*, O objective world), you are great, you are so great! You are so great that *haṭhāt janasya hṛdayānyā kramya yat nartayan*, you, *haṭhā*, by force, you enter in the brain of those philosophers and *nartayan*, you make them dance. O objective world, *bhaṅgībhir vividhābhir*, in various ways you make them dance here and there, *ātma hṛdayaṁ pracchādya*, and conceal your own [true] nature of your objectivity. Your [true] nature of objectivity you conceal and make them dance in another way. *Saṁkrīḍase*, and you joyfully play with them, play them. They are played by you. *Yastvām āha jaḍam jaḍaḥ sahṛdayam*,[844] and those philosophers who perceive and take for granted that "this, you, objective world, are *jaḍa* [unconscious], you are not *caitanya* [conscious], you are not one with God consciousness," he is

844 Their hearts (*sahṛdayam*) are lifeless (*jaḍaḥ*).

jaḍa himself! That philosopher is *jaḍa*, not you. You are one with *caitanya*, and he considers himself to be *caitanya*. But this consideration of his is a false decision. He has decided that he is *caitanya* [conscious] himself and [that] this objective world is *jaḍa* [unconscious]. Hence, he is *duḥśikṣita*, he is taught wrongly.

SCHOLAR: *Nirupadeśa*.

SWAMIJI: *Nirupadeśa*.[845] *Duḥśikṣita*, *duḥkhena śikṣita*, it is an incorrect teaching. He has received an incorrect teaching from his master. *Manye'muṣya jaḍātmatā*, this title of being *jaḍa*, which I have attributed to those philosophers, is really *stuti padam*, I sing glory to them because, in fact, they are [more] degraded than *jaḍa*.

JOHN: These philosophers.

SWAMIJI: These philosophers. *Tvatsāmya saṁbhāvanāt*, because I have given similarity [i.e., equivalence] to them with you, objective world. Otherwise, you, objective world, are . . . so you, objective world, are so great![846]

---

845 Confirming that those philosophers have been taught wrongly (*nirupadeśa*).

846 In this respect, Utpaladeva has sung the greatness of the objective world in his Śivastotravali:

> *jaḍe jagati cidrūpaḥ kila vedye'pi vedakaḥ /*
> *vibhurmite ca yenāsi tena sarvottamo bhavān //*
> Śivastotrāvalī 3.20

"O Lord, as You are *jaḍe jagati cidrūpaḥ,* in the world of unconsciousness, You are filled with consciousness, with awareness. In the unaware world, You are aware. *Kila vedye'pi vedakaḥ*, in the world of objectivity, You are the knower, You are the subject. *Vibhurmite ca yenāsi*, as You are all-pervading in limitation; in the world of limitation, You are unlimited. As You are such, *tena sarvottamo bhavān*, so You are the greatest and the highest Being existing in this universe." Paraphrase from *Festival of Devotion and Praise – Shivastotrāvali, Hymns to Shiva* by Utpaladeva, Swami Lakshmanjoo, ed. John Hughes, (Lakshmanjoo Academy, Los Angeles, 2014), 3.20.

SCHOLAR: *Stuti padam* is the praises of who?

SWAMIJI: It is the praises of those philosophers. It is a praise for them because I have nominated them as *jaḍa*.

JOHN: When they are really less than *jaḍa*.

SWAMIJI: They are [more] degraded [than] *jaḍa bhāva* also. So, in the same way, the *Tantrāloka* is blameless.

[Abhinavagupta says], "There is no fault in my *Tantrāloka*. Anybody who [finds] fault in my work, the *Tantrāloka*, he is false, he is filled with faults himself. The *Tantrāloka* is clear because this is the objective world, and this is one with God consciousness."

SCHOLAR: A great verse.

SWAMIJI: Yes.

Audio 12 - 28:51

इह गलितमलाः परावरज्ञाः
शिवसद्भावमया अधिक्रियन्ते ।
गुरवः प्रविचारणे यतस्तद्-
विफला द्वेषकलंकहानियाञ्चा ॥ ३३२ ॥

iha galitamalāḥ parāvarājñāḥ
śivasadbhāvamayā adhikriyante /
guravaḥ pravicāraṇe yatastad-
viphalā dveṣakalaṅkahāniyācñā //332//
[not recited in full]

Who are worthy to understand this *Tantrāloka*? Those rare persons are worthy to understand this *Tantrāloka* of mine who have absolutely freed themselves from all impurities (*āṇavamala*, *māyīyamala*, and *kārmamala*) and who are *parāvarājñāḥ*, who have acknowledged the truth of the first and the last, who have acknowledged the truth of '*a*' and '*ha*', who have acknowledged the truth of *ahaṁ* (universal-I, what is universal-I),[847] and *śiva sadbhāva mayā*, who are established in the state of Śiva-consciousness, established in the state of Śiva. Those are worthy, those masters (*guravaḥ*, those masters) are worthy to understand this *Tantrāloka* of mine. This *Tantrāloka* is not meant for disciples. This *Tantrāloka* is meant for masters to understand. Because (*yatas*) *tat pravicāraṇe*, so, if this is so, *tat* (thus), *dveṣakalaṅka-hāniyācñā viphala*, why should I say that that person is worthy and that person is not worthy to read this *Tantrāloka* of mine? So I have, in brief words, explained that the *Tantrāloka* can be understood by those masters who have absolutely removed all impurities, who have perceived the state of *ahaṁ* (universal-I), and who are established in the state of Śiva. Those are worthy to understand this *Tantrāloka*, not others.

The next [*śloka*]:

Conclusion of Tantrāloka First Āhnika

[Abhinavagupta's concluding *śloka*.]

Audio 12 - 31:02

तन्त्रालोकेऽभिनवरचितेऽमुत्र विज्ञानसत्ता-
भेदोद्गारप्रकटनपटावाह्निकेऽस्मिन्समाप्तिः ।

tantrāloke'bhinavaracite'mutra vijñānasattā /
bhedodgāraprakaṭanapaṭāvāhnike'sminsamāptiḥ //

Thus, in this first *āhnika* of the *Tantrāloka*, here ends the first *āhnika* of the *Tantrāloka* (*asmin tantrāloke*, *asmin samāptiḥ*, thus ends the first *āhnika* of the *Tantrāloka*), which

847 "'*A*' indicates the state of Lord Śiva, '*ha*' indicates the state of Śakti, and '*ma*' indicates the state of individuality." *Parātriśikā Vivaraṇa* (LJA archive).

is composed by Abhinavagupta (*abhinavaracite*). And this first *āhnika* is *vijñāna sattā bheda udgāra prakaṭana paṭau*, this *āhnika* is bent upon clearing the differentiated perceptions of the means (*āṇavopāya*, *śāktopāya*, *śāmbhavopāya*, and *anupāya*).

SCHOLAR: "*Vijñāna*" here means, *upāya*.

SWAMIJI: "*Vijñāna*" means *upāya* there. *Vijñāna sattā bheda udgāra prakaṭana paṭau asmin samāptiḥ*, so ends this *āhnika* of the *Tantrāloka*.

JOHN: *Jai Guru Deva*!

SWAMIJI: Jayaratha's *śloka* is also best. Jayaratha, the commentator of the *Tantrāloka*, was not a disciple of Abhinavagupta, but he had respect for Abhinavagupta, so he has commentated on his work. Otherwise, it was no use to comment [upon Abhinavagupta's] work as [Jayaratha] was from another order.[848]

Audio 12 - 32:33

श्रीशृङ्गाररथादवाप्य कृतिनो जन्मानवद्यक्रमं
श्रीमच्छङ्खधरात्परं परिचयं विद्यासु सर्वास्वपि ।
श्रीकल्याणतनोः शिवादधिगमं सर्वागमानामपि
व्याख्यातं प्रथमाह्निकं जयरथेनात्रावधेयं बुधैः ॥

śrīśṛṅgārarathādavāpya kṛtino janmānavadyakramaṁ
śrīmacchaṅkhadharātparaṁparicayaṁ vidyāsu
sarvāsvapi / śrīkalyāṇatanoḥ śivādadhigamaṁ
sarvāgamānāmapi vyākhyātaṁ prathamāhnikaṁ
jayarathen-ātrāvadheyaṁ budhaiḥ //[849]

Thus, Jayaratha has commentated upon the first *āhnika* of the *Tantrāloka*; Jayaratha, who was *śrī śṛṅgārarathādavāpya kṛtino janmānavadya kramaṁ*, who had got existence of [his]

848 "Jayaratha was attached to the Śrī Vidyā tradition." *Tantrāloka* 7.18.
849 Concluding *śloka* of Jayaratha's commentary on the *Tantrāloka*.

body from Sṛṅgāraratha. So, Sṛṅgāraratha was his father. *Anavadya kramam janma*, I have got this *janma* from Śṛṅgāraratha, and that *janma* of mine, that birth of mine, was absolutely flawless, faultless, absolutely great; *anavadya*, there was no defect, absolutely defect-less.

SCHOLAR: In its *krama*. Its *krama* was without defect.

SWAMIJI: Yes.

SCHOLAR: Its process.

SWAMIJI: Yes. *Śrīmat śaṅkhadharāt paraṁ paricayaṁ vidyāsu sarvāsva*, and all information of knowledge I have got from Śrī Śaṅkhadhara. Śaṅkhadhara was my master of theory. All theory I understood from Śaṅkhadhara, my master. *Śrīkalyāṇatanoḥ śivādadhigamaṁ sarvāgama*, and I got all information of all secrets of the *tantras* [from he] who was absolutely one with Śiva, Śrī Kalyāṇa. Śrī Kalyāṇa was his spiritual master. Śaṅkhadhara was his . . .

JOHN: *Vidyā guru.*

SWAMIJI: . . . *vidyā guru.*[850]

DEVOTEE: *Paricaya*?

SWAMIJI: *Paricaya* means, information. *Śrī kalyāṇatanoḥ śivādadhigamaṁ sarvāgamānām api vyākhyātaṁ pratham āhnikaṁ jayarathena āṣu*. So, Jayaratha has commented upon the first *āhnika* of the *Tantrāloka*. This must be accepted by those who have got absolute, complete information; *buddhaiḥ*, those who are informed already, they must know this.

Audio 12 - 35:12

HERE ENDS THE FIRST ĀHNIKA OF THE TANTRĀLOKA.

JAI GURU DEVA

850 Intellectual master.

APPENDIX

1. Bhairava

Bhairava is an appellation of Lord Śiva, which literally means, frightful, terrible, horrible, formidable. In Kashmir Shaivism, Parabhairava (supreme Bhairava) is synonymous with the state of *paramaśiva* (supreme Śiva).

"*Avayavāyamanair bhāva rāśibhir yuktāṁ*, so all this objective world has become the limbs of the Devī, of Lord Śiva, in his female form. *Maheśvarasya parabhairavasya abhedena vartamānām*, and this Devī is situated as one with Lord Śiva. It is not separated from Lord Śiva who is Parabhairava."
Parātriśikā Laghu Vṛtti, commentary verse 32 (LJA archive).

bhārūpaṁ paripūrṇaṁ svātmani
viśrāntito mahānandam /
icchāsaṁvitkaraṇair nirbharitam
anantaśaktiparipūrṇam //10
sarvavikalpavihīnaṁ śuddhaṁ
śāntaṁ layodayavihīnam /
yat paratattvaṁ tasmin vibhāti
ṣaṭtriṁśadātma jagat //11
(Paramārthasāra, verses 10-11)

"Now, the qualification of Parabhairava is described by Abhinavagupta. *Bārupam*, who is *bārupam*, who is *prakāśa*, who is filled with *prakāśa* (the light of consciousness), who is *pari pūrṇam*, who is *pūrṇam* (full), *svātmani viśrāntito mahānandam*, who is residing in His own way and is filled with *ānanda* (bliss, blissful state). *Bārūpaṁ pari pūrnaṁ* is He who is *cit*, who is the embodiment of *cit śakti* (energy of consciousness). *Svātmani viśrāntito mahānandam*, when He resides in His *cit śakti*, He becomes filled with *ānanda* (bliss). *Icchā-saṁvit-karaṇair*, *icchā nirbharitam*, He is also filled with *icchā śakti*, *saṁvit*, *jñāna śakti*, and *karaṇair*, *kriyā śakti*. *Icchā* means the energy of will, *saṁvit* means the energy of knowledge, and *karaṇair* means the energy of action. He is filled with these three energies. So He is filled with *cit śakti*, *ānanda śakti*, *icchā śakti*, *jñāna śakti* [viz., *saṁvit*], and *kriyā śakti* [viz., *karaṇair*]. And exclusively, He is *ananta-śakti-paripūrṇam*, He is not only filled with [these] five energies, He has got numberless *śaktis*. *Ananta-śakti-paripūrṇam*, He is filled with all energies, which are offshoots of these five energies. *Sarva vikalpa vihīnaṁ*, He who is *sarva vikalpa vihīnaṁ*, all varieties of thoughts have taken their end there. *Śuddhaṁ*, He who is clean, *śāntaṁ*, who is appeased, *layodaya-vihīnam,* who has rise and fall, and who is absent from rise and fall (He neither rises nor falls down). And that *para tattvaṁ*, that supreme state of God consciousness, the supreme state of Parabhairava, *tasmin*, in that, *śivatattvaṁ*, *tasmin śivādidharāntaṁ jagat viśvam*, *ṣaṭtriṁ-śadātma*, all this universe, which is from *pṛthvī* to Śiva *tattva*, it is existing in that *para tattva*."

Paraphrase taken from Swami Lakshmanjoo, trans., *Paramārthasāra–The Essence of the Supreme Reality*, verses 10-11 (1990).

bhiyā sarvaṁ ravayati sarvago vyāpako'khile /
iti bhairavaśabdasya saṁtatoccāraṇācchivaḥ //130//

"Just find out the meaning of "Bhairava." When you want to find out the meaning of Bhairava, you have to explain these three letters of Bhairava: "*bha*," "*ra*," and "*va*." "*Bha*" means, threat, fear; "*ra*" means, screaming, crying; "*va*" means, all-pervading, present, presence of God consciousness. There you find the presence of God consciousness. When you scream in fear, God is there."

Vijñāna Bhairava–The Manual for Self Realization, verse 130.

"Bhairava means, the terrible one who destroys the weakness of the lower self (ego). This is the name of Śiva. Bhairava is constituted of three letters, *bha*, *ra*, and *va*. The hermeneutic interpretation of Bhairava, therefore, is that '*bha*' indicates '*bharaṇa*', maintenance of the universe, '*ra*' indicates '*ravaṇa*' i.e., withdrawal of the universe, 'va' indicates '*vamana*', ejecting or letting go of the universe, i.e., manifestation of the universe. Thus, Bhairava indicates all the three aspects of the Divine, viz., *sṛṣṭi* (manifestation), *sthiti* (maintenance) and *saṁhāra* (withdrawal). Bhairava has been called 'three-headed', because the three heads are a symbolic representation of the three *śaktis* of Bhairava, viz., *parā*, *parāparā*, and *aparā* or because the three heads are a symbolic representation of Nara, Śakti, and Śiva."

Jaideva Singh, trans., *Pratyabhijña Hridayam*, p131, n 45.

vimalatamaparamabhairavabodhāt tatvad
vibhāgaśūnyamapi / Paramārthasāra 13a

"In the same way, that which is absolutely the purest element, Parabhairava (Parabhairava is the purest element of the supreme mirror), and in that supreme mirror, which is the purest element of Bhairava, *vibhaktama jagad etat*, from Śiva to *pṛthvī* (earth), it seems as if you perceive that universe as absolutely separate from that mirror, from Parabhairava. It appears as absolutely separate from Parabhairava. And not only that, it is separate from each other. *Pṛthvī* (earth) is separated from *jala* (water), *jala* is separated from *agni* (fire), *agni* is separated from *vāyu* (wind), *vāyu* is separate, *ākāśa* (ether) is separate, *antaḥkaraṇa*s (mind, intellect and ego) are separated, *śabda*, *sparśa*, *rūpa*, *rasa* and *ghanda*; *prakṛti, pṛthvī*, *jala*, and *māyā*, Śuddhavidyā, Īśvara, and Sadāśiva, are all separate; *vibhaktamābhāti*, in the same way this whole universe shines in the mirror of Parabhairava."

Paramārthasāra, *Essence of the Supreme Reality*, verse *13a*.

"Paramaśiva (supreme Śiva) is the life of all the thirty-six elements, and all these elements exist and posses their own states of being on the basis of Paramaśiva. But the thirty-six elements say that, "There is something greater than us!" So the thirty six elements are *uttara*, because there is something greater than the thirty six elements. Parabhairava *bodha* is the knowledge of that supreme state of Śiva, which means that Parabhairava is *anuttara* (supreme, unparalleled). Therefore, there is no element greater than Parabhairava."

Paraphrase from *Parātriśikā Vivaraṇa* (LJA archive).

2. **Thirty-six elements** (*tattvas*)

Though Kashmir Shaivism recognises 36 *tattvas* (elements), Abhinavagupta adds two additional states:

1) **Mahāmāyā*: Swamiji says, "It is the gap and power of delusion. Delusion, where you won't know that you are deluded. You will conclude that you are established on truth. But that is not truth, that is not the real thing." This is the abode of the *vijñānākalas*.

2) **Guṇa tattva*: The state where the three *guṇas* first manifest. Swamiji says, "In *prakṛti* you can't see the three *guṇas* [because] this is the seed state of the three *guṇas*. It is why in Shaivism, we have put another element, and that is the element of *guṇa tattva*."

Śuddha tattvas – Pure Elements

Śiva = I-ness (Being)
Śakti = I-ness (Energy of Being)
Sadāśiva = I-ness in This-ness
Īśvara = This-ness in I-ness
Śuddhavidyā = I-ness in I-ness / This-ness in This-ness

Ṣaṭ kañcukas – Six Coverings

(Mahāmāyā = gap of illusion)*
Māya = illusion of individuality
Kalā = limitation of creativity/activity

Vidyā = limitation of knowledge
Rāga = limitation of attachment
Kāla = limitation of time
Niyati = limitation of place

Puruṣa = ego connected with subjectivity
Prakṛti = nature
(Guṇa tattva = manifest guṇas)*

Antaḥkaraṇas – Three Internal Organs

Buddhiḥ = intellect
Ahaṁkāra = ego connected with objectivity
Manas = mind

Pañca jñānendriyas – Five Organs of Cognition

Śrotra = ear, organ of hearing
Tvak = skin, organ of touching
Cakṣu = eye, organ of seeing
Rasanā = tongue, organ of tasting
Ghrāṇa = nose, organ of smelling

Pañca karmendriyas – Five Organs of Action

Vāk = speech
Pāṇi = hand
Pāda = foot
Pāyu = excretion
Upastha = procreative

Pañca tanmātras – Five Subtle Elements

Śabda = sound
Sparśa = touch
Rūpa = form
Rasa = taste
Gandha = smell

Pañca mahābhūtas - Five Great Elements

Ākāśa = ether
Vāyu = air
Tejas = fire
Jala = water
Pṛthvī = earth

For a full explanation of the 36 *tattvas*, see *Kashmir Shaivism–The Secret Supreme*, chapter 1.

3. *Pramiti, pramātṛ, pramāṇa, prameya bhava* (supreme subjective, subjective, cognitive and objective consciousness)

"*Pramiti bhava* is the supreme subjective state, *pramātṛ bhava* is the pure subjective state, *pramāṇa bhava* is the cognitive state, and *prameya bhava* is the objective state. There is difference between *pramātṛ bhāva* and *pramiti bhāva*. *Pramātṛ bhāva* is that state of consciousness where objective perception is attached. When that state of *pramātṛ bhāva* is attached with objective perception, that is pure state of *pramātṛ bhāva*. When it moves to the state where there is no objective perception, there is no touch of objective perception, it is beyond objective perception, that is *pramiti bhāva*."
Tantrāloka 4.124, commentary (LJA archive)

"[*Pramiti bhāva* is an] objectless-subjective state. It is residing in only pure subjective consciousness. It has nothing to do with the object. When there is the objective state also attached to the subjective state, that is not *pramiti bhāva*, that is *pramātṛ bhāva*. And when that objective state is connected with the cognitive state, that is *pramāṇa bhāva*. When that objective state is completely a pure objective state, that is *prameya bhāva*. And *pramiti bhāva* is complete subjective consciousness without the slightest touch and trace of this object. In the long run, everything resides in *pramiti bhāva*; *pramiti bhāva* is the life of all the three. This is pure consciousness. And that *pramiti bhāva* is absolutely one with

svātantrya śakti, it is one with Lord Siva."
Ibid., 11.72-73a.

"For instance, when you are [giving a lecture while] reading your book, your consciousness is *with* an object. When you are giving a lecture without a book, without any support, your consciousness is *without* an object, it flows out. This is the state of *pramiti bhāva*."
Ibid., 6.180.

"In fact, this *pramiti bhāva* is the real source of understanding anything. Whatever you see, it must touch the state of *pramiti bhāva*, otherwise you won't understand it. For instance, you see [an object]. You'll only know [that object] when this sensation of [that object already] resides in *pramiti bhāva*, in that super state of subjective consciousness. And the super state of subjective consciousness is not differentiated. From that undifferentiated point of *pramiti bhāva*, the differentiated flow of *pramātṛ bhāva* and *pramāṇa bhāva* flow out."
Ibid., 11.62.

"It is *nirvikalpa*, it is a thoughtless state. And in that thoughtless state, it [i.e., all knowledge] must reside, otherwise it is not known. It will be unknown for eternity.
Ibid. 11.68-69.

4. ***Nirvikalpa*** (Lit., free from change or difference, unwavering, knowledge not depending upon or derived from the senses.)

> *saṁketādismaraṇaṁ ca tathā anubhavaṁ vinā kutaḥ ?*
> *(Parātriśikā Vivaraṇa)*

"In reality, everything, whatever exists, it is in *nirvikalpa* state [where] you can't define anything. You can define only in the *vikalpa* state, in the cycle of *vikalpa*, when you say, [for example], "This is a specks cover." But it is not a specks cover in the real sense in the state of God consciousness. It is just *nirvikalpa*–you can't say what it is, but it is! *Saṁketādi smaraṇam*, when you understand, "This is mine," "O, this was in my house and this is mine," this memory takes place in the *vikalpa* state, not the *nirvikalpa* state. And that *vikalpa* state cannot exist without *anubhavam*, the *nirvikalpa* state. *Nirvikalpa* is the cause of all *vikalpa*s; the undifferentiated state is the cause of all *vikalpas*. It is not something foreign [to *vikalpas*]. It is their life. It is the life of all *vikalpas*."

Parātriśikā Vivaraṇa (LJA archives).

tadevameva ihāpi śivatattvaṁ sadā avikalpameva vikalpasūti svātantryasarasamanādi . . . sarvādibhūtaṁ siddham / (Parātriśikā Vivaraṇa)

"So, this way, *ihāpi*, in this philosophy, Śiva *tattva* is *siddham*, understood as *avikalpameva,* it is thoughtless, *vikalpasūti svātantrya sarasam*, coated with *ānanda*, (that is, *sarasa*, with *rasa*), it is coated with that *rasa* which creates *vikalpa*s. This Śiva *tattva* is *nirvikalpa* Himself, and it is coated with the *rasa* of that state which creates *vikalpa. So vikalpa* is created from *nirvikalpa*, and from *vikalpa*, *nirvikalpa* is created, visa-versa. You won't find *vikalpa* without *nirvikalpa* and you won't find *nirvikalpa* without *vikalpa*. When you find it this way, that is the real knowledge. When you find only *nirvikalpa* as *nirvikalpa* and *vikalpa* as *vikalpa,* that is limited knowledge, that is a wrong notion."

Ibid.

yat yat svasāmarthyodbhūtottarakālikārthakriyāyogyatādivaśaniḥśeṣyamāṇasatyatāvaśāvāptāvicalasaṁvādaṁ virodhāvabhāsisaṁmatakramikavikalpyamānanīlādiniṣth avikalpapūrvabhāvi nirvikalpasaṁvidrūpaṁ (Parātriśikā Vivaraṇa)

"*Jalāharānāḍī kriyā*, when you are thirsty, you want a cup of water. At the first moment, there is some sensation, there is not thirst. After that, the sensation of thirst appears. And after thirst, you find some pot, and then you put water in that, *bas*, and drink it. But the first start, at the first start, there is only the sensation-*nirvikalpa*. You can't understand what it is, it is just one with Śiva. So you have to find out that state. That state of Śiva is to be observed in the whole cycle of this drama. Which drama? The sensation, the pot, and the taking, the pouring water, and drinking it. All this experience should be attached with that first vibration, *nirvikalpa*, where this whole drama is *asphuṭatāma*, it does not appear but it is there in seed form. So, there is first the sensation of thirst, [where] thirst has not yet appeared, then thirst appears, then craving for a tumbler appears, then craving for pouring water appears; then after pouring water, drinking this water appears; after drinking water, the sensation, the same sensation ends. Which sensation? *Nirvikalpa*. So, in the beginning, there is the *nirvikalpa* state, and in the end there is *nirvikalpa* state, in each and every activity of the world. [But] we don't look there, we don't look in the beginning and we don't look in the end. We look in the outside cycle, so we are lost."

Ibid.

> *sarvapramātṛṣu avikalpaka savikalpakatattva-saṁvedana daśāsu,* (*Shiva Sutras 3.19*)

There are two ways to observe this garland of letter: as *savikalpa* or as *nirvikalpa*. The Sanskrit word *savikalpa* means "with varieties of thoughts" and *nirvikalpa* means "without varieties of thoughts." The *nirvikalpa* way of observing sounds, letters, and sentences is experienced by *yogi*s. For example, if you say, "Get me a bucket of water, I want a bucket of water," then when you examine this statement in a *nirvikalpa* way, you won't get that bucket of water. Rather, you will observe this is only the flow of consciousness in its own nature. The word "get" will have no meaning. It is only the letters g-e-t and nothing else. There is no meaning in the separate letters. To derive meaning, you have to attach your individual consciousness. When individual consciousness is not attached to these letters, words and sentences, then you will become one with Lord Śiva. This is

the *nirvikalpa* reality of realization."
Shiva Sutras–The Supreme Awakening, 3.19

As long as the kingdom of God consciousness is there, there is no place for the kingdom of the mind.The junk of thoughts, in God consciousness, they don't come, they have no right to come, they have no room to come.

DENISE: But a person who's in God consciousness and in the world, don't they have to think a thought before they perform an action?

SWAMIJI: No, that thought is not thought. That thought is a fountain of bliss. You can't imagine unless you realize it, experience it.

JOHN: So we can't say that a man in God consciousness thinks, but he's in the world doing and acting and so many things.

SWAMIJI: But he is rolling in God consciousness. There is no worry about him. He can do everything, each and every act that an ordinary person, ignorant person, does, but for him, all is divine, all is lying in his nature (*svarūpa*).

JOHN: So thought is by its nature limited. The definition of thought is "something that is limited."

SWAMIJI: Limited, yes.

JOHN: And since a man in God consciousness doesn't have limited anything, then he doesn't have thoughts.

SWAMIJI: Unlimited thought is not thought, it is *nirvikalpa*. It is the state of your own nature where there is no limitation.
Special Verses on Practice, verse 65 (LJA archive)

5. **Seven States of *Ānanda*** (*turya*)

"The practical theory of the seven states of *turya*, also known as the seven states of *ānanda* (bliss), was taught to the great *Śaivite* philosopher Abhinavagupta by his master Śambhunātha. The first state of *turya* is called *nijānanda*, which means "the bliss of your own Self." When you concentrate in continuity with great reverence, with love, affection, and devotion, then your breath becomes very fine and subtle. Automatically, you breathe very slowly. At that moment, you experience giddiness. It is a kind of intoxicating mood. And when the giddiness becomes firm and stable, this is the second state of *turya* known as *nirānanda* which means "devoid of limited bliss." Here the aspirant falls asleep at once and enters that gap or junction which is known to be the start of *turya*. At that moment the aspirant hears hideous sound and sees furious forms. For example, he may experience that the whole house has collapsed upon him, or he may experience that there is a fire burning outside and this fire will burn everything including himself. He may actually think that he is going to die, but these thoughts are wrong thoughts and he must ignore them. When the aspirant desires to move from individuality to universality, all of these experiences occur because individuality has to be shaken off.

If you continue with tolerance, breathing and internally reciting your *mantra* according to the instructions of your master, then these terrible sounds and forms vanish, and pulling and pushing in your breathing passage begins to occur and you feel as if you are choking, that you cannot breathe. At that point you must insert more love and affection for your practice, and then after some time, this choking sensation will pass. This state of hideous sounds and forms, followed by the sensation that you are choking and that your breathing is about to stop, is called *parānanda*, which means "the *ānanda* (bliss) of breathing." Here, your breathing becomes full of bliss and joy, even though you are experiencing terrible forms and sounds. If you maintain your practice continuously with intense devotion, your breath stops at the center of what we call *lambikā sthāna*, which in English is known as the "soft palate." This *lambikā sthāna* is found on the right side near the pit of the throat. Here the aspirant experiences that his breath is neither moving out nor coming in. He feels that his breath is moving round and round, that it is rotating at one point. This state is called *brahmānanda*, which means, "that bliss which is all-pervading." Here, as his breathing has stopped, the *yogi* must put his mind on his *mantra* and only his *mantra* with great devotion to Lord Śiva. If he continues this practice with great devotion, then a myriad of changes take place on his face and the apprehension of death arises in the mind of this *yogi*. He feels now that he is really dying, [but] he is not afraid, he is apprehensive. This is the kind of death which takes place when individuality dies and universality is born. It is not a physical death, it is a mental death. The only thing the *yogi* must do here is shed tears of devotion and pray for the experience of universal "I." After a few moments, when the whirling state of breath becomes very fast, moving ever more quickly, you must stop your breath at once. You must not be afraid. At this point, it is in your hand to stop it or to let it go.

When you stop your breathing, then what happens next is, the gate of the central vein (*madhyanāḍī*) opens at once and your breath is "sipped" down and you actually hear the sound of sipping. Here, your breath reaches down to that place called *mūlādhāra*, which is near the rectum. This state of *turya* is called *mahānanda* which means, "the great bliss." After *mahānanda*, no effort is required by the aspirant. From this point on, everything is automatic. There is, however, one thing that the aspirant should observe and be cautious about, and that is that he should not think that everything is now automatic. The more he thinks that everything will be automatic, the more surely he will remain at the state of *mahānanda*. This is why masters never tell what will take place after *mahānanda*. From the Śaiva point of view, from *mahānanda* onwards, you must adopt *bhramavega* which means "the unknowing force." Here you have to put your force of devotion, without knowing what is to happen next. You cannot use your *mantra* because when your breath is gone, your mind is also gone, as the mind has become transformed into the formation of consciousness (*cit*). Here, breathing takes the form of force (*vega*). It is this *vega* which pierces and penetrates *mūlādhāra cakra* so that you pass through it.

When the penetration of *mūlādhāra cakra* is complete, then this force rises and becomes full of bliss, full of ecstasy, and full of consciousness. It is divine. You feel what you are actually. This is the rising of *cit kuṇḍalinī*, which rises from *mūlādhāra cakra* to that place at the top of the skull known as *brahmarandhra*. It occupies the whole channel and is just like the blooming of a flower. This state, which is the sixth state of *turya*, is called *cidānanda*, which means, "the bliss of consciousness." This force then presses the passage of the skull (*brahmarandhra*), piercing the skull to move from the body out into the universe. This takes place automatically, it is not to be done. And when this *brahmarandhra* is pierced, then at once you begin to breathe out. You breathe out once for only a second, exhaling from the nostrils. After exhaling, everything is over and you are again in *cidānanda* and you again experience and feel the joy of rising, which was already present. This lasts only for a moment and then you breathe out again. When you breathe out, your eyes are open and for a moment you feel that you are outside. You experience the objective world, but in a peculiar way. Then once again, your breathing is finished and your eyes are closed and you feel that you are inside. Then again your eyes are open for a moment, then they close for a moment, and then they again open for a moment. This is the state of *krama mudrā*, where transcendental "I" consciousness is beginning to be experienced as one with the experience of the objective world. The establishment of *krama mudrā* is called *jagadānanda*, which means "universal bliss." This is the seventh and last state of *turya*. In this state, the experience of Universal Transcendental Being is never lost and the whole of the universe is experienced as one with your own Transcendental "I" Consciousness.

All of the states of *turya* from *nijānanda* to *cidānanda* comprise the various phases of *nimīlanā samādhi*. *Nimīlanā samādhi* is internal subjective *samādhi*. In your moving through these six states of *turya*, this *samādhi* becomes ever more firm. With the occurrence of *krama mudrā*, *nimīlanā samādhi* is transformed into *unmīlanā samādhi*, which then becomes predominant. This is that state of extraverted *samādhi*, where you experience the state of *samādhi* at the same time you are experiencing the objective world. And when *unmīlanā samādhi* becomes fixed and permanent, this is the state of *jagadānanda*. In terms of the process of the seven states of the perceiver, the *sakala pramātṛ*, or the waking state, is the first state of *turya*, which is the state of *nijānanda*. *Vijñānākala* is the state of *nirānanda*. Śuddhavidyā is the state of *parānanda*. Īśvara is the state of *brahmānanda*. Sadāśiva is the state of *mahānanda*. Śiva is the state of *cidānanda*. And Paramaśiva is the state of *jagadānanda*."

Paraphrase from *Kashmir Shaivism–The Secret Supreme*, 16.107.

In respect of the above experiences, Swamiji once wrote the following poem.

There is a point twixt sleep and waking
Where thou shalt be alert without shaking.
Enter into the new world where forms so hideous pass;
They are passing–endure, do not be taken by the dross.
Then the pulls and the pushes about the throttle,[851]
All those shalt thou tolerate.
Close all ingress and egress,
Yawning there may be;
Shed tears–crave–implore, but thou will not prostrate.
A thrill passes–and that goes down to the bottom;
It riseth, may it bloom forth, that is Bliss.
Blessed Being, Blessed Being,
O greetings be to Thee.

851 Lit., throat or windpipe. As mentioned earlier, this is the place of *lambikā sthāna* on the right side near the pit of the throat.

For the full explanation of the seven states of *ānanda* (*turya*), see *Kashmir Shaivism–The Secret Supreme*, 16.107.

In the fifth *āhnika* of the *Tantrāloka* (5.43-45), Abhinavagupta explains God consciousness and the states of *turya* in relation to the five subtle *prāṇas*: *prāṇana*, *apānana*, *samānana*, *udānana*, and *vyānana*.

Nijānanda is no state. It is the beginning point of putting awareness on subjective consciousness, *pramātṛ bhāva*. The first state is *nirānanda*, when you go inside, inside, inside, inside. But this is not the point to be maintained. You have to rise from that (*nirānanda*). And the rising point is from *parānanda*.

When this *prāṇana* takes place, that is the state of *spanda*. When awareness resides in *śūnyatā* (voidness), then the rise of *prāṇana* takes place and then he enters in another world. And that is the world of *apānana vṛtti*.[852]

> Just close your eyes tightly, just close your eyes tightly–tightly, squeeze it–and you will hear that sound from inside. Don't you hear . . . ? In sexual intercourse also, that sound is there. That is the sound of *apānana* that gives you joy, happiness, and entire bliss.

Apānana vṛtti is the supreme *ānanda* (bliss). That is the next state of *yoga* called *parānanda*, the absolute state of happiness. There you feel that you have drowned in the sound of that bliss. In this state of *apāna vṛtti*, you feel that breathing in and out is gathered in one point. Not only breath, [but] all differentiated perceptions of the organic field and objective field are also gathered and balled in one point. It is

852. *Vṛtti* means the 'established state'. *Prāṇana vṛtti* is that kind of state of breath which is not moving–breath without movement. For instance, *prāṇana vṛtti* means, the established state of *prāṇa*, and *apānana vṛtti* means, the established state of *apāna*, etc.

why he sees that this whole universe has fallen down and is shattered to pieces; this whole world, all mountains have fallen down on him, in that *apānana vṛtti*. And it takes place on the right side here just below *tālu* (the soft palate). And when you establish your awareness in *apāna vṛtti*, then those fearful forms, fearful apparitions, and fearful impressions that take place in your awareness, they subside.

Now, when you find that everything is completely balled inside peacefully, and there is no breathing in and out, and all the objective and cognitive world is balled inside in one pointedness without fear, then what happens next? That *yogi* is absolutely filled with the state of joy, with the state of bliss, and that is the state of *samānana vṛtti* which is the state of *brahmānanda*. Then that fourth state of *udānana vṛtti* takes place, where the *yogi* finds this ball is melted in that sound of bliss: *Shsssssssssssssssssssssssssssssssssss*. This very long sound is produced there and this ball is melted inside. Finished, there is no breath, this breathing process is finished. This is the state of *mahānanda*. And that sound that is not only the *Shssssssssssssssssss* sound, sexual joy appears there with that sound. When you are fully established there and have settled your awareness fully there, then, in that supreme *tejas*, supreme light, he gets dissolved, he gets melted. He melts for good.

In the process of rising through these state, *prāṇa vṛtti* travels to *prāṇana vṛtti*, *apāna vṛtti* travels to *apānana vṛtti*, *samāna vṛtti* travels to *samānana vṛtti*, *udāna vṛtti* travels to *udānana vṛtti*, and *vyāna vṛtti* has to travel to *vyānana vṛtti*. And when *vyāna vṛtti* travels to *vyānana vṛtti*, this is the fifth state of *ānanda* called *cidānanda*. This is the state of *mahāvyāpti*, the great pervasion, where you pervade this whole universe. But, you don't pervade this whole universe only, you pervade the negation of this whole universe also. When the state of *cidānanda* takes place, nothing is excluded, nothing remains outside, *cidānanda* includes everything in its being.

Now, the sixth state of *ānanda* is called *jagadānanda*. This is that universal state which shines in the whole cosmos and which is strengthened and nourished by that supreme nectar of God consciousness, which is filled with knowledge which is beyond knowledge. Here there is no entry, there is no acceptance of remaining in *samādhi* or remaining in awareness and so on. That is the state of *jagadānanda*. Abhinavagupta concludes by saying, "This state of *jagadānanda* was explained to me by my great master Śambhunātha.
Tantrāloka (5.43-45)

The fifth *āhnika* of the *Tantrāloka* also explains God consciousness and the states of *turya* in relation to the five activities of Lord Śiva–creation (*sṛṣṭi*), protection (*sthiti*), destruction (*saṁhāra*), concealing (*tirodhāna*), and revealing (*anugraha*, grace): "Creation of God consciousness is in the state of *nirānanda*. Protecting God consciousness is in the state of *parānanda*. Destroying God consciousness (it is not destroying God consciousness, it is destroying differentiated God consciousness), is *brahmānanda*. Concealing of God consciousness is *mahānanda*, and revealing God consciousness is *cidānanda*. And *jagadānanda* is *anākhyā*,[853] where God consciousness is not felt, It becomes your nature."

6. **The Three Impurities** (*āṇava*, *māyīya*, and *kārmamala*)

"The three impurities are gross (*sthūla*), subtle (*sūkṣma*), and subtlest (*para*). The gross impurity is called *kārmamala*. It is connected with actions. It is that impurity which inserts impressions such as those which are expressed in the statements, "I am happy," "I am not well," "I have pain," "I am a great man," "I am really lucky," etc., in the consciousness of the individual being. The next impurity is called *māyīyamala*. This impurity creates differentiation in one's own conscious-

853 The literal meaning of *anākhya* is unspeakable. Here *anākhya* is being used in the sense of "the absolute void which is known in the state of the unknown. It is unknown and at the same time it is known." *Tantrāloka* 11.86, (LJA archives).

ness. It is the impurity of ignorance (*avidyā*), the subtle impurity. The thoughts, "This house is mine," "That house is not mine," "This man is my friend," "That man is my enemy," "She is my wife," "She is not my wife," are all created by *māyīyamala*. *Māyīyamala* creates duality. The third impurity is called *āṇavamala*. It is the subtlest impurity.* *Āṇavamala* is the particular internal impurity of the individual. Although he reaches the nearest state of the consciousness of Śiva, he has no ability to catch hold of That state. That inability is the creation of *āṇavamala*. For example, if you are conscious of your own nature and then that consciousness fades away, and fades away quickly, this fading is caused by *āṇavamala*. *Āṇavamala* is *apūrṇatā*, non-fullness. It is the feeling of being incomplete. Due to this impurity, you feel incomplete in every way. Though you feel incomplete, knowing that there is some lack in you, yet you do not know what this lack really is. You want to hold everything, and yet no matter what you hold, you do not fill your sense of lacking, your gap. You cannot fill this lacking unless the master points it out to you and then carries you to that point. Of these three impurities, *āṇavamala* and *māyīyamala* are not in action, they are only in perception, in experience. It is *kārmamala* which is in action."

Paraphrase from *Kashmir Shaivism–The Secret Supreme*, 7.47-49.

*"*Āṇavamala* is the root of the other two impurities. Which are those other two impurities? *Māyīyamala* and *kārmamala*."

Parātriśikā Vivaraṇa (LJA archive)

"This whole universal existence, which is admitted by other thinkers, that it is ignorance, that it is *māyā* (illusion), that is pain, it is torture–they explain it like that–but we Shaivites don't explain like that. We Shaivites explain that this [universe] is the expansion of your own nature. *Mala* is nothing [substantial], *mala* is only your free will of expanding your own nature. So we have come to this conclusion that *mala* is not a real impurity [i.e., substance]. It is your own choice; it is the choice of Lord Śiva. The existence of impurity is just the choice of Lord Siva, it is not some thing. It is *svarūpa māṭraṁ*, it is just your will, just your independent glory. If you realize that it is *svarūpa svātantrya māṭraṁ*, [that] it is your own play, then what will an impure thing do? An impure thing will only infuse purity in you . . . if you realize that impurity is not existing at all, it is just your own play, just your own independent expansion. So, *mala* is neither formless nor with form. It is just ignorance. It doesn't allow knowledge to function–knowledge is stopped. *Mala* is the absence of knowledge. *Mala* is not something substantial. So, this absence of knowledge takes place only by ignorance, otherwise there is no *mala*. In the real sense, *mala* does not exist, impurity does not exist."

Tantrāloka 9.79-83 (LJA archives).

See also Appendix 10 (p394) for the relationship between the *mala*s and the seven perceivers (*pramātṛ*s).

7. ***Svātantrya*** (independent freedom)

"All these five energies of God consciousness are produced by His *svātantrya śakti* of freedom, His free power. That is called *svātantrya śakti*. *Svātantrya śakti* produces these five energies of Lord Śiva. And *cit śakti* is actually based on His nature, *ānanda śakti* is based on His *śakti* (on His Pārvatī), *icchā śakti* is based in Sadāśiva, and *jñāna śakti* (the energy of knowledge) is based on Īśvara, and the energy of *kriyā* is based on Śuddhavidyā. All these five pure states of Lord Śiva are one with Lord Śiva. *Cit śakti* indicates Lord Śiva's actual position, *ānanda śakti* indicates Lord Śiva's position of Śakti, and *icchā śakti* indicates Lord Śiva's position of Sadāśiva, and *jñāna śakti* indicates His position of Īśvara, and Śuddhavidyā is [His] fifth position [viz., *kriyā śakti*]. All these five positions are filled with God consciousness. Below that is the scale of *māyā*, illusion. That will go from *māya* to earth."

Special Verses on Practice (LJA archive)

"The definition of *svātantrya* is "freedom in action and freedom in knowledge," when you know with your freedom, when you act with your freedom. When you know and you don't succeed in that knowledge, there is not *svātantrya*. When there is not *svātantrya*, it is not really knowledge. When there is not *svātantrya*, it is not really action. The action of individuals is just like that. Individuals know, they know something–you can't say that they don't know anything–they know something, but that knowledge has not *svātantrya*. And they act also, they do something, but that doing also has not *svātantrya*. So, without *svātantrya*, doing and knowing has no value. When there is *svātantrya*, it is fully valued. That essence of *svātantrya* is *anavacchinna* (beyond limitation), all-round beyond limitation. There is no such limit found in that state. *Vicchinna camatkāra maya viśrāntyā*, and this limited state of being is also found there. [Lord Śiva] is unlimited, but the limited cycle of God consciousness is also found there. So it is both limited and unlimited. That being who is limited only, he is not true. That being who is unlimited only, he is not true. Why? Because he is limited. The being who is unlimited is not true because he is unlimited only and not limited. That fullness of God consciousness is found [in one] who is limited and, at the same time, unlimited also. That is the fullness of God consciousness. The fullness of God consciousness is where nothing is excluded. Whatever is excluded, it is also one with That. That is the fullness of God consciousness."

Parātriśikā Vivaraṇa (LJA archive).

"Lord Śiva creates this external universe for the sake of realizing His own nature. That is why this external universe is called "Śakti," because it is the means to realize one's own nature. Therefore, in order to recognize His nature, He must first become ignorant of His nature. Only then can He recognize it. Why should He want to recognize His nature in the first place? It is because of His freedom, His *svātantrya* (independence). This is the play of the universe. This universe was created solely for the fun and joy of this realization. It happens that when His fullness overflows, He wants to [become] incomplete. He wants to appear as being incomplete just so He can achieve completion. This is the play of His *svātantrya*: to depart from His own nature in order to enjoy it again. It is this *svātantrya* that has created this whole universe. This is the play of Śiva's *svātantrya*. This kind of action cannot be accomplished by any power in this universe other than Lord Śiva. Only Lord Śiva can do this. Only Lord Śiva, by His own *svātantrya*, can totally ignore and mask His own nature. This is His *svātantrya*, His glory, His intelligence. Intelligence does not mean that in this super-drama called creation you will only play the part of a lady or a man. With this kind of intelligence, you will also play the part of rocks, of trees, of all things. This kind of intelligence is found only in the state of Lord Śiva and nowhere else."

Self Realization in Kashmir Shaivism–Fifteen Verses of Wisdom, chapter 1, Verses 5, 6 and 7, pp23-26.

"*Svātantrya śakti* and *māyā* are one. *Svātantrya śakti* is that state of energy which can produce the power of going down and coming up again. And *māyā* is not like that. *Māyā* will give you the strength of coming down and then no ability of going up–then you cannot go up again. This is the state of *māyā*. And all these three *mala*s ("impurities") reside in *māyā śakti*, not *svātantrya śakti*, although *svātantrya śakti* and *māyā śakti* are one. *Māyā śakti* is that energy, universal energy, which is owned by the individual being, the individual soul. The same energy, when it is owned by the universal Being, is called *svātantrya śakti*. *Svātantrya śakti* is pure universal energy. Impure universal energy is *māyā*. It is only the formation that changes through a difference of vision. When you experience *svātantrya śakti* in a crooked way, it becomes *māyā śakti* for you. And when you realize that same *māyā śakti* in Reality, then that *māyā śakti* becomes *svātantrya śakti* for you. Therefore, *svātantrya śakti* and *māyā śakti* are actually only one and the three impurities (*mala*s), which are to be explained here, reside in *māyā śakti*, not in *svātantrya śakti*."

Kashmir Shaivism–The Secret Supreme, 7.47.

"In Vedānta, [*māyā* is] unreal. In Shaivism, *māyā* is transformed at the time of knowledge. At the time of real knowledge, *māyā* is transformed in His *śakti*, in His glory. *Māyā* becomes the glory of Paramaśiva then. When *puruṣa* realizes the reality of his nature, *māyā* becomes glory for him–*śakti*, His energy, great energy, [i.e., *svātantrya śakti*]."
Kashmir Shaivism–The Secret Supreme (LJA audio archive).

8. ***Kañcukas*** (coverings)

"Directly, universal consciousness can never travel to individual consciousness unless universal consciousness is absolutely disconnected. *Māyā* is the disconnecting element from God consciousness. *Kalā* (limited action) is the connecting element to that dead being in some limited thing. So he does something by *kalā*. When he does something, then individuality shines. Otherwise, direct from God consciousness, individual consciousness would never come in existence." *Tantrāloka* 9.175-6 (LJA archive). "*Kalā*, *vidyā*, *rāga*, *kāla*, and *niyati* are the limiting connecting rods [between the individual and God]."
Tantrāloka 9.257 (LJA archive).

"[The five pure states of Lord Śiva] take the formation of *ṣaṭ kañcuka* in the individual. Because, whatever is manifested in the universe, it is not manifested as other than Śiva. The same thing has come out in manifestation; the same thing what existed in Paramaśiva, that same thing is manifested outside also."
Tantrāloka 6.41 (LJA archive).

"*Kalā*, *vidyā*, *rāga*, *kāla*, and *niyati*, these five elements are just offsprings of, offshoots of, *māyā*. *Kalā* means, "the capacity of doing something," *vidyā* means "the capacity of knowing something," *rāga* means "the capacity of some attachment" (not universal attachment), *niyati* means "the capacity of the limitation of space," *kāla* means "the limitation of time." Ibid., 9.41.

"These [*kañcukas*] are pertaining to the individual being. It is why [the grammarian] Pāṇini has also accepted these, the representatives of these [*kañcukas* as the letters] *ya*, *ra*, *la*, *va*. These letters as *antaḥstha*, these [subtle] energies are found, not outside the individual being, but inside the individual being, inside the thought of the individual being, inside the perception of the individual being. So they are named, nominated, by the grammarian [Pāṇini], as "*antaḥstha*." *Antaḥstha* means "that which is residing inside of the individual being." We say that it is not *antaḥstha*. [We say that] it is *dhāraṇā* [lit., the bearing or support] because it gives *life* to the individual being. The individual being is created, the individual being is glorified, by these five elements ("five" means, the five coverings); the glory of his own place, not the glory of Śiva; glorified with his own limited sphere."

Shiva Sutra Vimarśinī (LJA archive).

"In [the Śaiva] *tantras*, they are nominated as "*dhāraṇā*." These five elements (*kalā*, *vidyā*, *rāga*, *kāla*, *niyati*, with *māyā*) are called "*dhāraṇā*" because they give life to the individual being; the individual being lives in these five elements. Without these five elements, there was no life to the individual being, there was only the sphere of Lord Śiva. If these five elements would not be there, there was no question of the individual being to exist. The individual being lives only on the basis of these five elements, so they are nominated as *dhāraṇā*. *Dhāraṇā* means, that which gives you life to exist."

Ibid.

For a further explanation of the *ṣaṭ kañcukas* (the six coverings), see *Kashmir Shaivism–The Secret Supreme*, 1.7-8.

9. ***Parāmarśa*** (the state of 'awareness')

The literal meaning of *parāmarśa* is: seizing, affection, recollection, remembrance, consideration, inference [logic], conclusion [logic], reflection. *Para*: extreme. *Āmarśa*: similarity, contact, touching and nearness. *Parāmarśa* is variously described in Kashmir Shaivism as 'direct experience', 'direct perception', and 'intense awareness'. Simply stated, *parāmarśa* is *para* (extreme) awareness (*āmarśa*). Here, *parāmarśa* is not a static experience, but a dynamic pulsation (*spandana*) of awareness, as explained by Swamiji in the following extracts:

"*Parāmarśa* is always in movement; *parāmarśa* is not only one-pointed. It is movement, not in one pointedness, not in one thousand pointedness, it is innumerable movements, innumerable times (*ananta*). This is what he says: *parāmarśo hi spandanātmaiva*, *parāmarśa* is always in *spandana*, in movement. It is the chain of movement. I would call it "chain of movement." It is not only sparks of movement. There is the possibility in sparks [that] there is a gap, [but] there is no gap [in *parāmarśa*]. It is movement in such a way that this movement is without any gap, and in this movement you feel as if there is no movement. It is only one movement, just like when you draw one line, this is the movement of these points."
Parātriśikā Laghu Vṛtti (LJA archive).

The conclusion of the third *āhnika* of the *Tantrāloka* is devoted to the subject of *ahaṁ parāmarśa*, which is defined as 'supreme I-consciousness'. To understand *aham parāmarśa*, one has to see how this word *ahaṁ* is divided into three parts: *a-ha-aṁ*.

anuttarādyā prasṛtirhāntā śaktisvarūpiṇī / /
pratyāhṛtāśeṣaviśvānuttare sā nilīyate /
(*Tantrāloka 3.204-205a*)

"Now he gives the conclusion of this *ahaṁ parāmarśa*:

Anuttarādyā prasṛti, *ahaṁ parāmarśa* begins from the flowing out of creation. Creation of what? Creation of your own nature. You have not to create any foreign matter. *Anuttarādyā prasṛti*, this flowing nature of His being, which begins from *a* and ends in *hāntā* (ends in *ha*)–and this *prasṛti* is in fact from *a* to *ha*–in conclusion this is the *prasṛti* of His energy. *Prasṛti* means, flowing out, *prasara*. This flowing out from *a* to *ha* is the flow of His energy, not anything else–*śakti svarūpiṇī*.[854] And it is *pratyāhṛtāśeṣaviśva*, and it has digested this whole universe in Her own nature. When She has digested–this Śakti, this energy of Lord Śiva–has digested in Her own nature, in Her own being, this situation of the whole universe, *garbhikritānantaviśva*, and after having digested this whole differentiated world in Her own nature, *anuttare sā nilīyate*, in the end She absorbs Her nature inside Śiva again, in the end. And that is *aṁ*. So it is *ahaṁ*.[855] This is a very important point in our Śaivism."

Tantrāloka 3.204 commentary (LJA archive).

In the following extract, Swamiji explains how *ahaṁ parāmarśa* is also functioning on the individual level in every day experience:

"So, for instance, just take the individual way of experience for this *ahaṁ parāmarśa*. When you look at this pencil, just at the very beginning of looking towards the pencil–this is *ahaṁ*, this is the conducting way of *ahaṁ*, in the individual way for *sādhaka*s, for those who have to experience this *ahaṁ parāmarśa*–when your consciousness flows out to perceive this pencil, in the beginning your consciousness is established in *a*, when your consciousness travels up to the point of the pencil and it has not reached the point of pencil, this traveling span of space is the traveling from *a* to *ha*. And when you perceive

854 This is *vimarśa śakti*, the energy of universal self awareness. See Appendix 13 (p399) for an explanation of *prakāśa* and *vimarśa*.

855 This movement from *anuttara* (Śiva), to Śakti, to *aṁ* (Śiva) in the end.

[that] this is a pencil and you close your eyes [after confirming that], "Oh, this is a pencil," when you close your eyes, this is reality of *aṁ*. So, in each and every action of the universe, in worldly action also, you can realize this *aṁ*. You have to realize it. If you don't realize, you are kept away from Śaivite thought."

Ibid., 3.204 (LJA archive).

10. **The Seven Perceivers** (*pramātṛs*)

Kashmir Shaivism posits the existence of seven perceivers (*pramātṛs*): *sakala*, *pralayākala*, *vijñānākala*, *mantra* (Śuddhavidyā), *mantreśvara* (Īśvara), *mantra maheśvara* (Sadāśiva), and Śiva (Śiva and Śakti are actually one element).

The first state is called *sakala*. The *sakala* state is that state where perception takes place in the objective world and not in the subjective world. In other words, I would call this state the state of *prameya*, the state of the object of perception. It is realized by its *pramātṛ*, the observer, who resides in this state, in the field of objectivity and its world.

The second state is called *pralayākala*. This is the state of negation, where the whole world is negated. And the one who resides in this world of negation is called *pralayākala pramātṛ*, the observer of the *pralayākala* state. And this *pramātṛ*, this perceiver, does not experience the state of this voidness because it is actually the state of unawareness. This state would be observed at the time of *mūrcchā*, when one becomes comatose, which is like unnatural and heavy sleep, like deep sleep devoid of dreams. And the observer, *pralayākala pramātṛ*, resides in that void of unawareness.

These two states (*sakala* and *pralayākala*) function in the state of individuality, not in the state of your real nature. These are states of worldly people, not spiritual aspirants.

The third state is called *vijñānākala pramātṛ*. This state is experienced by those who are on the path of *yoga*. Here, the *yogi* experiences awareness at times (but this awareness is not active awareness), and at other times, his awareness is active but he is not aware of that active awareness. This *vijñānākala pramātṛ*, therefore, takes place in two ways: sometimes it is full of action (*svātantrya*) without awareness, and sometimes it is full of awareness without action.

The fourth state of the observer is called Śuddhavidyā and its observer is called *mantra pramātṛ*. In this state, the observer is always aware with *svātantrya*.

The next state is called Īśvara and its observer is called *mantreśvara pramātṛ*. The word "*mantreśvara*" means "the one who has sovereignty on *mantra* (*ahaṁ*–I)." This state is like that of *mantra pramātṛ*, full of consciousness, full of bliss, full of will, full of knowledge, and full of action, however, this is a more stable state. The aspirant finds more stability here. The *mantra* for this state is "*idaṁ-ahaṁ*." The meaning of this *mantra* is that the aspirant feels that this whole universe is not false. On the contrary, he feels that this whole universe is the expansion of his own nature. In the state of *mantra pramātṛ*, he felt that the universe was false, that he was the truth of this reality. Now he unites the state of the universe with the state of his own consciousness. This is actually the unification of *jīva*, the individual, with Śiva, the universal.

The next state is the state of Sadāśiva. The observer of this state is called *mantra maheśvara*. In this state, the observer finds himself to be absolutely one with the universal transcendental Being. He experiences this state to be more valid, more solid, and deserving of confidence. Once he enters into this state, there is no question at all of falling from it. This is the established state of his Self, his own Real nature. The *mantra* of this state is "*ahaṁ-idaṁ*." The meaning of this *mantra* is, "I am this universe." Here, he finds his Self in the universe, while in the previous state of *mantreśvara*, he found the universe in his Self. This is the difference.

The seventh and last state is the state of Śiva and the observer of this state is no other than Śiva Himself. In the other six, the state is one thing and the observer is something else. In this final state, the state is Śiva and the observer is also Śiva. There is nothing outside Śiva. The *mantra* in this state is "*ahaṁ*," universal-I. This-ness is gone, melted in His I-ness. This state is completely filled with consciousness, bliss, will, knowledge, and action.
Kashmir Shaivism–The Secret Supreme, 8.51-54.

The seven perceivers in relation to the three *malas*:

"In the first state, the state of *sakala pramātṛ*, all the three *malas* (*āṇava*, *māyīya*, and *kārma mala*) are active. In the second state, the state of *pralayākala pramātṛ*, *kārmamala* is gone and only two *malas* remain–*āṇavamala* and *māyīyamala*. These two *malas* are concerned with thought rather than action whereas *kārmamala* is concerned with action. In the third state of the perceivers, the state of *vijñānākala pramātṛ*, only one *mala*, *āṇavamala*, remains while the other two *malas*, *māyīya mala* and *kārma mala*, have ceased functioning. The fourth state of the observer is called Śuddhavidyā and its observer is called *mantra pramātṛ*. In this state, the observer is always aware with *svātantrya*. All the *malas* have been removed and its observer observes only the state of his own Self, his own Real nature, full of consciousness, full of bliss, full of independent will, full of knowledge, and full of action."
Kashmir Shaivism–The Secret Supreme, "Seven States of the Seven Perceivers," Chapter 8.

The seven perceivers are discussed in *Tantrāloka* in *āhnikas* 4, 6, 9, and 10. In *āhnika* 9, Abhinavagupta explains how *āṇavamala* remains active up to the state of Sadāśiva until finally expiring in the state of Śiva/Śakti.

11. *Bauddha jñāna* and *puruṣa jñāna*

"Our Śaivism explains that *jñāna* (knowledge) is knowing one's own nature, which is all-Being (*sat*), all-consciousness (*cit*), and all-bliss (*ānanda*). *Ajñāna* (ignorance) is ignoring this nature and this is the cause of the *saṁsāra*, which carries one in the cycle of repeated births and deaths.

Kashmir Śaivism explains that ignorance (*ajñāna*) is of two kinds: *pauruṣa ajñāna* and *bauddha ajñāna*. *Pauruṣa ajñāna* is that kind of ignorance wherein one is unaware of realizing one's own nature in *samādhi*. This kind of ignorance is removed by the grace of masters and by meditating upon one's own Self. And when this ignorance is removed, you find yourself in the real knowledge of Śaivism, which is all-being, all-consciousness, all-bliss. This kind of knowledge is called *pauruṣa jñāna*. When you possess *pauruṣa jñāna*, you realize your nature of Self perfectly.

Bauddha ajñāna (intellectual ignorance) occurs only when you are completely ignorant of the philosophical truth of the monistic idea of Śaivism. And *bauddha ajñāna* is removed by studying those monistic Śaiva texts which explain the reality of the Self. Therefore, these texts are the cause of your being carried from *bauddha ajñāna* to *bauddha jñāna*. *Bauddha jñāna* is thought-based and is developed through the intellect. *Pauruṣa jñāna*, on the other hand, is practical and is developed through practice. *Pauruṣa jñāna* is predominant over *bauddha jñāna* because when you possess only *pauruṣa jñāna*, even then you are liberated in the real sense. In this case, however, liberation is attained only after leaving your body. When, however, at the same time, you attach *bauddha jñāna* to *pauruṣa jñāna*, which means that, on the one hand, you practice on your own Being and, on the other hand, you go into the philosophical thought of the monistic Śaiva texts and elevate your intellectual being, then you become a *jīvanmukta*, one who is liberated while living. If, however, you possess only *bauddha jñāna* and not *pauruṣa jñāna*, then you will not attain liberation either while living in the body or at the time of death. *Bauddha jñāna* without *pauruṣa jñāna* is useless and will not take you anywhere. The study of texts shines perfectly only when there is practical knowledge at the same time. Without practical knowledge, philosophical study is useless. *Bauddha jñāna* will bear fruit only when *pauruṣa jñāna* is present and not otherwise.

If an aspirant is attached only to practical knowledge and not to theoretical knowledge, believing that the only real knowledge is practical knowledge, which is the realizing of ones own nature, then from a Śaiva point of view he is mistaken. If only *pauruṣa jñāna* is cultivated and *bauddha jñāna* is totally ignored, then there is every possibility that *pauruṣa jñāna* may decrease day-by-day, slowly fading away so that in the end, it does not remain at all. It is the greatness of *bauddha jñāna* that, with its power, it firmly establishes *pauruṣa jñāna*. In this respect, therefore, *bauddha jñāna* is more important than *pauruṣa jñāna*.

In our Śaivism, it is said that when you go in search of a master so that you can be initiated, you should first seek that master who is full of both *bauddha jñāna* and *pauruṣa jñāna*. Finding him, you should consider him a real master. If, in this world, such a complete master is not to be found, then you should seek one who is only filled with *bauddha jñāna*. He is to be preferred over that master who is filled only with *pauruṣa jñāna* because intellectually he will carry you by-and by-to the end point. That master who resides only in *pauruṣa jñāna* would not ultimately be successful in carrying you to that which you seek."

Kashmir Shaivism–The Secret Supreme, 98-100.

12. ***Vedha Dīkṣā*** (the initiation of piercing)

"This *vedha dīkṣā* takes place in varieties: *mantra vedha*, *nāda vedha*, *bindu vedha*, *śakta vedha*, *bhujaṅga vedha*, and *para vedha*. *Mantra vedha* is when he hears some sound with *mantra*. The *yogi* hears that when penetrated by some *mantra* like "*oṁ*" or "*Śiva*" or like that. It appears to him, and through the mind he experiences that. That is *mantra vedha*. Another kind of *vedha* is *nāda vedha*. *Nāda vedha* is a sound or a drum beating, e.g., '*dum dum*', that constant sound of a drum takes place. *Bindu vedha* is when it rises, when [sound] takes the formation of sexual joy. Sexual joy is also with that when it rises as *bindu vedha*. And another is *śakta vedha*; *śakti*, he thinks it is powerful, its sound is creating power and the greatest stimulation. In *bhujaṅga vedha*, he feels that a serpent is rising and producing this sound: *ssssssssssssssh*. That is *bhujaṅga vedha*. And the last is *parā vedha*. *Parā vedha*, the supreme *vedha*, is experienced by those *yogin*s who are always bent upon finding the Lord, nothing else, and who are fed up with this universe."

Self Realization in Kashmir Shaivism, "*Kuṇḍalinī Vijñāna Rahasyam*," 5.109-112.

For *Vedha Dīkṣā*, see also *Kashmir Shaivism–The Secret Supreme*, "*Variations in the Rise of Prāṇa Kuṇḍalinī*," ch 18.

13. ***Prakāśa* and *Vimarśa*** – The Self Reflective Light of God Consciousness

In the world of Shaivite philosophy, Lord Śiva is seen as being filled with light. But more than this, Lord Śiva is the embodiment of light and this light is different than the light of the sun, of the moon, or of fire. It is light (*prakāśa*) with Consciousness (*vimarśa*), and this light with Consciousness is the nature of that Supreme Consciousness, Lord Śiva. What is Consciousness? The light of Consciousness is not only pure Consciousness, it is filled with the understanding that, "I am the creator, I am the protector, and I am the destroyer of everything." Just to know that, "I am the creator, I am the protector, and I am the destroyer," is Consciousness. If Consciousness was not attached to the light of Consciousness, we would have to admit that the light of the sun or the light of the moon or the light of a fire is also Lord Śiva. But this is not the case. The light of Consciousness (*vimarśa*) is given various names. It is called *cit-caitanya*, which means, the strength of consciousness; *parā vāk*, the supreme word; *svātantrya*, perfect independence; *aiśvarya*, the predominant glory of supreme Śiva; *kartṛtva*, the power of acting; *sphurattā*, the power of existing; *sāra*, the complete essence of everything; *hṛdaya*, the universal heart; and *spanda*, universal movement. All these are names in the *tantras*, which are attributed to this Consciousness.

This I-Consciousness, which is the reality of Lord Śiva, is a natural (*akṛtrima*), not a contrived, "I." It is not adjusted I-Consciousness. Limited human beings have adjusted I-Consciousness. Lord Śiva has natural or pure I-Consciousness. There is a difference between adjusted Consciousness and natural Consciousness. Adjusted or artificial consciousness exists when this I-Consciousness is attributed to your body, to your mind, to your intellect, and to your ego. Natural consciousness is that consciousness that is attributed to the reality of the Self, which is all-Consciousness. This universe, which is created in His Consciousness, is dependent on that Consciousness. It is always dependent on that Consciousness. It cannot move outside of that Consciousness. It exists only when it is residing in His Consciousness. This is the way the creation of His universe takes place."

Self Realization in Kashmir Shaivism, 3.56-57."

"There are two positions of Śiva. One is *prakāśa* and another is *vimarśa*. When He feels this blissful state as His own nature, that is *prakāśa*. When He feels, "That blissful state is My glory," that is *vimarśa*. When He feels that, "This blissful state is My being," that is Śiva. When He believes that, "this is My glory," that is Śakti. The cycle of glory is residing in Śakti, and the cycle of *prakāśa* is residing in Śiva. Both are in one. That is indicated by *visarga* in Śiva, i.e., [the vowel] '*aḥ*' or ':'. So, *vimarśa śakti* is supreme *parā parameśvarī* attributed to *svātantrya śakti*. It is the intensity of independence of the *svātantrya* of Bhairava."

Parātriśikā Vivaraṇa (LJA archives).

Advaita Vedānta considers God to be the embodiment of *prakāśa*, but not *vimarśa*. "In the world of Shaivite philosophy, Lord Śiva is seen as being filled with light. But more than this, Lord Śiva is the embodiment of light and this light is different than the light of the sun, of the moon, or of fire. It is light (*prakāśa*) with consciousness (*vimarśa*), and this light with consciousness is the nature of that Supreme Consciousness, Lord Śiva." *Vimarśa* is Self-reflective awareness.

14. *Turya* and *Turyātītā*

"When, by the grace of a master, this subjective body enters into subjective consciousness with full awareness, and maintaining unbroken awareness becomes fully illumined in its own Self, this is called the fourth state, *turya*. From the Trika Shaivite point of view, predominance is given to the three energies of Śiva: *parā śakti* (the supreme energy), *parāparā śakti* (medium energy), and *aparā śakti* (inferior energy). The kingdom of *aparā śakti*, the lowest energy, is found in wakefulness and dreaming. The kingdom of *parāparā śakti*, the medium energy, is established in the state of sound sleep. And lastly, the kingdom of *parā śakti*, the supreme energy, is found in the state of *turya*. The state of *turya* is said to be the penetration of all energies simultaneously, not in succession. All of the energies are residing there but are not in manifestation. They are all together without distinction. *Turya* is called "*savyāpārā*" because all of the energies get their power to function in that state. At the same time, this state is known as "*anāmayā*" because it remains unagitated by all of these energies. Three names are attributed to this state; by worldly people, by *yogin*s, and by illuminated humans (*jñāni*s). Worldly people call it "*turya*," which means "the fourth." They use this name because they have no descriptive name for this state. They are unaware of this state and, not having experienced it, simply call it "the fourth state." *Yogin*s have attributed the name "*rūpātītā*" to this condition because this state has surpassed the touch of one's self and is the establishment of one's Self. The touch of one's self was found in sound sleep, however, the establishment of one's Self takes place in *turya*. For illuminated humans, *jñānis*, the entire universal existence is found in this state of *turya*, collectively, as undifferentiated, in the state of totality. There is no succession here. *Jñānis*, therefore, call this state "*pracaya*," the undifferentiated totality of universal existence."

"*Turyātītā* is that state which is the absolute fullness of Self. It is filled with all-consciousness and bliss. It is really the last and the supreme state of the Self. You not only find this state of *turyātītā* in *samādhi*, you also find it in each and every activity of the world. In this state, there is no possibility for the practice of *yoga*. If you can practice *yoga*, then you are not in *turyātītā*. In practicing *yoga*, there is the intention of going somewhere. Here, there is nowhere to go, nothing to achieve. As concentration does not exist here, the existence of the helping hand of *yoga* is not possible. There are only two names actually attributed to this state of *turyātītā*, one given by worldly people and one by *jñānis*. Worldly people, because they know nothing about the state, call it "*turyātītā*," which means "that state which is beyond the fourth." *Jñānis*, on the other hand, also have a name for it. They call it "*mahā-pracaya*," which means "the unlimited and unexplainable supreme totality." *Yogins* do not actually attribute any name to this state because they have no knowledge of it. It is completely outside of their experience. *Yogins* have though, through the use of their imagination and guesswork, imagined one name which might be appropriate for this state: "*satatoditam*," which means "that state which has no pause, no break." It is a breakless and unitary state. In *samādhi*, It is there. When *samādhi* is absent, It is there. In the worldly state, It is there. In the dreaming state, It is there. And in the state of deep sleep, It is there. In each and every state of the individual subjective body, It is there."

Kashmir Shaivism–The Secret Supreme, 11.72-84.

"The difference between *turya* and *turyātītā* is, in *turya*, you find in *samādhi* that this whole universe is existing there in the seed form, germ. The strength, the energy, of universal existence is existing there, but here he has [yet] to come out [into activity]. In *turyātītā*, he comes out in action and feels universal consciousness. This is the difference between *turya* and *turyātītā*."

Tantrāloka 10.288 (LJA archive).

15. ***Unmīlanā samādhi* and *nimīlanā samādhi***

"*Nimīlanā samādhi* is internal subjective *samādhi*. In your moving through these six states of *turya*, this *samādhi* becomes ever more firm. With the occurrence of *krama mudrā*, *nimīlanā samādhi* is transformed into *unmīlanā samādhi*, which then becomes predominant. This is that state of extroverted *samādhi*, where you experience the state of *samādhi* at the same time you are experiencing the objective world. And when *unmīlanā samādhi* becomes fixed and permanent, this is the state of *jagadānanda*. The establishment of *krama mudrā* is called *jagadānanda*, which means, universal bliss. This is the seventh and last state of *turya*. In this state, the experience of universal transcendental Being is never lost and the whole of the universe is experienced as one with your own transcendental I-consciousness."

Kashmir Shaivism–The Secret Supreme, 16.114-115.

16. **The Sixfold Path of the Universe** (*Ṣaḍadhva*)

"In Shaivism, this objective universe is said to be threefold, because it is composed of three paths (*adhvan*s). These *adhvan*s are gross (*sthūla*), subtle (*sūkṣma*), and subtlest (*para*). The gross path is called *bhuvanādhva*, "the path of all the worlds." In Śaivism, these worlds are said to number one hundred and eighteen. By "one world," I do not mean, one planet. This whole cosmos, including suns, moons, stars, and planets, is called one world. It has been found by *yogin*s in *samādhi* that there are one hundred and eighteen worlds like this cosmos which have been created."

"*Tattvādhva* means "the course of all elements," the path of the thirty-six *tattvas*. This is that path which is subtle. That path which is more refined than *tattvādhva* is known as *kalādhva*. That path is the subtlest. *Kalādhva* consists of five *kalās*, which are five boundaries or enclosures. These *kalās* are enclosures for all of the thirty-six elements, the thirty-six *tattvas*, from earth up to Śiva. The first and outermost enclosure is called *nivṛtti kalā*. In *nivṛtti kalā* you will find *pṛthvī tattva*, the element earth. The next *kalā* or enclosure is *pratiṣṭhā kalā*. In *pratiṣṭhā kalā* you find the twenty-three *tattvas* from *jala tattva*, the element water up to and including *prakṛti tattva*. The next enclosure is known as *vidyā kalā*. *Vidyā kalā* contains the seven *tattvas*, from *puruṣa tattva* up to and including *māyā tattva*. The next enclosure is called *śāntā kalā*. *Śāntā kalā* contains the four *tattvas* from Śuddhavidyā *tattva* up to and including Śakti *tattva*, the thirty-fifth *tattva*. The fifth and last enclosure is known as *śāntātītā kalā*. Here, you will only find the existence of Śiva *tattva*."

"This course of the threefold *adhvans* is called *vācyādhva*. The word *vācya* means "that which is observed, spoken, told." It is called *vācyādhva* because it is seen, it is observed, it is created, it is felt. It is the objective cycle of this creation. The creator of the threefold path of the universe known as *vācyādhva* is called *vācakādhva*. The meaning of the word *vācaka* is "that which observes, sees, and creates." It is the subjective cycle of this creation. And, like *vācyādhva*, *vācakādhva* is also composed of three paths: gross (*sthūla*), subtle (*sūkṣma*), and subtlest (*para*). Gross (*sthūla*) *vācakādhva* is called *padādhva* and consists of sentences; sentences are said to be gross. Subtle (*sūkṣma*) *vācakādhva* is called *mantrādhva* and consists of words, because words are known to be more subtle than sentences. Subtler than *mantrādhva*, the world of words, is the path of letters, called *varṇādhva*. Take any object such as a pot. That object will fall in the threefold world of *vācyādhva*. It is an offshoot of the thirty-six elements. On the other hand, the word "pot" is *vācakādhva* for this object. So, this object (the physical pot) is *vācya*, and its *vācaka* is the word "pot.""

"The combination of these three objective *adhvans* and the three subjective *adhvans* is called *ṣaḍadhva*, the sixfold *adhvans*. This is the explanation of this whole universe, both subjective and objective. The word *adhva* (path) has a twofold meaning: it is either that path on which you tread or that path which you must dispose of, must discard. You have either to tread on the path or discard the path. You can dispose of this path only by the grace of your Master. And when you dispose of this path, you reach the state of Paramaśiva. There is no question of realizing God through treading on this path. You may tread for centuries and centuries and still you will be treading. So you must discard this path, dispose of it. When you do dispose of the path, that is also called *adhvan*. Disposing of it, however, can only be done by the grace of the Master, who is the embodiment of Paramaśiva."

Paraphrase from *Kashmir Shaivism–The Secret Supreme*, "The Sixfold Path of the Universe (*Saḍadhvan*)," ch 2.

17. The *praṇava mantra, auṁ* (*oṁ*)

In sanskrit, the word *akāra* means the letter '*a*', *ukāra* means the letter *u*, and *makara* means the letter *ma*, which together constitute the *mantra*, *auṁ* (*oṁ*).

> *akāraśca ukāraśca makāro bindureva ca* | |
> *ardhacandro nirodhī ca nādo nādānta eva ca* |
> *śaktiśca vyāpinī caiva samanaikādaśī smṛtā* | |
> *unmanā ca tato 'tītā tadatītaṁ nirāmayam* | |[856]

"*A*, *u*, and *ma*. *A* is the first ray of God, *u* is second, *ma* is third, *bindu* is fourth, *ardhacandra* is fifth, *nirodhī* is sixth,

856 These verses, often quoted by Swamiji, appears in numerous Śaiva texts, and feature predominantly in the *Netra tantra* 22.21-22, and the *Svacchanda tantra* 4.430-431.

nāda is seventh, *nādānta* is eighth. *Bas*, this is *āsana* (the seat). [Then] *śakti*, *vyāpinī*, and *samanā* are three other states of energies on that seat, on that corpse[857]–*śakti, vyāpinī*, and *samanā*. *Śakti* is *aparā*, *vyāpinī* is *parāparā* energy, *samanā* is *parā* energy."

Parātriśikā Vivaraṇa (LJA archive).

"*Oṁ* is the combination of four letters: *a-kāra*, *u-kāra*, *ma-kāra*, and *bindu* (*ṁ*). These four letters will produce the sound of *oṁ praṇava*. But actually, this *praṇava* is incorrect. After producing these four sounds, there are other sounds which are not spoken, which are not uttered. That is *akāraśca ukāraśca makāro bindurevaca*, these four letters are produced in the cycle of the utterance of *oṁ*. After uttering *oṁ*, this *śabda* (sound), there is something else. That is, *ardhacandra-nirodhīka-nāda-nādānta-śakti-vyāpinī-samanā-unmanā*, these eight words are yet to be produced when you utter the *mantra* of *oṁ*. After *oṁ*, you have to go in *ardhacandra*, then you have to get entry in *nirodhī*, then *nāda*, then *nādānta*, then *śakti*, then *vyāpinī*, then *samanā*, and then *unmanā*. So, there are twelve letters in the cycle of the reciting of the *praṇava* (*oṁ*). You have to get entry in *ardhacandra*, then *nirodhinī*, then *nāda*, *nādānta*, *śakti*, *vyāpinī*, *samanā*, and *unmanā*. Where *unmanā* is situated, there you find the actual position of God consciousness. That is *parā*."

Ibid.

"*Unmanā state* is that state of *oṁ-kāra* where the mind is over, the functioning of the mind stops altogether–that is *unmanā*. When reciting this *oṁ-kāra*, you reach to the topmost point of *unmanā* (*unmanā* is not a state). After *unmanā*, you enter in the state of Śiva."

Vijñāna Bhairava, The Manual for Self Realization, Dhāraṇā 19, verse. 42

857 *Mahāpreta* (the great corpse), or Sadāśiva in the pure transcendental state.

"*Oṁ-kāra*, *oṁ* is only the gross *mantra*. Beyond that *oṁ* you have to do "*oṁṁṁṁṁṁṁ* . . . .," then go in the depth of that subtle word inside, internally. And *unmanā* is where there is no approach of mind, beyond mind–super-mind. Bhaṭṭa-nārāyaṇa says, "The stage of *praṇava*, which is residing in the state of super-mind, that twelfth step (*unmanā*), Lord Śiva's consciousness, *praṇavo ūrdhva ardha mātrat'pyanave*, is subtler than that state of *praṇava* (*oṁ*)."
Stava Cintāmaṇi, verse 7.

tasya nābhyutthitaṁ mūrdharandhratrayavinirgatam /
nādāntātma smarecchaktivyāpinīsamanojjvalam / /
Tantrāloka 15.313

"Above that seat of *nādānta* (i.e., *brahmarandhra*) is *parā śakti*. As long as the question of that body is concerned, Sadāśiva has no navel. In place of a navel, he has got *mūlādhāra*, and the point where *parā śakti* rises, that is *nabhi*, that is his navel. And this is the *nabhi* (navel) of Sadāśiva, that *preta*. Which *preta*? *Mahāpreta* (the great corpse). *Mūrdha* means *brahmarandhra*, *randhra traya* means, three openings. From those three openings of *brahmarandhra* (that is the navel of Sadāśiva), and which is residing in *nādāntātma* (*nādānta*, *smaret*), the aspirant of the Trika system has to concentrate on three other energies–*śakti*, *vyāpinī*, and *samanā*. *Śakti* is ninth, *vyāpinī* is tenth, *samanā* is eleventh. These three energies are to be contemplated on the three openings of *brahmarandhra* of Sadāśiva. [There] it is called *ūrdhva dvadaśānta*. *Ūrdhva dvadaśānta* means, *brahmarandhra*. This is the surface of *brahmarandhra*, covered by all these three aspects–*śakti*, *vyāpinī*, and *samanā*."
Tantrāloka 15.313 (LJA archive)

tanmadhye tu parādevī dakṣine ca parāparā /
aparā vāmaśṛṅge tu madhyasṛṅgo'rdhvatah śṛṇu / /
yā sā saṁkarṣinī kālī parātītā vyavasthitā / /[858]

"*Parā devī* is in the center (*tanmadhye tu parādevī*). *Dakṣine ca parāparā*, on the right side is *parāparā* energy. On the left side is *aparā*. *Madhya sṛṅgo*, from supreme *parā* there is another spoke above, *yā sā śakti parā sūkṣma parātītā vyavasthitā,* that is, *kālākarṣinī.*[859] And above that is the position of Lord Śiva. This will all go and cover the seat (*āsana*) of Lord Śiva."

iti śakti-vyāpinī-samanāntaka-śṛṅgatrayam uktam /

"*Śakti*, *vyāpinī*, and *samanā* are the three spokes explained there on that *āsana*."[860]

tatrāpi unmanasordhvakuṇḍalikāpada-paramadhāma-sitakamalatraya-rūpatayā nirūpitam.

"On that state of *śakti*, *vyāpinī*, and *samanā*, there are three white lotuses, which are one with that supreme *parā kuṇḍalinī śakti. Parā kuṇḍalinī śakti*, the greatest universal serpent power is there. And *paramadhāma*, that is the supreme state of God consciousness. There you find *sita-kāla-traya-rūpatayā,* three absolutely white lotuses, and there also you'll find *śakti, vyāpinī*, and *samanā*."
Parātriśikā Vivaraṇa (LJA archive).

---

858 Jayaratha has quoted this verse twice in his commentary on the *Tantrāloka* (3.70 and 31.97), and Swamiji has included it as a very important verse relating to the supreme energies (Goddesses) of the Trika.
859 This is Kālasaṁkarṣinī Kālī, the Supreme *paradevī* who draws all time into herself and dances on the lord of death.
860 *Śakti*, *vyāpinī*, and *samanā* reside on the three spokes (prongs) of the *triśūla*. These three spokes are all in the same level.

"And those [three white] lotuses are residing in the cycle of *unmanā* state.[861] *Unmanā* means, above the cycle of mind, above the cycle of thought. You can't concentrate on them. It is *aunmanasaṁ*, that is why it is called *unmanā*."
Tantrāloka 15.313 (LJA archive)

18. ***Samāveśas* in *śāmbhavopāya*** (fiftyfold and threefold)

The fiftyfold practices of *śāmbhavopāya* are:

- Fivefold is *bhūta samāveśa:* five elements from earth to ether.
- Thirtyfold is *tattva samāveśa*: thirty elements from *gandha* (smell) to *śakti tattva*.
- Threefold is *ātmā samāveśa*: *ātmā* (*puruṣa*), *vidyā*, and Śakti.
- Tenfold is *mantra samāveśa*: *a-u-m*, up to *vyāpinī*.[862]
- Twofold is *śakti samāveśa*: Śakti and Śiva.

The threefold *samāveśa* of *ātmā* (*puruṣa*), *vidyā*, and *śakti*, below is explained separately because these threefold elements pervade the whole world of elements, whereas the other elements in the fiftyfold *samāveśa* are *avyāpaka*, they don't pervade each other. In these thirty-six elements, the threefold elements, *ātmā* (*puruṣa*), *vidyā*, and *śakti*, are said to be fourfold, tenfold, and threefold respectively.

- Fourfold is *ātmā-puruṣa samāveśa*: *sakala*, *pralayākala*, *vijñānākala*, and *śuddhavidyā*.
- Tenfold is *vidyā samāveśa*: *aum* to *unmanā*.[863]
- Threefold is *śakti*[864] *samāveśa*: *icchā śakti* (will), *jñāna śakti* (knowledge), and *kriyā śakti* (action).

---

861 This is the abode of that supreme *paradevī*, which Abhinavagupta has praised in verse 2 of this *Tantrāloka*: *naumi citpratibhāṁ devīṁ parāṁ bhairava-yoginīm*.
862 See Appendix 17 (p405).
863 The tenfold *vidyā samāveśa* of *auṁ* to *unmanā* are included in the twelvefold divisions (*kalā*s) of the *praṇava mantra*, *auṁ*. See Appendix 17 (p405).
864 Here, Śakti is *svātantrya śakti*.

19. ***Kuṇḍalinī*** in Kashmir Shaivism

"*Kuṇḍalinī śakti* is the revealing and the concealing energy of Lord Śiva. On the one hand, it is the revealing energy, and on the other hand, it is the concealing energy. It reveals and it conceals. This *kuṇḍalinī śakti* is not different from the existence of Lord Śiva, just as the energy of light and the energy of heat are not separate from the fire itself. *Kuṇḍalinī*, therefore, in the true sense, is the existence of Śiva. It is the life and glory of Śiva. It is Śiva Himself. In our Trika Shaivism, *kuṇḍalinī*, which is that internal serpent power existing in the shape of a coil, is divided in three ways:

1. *Parā kuṇḍalinī–kuṇḍalinī* functioned by Lord Śiva.
2. *Cit kuṇḍalinī–kuṇḍalinī* functioned in consciousness.
3. *Prāṇa kuṇḍalinī–kuṇḍalinī* functioned in breath.

"The supreme *kuṇḍalinī* is called *parā kuṇḍalinī*. This *kuṇḍalinī* is not known or experienced by *yogins*. It is so vast and universal that the body cannot exist in its presence. It is only experienced at the time of death. It is the heart of Śiva. This whole universe is created by *parā kuṇḍalinī*, exists in *parā kuṇḍalinī*, gets its life from *parā kuṇḍalinī*, and is consumed in *parā kuṇḍalinī*. When this *kuṇḍalinī* creates the universe, Śiva conceals His real nature and is thrown into the universe. When the universe is created, He becomes the universe. There is no Śiva left which is separate from the universe. This is His creative energy. And when *kuṇḍalinī* destroys the universe, Śiva's nature is revealed. So, the creative energy for the universe is the destructive energy for Śiva; it is the revealing energy for the universe and the concealing energy for Lord Śiva. And the destructive energy for the universe is the creative energy for Śiva; it is the concealing energy for the universe and the revealing energy for Lord Śiva. *Parā kuṇḍalinī* is the supreme *visarga* of Śiva. As you know from studying the theory of *mātṛkā cakra*, *visarga* (:) comprises two points. These points are said to be Śiva and Śakti. In the real sense, however, these points are not Śiva and Śakti, they are the revealing point and the concealing point."

"*Cit kuṇḍalinī* is experienced by *yogin*s by means of concentrating on the center between any two breaths, thoughts, or actions; between the destruction and creation of any two things. The happiness and bliss that you experience here [in *cit kuṇḍalinī*] cannot be described. It is ecstasy beyond ecstasy, just like sexual bliss. In comparing sexual happiness with the happiness experienced in *cit kuṇḍalinī*, however, you will find that sexual happiness is one millionth part of the happiness experienced in *cit kuṇḍalinī*. In addition, simultaneously with the experience of ecstasy, you also realize the reality of Self. You recognize your real nature and you know, "I am only bliss (*ānanda*) and consciousness (*cit*)." In the actual rise of *cit kuṇḍalinī*, you will only get a glimpse of it and then come out. The full rise of *cit kuṇḍalinī* takes place only by the grace of your master and by the grace of your own strength of awareness."

"*Prāṇa kuṇḍalinī* also comes about through the process of centering. *Prāṇa kuṇḍalinī*, however, is only experienced by those *yogin*s who, along with their attachment to spirituality, also have attachments to worldly pleasures. If your desire and attachment is only for spirituality, then *cit kuṇḍalinī* takes place. Whether you experience the rise of *kuṇḍalinī* as *cit kuṇḍalinī* or as *prāṇa kuṇḍalinī* depends on your attachments. If you have attachment for spirituality and also for worldly pleasures, then the rise of *kuṇḍalinī* takes place in the form of *prāṇa kuṇḍalinī*. If you do not have attachments for worldly pleasures and are only attached to spirituality, then the rise of *kuṇḍalinī* takes place in the form of *cit kuṇḍalinī*. There is nothing you can do to determine how the rise of *kuṇḍalinī* will take place. It rises in its own way, depending on your attachments."

Kashmir Shaivism–The Secret Supreme, 17.117-121.

20. **Twelve Kālīs** in Kashmir Shaivism

In the fourth *āhnika* of the *Tantrāloka*, Abhinavagupta list the names of the twelve *kālī*s and their respective functions of creation (*sṛṣṭi*), protection (*sthiti*), destruction (*saṁhāra*), and *turya* (*anākhya*),[865] in the three states of objective (*prameya*), cognitive (*pramāṇa*), and subjective (*pramātṛ*) consciousness.

Four Kālīs in the objective cycle (*prameya*)

1. Sṛṣṭikālī: creation in the objective cycle
2. Raktakālī: protection in the objective cycle
3. Sthitināśakālī: destruction in the objective cycle
4. Yamakālī: *anākhya* in the objective cycle

Four Kālīs in the cognitive cycle (*pramāṇa*)

5. Saṁhārakālī: creation in the cognitive cycle
6. Mṛtyukālī: protection in the cognitive cycle
7. Bhadrakālī:[866]destruction in the cognitive cycle
8. Martāṇḍakālī: *anākhya* in the cognitive cycle

Four Kālīs in the subjective cycle (*pramātṛ*)

9. Paramārkakālī: creation in the subjective cycle
10. Kalāgnirudrakālī: protection in the subjective cycle
11. Mahākālakāl: destruction in the subjective cycle
12. Mahā-bhairava-ghora-caṇḍa-kālī:[867] *anākhya* in the subjective cycle

"What is the purpose of these twelve *kālī*s? In *prameya*, the objective world, in [*pramāṇa*], the cognitive world, and in [*pramātṛ*], the subjective world, you have to find *sṛṣṭi*, *sthiti*, *saṁhāra*, and *anākhya* (creation, protection, destruction and withdrawal). [*Anākhya*] is more than *turya*. The purpose of

865 *Anākhya* means the gap between each of the cycles of objective, cognitive and subjective. Although related to the fourth state (*turya*) Swamiji says the *anākhya* is more than *turya*.

866 Also nominated as Rudrakālī.

867 Also nominated as Mahā-bhairava-ghora-ugra-caṇḍa-kālī.

twelve *kālīs* is to find that state in each and every state. The twelve *kālīs* are the explanation of *anākhya cakra* only. It is not the explanation of objectivity or cognitively or subjectivity. You have to find that real transcendental state of nothingness in each and every act. It is why it is called *anākhya cakra*."

Paraphrase from the *Tantrāloka*, 4.142 (LJA archive).

"And this explanation of the twelve-fold energies is the explanation of the kingdom of Trika. This is the kingdom of Trika *śāstra*."

Ibid., 4.146.

21. **Twelvefold *cakra*** (names of the energies)

ekavīro yāmalo'tha triśaktiścaturātmakaḥ /
pañcamūrtiḥ ṣaḍātmāyaṁ saptako'ṣṭakabhūṣitaḥ / /109/ /
navātmā daśadikchaktirekādaśakalātmakaḥ /
dvādaśāramahācakranāyako bhairavastviti / /110/ /

1. *Ekavīra* means, when there is only Śiva everywhere.
2. *Yāmala*, when there is Śiva and Śakti.
3. *Triśakti*, when there are three energies shining (*parā*, *parāparā*, and *aparā*).
4. *Caturātmā*, when there are four states: wakefulness (*jāgrat*), dreaming (*svapna*), dreamless sleep (*suṣupti*), and the fourth (*turya*).
5. *Pañcamūrti* means, *sṛṣṭi*, *sthiti*, *saṁhāra*, *pidhāna*, and *anugraha* (creation, protection, destruction, concealing, and revealing).
6. *Ṣaḍātma,* the sixfold energies are the goddesses: Viśvā, Viśveśā, Raudrī, Vīrakā, Tryambikā, Gaurvī.
7. *Saptaka,* sevenfold are: Brāhmī, Māheśvarī, Kaumārī, Vaiṣṇavī, Vārāhī, Indrāṇi, and *Cāmuṇḍā*.
8. *Aṣṭakena* (eightfold) means, when Aghorā is also there.
9. *Navātma,* ninefold is the one who governs the eightfold *cakra*–Navātma Bhairava.
10. Tenfold energies are Umā, Durgā, Bhadrakālī,

Svastī, Svāhā, Subhāṅkarī, Srīḥ, Gaurī, Lokadhātri, Vāgīśī.

11. According to Jayaratha, the elevenfold *cakra* is discussed in the *Khaṇḍacakra śāstra*.
12. The energies (*śaktis*) of the twelvefold *cakra* are the twelve *kālīs* (See Appendix 20, p412).

Dvādaśāraṇam mahā cakra nāyako bhairava, Bhairava is *nāyaka*, the leader of the twelvefold energies.

22. ***Śaktipāta* (grace)** – The Five Great Acts of Lord Shiva

"The five great acts of Lord Śiva are *sṛṣṭi* (the creative act), *sthiti* (the protective act), *saṁhāra* (the destructive act), *tirodhāna* (the act of enfolding or concealing His nature), and *anugraha* (the act of unfolding or revealing His nature). In the kingdom of spirituality, Lord Śiva creates masters and disciples through His fifth act, the act of grace (*anugraha*). This grace is ninefold and, therefore, He creates masters and disciples in nine different ways."

"The first and highest level of grace is called "*tīvratīvra śaktipāta*." *Tīvratīvra śaktipāta* means "super-supreme grace." When Lord Śiva bestows super-supreme grace on anyone, then that person becomes perfectly Self-recognized. He knows his real nature completely and in perfection. At the same time, however, this kind of intense grace cannot be resisted by his body, so he throws away his body and dies."

"The second intensity of grace is called "*tīvramadhya śaktipāta*." This is "supreme-medium grace." The effect of this grace of Lord Śiva is that the recipient becomes completely and perfectly illumined but does not leave his body. He is said to be a *pratibhā guru*, that is, a master who is made not by another master's initiation, but by his self, by his own grace."

"The third intensity of grace is called "*tīvramanda śaktipāta*," which means "inferior supreme grace." In one who has received this grace, the desire appears for going to the feet of a spiritual master. And the master that he finds has received the second intensity of grace, *tīvramadhya śaktipāta*. This master is perfect. He is all-knowing. There is no difference between this master and Śiva. Lord Śiva, through these three supreme intensities of grace, creates masters in the kingdom of spirituality. With lower intensities of grace, Lord Śiva creates worthy disciples."

"The fourth intensity of grace is called "*madhyatīvara śaktipāta*." This is "medium-supreme grace." Through the effect of this intensity of grace, the disciple reaches the feet of that master who is absolutely perfect. But because the foundation established in the mind of this disciple is not quite completely perfect, the mere touch or glance of this perfect master will not bring this disciple to enlightenment. He, therefore, initiates this disciple in the proper fashion by giving him a *mantra* and teaching him the proper way of treading."

"The fifth intensity of grace is called "*madhyamadhya śaktipāta*," which means "medium-middle grace." When Lord Śiva bestows this particular intensity of grace upon someone, the intense desire for achieving the existence of Lord Śiva arises in this person's mind. At the same time, however, he does not want to ignore the enjoyments of the world. He wants to enjoy worldly pleasure along with wanting to realize the existence of Lord Śiva. Yet the intensity of his desire is only for achieving Lord Śiva's state."

"The sixth intensity of grace is called "*madhyamanda śaktipāta*," which means "medium-inferior grace." The effect of this grace is very much like the effect of medium-middle grace, however . . . the predominant desire here is for experiencing worldly pleasures. The above three medium intensities of grace take place in the field of aspirants living in the kingdom of *śiva-dharma*. Those aspirants have the inclination to achieve the state of Self-realization at least half-hourly during the day and at least twice during the night. The remaining period they keep aside for worldly pleasures."

"The following three inferior intensities of grace–*manda-tīvra* (inferior-supreme), *manda-madhya* (inferior-medium), and *manda-manda* (inferior-inferior)–take place in the field of aspirants living in *loka dharmaḥ*, the kingdom of worldly life. These aspirants have the desire for achieving Self-realization, the state of Lord Śiva, only when the pains and pressures of this world become too much to bear. At that moment, they want to abandon everything and achieve Self-realization but they are not able to, and though they want to leave this worldly life, they cannot. These aspirants have more tendency for worldly pleasure and less tendency for realizing their Self. But, as the grace of Lord Śiva shines in them, in the end–which may take many lifetimes–they become one with the supreme Being. This is the greatness of Lord Śiva's grace–that no matter what intensity of His grace is with you, it will carry you to His nature in the end."

Kashmir Shaivism–The Secret Supreme, 10.65-70.

23. ***Samādhi***

In classical yoga texts, the state of *samādhi* is recognized as the last limb (*aṅga*) of Patañjali's eight limbed *Aṣṭaṅga Yoga*. These are *yama*, *niyama*, *āsana*, *prāṇāyāma*, *pratyāhāra*, *dhāraṇā*, *dhyāna*, and *samādhi*. In these texts, the state of *samādhi* is considered to be the highest state of achievement on the path of yoga. Kashmir Shaivism on the other hand, treats this eighth limb of yoga as a purely internal state, akin to *nimīlanā samādhi*.

"*Nimīlanā samādhi* is internal subjective *samādhi*. In your moving through these six states of *turya*, this *samādhi* becomes ever more firm. With the occurrence of *krama mudrā*, *nimīlanā samādhi* is transformed into *unmīlanā samādhi*, which then becomes predominant. This is that state of extroverted *samādhi*, where you experience the state of *samādhi* at the same time you are experiencing the objective world. And when *unmīlanā samādhi* becomes fixed and permanent, this is the state of *jagadānanda*. The establishment of *krama mudrā* is called *jagadānanda*, which means, universal bliss. This is the seventh and last state of *turya*. In this state, the experience of universal transcendental Being is never lost and the whole of the universe is experienced as one with your own transcendental I-consciousness."

Kashmir Shaivism–The Secret Supreme, 16.114-115.

"So if you want to perceive the state of Lord Śiva as it ought to be perceived, in its real sense, you must enjoy this universe. You won't find the real state of Lord Śiva in *samādhi*. In the state of *samādhi*, you will find His non-vivid formation. You will find the exact state of Lord Śiva in the universe."

Shiva Sutras, The Supreme Awakening, 2.7.101.

"When such a yogī experiences the state of universal consciousness of Lord Śiva, not only in his internal state of consciousness of self but also in the very active life of the universe, this is called real *samādhi*."

Ibid., 3.6.148.

24. ***Svarūpa*** in Kashmir Shaivism

The literal meaning of *svarūpa* is, real nature, quality, own condition, or having one's own original form or character.

> *evaṁ siddhaṁ vedyatākhyo dharmo bhāvasya bhāsate / /*
> *tadanābhāsayoge tu svarūpamiti bhaṇyate /*
> *(Tantrāloka 10.91-92a)*

"So, this is decided that the aspect of perceiving the object is of the object, not of the perceiver. And when this perceiving function does not take place of the object, that is the *svarūpa*, that is the real nature, of the object–when it is not perceived. When the object is not perceived, then it is *svarūpa*, then it is the real object. When the perceiving function takes place, then it is not the object, it is in *pramātṛ bhāva* (subjective state) and in the energy of *pramātṛ*. When *pramātṛ*s and the energies of *pramātṛ*s are not functioning exclusively, the state of that object is *svarūpa,* i.e., when it is not known. When the perception of the object does not take place, that is in the real sense the *svarūpa* of the object i.e., unperceived, untouched. When *svātma*, when the perceiver, that individual being, has nothing to perceive, when he keeps away the mode of perceiving and he does not perceive anything, *yena vapuṣā bhātyartha*, at that moment that object before him, whatever it may be, whatever is existing there (the object which is not perceived), *tat svakaṁ vapuḥ*, that is the real formation of that object, that is the *svarūpa* of the object. If it was the theory of the Nyaiyakas, logicians, then we would argue that it does not exist if it is not perceived. [But] as long as our theory is [concerned], that the whole totality of objective and subjective totality is one with Lord Śiva, so then this question does not arise there. Everything is residing in Lord Śiva, and Lord Śiva is all-consciousness. So when this [object] is not perceived, [still] it is existing in its own way as Lord Śiva."[868]

Paraphrase from *Tantrāloka* 10th *āhnika* (LJA archive).

25. ***Upāyas*** (the "means" or "ways")

Upāya	**Upāya**	**Energy**	**Tattva**
anupāya	ānandopāya	ānanda	Śakti
śāmbhavopāya	icchopāya	icchā	Sadāśiva
śāktopāya	jñānopāya	jñāna	Īśvara
āṇavopāya	kriyopāya	kriyā	Śuddhavidyā

"The difference between *āṇavopāya*, *śāktopāya*, and *śāmbhavopāya* is this: In *āṇavopāya*, the strength of your awareness is such that you have to take the support of everything as

868 "*Śivatvam*, He is Śiva. If you know Him, He is there. If you don't know Him, He is still there. Don't worry about it." *Special Verses on Practice*, vs. 57. See commentary of verse 137 for a full explanation of this quote from Somānanda's *Śivadṛṣṭi*.

an aid to maintain and strengthen your awareness. In *śākto-pāya*, your awareness is strengthened to the extent that only one point is needed as a support for your concentration and that point is the center. In *śāmbhavopāya*, the strength of your awareness is such that no support is needed. You are already residing in the meant (*upeya*). There is nowhere to go, just reside at your own point. The rest is automatic. It is important to realize that though there are different *upāya*s, all lead you to the state of one transcendental consciousness. The difference in these *upāya*s is that *āṇavopāya* will carry you in a long way, *śāktopāya* in a shorter way, and *śāmbhavopāya* in the shortest way. Although the ways are different, the point to be achieved is one."

Kashmir Shaivism–The Secret Supreme, 5.39-40.

26. ***Kashmir Shaivism***, *The Secret Supreme* and *Tantrāloka* (*TĀ*).

The following is a list of the chapters from *Secret Supreme*, and their equivalent chapters in *Tantrāloka*:

Chap 1: Thirty-Six Elements (*Tattvas*) – *TĀ* chs 9 and 10.
Chap 2: Sixfold Path of the Universe (*Ṣaḍadhvan*) – *TĀ* chs 6, 10, 11 and 12.
Chap 3: Theory of the Alphabet *Mātṛkā cakra* – *TĀ* ch 3.
Chap 4: Theory of Reflection *Pratibimbavādaḥ* – *TĀ* ch 3.
Chap 5: Explanation of the Means (*Upāyas*) – *TĀ* ch 1.
Chap 6: The Theory of Speech (*Vāk*) – *TĀ* ch 3.
Chap 7: The Three Impurities (*Malas*) – *TĀ* ch 9 and 13.
Chap 8: Seven States of the Seven Perceivers – *TĀ* ch 10.
Chap 9: Seven Processes of the Seven Perceivers – *TĀ* ch 10.
Chap 10: The Five Great Acts of Lord Śiva including His Grace (*Śaktipāta*) – *TĀ* ch 13.
Chap 11: The Five States of the Individual Subjective Body – *TĀ* ch 10.
Chap 12: Fivefold Contacts of Masters and Disciples – *TĀ* ch 1.
Chap 13: The Birth of the Tantras – *TĀ* ch 36.

Chap 14: *Mokṣa* in Kashmir Shaivism and Indian Philosophy – *TĀ* 13.
Chap 15: Kashmir Shaivism and Advaita Vedānta – in various chs of *TĀ*.
Chap 16: The Seven States of *Turya* – *TĀ* 6.
Chap 17: *Kuṇḍalinī* and Its Purpose – *TĀ* ch 3, 5, 7 and 29.
Chap 18: Variations in the Rise of *Prāṇa Kuṇḍalinī* – *TĀ* ch 1 and 29.
Chap 19: Kashmir Shaivism – Outline of the different schools – Pratyabhijñā, Kula, Krama and Spanda. Each of these schools is mentioned in various chapters of *Tantrāloka*.

Bibliography

Published text of Lakshmanjoo Academy Book Series:

The Mystery of Vibrationless-Vibration in Kashmir Shaivism, Vasugupta's *Spanda Kārikā and* Kṣemarāja's *Spanda Sandoha*, Revealed by Swami Lakshmanjoo, Lakshmanjoo, ed. John Hughes, (Lakshmanjoo Academy, Los Angeles, 2016).

Essence of the Supreme Reality, Abhinavagupta's Paramārthasāra, with the commentary of Yogarāja, translation and commentary by Swami Lakshmanjoo with original video recording, (Lakshmanjoo Academy Book Series, Los Angeles, 2015).

Bhagavad Gita, in the Light of Kashmir Shaivism (*with original video*), Swami Lakshmanjoo, ed. John Hughes, (Lakshmanjoo Academy Book Series, Los Angeles, 2015).

Festival of Devotion and Praise, Shivastotrāvali, Hymns to Shiva by Utpaladeva, Swami Lakshmanjoo, ed. John Hughes, (Lakshmanjoo Academy Book Series, Los Angeles, 2015).

Kashmir Shaivism, The Secret Supreme, Swami Lakshmanjoo, ed. John Hughes (Lakshmanjoo Academy Book Series, Los Angeles, 2015).

Shiva Sutras, The Supreme Awakening, Swami Lakshmanjoo, ed. John Hughes, (Lakshmanjoo Academy Book Series, Los Angeles, 2015).

Vijñāna Bhairava, The Manual for Self Realization, Swami Lakshmanjoo, ed. John Hughes (Lakshmanjoo Academy Book Series, Los Angeles, 2015).

Self Realization in Kashmir Shaivism, The Oral Teachings of Swami Lakshmanjoo, ed. John Hughes (State University of New York Press, Albany, 1995).

Unpublished texts from the Lakshmanjoo Academy (LJA) archives:

Bhagavad Gitartha Samgraha of Abhinavagupta, translation and commentary by Swami Lakshmanjoo (original audio recording, LJA archives, Los Angeles, 1978).

Janmamaraṇavicāragranthaḥ, Janma Maraṇa Vicāra of Bhaṭṭa Vāmadeva, Swami Lakshmanjoo (original audio recording, LJA archives, Los Angeles, 1980).

Parātriśikā Laghuvṛtti with the commentary of Abhinavagupta, translation and commentary by Swami Lakshmanjoo (original audio recording, LJA archives, Los Angeles, 1982).

Parātriśikā Vivaraṇa with the commentary of Abhinavagupta, translation and commentary by Swami Lakshmanjoo (original audio recording, LJA archives, Los Angeles, 1982-85).

Special Verses on Practice, translation and commentary on selected verses from various texts. Swami Lakshmanjoo (original audio/video recording, LJA archives, Los Angeles, 1988).

Stava Cintāmaṇi of Bhaṭṭanārāyaṇa, translation and commentary by Swami Lakshmanjoo (original audio recording, LJA archives, Los Angeles, 1980-81).

The Tantrāloka of Abhinavagupta, Chapters 2 to 18, translation and commentary by Swami Lakshmanjoo (original audio recording, LJA archives, Los Angeles, 1972-1981).

Vātūlanātha Sūtras of Anantaśaktipāda, translation and commentary by Swami Lakshmanjoo (original audio recordings, LJA archives, Los Angeles, 1979).

Additional sources - Books

Mālinīvijayottara Tantram, Edited with Preface and English Introduction by Pandit Madhusudan Kaul Shastri, *Kashmir Series of Tests and Studies* (*KSTS*), Vol. XXXVII, Srinagar, Kashmir, 1922.

Netra Tantram, with commentary by Kṣemarāja. Edited by Pandit Madhusudan Kaul Shāstrī, *Vidyāvāridhi*, Superintendent of The research Department of The Kashmir State, (*KSTS*), Vol. XLVI, Srinagar, Kashmir, 1926.

Pratyabhijñāhṛdayam, *The Secret of Self-Recognition*, Sanskrit Text with English Translation, Notes and Introduction by Jaideva Singh (Motilal Banarsidass, Delhi, 1963-2011).

The Śivadṛṣṭi of Sri Somānandanātha, with the *vṛtti* by Utpaladeva, Edited with Preface, Introduction and English Translation by Paṇḍit Madhusudan Kaul Shastri, (*KSTS*), Vol. LIV, Srinagar, Kashmir, 1934.

Svacchandatantra, with commentary by Kṣemarāja. Edited with Notes by Paṇḍit Madhusudan Kaul Shastri, Superintendent of The research Department of The Kashmir State, (*KSTS*), Vol. XXXI, Srinagar, Kashmir, 1921.

Tantrāloka of Abhinavagupta with the commentary of Rājānaka Jayaratha, Edited with notes by Mahāmahopādhyāya Paṇḍit Mukunda Rāma Śāstrī, Officer in Charge, Research Department, (*KSTS*) Vol XXIII, Allahabad, 1918.

INDEX

Teachings of Swami Lakshmanjoo published by The Lakshmanjoo Academy

Bhagavad Gita, In the Light of Kashmir Shaivism

Festival of Devotion & Praise, Hymns to Shiva
Shivastotrāvali by Utpaladeva

Vijñāna Bhairava, The Manual for Self Realization

Shiva Sutras, The Supreme Awakening

Kashmir Shaivism, The Secret Supreme

Self Realization in Kashmir Shaivism,
The Oral Teachings of Swami Lakshmanjoo

Essence of the Supreme Reality,
Abhinavagupta's Paramārthasāra

The Mystery of Vibrationless-Vibration
in Kashmir Shaivism,
Vasugupta's Spanda Kārikā & Kṣemarāja's Spanda Sandoha

Lakshmanjoo ACADEMY

The teachings of Swami Lakshmanjoo are a response to the urgent need of our time: the transformation of consciousness and the evolution of a more enlightened humanity.

The Universal Shaiva Fellowship was established under Swamiji's direct inspiration, for the purpose of realizing Swamiji's vision of making Kashmir Shaivism available to the whole world. It was Swamiji's wish that his teachings be made available without the restriction of caste, creed, color or gender. The Universal Shaiva Fellowship and the Lakshmanjoo Academy, along with the Kashmir Shaiva Institute (Ishwar Ashram Trust), India, have preserved Swamiji's original teachings and are progressively making these teachings available in book, audio and video formats.

This knowledge is extremely valuable and uplifting for all of humankind. It offers humanity a clear and certain vision in a time of uncertainty. It shows us the way home and gives us the means for its attainment.

For information on Kashmir Shaivism or to support the work of The Universal Shaiva Fellowship and the Lakshmanjoo Academy and Kashmir Shaiva Institute (Ishwar Ashram Trust) visit the Lakshmanjoo Academy website or email us at info@LakshmanjooAcademy.org.

www.UniversalShaivaFellowship.org

www.LakshmanjooAcademy.org

www.IshwarAshramTrust.com

Instructions to download audio files

1. Open the link below to download the free audio https://www.universalshaivafellowship.org/TantralokaOne

   You will be **directed** to "**Light on Tantra in Kashmir Shaivism, Abhinavagupta's Tantraloka, Chapter One - Audio**."

2. Select "**Add to basket** " which will send you to the next page.

3. Copy **"Tantraloka One"** into the "**Add Gift Certificate or Coupon"** box

4. Click "**Checkout**" and fill in your details to process the free downloads.

If you have any difficulties please contact us at:
www.LakshmanjooAcademy.org/contact

Made in the USA
Monee, IL
30 May 2021

69620660R00262